ECONOMICS OF INCOME AND CONSUMPTION

By

HELEN G. CANOYER

PROFESSOR OF ECONOMICS AND MARKETING,
UNIVERSITY OF MINNESOTA

and

ROLAND S. VAILE

PROFESSOR OF ECONOMICS AND MARKETING,
UNIVERSITY OF MINNESOTA

THE RONALD PRESS COMPANY ⟋ NEW YORK

FOREWORD

The drama-packed years of the last decade have wrought many changes in its political economy. These changes have accrued with kaleidoscopic suddenness and inconsistency, and have changed both the tempo and the temper of our living. There are, however, some economic principles or truisms which history does not alter, and a changed world has made it ever more important that they be recognized and understood. We hope that our description and illustration of the simple unchanging economic laws which still govern our lives will help those who read these pages to understand and to cope with the very human economic world in which all of us live. And we believe that our approach, which is from the viewpoint of the consumer, will lead more quickly to an understanding of these economic problems than if they were considered from the viewpoint of the producer.

We have written this book with two groups of students in mind. First, we have written for students who have already had a course in which the principles of economics have been given formal statement. For many such persons, we believe that the day-to-day applications and continuing interrelations of economic principles may be clarified and made real when discussed in their application to consumers' problems. We have tried to present the subject in a manner that will stimulate their thinking, give them a greater degree of literacy in the field of economics, and orient them and their problems in the working world's scheme of things.

In the second place, we have written for that large group who, some time in their first two years of college, want to acquire some degree of literacy in the field of economics but who shy away from the conventional and formal course in principles of economics. For many of this group, this may be their only course in economics, but we hope some may be persuaded by it to continue their studies in the field.

Of all the pressing problems of our time, perhaps the most important, both for the individual and society, is that of governing ourselves wisely. Democracy can work only when its citizens are capable of intelligently exercising their duties under the guidance of competent leadership. We will be more intelligent and happier citizens,

iii

and have more competent leaders, if we and those whom we ask to lead us understand and appreciate the economic principles which, inescapably, operate in this and other nations.

The first chapter of the book is devoted to a thumbnail description of the two basic components of an economic society: human desires and raw materials; the second chapter considers the manner in which an economy functions and how it is controlled; the third sets forth the prime controlling factors of production and consumption and the permissive factor of income. These introductory chapters are followed by others which analyze the role of specialization and the mechanics of exchange, and these in turn are followed by a rather detailed chapter on markets and marketing.

The text then proceeds to its major task of relating economic principles to the many aspects of consumption, to which Chapters 8-14 are devoted. Nearly every day of our productive years is devoted to some kind of activity which serves ourselves or other people. Nearly everything we do has its economic aspect. We sell things, or labor, or advice. We work for wages. We *consume*. The sum of what we sell and buy and consume is the sum of our economic activity. The sum of what each of the two billions of us, who inhabit the earth today, buy and sell and consume is the sum total of the world's economic activity.

We engage in economic activity for two excellent reasons: we want to keep alive and we want to satisfy as many of our desires and ambitions as possible. But there is a large gap between what we can obtain of life's satisfactions if we are alert and knowing about what we and others can do to obtain them, and what we can get if we are ignorant of such matters. Every day, economic ignorance robs us of happiness in many ways. It makes us wasteful. It leads us to buy and sell at the wrong time and at the wrong price. It causes us to blame our political and economic leaders for troubles that stem directly from our individual or mass poor judgment. In sum, economic ignorance makes it difficult for us to govern ourselves wisely.

Governing ourselves with greater wisdom obviously requires that consumers develop an improved ability to increase the national income and their individual share of it. We hope that Chapters 15-20, which we have devoted to the diverse problems of increasing consumer income, and to the private and governmental efforts which have been exerted in this direction, will, indeed, show students how they may govern their productive lives more wisely.

The science of economics furnishes tools for the analysis of any kind of economic order. Professional skill in the use of these tools can be obtained only through technical training in colleges, professional schools, and in business or industry itself. An introduction to the study of economics, admittedly, cannot go far in giving this technical training. It can, however, give students an appreciation of the difficult but interesting problems involved in satisfying human wants. It can describe existing economic conditions, the ways in which these conditions are changing, can give the student some idea of the measures that are being proposed for modifying or controlling these trends, and can also afford him a basis for judging the practicality and consistency of the proposed solutions. It may, finally, encourage some to continue the study of economics until full competence in the use of the tools of economic analysis has been attained.

Limited portions of this book are based on our earlier book, *Income and Consumption.* We are indebted to Henry Holt and Company for their kind permission to utilize this material.

HELEN G. CANOYER
ROLAND S. VAILE

Minneapolis
July, 1951

CONTENTS

INTRODUCTION, *3*. Human desires.

THE RAW MATERIALS OF AN ECONOMIC SOCIETY, *4*. We start with natural resources. Man has added capital goods. People are important, too. Our institutions facilitate and restrict. Raw materials are used to satisfy desires.

THE BASIC DECISIONS, *9*. The rationing of limited supplies. The determination of what shall be produced. The determination of occupations. The determination of the rate of capital accumulation.

A PRICE-DIRECTED ECONOMY, *11*. Prices direct economic activity. How prices guide business. Prices reflect relative demands. Wages attract individuals. The future is different from now.

AN ECONOMY WITH MULTIPLE CONTROLS, *15*. Government shares the control with prices. The use of price varies among industries. Government spends money for us. Should you have more to spend—or less?

OUR INDETERMINATE OBJECTIVES, *19*.

PRODUCTION, *22*. Rearrangement of matter to make it more useful. Tangible and intangible products. Roundabout production. Payment for production.

CONSUMPTION, *24*. Destruction by use. Production precedes consumption. Rates of destruction differ widely. Consumption and satisfaction of wants.

INCOME, *26*. Income permits us to consume. Income is hard to define. Income is a flow. Purchasing power and realized income.

THE NEED FOR A "YARDSTICK," *31*.

THE HELLER COMMITTEE METHOD, *32*.

DIFFERENCE BETWEEN STANDARD AND PLANE OF CONSUMPTION, *32*. A standard is a criterion. A plane is a result or accomplishment. Standards must fit the circumstances.

THE ESTABLISHMENT OF STANDARDS, *34*.

THE PURPOSES OF STANDARDS, *35*. The cost of living.

ILLUSTRATIONS

TABLES

ECONOMICS OF
INCOME AND CONSUMPTION

Chapter 1

POLITICAL ECONOMY: A THUMBNAIL SKETCH

INTRODUCTION

"The aim of economics is the seeking after such knowledge as will raise the quality of human life."—Alfred Marshall.

No one who reads Marshall's words will have been satisfied with his lot throughout the past year. No one will have had everything he dreamed of and desired. All but the most naïve, fatalistic, or credulous will have asked *why* they cannot have what they want, when they want it, and in ample quantity. Few indeed are those who have found contentment with their lot. Through the ages men have wanted things that were scarce, and they have fought each other for treasured possessions. They have seen the greener grass on the other side of the fence and have climbed over; they have heard voices calling "Something lost behind the Ranges. Lost and waiting for you— GO!" They have tried eagerly, boldly, albeit not always wisely, to go and do and have.

Many systems have been tried to aid people, individually and as groups, to gain their desires. A major purpose behind each socio-economic system has been to maximize the flow of income to the present generation without impairing the heritage it leaves to posterity. No system so far devised, however, has been entirely successful in accomplishing this purpose.

As prelude to a discussion of the reasons for failure—to a discussion, that is, of why we are as poor as we are—it is essential that we have in mind something about the nature of human wants and also something about the materials out of which an economic society is shaped.

Human Desires.—Human desires are both negative and positive. Most of us are lazy: we want to conserve our energy, avoid physical effort, evade responsibility, and escape future uncertainty. At the same time we are ambitious; we want to acquire, accomplish, attract attention, consume, control, or discover the unknown. Each of these general desires may be satisfied, of course, in any of many ways.

3

They lead to such things as laborsaving gadgets in industrial plants and in the kitchen; to life insurance and social security programs; to highly styled clothes, huge corporation mergers, airplanes, television, and atomic bombs.

Some of our wants are more insistent than others. This is illustrated by our response to a rise or a fall in price. When prices rise relative to our money incomes we continue to buy those things which we hold essential; when prices fall we add less essential things to our shopping list. Similarly, when our incomes fall we continue our purchases of some things but not of others. In the depression of the 1930's for example, we bought about as much gasoline for our automobiles as we had before, but our purchases of clothing, insurance, and new houses fell off materially. This matter of insistence of demand for specific things is examined in some detail in a subsequent chapter.

Perhaps it is correct to say that no specific things are necessities in any absolute sense. We need air, food, control of bodily temperature and, perhaps, some other basic or generic things. But each of these wants may be supplied in numerous ways. Usually air is so plentiful and satisfactory that it is free. Occasionally, however, as in deep mines and on stratosphere flights, it must be supplied, and an important market is developing for air-conditioning equipment in factories, offices, and even in homes. The menus of different cultural groups not only make "eating one's way around the world" a fascinating adventure, but demonstrate the fact that no single item of food is essential to health and well-being. Moreover, it is obvious that appetite and taste are influenced by sales promotion as well as by habit and environment, and that they are subject to development and change.

In subsequent chapters the attempt is made to depict the present pattern of consumption in the United States together with some of the recent changes. This description will show the kinds of desires we now are satisfying, the amounts of specific goods and services used in their satisfaction, and will lead to a discussion of many problems resulting from our efforts to satisfy them.

The Raw Materials of an Economic Society

Every attempt to satisfy the wants of a people will be limited and directed in part by the raw materials available to the society. Here we are using the term "raw material" in a very broad, inclusive sense.

We Start with Natural Resources.—In the first place, the natural, material resources are of great importance. These include such things as land, water, mineral resources, climate, indigenous animal and plant life, and the interplay of these on agricultural and industrial potentials. It has been estimated by one authority,[1] for example, that the United States possesses two and one half times the wealth of raw materials of these sorts per capita of present population that Russia's population does, ten times as much as India's, but only two thirds as much as Australia's. That fact furnishes an important part of the explanation of the different levels of living in those several countries. It also raises some troublesome questions concerning the possibility of maintaining a peaceful world so long as such disparities exist, especially in view of the world-wide improvements in education and communication that are developing, since with these developments each of us comes to know what all the others possess.

Man Has Added Capital Goods.—Like Robinson Crusoe, men in all industrialized countries have taken time to make some tools with which to work. In this country these tools now are both numerous and complicated. They include our factories and the machines in them used to shape material; our railroads, highways, trains, trucks, and planes to move materials; our stores and office buildings in which to carry on our commercial business. These things are spoken of both specifically and collectively as man-made capital goods. We now achieve far greater consumption because our fathers undertook the building of a great and diverse capital plant. We in each generation must maintain, modify, and add to with the hope of improving this supply if we and our children are to enjoy as rich an opportunity to consume.

People Are Important, Too.—Third among the group of raw materials for an economic society is people. Anthropologists tell us that there are few, if any, basic inherent differences among the peoples of the world. Nevertheless the people of different areas do differ in many ways. Among the important characteristics that may be mentioned are their physical strength and skills, their mental abilities, their innate desires and ambitions, their willingness to move and to pioneer. Many of these characteristics are the result of environment, of course, including in "environment" such things as early training, community mores and taboos, sanitation and health care, industrial

---

[1] Herman Kranold, *The International Distribution of Raw Materials* (London: G. Routledge & Sons, Ltd., 1938).

opportunity, and leadership. In the United States from 1750 to 1850, for example, there was the fortunate conjuncture of almost unpopulated land, favorable climate, and good supplies of minerals, with a people full of ambition and relatively free from taboos. This combination resulted in the westward surge of population, accompanied and made possible by the development of industry and transportation. In the Netherlands Indies during the 1930's, to mention one contrasting case, strenuous and well-intentioned efforts on the part of governmental agencies to get people to move from the overcrowded parts of Java to the outer islands were almost completely thwarted by the lack of willingness of the people to pioneer. Consequently, the overcrowding continued to increase and resulted in a progressive lowering of the scale of living. Japan had much the same difficulty in her attempt to colonize in Manchuria. Without vision for the future, the people stay at home to perish.

Our Institutions Facilitate and Restrict.—A fourth group of the essentials for an economy includes the institutions with which the people have surrounded themselves. These are of many kinds. Included would be the legal framework that both facilitates and restricts all sorts of actions; the practical knowledge of science and mechanics; the physical plants such as factories, railroads, highways, and stores that already have been constructed and are available for use; and the cultural traditions, customs, and habits of the social group.

Babies are born naked with nothing in either their hands or their heads with which to meet the complex problems of the modern world. They are bequeathed an inheritance, however, that includes an intricately intertwined and finely balanced set of privileges and restrictions. Take the matter of legal ownership of property, for example. An individual may have a bundle of rights which we call ownership in a pair of shoes. He may wear the shoes, polish them, kick a football with them, use them to pound a nail, or leave them under his bed. But he may not throw them through his neighbor's window. Or a man may own a city lot on which he may build a home. But if it is in an area which common authority has zoned for residential purposes only, the owner may not build a store or a factory on it. The privileges of ownership are extended by society, and may be restricted by the same authority. In fact, both the privileges and restrictions are subject to continual change. The rights and responsibilities of contract, the establishment of units of weights and measures, of money as a medium of exchange—each of these is an institutional part of the political economy. The opportunity for individuals to band together for joint action in corporations or labor unions is the result of man-made rules subject to restriction and control.

The great tradition of the English classical economists is built on the assumption that each individual will strive rationally to maximize his own well-being and that the sum of such maxima will be a maximum for the social group. Cooperative effort, however, whether in a corporation, labor union, or other legalized institution may give the organized group such an advantage over those with whom they would deal as to make political restrictions desirable or even essential to the group well-being.

The inheritance of wealth is another institution devised by men. It is differently provided and regulated in different countries and it is subject to change anywhere. But in many cases it provides a method through which some young people acquire great financial advantage over others. This and similar advantages which our legal institutions provide have led some persons to conclude that the sum of individual striving for well-being will not maximize the well-being of the commonwealth. Consequently graduated inheritance and income taxes have been instituted partly in the effort to equalize the opportunities of individuals. Such action has been justified in the minds of the people partly on the grounds that the original advantages which made the incomes possible were the result of man-made institutions or rules and that privileges granted by the people might by the people be taken away. Or perhaps it would be more accurate to say that the things resulting from use of the privileges belong at least in part to those who granted the privileges.

Raw Materials Are Used to Satisfy Desires.—The raw materials of political economy just discussed are combined and used in the effort to satisfy as completely as possible the human desires of individuals in the commonwealth. The manner in which this is done and the degree of success vary among different nations and sometimes even among areas within a nation. Many of the ramifications of this complex matter, as worked out in the United States, are described and discussed in subsequent chapters. In fact, this is the core and purpose of this book.

PROJECT QUESTIONS

1. Make a list of the items in your state which you would classify as natural resources. Then write a brief paragraph descriptive of the way they are used.

2. What would you consider the most important form of "man-made capital goods" in your community? Why do you rate it as most important?

3. Who is Alfred Marshall? When and where did he live and what are some of the books which he wrote?

4. Go to your library and refer to Marshall's *Principles of Economics*. By examining the footnotes, index, or text, find the names of at least five other economists. What is the best known book of each? When was it written?

Chapter 2

HOW THE ECONOMY PRODUCES OR WORKS

The Basic Decisions

During the past several centuries individuals have cooperated in many ways in the attempt to satisfy their own and others' desires. These attempts have led to a high degree of specialization in the use of the raw materials discussed above.[1] Geographically, we have our wheat belt, corn belt, cotton belt, and so on. Personally, some of us are doctors, mechanics, inventors, painters, merchants, ditchdiggers, teachers, and so on. Each area and person contributes to the total supply of goods and services—the national income—and then extracts a share to use or consume. If any system of specialization-exchange-cooperation [2] is to work, it must be subjected to some sort of regulation and control.

Any system by which the activities of men are modified, regulated, or controlled must provide a more or less orderly method of arriving at certain basic decisions. Some of the fields in which these decisions must be made will first be indicated; then the problems concerning each field will be elaborated and illustrated.

The principal tasks with which any system of political economy must be concerned are:

1. The rationing of limited supplies of goods and services among those desiring them.
2. The determination of what shall be produced from the available supply of natural resources, with the aid of human effort.
3. The determination of the particular tasks to be performed by each individual.
4. The determination of the rate at which capital plant shall be built as an aid to future production and consumption.

---

[1] Both regional and personal specialization are discussed in some detail in Chapter 5.

[2] Any system, that is, in which persons and areas specialize in the things they do or produce, then exchange products among themselves, thus cooperating in achieving their scale or plane of living.

9

Each of these fields is of direct concern to the individual because it affects both the total income of a group of people and the share of this total that goes to each individual.

The Rationing of Limited Supplies.—As already suggested, the supply of many things is insufficient to satisfy the desires of all people. Of course some things are so plentiful relative to their usefulness as to be a nuisance; weeds, for example, or mosquitoes, or noise. Such things call for no rationing and enter the economic system only when effort is necessary to remove or avoid them. Other things are so plentiful that no single unit of them is important, but they are never particularly in the way; under normal living conditions no one is concerned, for example, about any particular cubic yard of air. Such things, also, are outside any system of political economy, but there are not many such. Most things of which we are conscious at all are limited in supply and must be rationed; this applies to our supplies of food, clothing, housing, and so on.

The Determination of What Shall Be Produced.—Before goods can be consumed they must be produced. Before we can eat our Thanksgiving plum pudding, for example, many persons will have performed many tasks. Farmers will have planted and harvested wheat, currants, sugar cane; plows and stoves and steam kettles will have been fashioned; flour mills, packing plants, and iron mines will have given employment to men. Someone will have decided to do each of these things and some of them will have been decided long before our pudding appears. The decision to do them will have been based in part, however, on the expectation that we will demand our pudding when the day arrives. In other words, anticipation of the pattern by which consumer goods and services will be rationed determines what will be produced. Since all the activities necessary to produce the pudding—or any other good—proceed somewhat continuously, it may be said that in a sense the Thanksgiving Day demand directs and pays for all the steps.

The Determination of Occupations.—There are many different things to be done in the world. Particular tasks often require special abilities and carry special satisfactions to individuals. If all tasks were equally useful to others, each of us could do whichever ones we enjoyed the most or disliked the least. The results of individual activity are not all equally appreciated, however, by the rest of society. Someone might get great personal satisfaction, for example, out of throwing stones through windows, but it is not likely that the rest of society would pay the individual for that activity. Much arduous preparation and many sleepless nights are included in the life of a physician, but society thinks so much of the results of these efforts that the income of a good physician is relatively large and, consequently, a considerable number of individuals clamor for admission to medical schools.

In general, people are free to choose their occupations, within the limitations of their abilities, on the basis of the expected income to be derived. There are, however, some important exceptions to this rule, which will be referred to again shortly. (See Chapter 5.)

The Determination of the Rate of Capital Accumulation.—Perhaps the outstanding characteristic of twentieth-century life is the large accumulation of capital plants of all sorts—factories, stores, railroads, telephone and other communication systems, motorized farms, highways, public buildings. All these things are designed to make production both easier and greater in the future. These accumulations were accomplished only through some temporary reduction in immediate consumption, for it is not possible to produce as much for immediate consumption when a part of the total energy available is devoted to the making of capital goods. Russia has found this strikingly and, perhaps, bitterly true ever since she started her rapid development of industrial plants. In the long run, the ability of Russia to produce for immediate consumption will be greatly increased by the enlargement of capital plants, but during the construction period the people have gone without many things they might have enjoyed.

These four basic tasks are the essential parts of any economic order. They are performed in every political commonwealth, whether the form of government be a monarchy, a democracy, a socialist state, or a communist state, although the methods used will be different in the several cases. Later on in this book we examine some of the results, good and bad, that have accompanied recent methods of making the necessary decisions in the performance of these four basic tasks. Finally, we shall consider some of the many suggestions that are current for other methods of directing economic activities to see how they might affect total consumption and the lot of the individual consumer.

A PRICE-DIRECTED ECONOMY

There are many ways by which each of these basic decisions might be carried out. Most of these ways have been tried and are still used under special circumstances. During the emergencies created by war or famine, for example, dictators use resources and give shares of the essential commodities in accordance with their own interpretation of need or desirability. Whether the distribution is beneficent or not depends upon the temper of the dictator. Under very primitive social conditions, the physically strong take what they want and leave the remainder to the weak. Ancient patriarchs, absolute monarchs, medieval barons, each have had their ways of rationing through the use of a high degree of centralization of the power of decision.

Prices Direct Economic Activity.—For example, during the nineteenth century and so far in the twentieth, rationing has been accomplished in the main by the mechanism of price. A rise in the price discourages consumption, on the one hand, and encourages production, on the other. A fall in price has the opposite effects. When prices are free to move, they tend to adjust to that point where the available supply is just taken from the market and where the cost of producing the supply for the immediate future is just met. Price is a simple and efficient mechanism for equating demand and supply. In the process, it rations the supply to those who can and will pay the price.

In a price-controlled society, each step in the complicated process of production receives a portion of what people are willing to give for the finished good. If the amount is sufficient to interest the producer, human efforts and natural resources continue to be devoted to this activity; if insufficient, the producer turns his attention elsewhere and other things are produced.

How Prices Guide Business.—Perhaps an illustration will make the point clearer. The large meat packers are said to base their purchases of beef cattle on the equation of costs and probable selling prices each day. Their calculations proceed somewhat as follows:

Start with today's selling price of beef cattle   _____
Add—estimated cost of processing   _____
Subtract—estimated value of by-products   _____
Remainder—estimated cost of dressed beef   _____
Compare with—today's market price of dressed beef   _____

If the comparison shows that the market price of dressed meat is above cost, the packers purchase cattle; if not, they delay purchase until either the price of beef cattle goes down or the price of dressed meat goes up. Thus they permit price relationships to shape their decisions and govern their production. If packers persist in their restriction of purchases of cattle, farmers, in turn, will reduce their cattle-feeding and -breeding programs. Similar calculations are made throughout industry wherever society is organized under a price economy.

Prices Reflect Relative Demands.—A perfectly free operation of the price mechanism would give a more or less accurate reflection of the willingness and ability of the people to pay for any certain use of energy and resources; it would be democratic in the extreme. It must not be inferred, however, that the authors, or anyone else, believe that a freely operating price system exists in any part of the world today. The truth is quite the contrary; the price mechanism has been "frozen" and arbitrarily "set" at many points so that it is quite incapable at those points of expressing the democratic choice to which reference has just been made.

Even though the price system is not permitted to move freely in control of economic activities, decisions concerning what to produce, and when, must still be made. The introduction of other methods of deciding these matters appears to be based on the assumption that some particular individual or group should make decisions for the rest of us. This point is discussed in more detail later.

Wages Attract Individuals.—In a price-directed economy, individuals choose their occupations to a considerable extent on the basis of the income they hope to get. As is pointed out specifically in Chapter 11, personal income is dependent to a large degree on wages, which are a form of price. There are, however, some special circumstances that prevent the price mechanism from being as satisfactory in the allocation of human resources as it is in other fields. Among these circumstances the following seem particularly important.

1. Perhaps the first limitation on the freedom of young people to choose their occupations is the influence of parents. Frequently a boy is expected to enter the firm or profession of his father without regard to his own desires or abilities. In other cases parents want their children to enter a different line of work and perhaps a stratum of society different from their own. This has led to overemphasis on the desirability of white collar jobs and perhaps of college education. In some instances at least it has resulted in frustration and maladjustment on the part of the individual.

2. Even in a new and democratic country like the United States there are social groups, and it is difficult for individuals to get started in any occupation which traditionally "belongs" to some other group. This difficulty is much greater, of course, in an older country like England or India.

3. Some occupations can be undertaken only by persons who possess some money or other capital resource. It is much more difficult in this country, for example, to start independent farming than it was fifty years ago because of the higher price of farm land and the cost of machinery which now is almost universally used in farming. The same difficulty is even more pronounced in many lines of manufacturing in this era of large-scale industry. It is much easier, financially, to enter the field of grocery retailing or shoe repairing as an owner-manager than that of automobile manufacturing or railroading. In fact, it is easier, financially, to enter almost any particular field as an employee than as an employer. The professions require longer and more expensive preparation than most of the trades, while the trades require more than common labor. Since these things are so, some persons with first-rate ability doubtless are kept by lack of funds from undertaking important things for which they could be fitted and which they would really like to do.

4. Frequently individuals do not know their own abilities, nor do they have any easy way to find out what they might do well. Psychologists have made important progress in adapting tests of interests and abilities that will forecast for young people the lines for which they can expect to develop aptitudes, and a more general use of such tests probably is to be recommended. It is still true, however, that many young people never do get started in the thing for which they would be best fitted, because they do not know their own abilities.

5. It is often true, also, that people misjudge the opportunities in various occupations or specific jobs. A fairly obvious and simple case might be that of the professor in a midwestern college who is offered $1,000 more salary at a large eastern university. The higher salary leads him to accept, only to find after moving that the higher cost of living in the East approximately offsets his increase in salary. A more complicated case—and perhaps more typical—would be that of the child-woman who accepts employment in a poorly lighted tailor shop at a wage which is, perhaps, adequate for the weariness of the day, but which in no sense compensates for the eyestrain and future semiblindness that result. Certainly the degree of freedom to choose one's occupation that is available here and now does not guarantee wisdom of choice from the standpoint either of the individual or of the national economy.

The Future Is Different from Now.—Unforeseen changes that come with the passage of time interfere with the accuracy with which price allocates the use of resources. This is particularly the case in

connection with the building of capital plant as an aid to future production of consumer goods. One reason why the scale of living in
present-day China is lower than in America is because the earlier
generations of Chinese did not build railroads and factories which the
present generation might use. One reason why the scale of living in
Russia was low during the 1930's was that Russia was devoting a
great amount of energy to the building of capital plant rather than to
immediate consumption goods.

It is not our purpose here to discuss the wisdom or the hardship
associated with these Chinese and Russian decisions concerning the
building of capital plant, nor to seek the reasons for the decisions.
Rather, it is to emphasize that such decisions must be made and that
they have both a present and a lasting effect on the ability to consume.
In America, so far, the decisions even in this field have been made
largely by individuals or private corporate groups as a result of the
lure of gain. Such experiments as TVA and REA suggest, however,
that we are not entirely satisfied with the results. Perhaps, therefore,
the future will see departures on a growing scale from a price control
of capital investment.

An Economy with Multiple Controls

Early in the use of the price system it was decided that this form
of rationing did not always bring the desired results. For example,
in the United States many years ago, it came to be commonly believed
that the youth of the country should receive more educational opportunities than they or their parents could or would pay for. Education
at public expense, without direct cost to the individual receiving it,
was the result. The postage-stamp method of payment for mail service is another illustration of a departure from rationing through the
mechanism of a price that is nicely adjusted to cost. If prices that
covered the costs of specific services were charged, mail might never
be sent to some remote places. Tariffs, subsidies, sales and excise
taxes, and many other institutional devices are employed to modify
both the kind and the amount of goods and services used by individuals. Social considerations other than the ability and willingness of
the individual to pay a price set by cost clearly enter into these cases
of rationing and the number of such cases has grown to large proportions through the years. At present about 25 per cent of our total
national income is spent for us by government agencies.

Government Shares the Control with Prices.—In such cases
government steps in to modify the rationing. Thus we have a dual

system of control partly economic and partly political, justifying the term "Political Economy." Once the dual use of these two forms of control is started there is no *logical* proportionality between them. Neither is there any final *legal* limit to the extent of political control. The division becomes a matter of social expediency and it is constantly being shifted. In spite of much controversy over the form of control, the major task remains, however, and must not be overlooked: limited supplies both of raw materials and of finished goods must be rationed. The details of the rationing will depend on the character of those handling the dual controls and may be either beneficent or selfish, merciful or ruthless, stable or vacillating, cooperative or dictatorial, wise or foolish.

The Use of Price Varies Among Industries.—Even among industries that are operated as private enterprises, there are some in which the price system does not fully control the rationing or allocation of resources. In the case of magazines and newspapers, for example, the subscription or newsstand price pays only about half of the total cost of publication and distribution. The rest of the income available to the publishers comes from the sale of advertising space. If you and I had to pay the total cost of magazines and newspapers when we bought them it is probable that their total circulation would be curtailed sharply; perhaps many would not be published at all. In the case of radio programs the listeners pay nothing directly towards the costs either of talent or of broadcasting expenses. The sale of advertising time is the sole source of revenue for the industry. Probably we should listen less often and choose our programs with greater care if we had to pay for each one individually. These industries of great educational and recreational importance surely would be very different in both volume and quality of output if consumer prices were their sole source of revenue.

We do not mean to imply that the quality of publications and of radio programs necessarily would be improved if consumers paid all the costs directly. The moving picture industry may be cited for comparison on this point. In this case, the box-office receipts—what individual patrons pay at the movie-house door—are the entire income from which all expenses of exhibition and of production must be paid. In other words, patrons must be satisfied with the show or income is curtailed at its source. It is not clear, however, that this direct-payment method of influencing the quality of product has resulted in better movies than has the indirect-payment method in the case of periodicals and radio programs. Perhaps the self-interest

involved in holding an audience for the advertiser is as accurate a
way to give consumers what they want as is reliance on their own
individual expenditures.

Government Spends Money for Us.—Government agencies take
about 25 per cent of our total national income through the medium
of taxation and expend it for us in accordance with some centrally
determined program.[3] In the use of government funds there is considerable variation in the relationship between who pays the tax and
who gets the benefit. In the case of the gasoline tax, for example, the
users of public highways pay about in proportion with their use. The
tax on gasoline used on some highways, however, may be much more
than the cost of the highway, which results in funds available for some
roads that never would pay for themselves. Thus, in total, the payment for highways is distributed among users in much the same way
as though the private-enterprise price mechanism prevailed, but the
choice of roads to be improved is not directed in the same manner.

In the case of public schools, in contrast, tax payment is based
largely on "ability to pay"; that is, it is proportioned to individual or
family income. The father who sends his children to a private school
pays as much towards the support of the public school as does his
neighbor whose children attend the public school—and the bachelor
next door pays a higher proportion of his income towards school
support than does either of the parents. This results in a distribution
of expenditure that is quite different from that which would prevail
under a free-enterprise price system. In other words, taxation and
expenditure by governmental agencies modify the distribution of
purchasing power among individuals and families, and also change
the pattern of consumer expenditure.

Individuals in this country still are free to spend whatever income
they have after taxes in almost any way they like. They may choose
among the wares of all the merchants in the country, they may engage
in any form of recreation, or they may invest in any enterprise designed to yield income in the future.

In general each individual does those things which, within the
limitations of his income and his tastes, he believes will give him the
greatest satisfaction and permit him most completely to avoid pain
and suffering. We wear leather shoes rather than wooden ones be-

---

[3] In this country this share has been increasing for many years. In 1900 it was
only about 10 per cent. During World War II it became nearly 50 per cent and
probably it would rise again to some such figure if there were another all-out war.

cause we believe them more comfortable and better looking; we spend more money in this country on cigarettes than on symphony concerts because as individuals we believe we shall enjoy more dimes spent on smoking than on listening to symphonies. And so with all our choices; in each one we try to get as much satisfaction out of any one dollar as out of any other. Of course, it often is difficult to make direct comparisons between the satisfactions gained from two different acts of consumption, but the continued repetition of purchases by many people becomes realistic testimony of personal judgments in the mass. The array of choices so made becomes the evidence on which the four basic decisions previously discussed are founded.

Not only do individuals want to maximize their personal satisfactions, but groups and nations likewise strive to get the largest possible group or national consumption. Whether the sum of "best" uses of income by individuals gives the "best" use for an entire country is a moot question that need not detain us long at present. We may point out, however, that as a nation we decided long ago that everyone should consume certain things regardless of his ability or willingness to pay the cost. For example, all the youth of the country should have an opportunity for education regardless of the financial status of individual families, in the belief that a high degree of literacy is a desirable social end. Moreover, adequate supplies of pure water and the sanitary disposal of sewerage are considered so clearly in the interest of general welfare that they frequently are furnished by communities without reference to individual ability to pay. These cases are illustrative of the important program of "enforced consumption" that is undertaken by representative governments and that is paid for through our system of tax collections without allowing chance for personal choice in the matter. The existence of such items is evidence that the group has decided that greater good will come to the commonwealth if part of the pattern of consumption is centrally planned and administered.

Should You Have More to Spend—or Less?—In any program of socially planned consumption, questions concerning both the *willingness* and the *ability* of the individual to pay are involved. At most points in our present system of taxation and governmental expenditure, people with large financial ability are expected to contribute more liberally than those with less ability, regardless of the personal use made of the particular governmental service. This arrangement is based on the belief that the welfare of the community as a whole is important both to the earning power and to the enjoyment of every citizen in it. Generally speaking, this position is accepted by those who are fortunate enough to have high purchasing power, but there are limits beyond which taxation in the interests of others will not be tolerated.

Another reason, or justification, for modifying the distribution of income through taxation and public expenditure is often advanced. Individual incomes do differ markedly, and there is a feeling that persons with very large incomes do not get as much satisfaction out of any particular dollar's worth of consumption as do individuals with small incomes. The corollary is that if some dollars are taken away from those with large incomes and given to those with small, the total well-being of the nation will be increased; under this reasoning it would reach a maximum only when all incomes were equal. This is not the place to attempt a complete justification of inequality of incomes, nor would we ever undertake to justify in its entirety the present distribution, but we should point out that just as there are differences of ability in other respects, so there doubtless are in the ability to gain satisfactions from consumption. Probably ability to gain title to a share in the world's production is not correlated precisely with ability to appreciate the fine things of life in consumption, but with equal assurance we can say that there is a fairly strong tendency towards such correlation. To the extent that this is true, unequal distribution of income available for consumption will tend to maximize the well-being of a nation. As yet we have no scientific measurement of the well-being of a nation that permits comparisons either among different nations at the same time or for the same nation at different times.

Our Indeterminate Objectives

A principal difficulty confronting any system of political economy lies in reaching a clear-cut agreement on objectives. Exact measurement is one of the basic requirements of any science, but in order for measurement to be useful at least three things are necessary:

   a) Definition of the characteristic to be measured
   b) A unit of measurement
   c) A standard of comparison

There are many problems of measurement in the social sciences. Too frequently there is lack of definition of the characteristic to be measured; more frequently there is lack of satisfactory unit of measurement; most frequently, perhaps, there is lack of adequate standards of previous performance for purposes of comparison.

It is said that in Persia distances between towns often are measured by the time required to go on horseback from one to the other. This would be a satisfactory measurement provided time of travel for horsemen is the important characteristic; it might not do at all for the purpose of estimating the cubic yards of concrete required to surface a road, or the distance in terms of airplane flight. Or you may have heard of the wartime rabbit pie made, so it was said, half of rabbit and half of horse meat—that is, at least one rabbit to one horse. The single animal as a unit might be all right for some purposes, but it hardly would be considered accurate in describing a meat pie. Nor is it possible to know whether or not the athlete has made a good jump unless one knows how far other men have jumped.

Similarly, in our problem of measuring the well-being of individuals and nations we have wide differences of opinion concerning the relative values of specific consumer goods and we are slow in developing precise methods of comparison. Do we want a nervous thrill or serene complacency; what is the desirable balance between security and freedom; is contract bridge a fine matching of wits or a stupid bore; is Roquefort cheese a delicacy or something rotten; is comfort or appearance to be rated highest in the selection of a pair of shoes? At present there are neither right nor wrong answers to these and countless similar questions; they are matters of individual judgment. When individual choice prevails each person generally can answer them in his own way, while any other method of decision leads to some sort of compromise based on "average" or "authoritarian" opinion.

People are constantly looking for better ways to make all the decisions that are necessary in a complex society. This is no simple task. To this end it is important that each of us know as much as possible about our social institutions, how they work, and what they have accomplished for us. Only when we are equipped with that knowledge are we in a position to consider the possibility of improvements. Perhaps as individuals we are careless and inexpert in planning our consumption. But our per-capita use of automobiles and television sets, our air-conditioned homes, the annual volume of our books and magazines, the growing proportion of college-trained men and women, and the increase in our average length of life all testify that as a nation we have shown amazing ambition and considerable wisdom.

Project Questions

1. Write a brief discussion, with factual illustrations, of different methods of rationing limited supplies such, for example, as the rationing of food by Captain Bligh in the small boat after the mutiny on the *Bounty*. Include at least one illustration of rationing by price.

2. List as many *specific* cases of restriction in the freedom of competitive price movements as you can discover. In each case what type of authority or organization imposed the restriction?

3. See what you can find concerning the rate of capital accumulation. Individual students may be assigned specific countries such as the United States, Russia, or Sweden; or specific periods such as the middle nineteenth century in England or the first third of the twentieth century in the United States.

4. Is there any such thing in this country as "enforced consumption"? If so, give illustrations and explain how the "enforcement" occurs.

Chapter 3

PRODUCTION, CONSUMPTION, AND INCOME: SOME BASIC DEFINITIONS

Long ago someone wisely said, "If you would talk with me define your terms." This book is largely concerned with analyzing *consumption* and *income,* and *production* is an essential element of both concepts. Each of these terms may be defined differently. Therefore, in order to minimize misunderstandings we must describe how we shall use these terms in this book.

PRODUCTION

Rearrangement of Matter to Make It More Useful.—Production has been defined as the rearrangement of matter. To be economically useful the rearrangement must increase the usefulness of the matter. Usefulness may be created through change in form, place, time, or possession. Such changes are called by economists the creation of utilities. Change in form most frequently occurs in connection with those business activities commonly called farming, mining, and manufacturing. The other changes involve activities frequently classed together under the terms *transportation* and *marketing.* The term *production* properly applies to them all. That is, production is the creation of form, place, time, or possession utilities.

Thus, the storage of seasonally produced goods such as eggs creates primarily time utility although often other utilities may increase during the storage process, such as the ripening of bananas or the aging of cheese and wines. Storing such goods at the time of their abundant supply for use during a time of reduced supply creates time utility because it makes such goods available at all times when they are wanted. For example, not many years ago in the small towns of our northern states no lettuce, tomatoes, or oranges could be bought during the winter months. Today, as a result of expanded and improved transportation and storage facilities, it is possible in those same towns to buy fresh fruits and vegetables throughout the year.

Tangible and Intangible Products.—There are other aspects of production which are important to an understanding of our economy. Sometimes those activities which do not result in tangible goods are overlooked in a consideration of production. Actually, the violinist is as much a producer as the man who makes the violin. Even when a concert violinist plays to a live audience, economic utility or human satisfaction is produced for the audience. In this case, production and consumption are simultaneous. When a recording is made of the violinist's playing in a studio, production and consumption may be quite separate in time, the result of the production is less ephemeral and more tangible, and the recording may be sent for the enjoyment of people (audiences) to any part of the world. Thus time utility and place utility are increased by the recording, but we must not lose sight of the fact that the playing in the concert hall was productive even though no tangible thing resulted. The purpose of economic activity is the satisfaction of wants, and that purpose is frequently fulfilled without the production of any tangible good.

Roundabout Production.—Production of goods and services from which satisfactions may be derived frequently is "roundabout." That is, rearrangement of matter may proceed through several steps or stages and considerable time may elapse before anything is available for direct consumption. Because of this "roundaboutness," consumption and the consumer are not always easily defined. The recording of the violinist's concert is but one case in point. Throughout our complex industrial system the finished product of one industry becomes the raw material of another. Wheat, for example, is a finished product of the farm, but a raw material for the flour miller. Flour is the finished product of the mill, but a raw material for the bakery. While the housewife may purchase flour, she further processes it into biscuits or cakes before it is consumed in the sense of supplying satisfaction or utility directly to an ultimate consumer. Much of our in-industrial or commercial production consists, therefore, of making raw materials, semimanufactured articles, machines, factories, railroads and the like which are used in further processing before goods and services for final consumption can be made available. The goods which are ready for final consumption in the satisfaction of wants are frequently distinguished from those used in further processing by calling the former "consumption goods" and the latter "production goods."

Payment for Production.—In the making of each type of good, money is supplied by someone and distributed to wage-earners, landlords, suppliers of raw materials, transportation facilities, and so on. Frequently, and especially in the case of production goods, considerable time elapses between the distribution of money income to these several claimants and the final appearance of the consumer good. During this time the makers of the producer goods face the risk that the subsequent steps in the process will not be completed, or that consumers finally will not be willing to pay prices for the consumer goods that will compensate fully for all the advance distribution of money income. Thus the "roundaboutness" of our business processes is a major cause of business risk.

Consumption

Destruction by Use.—A dictionary definition of consumption is "destruction by use." That definition is both too arbitrary and too narrow for our purposes. Alfred Marshall has said that "consumption may be regarded as negative production." That is, man's production of material products really is nothing more than a rearrangement of matter which gives it new utilities, while his consumption is a disarrangement of matter which diminishes or destroys its utilities. Sometimes, in fact, man's part in either process is slight. All he does towards the production of wheat is to put seed where nature will make it grow. As a consumer of pictures or curtains, or even of a house, he does little to wear them out, but he enjoys them while time destroys them.

Production Precedes Consumption.—In general, it follows that production must precede consumption. Man must rearrange matter through productive processes before he can disarrange it through consumption. In fact, the economist's definition of production is the providing of utilities that may be enjoyed by man. There are a few cases of consumption, to be sure, which do not depend upon human productive effort. The sunset across the lake, the call of the loon, the fragrance of desert wild flowers, the panoramic view from a mountain top, man neither produces nor destroys by consuming, yet from them he gets memorable joy. They are as surely part of his consumption as anything else.

Consumption, then, is man's harvesting of utilities or satisfactions from matter. Usually, but not always, the matter has been arranged in a particular form—i.e., produced—by man so that the utilities may be harvested. Sometimes, but not always, the arrangement is destroyed by the process of consumption. Consumption is maximized when the total harvest of utilities is greatest or, in more direct words, when human enjoyment or satisfaction is greatest.

Rates of Destruction Differ Widely.—The extent to which matter is disarranged in consumption differs greatly among the many types of goods. A lighted match, for example, quickly burns up its usefulness, and food is converted into energy, muscle, or fat almost as soon as it is eaten. Consumption in such cases results in immediate and complete destruction of the specific good. In contrast, a day's use of an automobile, house, or factory destroys only a small fraction of the item's usefulness. Thus the rate at which the utilities of specific goods may be harvested varies greatly.

Frequently the commodities which give up their utilities over a considerable period of time are physically durable. In some cases, however, fragile or physically perishable things may be handled so that they give satisfaction for many years—fragile bric-a-brac for example, that breaks easily if dropped. Consequently the two dichotomous classifications, namely perishable versus durable and immediate-consumption versus instalment-consumption goods, are not the same. In other words, the rate at which utilities may be harvested from specific goods depends in part on physical durability in the ordinary sense and in part upon the way in which use actually rearranges or destroys the particular form of the commodity.

This classification of goods into immediate-consumption or instalment-consumption commodities is of considerable economic importance. In each case, money income is distributed to wage-earners, suppliers of raw materials, and the like at the time of production. Someone must have advanced this money income prior to consumption, perhaps with the aid of the credit facilities of our banking and general monetary system. In the case of the single-instalment or immediate-consumption goods the consumer may buy a single consumption unit at a time and consequently the total amount produced may be closely related to the amount to be consumed in the near future. In the case of instalment-consumption goods, in contrast, the consumer must buy many consumption units at one time, and likewise, the producer must make a supply that will last a long while. This involves the payment of the costs of production months or even years before the utilities may be harvested and is one of the things which makes necessary our complicated financing and credit-extending institutions and practices. A frequent result is that many families find it more practical to rent rather than own a home.[1]

---

[1] Further discussion of the influence of commodity characteristics on consumer purchase and consumption patterns is found in Chapters 10 and 13.

Consumption and Satisfaction of Wants.—Determining when human satisfaction is at a maximum is no easy matter. Economic society presents a pattern too complicated for easy measurement. You and I will not agree on what wants are most urgent or what activities are most satisfying. Even philosophers (not to mention politicians) do not agree on what constitutes the Good Life. How do we rate, for example, the emotional strength or the social desirability of the thrills that come from an airplane ride, an evening of symphony music, or the "never-never land" of an opium dream? Or, and this is even more nebulous, how do we value any of these thrills compared with the satisfactions to be gained from wearing a durable and comfortable pair of shoes, or a suit in the latest fashion? Perhaps, someday, psychologists and philosophers will give us a complete and scientific method of making these comparisons; of measuring the satisfaction derived from enjoying a beautiful sunset so that it may be compared with that resulting from wearing a warm coat on a cold day. Until that distant day, we must find consolation in our ignorance concerning that "better world that might have been."

The nearest approach we have at present to a measurement of relative satisfactions is found in the prices and total expenditures we are willing to pay either in money or in time and energy—in the proportion, that is, of our income—required to obtain them.

There are some shortcomings to this measurement. Frequently, for one thing, we underestimate the worth of those things for which we spend no money, but only time and energy. Then, too, we spend money on impulse for things which later we find unsatisfactory. The old adage that "anticipation is better than realization" leads us astray. What we eat for breakfast may affect our subjective evaluations all day long. For these and other similar reasons, relative prices and total expenditures on specific goods and services are only a rough approximation at best of relative satisfactions or utilities. In spite of its shortcomings, this method of measuring satisfactions obtainable through consumption gives us the best evidence so far discovered concerning the most useful rearrangement of matter.

INCOME

Income Permits Us to Consume.—Income is the result of production and the source of consumption. Our income greatly interests us as consumers, for the size of one's income limits the extent of one's consumption of economic goods and services.

Income Is Hard to Define.—Income is not easy to define. It may be considered, for some purposes, as the total of all money and credit received. This does not serve our present purpose very well, for one's gross income or total receipts may be very large while the part available to spend on consumption is small. A retail grocer may have sales of $75,000 a year, for example, but when he has paid for his stocks of merchandise, his clerk hire, his fuel and light bills, and the other necessary expenses of his business, only a small part of his total sales will be left to him; perhaps not over $1,500—or $2,500 if he has been an unusually good manager. Even of this amount some may have to go for taxes, or repayment of previous loans, or some purpose other than current family consumption.

The federal government and many of the states have undertaken to establish legal definitions of personal income as a basis for levying taxes. They have had great difficulty in deciding what should be counted and what not. One of the troubles has been that individuals often take ownership in land, or capital plant, or inventories of goods, at some appraised value as part of their apparent income. Then when they dispose of their ownership they may realize either more or less than they expected and the question arises, "Is the gain or loss from expected value to be added to or deducted from current income?" This is but one of many complicated questions concerning income that have bothered income tax departments for many years. None of the definitions of income tax authorities quite meets the purposes of our discussion in this book.

Income Is a Flow.—One thing we can say with assurance concerning income—it is a *flow* of value and can be counted only in relation to a period of time. Wealth, in contrast, is a *store* of value, existing and possessed by someone at a moment of time. If I receive a wage for services, a price for the sale of a city lot, an inheritance of a farm or a factory, I have in a sense received an income. If I still possess the farm or factory the next year, it is not income to me, for there has been no further flow of its ownership. It is, however, now a part of my store of wealth.

Some authorities would go still further in limiting the concept of income. These would claim that people do not really receive income until they actually obtain goods and services to consume. In this sense my inheritance of a farm is not income to me, but an increase in my ownership of wealth. I could convert this into income by selling the farm—or by borrowing on it—and using the money for a vacation trip or other form of consumption. Perhaps this is the most accurate concept of income, but it is not the one most commonly used.

Purchasing Power and Realized Income.—For our purposes it is not necessary that we choose one best definition, but that we understand the differences among the several definitions and that we take care to determine the sense in which the term is used whenever we see it. Perhaps it will be helpful if we think of net intake or receipt of money or goods available for consumption as income in the sense of *purchasing power,* and of actual consumption as *realized income.*

When we examine the last mentioned concept of income we see that by its terms the final consumption of goods and services constitutes the total of income. The building of factories is a necessary step towards the production of future income, but it is not income. In the process of building, however, someone is willing to pay money wages to carpenters, bricklayers, and others in anticipation of subsequent business earnings. These wages are, in the main, promptly converted into income in the form of groceries, clothing, and the other goods and services consumed by the wage-earners and their families. Durable consumer goods, such as houses and automobiles, present another complication. Strictly speaking, only their depreciation is realized income, although frequently their purchase for individual use is to be considered. If a house burns down or is otherwise destroyed immediately after completion, no "realized income" i.e., consumption, resulted from its building.

Income, both national and personal, has been defined by one leading authority as follows: [2]

National income may be defined as the net value of commodities and services produced by the nation's economic system. It is "net" in that the value of output of all commodities and services is reduced by the value of commodities (fuel, raw materials and fixed equipment) consumed in the process of production. And it refers, by design, to the net product of the economic system, which, for the advanced nations during recent decades, may be identified with the market economy; provided "market" is understood broadly as the meeting-place of all buyers and sellers, no matter how much the freedom of transactions may be curbed by custom or regulation.

National income is thus that part of the national product which is largely imputable to individuals who contribute to production either their labor or the services of their property. In return for this participation these individuals receive compensation, which accounts for the preponderant share of national

---

[2] Simon Kuznets, *National Income, 1919-1935* (New York: National Bureau of Economic Research, Bulletin 66, 1937).

income produced in any given year. But there may be two other elements in national income. First, the producing enterprises may make payments not only to individuals who, in a given year, participate in the productive process, but also to individuals who participated in it in the past or have not participated at all. Pensions, compensations for injuries, relief payments, and charity contributions by business enterprises are channels through which income produced in a given year may be paid to individuals other than those sharing in the process of producing it. Second, enterprises may distribute to individuals amounts not necessarily equal to the part of national income that these enterprises produce. In some years a business firm or other producing enterprise may pay out to individuals an amount smaller than its share in national income thus retaining what we designate as positive savings of enterprises. In other years an enterprise may distribute to individuals an amount larger than its own share in the national total, thus giving rise to negative savings of enterprises. If we designate all receipts by individuals from the producing enterprises as income payments to individuals, national income is equal to the algebraic sum of incomes paid to individuals and of savings of all enterprises.

Income generally is reported in terms of money. This is convenient because nearly all business transactions are completed by money payments and because money is a convenient common denominator with which to obtain the sum of satisfactions derived respectively from a new pair of shoes, a month's supply of milk, a week end at a lake resort, a carton of cigarettes, a symphony concert, and any quantity of other things. As will be pointed out in Chapter 6, however, money is both inadequate and inexact as a measure of income to such an extent that great care must be used in comparing the consumption possibilities associated with specific money incomes.

Whenever the term *income* is used in this text we hope that its meaning will be clearly understood from explicit modifying phrases or from the context in which it is used.

PROJECT QUESTIONS

1. Locate the oldest house in your community. When was it built? How is it being used at present? How old is the house in which your family lives?

2. Answer the above questions for the following commodities in your immediate neighborhood or among your close acquaintances:

   a) Automobile
   b) Dining-room table
   c) Winter overcoat
   d) The oldest item of food or beverage
   e) Musical instrument

3. Visit any manufacturing concern and then describe the process through which the raw material goes and the resulting changes in form. Where did the raw material come from and what man-made changes in form had it already undergone before it reached this factory? Is the product of this factory ready for ultimate consumption? If not, how will it be used?

4. Have each student estimate the "value" of specific forms of non-monetary income received by his family, relative either to total money income or to expenditures in retail stores.

Chapter 4

STANDARDS AND PLANES OF CONSUMPTION

The Need for a "Yardstick"

There are numerous reasons for wanting a method of comparing patterns of consumption. Some important ones are suggested by the following questions:

Do we live as well as our fathers did?

How much better off are we than the people in India or England?

Does the rank and file of population live better in California, or Minnesota, or Pennsylvania?

Do mechanics live better than accountants?

Do any of us live as well as our money income [1] would permit?

Does today's wage buy as much as last year's?

A "yardstick" by which these and similar questions might be tested would be most welcome. Unfortunately, none exists that is entirely satisfactory. Money expenditures are, perhaps, the best simple index by which to compare different patterns of consumption. This is inadequate, however, for many reasons, some of which are the following:

Money changes in value or purchasing power with the passage of time, thus becoming a "rubber yardstick." This point is explained more fully in Chapter 6.

Government consumes different forms and amounts of goods in different countries at the same time, and at different times in the same country.

Different environments necessitate different expenditures to gain similar results. This point is explained in Chapters 9 and 10.

Differences in the cultural complex—i.e., experiences, traditions, education, and training, awareness of the existence of some consumption goods, tastes, taboos, legal privileges and restrictions, and personal whims—make monetary comparisons almost meaningless in terms of human satisfactions.

---

[1] Money income, its origins and distribution, is discussed further in Chapters 11 and 12.

THE HELLER COMMITTEE METHOD

As a pragmatic solution to the problem of comparisons, the approach followed by the Heller Committee of the University of California has much merit. This committee has undertaken for some years to prepare lists of specific possessions and annual expenditures that seem proper and attainable under the production and general environmental conditions prevailing in the San Francisco Bay region. They have prepared three lists, one each for the rank and file of (1) factory employees, (2) office employees, and (3) professional workers. The lists are changed every few years to accommodate changes in such things as relative productivity, prices, general modes of living, and so on. The lists are very different in detail from such lists in Butte, Montana where the climate, for example, is radically different, or in New York City where the custom of owning automobiles differs, or in a rural farming district where the whole mode of living is different.

What the Heller Committee has set up is a somewhat idealized and highly generalized pattern of consumption for each of three groups of families. They represent "standards" that are possible of attainment with present purchasing power, provided the latter is well managed by the individual family. They are also standards that are acceptable to many, perhaps to most, of the families in each group. They are not, however, standards that would be equally possible of achievement or acceptable if achieved under other income or environmental conditions. Families in Minneapolis, for example, would not be warm enough in winter with the same expenditure for fuel and overcoats, while because of lower prices they might require less money for eggs and milk. Moreover, no individual family may have followed precisely the pattern of the standard.

This discussion clearly suggests the need for two steps in the measurement of consumption. First a standard must be established. Then actual consumption must be compared to this standard. Let us amplify the definition of the term "standard" somewhat and also the distinction between "standard" and "plane" of consumption.

DIFFERENCE BETWEEN STANDARD AND PLANE OF CONSUMPTION

A Standard Is a Criterion.—A *standard* may be defined as a "criterion" or a bench mark for comparison, or as "that which is established as a model or example by authority, custom, or general consent." In other words, a standard is a record or a unit of measurement of some sort against which an actual object or performance may be judged. Ten seconds might be agreed upon, for example, as a *standard* time for the 100-yard dash; anything faster than that might be called excellent, or phenomenal, while anything slower might be called mediocre, or poor. This illustration suggests that the standard should be possible of objective measurement and comparison, and also that it may be chosen quite arbitrarily. The term, *standard of consumption,* as we shall see presently, is at least partially possible of objective measurement, but its choice is certainly arbitrary.

A Plane Is a Result or Accomplishment.—A *plane* of consumption is the actual use or consumption of goods and services that has been reached at a particular time by specific individuals and groups. In other places in this book we have spoken of "the pattern of consumption"; when this term includes all types of consumption it is identical with the plane of consumption. *Scale* and *level* of consumption are also used as synonyms for plane of consumption.

A distinction may be made between that portion of consumption which consists of the use of economic goods and services on the one hand, and the portion which consists of the use of free goods on the other hand. Economic goods, as the term implies, are those for which the individual must pay a price. We already have intimated that a part of one's happiness comes from the enjoyment of things which are free, such as sunsets and other natural views.

Standards Must Fit the Circumstances.—Moreover, in Florida or California one enjoys the sunshine and avoids some expenditure for fuel and heavy clothing. In contrast, in New Hampshire and Vermont one enjoys certain winter sports not available to persons living in warmer climates. All these things make it necessary that comparisons of the plane of living be made against different standards for different parts of the country. There is a point to be made beyond this, however, which is that for some purposes the noneconomic or free goods must be included in comparing opportunities for living under different geographical or cultural circumstances. It would be interesting to establish two sets of standards, one including only the economic goods and services for which we have to pay and the other including in addition all the noneconomic advantages to which we have access. However, this latter set of standards would include so many intangible items for which no good unit of measurement is available that it would be difficult to prepare. For the balance of our discussion we shall confine ourselves primarily to standards and planes measured entirely by economic goods and services. Moreover, we shall consider the terms *standard of living* and *standard of consumption* as being synonymous. This will be true also with plane of living and plane of consumption. Common practice has identified standard of living, plane of living, and cost of living as being concerned exclusively with matters of economic cost and value.

THE ESTABLISHMENT OF STANDARDS

The establishment of a standard, or standards, of consumption is not easy. This is true, in the first place, because the final criterion of consumption is the satisfying of wants or desires, and personal satisfactions are subjective. They are "feelings" rather than "facts" and there are no definite units for measuring them.

In the second place, there are many satisfactions which, as we have already pointed out, do not enter the commercial economic system; that is, things like a swim in the surf or a romp with a dog or a child are outside our system of exchange-cooperation and generally are omitted from formal standards of living.

In the third place, standards of living are the products of experience and, as such, are constantly changing. They mirror history and the psychological interests and attitudes of given people at a given time. It is a commonplace, for example, that the standards in art, clothes, games, food, and bathrooms of the Middle Ages were vastly different from those of today, and it has been pointed out earlier that a standard of living involving automotive transportation was impossible until technology had developed automobiles that were economically practical. Comfort in beds, variety and vitamins in food, speed in travel, cleanliness of person and clothing, are refinements of the last one hundred years. So, also, are the radio, the telephone, sanitary plumbing, and practically all of modern medicine and surgery. It is only a long generation ago that when one of the wealthier families in southern Minnesota entertained guests overnight, some member of the household had to sleep in the haymow. A reading of *Life in a Medieval Barony,* by William Stearns Davis, or *Famine,* by Liam O'Flaherty, or any of Dickens' novels portraying the beginnings of the industrial revolution, or a view of the motion picture on the life of Henry VIII, will impress one with this fact of continuous change, in view of which a standard for yesterday is of little interest in measuring today's scale of living.

In the fourth place, even for today there will be many standards. "That which is established as a model or example by authority, custom, or general consent" differs greatly for different regions and communities. This means that many standards may be desirable for a country like the United States in which conditions differ so widely among the different sections. Housing and clothing that are adequate in Florida, for example, might not keep people from freezing to death in North Dakota. Moreover, custom dictates that schoolteachers and farmers shall wear different clothes as also shall office clerks and factory workers. The fisher folk of Maine, the apartment dwellers of New York, the Babbitts of the middle western small cities, and the ranchers of Montana each have their pattern of living, accepted by general consent. The distinctions are not so great as they were before the time of rapid transportation, instantaneous communication, ubiquitous movies, and national advertising, but they still exist to baffle the maker of standards.

Finally, there will always be some dispute as to whether a standard should be merely a measure of something already attained and temporarily accepted by a social group, or whether it should be an ideal towards which the group is straining. Except where otherwise noted, we shall refer to accepted standards that have been realized by enough persons in each group to make them appear practical of general attainment, leaving the reader free to establish his own ideal standards.

THE PURPOSES OF STANDARDS

Standards properly conceived will provide a measuring rod or pattern of consumption against which the actual plane of living of each group in society may be judged. Emphasis must be given, however, to the fact that different standards are applicable to different groups of people. Frequent reference is made to the "American standard of living," but it is clear that a single standard cannot be applied usefully to such heterogeneous situations as exist in the United States. Peixotto has called the present scale of living among the professional classes in the country "the American standard of living," because, she says, "the aspiration of all Americans strains toward the professional life and toward a professional standard of living." [2] It is not certain, however, that all Americans strain toward the professional life and perhaps it would be very unfortunate if they did. Some individuals probably actually prefer to be trappers, or woodsmen, or farmers, or mechanics, or salespeople, or what not, and to live as these groups customarily do rather than as the present lawyers, doctors, or university professors live. Only if this is true can we

---

[2] Jessica Peixotto, *Getting and Spending at the Professional Standard of Living* (New York: The Macmillan Co., 1927), p. 35.

continue happily to operate an exchange economy with its large total production and its colorful variety of life. The probability that people do have this diversity of preferences is supported, certainly, by a mass of evidence on individual differences in abilities, discrimination, and the like. It is supported, further, by the fact that people always have selected a wide variety of personal activities in their choices both of work and of play. In any case it has been more common practice, and perhaps more useful, to apply the term "American standard of living" separately to each of several economic groups within the country. Under this usage of the term the American standard of living for workmen, for example, would be that attained by the better-paid and more continuously employed wage-earners in the common industries of the country.

Even this concept might well be given separate consideration and measurement not only for different income levels but also for different parts of the country. Whether or not the coal miner in Pennsylvania, the automobile worker in Michigan, the sheepherder in Montana, the cotton picker in Alabama, the packing-house hand in Chicago, and the butter-maker in Minnesota, *should* live differently does not concern us here; the fact is that they do. The differences are so great that a leveling of the real income of workers and a standardizing of their patterns of consumption throughout the different regions would have a profound effect on the production programs and the general economy of the entire country. If all were leveled *up* to the standard of automobile workers, there would be a great increase in the production and consumption of houses, automobiles and gasoline, upper-middle-class clothing, and so on. If all were leveled *down* to the standard of coal miners, cotton pickers, or sheepherders, there would be a great decline in these and many other items of consumption.

Either a standard or a plane of living may be thought of as: (a) psychological feelings of satisfaction; (b) money income devoted to different lines of goods and services as a forerunner of consumption; or (c) actual use or consumption of goods and services in physical terms. We are forced, however, largely to disregard the first concept, because of lack of measuring devices. Consequently, we shall consider both standards and planes of living in terms of money expenditures and, whenever practical, in terms of physical quantities.

The Cost of Living.—Because of the complications of changing levels of prices and changing money values of specific goods and services, however, it is necessary for clarity to use still another term. We shall confine the use of the terms *standard* and *plane* of consumption to physical quantities unless otherwise noted, while *cost of living* will be used in reference to the money expenditure necessary for any particular standard or plane at a particular time. Care must be taken in the use of *cost of living,* of course, to make clear whether it refers to a standard or a plane of consumption.

PROJECT QUESTIONS

1. If possible, get a copy of one of the Heller Committee's Quantity and Cost Budget studies. Compare the items in the wardrobes suggested with those in your own family. What do you think of the differences?

2. How would you go about establishing standards for two or three families which differ by income, size, and occupation?

3. How many students in this class have been led to believe that they can become either President of the United States or millionaires? How realistic are these assumptions? Discuss the extent to which such assumptions may lead to frustration and maladjustment. Do such assumptions motivate individuals to great achievement?

4. Discuss the differences between your "standard" and your "plane" of living; specify in terms of commodities and services.

Chapter 5

THE ROLE OF SPECIALIZATION

The Development of Specialization

Somehow men never have been able to discover an effortless approach to the satisfaction of their desires. They always have wanted things which are scarce. The pages of history are colorful with the exploits of individuals whose discoveries in geographic, scientific, and other areas were motivated by the desire for new or scarce things. The fabulous Mongol warrior-king, Genghis Khan, who dreamed of establishing control over the great area from the Pacific coast of China to the Atlantic coast of Europe, was motivated by both a burning desire for power and an equally overpowering desire for wealth in the form of precious stones, gold, and other priceless things. Through the ages, men have wanted scarce things and have fought each other for what they thought were treasured possessions.

Many systems have been tried to permit people individually and in groups to gain their desires. To a considerable extent, these trials result from the attempt of people to adapt their economy to their environment. Since environments differ, there has been no precise order in the evolution from one economy to another. Nevertheless, throughout history, one trend is crystal clear. As the world has moved from epoch to epoch, individuals and areas in general have become continuously more specialized. In the early hunting and fishing stage, the men captured the game while the women did just about everything else, but this was as far as specialization went. There was little or no trading between families or tribes. In the pastoral stage, the nomadic peoples gained some regional specialization by following the seasons, from the warm lowlands in winter to the cool mountain highlands in summer. Thus they kept their flocks in grass throughout the year, and got their meat supply with less effort and more certainty than did their forebears.

Here and there peoples gave up nomadic life for the more productive and safer domestic economy with its increasing specialization of labor. Transition has been slow and remnants of pastoral economies still persist in a few places. But as early as 1700 the diary of a

French Countess tells of her supervising the work of carders, spinners, weavers, seamstresses, builders, wig-makers and other workers.[1] In humbler homes, the members of the family made what they needed, aided by village or wandering craftsmen.

The characteristics of the domestic economy were that workers were partly in agriculture and partly in hand manufacture, and production for one's own use was increasingly supplemented by production for exchange. The merchant-capitalist or middleman was needed to assist in the distribution of goods when the worker could no longer finance his own production. The individual no longer consumed all he produced nor produced all he consumed. The task of getting goods from the producer to the consumer gradually became an important one, with more and more specialized functions and institutions requiring more and more people to perform the jobs and staff the institutions.

Domestic economy gradually developed into the factory or industrial stage, which resulted in the greatest growth of specialization both geographic and personal. The characteristics of the factory or industrial stage are: (1) introduction of power machinery, (2) ownership by employers of plant and equipment, (3) concentration of workers in factories or under one roof instead of working in their own scattered homes, (4) resultant growth of specialization and division of labor, and (5) separation of consumer and producer.

This stage has been coincidental with the industrial revolution which had been "in process" for two centuries before its effects were numerous enough and important enough to demand recognition. Certainly by 1760 the industrial revolution was under way in many parts of the world. The system of political economy engendered by it still is evolving and maturing, until none of us produces much of anything for our own uses. Even large areas like states or countries produce only part of what is consumed in the area, as we shall illustrate in a moment.

Whenever people get together—whether it be in primitive tribes, more sophisticated cities and nations, in a world economy, or on a college campus—they find they possess different skills, abilities, and preferences. One enjoys hunting wild game and excels at it, another can carve wood or shape metal with great skill; some are extroverts who can sell anything while others are much better at independent laboratory research. Some college students edit the college paper,

---

[1] Herbert Heaton, *Economic History of Europe* (New York: Harper & Bros., 1936), p. 335.

others play football or pole-vault, others organize political parties, while a few apparently do nothing but study. As these differences become evident individuals tend to specialize and to do those things for which each is best fitted. Whenever they undertake to earn their own living, their special products are exchanged for those of others.

This process of specialization has been carried so far that, as pointed out above, division of tasks is a major characteristic of economic society. The surgeon does not practice law and the tool designer is not a C.P.A. While the farmer must do many things, he neither weaves cloth for his family nor makes his own tractor; frequently he does not even grow his own seed.

Regional specialization also has become commonplace, especially since the development of modern methods of transportation. In this country we have a Cotton Belt, a Corn Belt, a Wheat Belt, and so on. Steel is produced in a few locations only, and the automobile industry is concentrated in and near its Michigan center. We import products such as natural rubber, tin, nickel, coffee, and tungsten from countries where they are produced cheaply. Through trade these things are made available for use at points far removed from their production.

When specialization operates so that each person and area is producing the things which he or it can do best, total production is maximized. No society ever has directed the use of human and other resources so perfectly as to reach the maximum product. Even our government-directed army has failed miserably in some cases to utilize the special skills of individuals. Nevertheless, the principle of specialization is so important in economic development that it needs to be thoroughly understood.

The Principle of Comparative Advantage

If production is to be maximized, both regions and individuals must specialize in accord with the Principle of Comparative Advantage or Least Comparative Disadvantage. In practical situations, this principle is related to—and measured by—costs of production. Consequently it sometimes is discussed as the Principle of Comparative Costs. The rest of this Chapter is devoted to explaining and illustrating this principle.

As Stated by the Businessman.—The businessman, thinking of the day-to-day transactions in his business, will state the principle about as follows: a region will do well to export those products which are lower in price within its borders than elsewhere, and to import those which are higher in price nearby than elsewhere. The differences in price, of course, must be more than the cost of transporting the goods from the low-cost to the high-cost area if they are to be moved with profit. Consequently a well-developed, low-cost transportation system is a great aid in the practical application of the principle of comparative advantage. Regional specialization has been carried much further in the United States than in China, for example, partly because of the great difference in transportation facilities in the two countries.

As Stated by the Job Seeker.—Individuals attempting to decide what job to take will phrase the principle of comparative advantage in much the same way: it will pay to undertake those activities for which others will pay the highest price for one's time, and to buy those goods the making of which would require the foregoing of other earnings greater than their price. Perhaps, for example, an insurance salesman cannot afford to wash his own automobile—which he could hire done for a dollar—if in the time so used he could sell a policy on which his commission would be ten dollars.

The Principle of Opportunity Costs.—When stated this way the principle of comparative advantage suggests another, namely, the Principle of Opportunity Costs. In many cases the term "cost" implies merely a measurement of the direct expenditures of money or time and energy. In other cases, however, "cost" properly includes whatever alternative is given up. If one goes to the football game on Saturday afternoon, for example, the "costs" may include not only the price of the ticket, but also the loss of money that might have been earned clerking in the drugstore. This is on the assumption, of course, that one had opportunity to work in the drugstore and must take a "vacation" to go to the game. Whenever real alternatives exist the individual and the region must consider the opportunities that are foregone in estimating the cost of each alternative. If a farmer can rent his land for $10 an acre, that becomes his "opportunity cost" of using the land for any crop and should be added to the calculation of all his other costs in determining whether to rent or to farm his land. Or if a man is considering starting his own grocery store, his calculation of "costs" should include his "opportunity" to work for someone else at a salary and to place his money in a savings organization where it would be federally insured. When items like these are estimated realistically they are very helpful in pointing to the most profitable use of resources.

As Stated by the Economist.—Economists state the Principle of Comparative Advantage as follows : A country tends to export those products in the production of which it has the greatest advantage or the least disadvantage compared with other countries, and it tends to import those products in which it has the least advantage or greatest disadvantage. Stated slightly differently, a country tends to export those products which are produced at a lower comparative cost within its borders than elsewhere and to import those which are produced at a higher comparative cost at home than elsewhere. In this form the principle becomes the Law of Comparative Costs.

However the principle is stated, so long as men are free to do what they will they tend to do those things that give them the greatest power of exchange. While this is a strong tendency there are, unfortunately, some things that partially offset it and thus prevent the maximization of income. Information is frequently inadequate on which to base wise decisions. Then, too, the emotional urge for national or regional self-sufficiency is often a barrier to interregional trade. Each of these offsetting forces is discussed later in this chapter.

GEOGRAPHIC SPECIALIZATION

Geographic specialization has been carried to such a point that much of the world's economy has become a closely knit and integrated structure. Each country and, in fact, each section within each country is dependent to a considerable extent upon other areas for many things. Elaborate transportation and communication systems have been built to facilitate interchange of goods and to give each area the benefit of the other areas' advantages. The result is an integrated economic organization composed of highly dependent areas and individuals. Certain strategic points, spoken of as metropolitan centers, serve as clearing houses in the exchange of goods. Here the materials produced in the immediate hinterland are concentrated for processing and distribution, perhaps over wide areas. Here also materials are brought from everywhere for distribution and use within the area served by the agencies in the metropolitan center.

Rivalry between metropolitan centers frequently is keen. In the development of the Mississippi Valley, for example, Chicago and St. Louis competed for the trade of the Twin Cities. Earlier, the seaboard cities of Boston, New York, and Philadelphia had been in strong rivalry for supremacy in eastern commercial circles. San Francisco and Los Angeles each desires to be the maritime center for trade with the Orient. North Carolina is attempting to develop cotton mills that will partially displace those in New England, as the shoe factories of St. Louis already have, and as the flour mills of Buffalo have partially displaced those of Minneapolis. This sort of rivalry is occurring continuously throughout the world. Moreover, specialization and rivalry are as natural between different countries as they are between areas within any one country.

Why Each Country Is Not Self-sufficient.—There are two reasons why countries are not self-sufficient; the one is physical and the other economic. In the first place, no country has a geographical endowment of climate, soils, minerals, and other natural resources which make it suitable for the production of all commodities. For instance, wheat cannot readily be produced in the tropics, nor can bananas be grown anywhere but in the tropics. Thus a great deal of international commerce arises out of the interchange of commodities which may be produced only in certain areas. Such trade is mutually advantageous since it enables the consumers in each country to choose from a wider variety of goods, and thus to improve their standard of life.

Western United States, Argentina, New Zealand, and Australia are abundantly supplied with productive land relative to their present population density, compared with that of England, Japan, and the continent of Europe. Therefore they have a comparative advantage in the production of those commodities that require much land and little labor, such as meat, hides, and wool. The rich nickel deposits of Ontario and the tin deposits of Southeast Asia give those areas decisive advantages as world centers of production for nickel and tin. In Japan and China human labor is relatively plentiful and so those areas find it more profitable to produce handmade products rather than automobiles or machine tools which require much capital equipment.

California produces oil but no automobiles, while Michigan produces automobiles but very little oil. Florida and Texas produce many more grapefruit than are consumed in those states while they produce less wheat than they consume. Although over 70 per cent of our raw wool is produced in our western states, nearly all woolen manufacture is in the East. Wherever one may live, it is interesting to list the things one uses which are made nearby, and then list those that originate elsewhere. The latter list is almost certain to be much the longer. And then a third list may be made of the things sent out from the area in exchange for those sent in. These lists will dramatize the importance of interregional trade.

If each region and country specialized in the production of the goods which it could produce most advantageously, and exchanged the surplus for other goods, a social gain would result since more and a greater variety of goods could be produced and therefore consumed. The United States buys coffee from Brazil, and tea from the Orient, because those goods cannot be advantageously produced at home. In exchange we produce and export cotton, wheat, automobiles, and other goods which may be more advantageously produced here. If such a policy were followed for more commodities by more countries, each country could enjoy a greater variety of goods, and at a lower cost.

Science and Technology Tend to Reduce Regional Differences. —However, beginning in the latter part of the nineteenth century and accelerating in the twentieth century, the advance of science and technology began to weaken the necessity for interdependence of regions and countries. The development of electrical power weakened the influence of coal deposits in the localization of industries. "It is believed by many—the evidence thus far is certainly inconclusive— that the development of electrical power may become an important factor tending toward the decentralization of industry and toward greater national and local self-sufficiency."[2] Moreover, the rise of modern chemistry has made possible the raising of crops in regions by nature not advantageous to them. For example, prior to World War II Germany reached a position of virtual self-sufficiency in food —a prospect hardly dreamed of by anyone two decades ago.

War Tends to Increase Nationalism.—An additional impetus toward nationalism is found in the depression of 1929-35. During this period of drastic maladjustment of production and consumption many governments came to the conclusion that their citizens could be kept more fully employed if no foreign-made goods were permitted in their markets. Consequently, trade barriers were carried to heights never dreamed of before.

Moreover, the terrific impact of wars results in an almost universal craving for the utmost measure of self-sufficiency as a means of national security. War engenders, of necessity, an intense political nationalism. This in turn develops and strengthens the trend toward economic self-sufficiency. One can well understand that Germany, starved into submission by World War I and the post-armistice

---

[2] Alvin Hansen, *International Economic Relations* (Minneapolis: University of Minnesota Press. 1934). p. 106.

blockade, was willing to pay a very considerable price for self-sufficiency in food and essentials of national defense. A strong impulse was given most countries involved in that devastating war to develop those industries which were important for the feeding of its people and for the manufacturing of munitions and other war materials to protect their boundaries. This meant a reorientation of productive channels, of capital investment, and of the use of natural resources—a reorientation farther removed from and less economic than those based on comparative advantage.

Political Areas Should Conform More Closely to Economic Areas.—World War II has intensified this struggle for greater economic security but on a somewhat different plane. Certain nations, suffering from almost overwhelming economic instability and insecurity, seem to be willing to make considerable sacrifices of economic progress and even of real income in the interest of a domestic supply of essential commodities. In contrast, as never before, it is becoming clear that a high standard of living (and perhaps even survival for certain segments of the world) depends upon a revival and maintenance of international trade based on the Principle of Comparative Advantage. Barbara Ward argues for a Western Association of European Nations.[3] She maintains that the pre-World War II economic framework failed not only because the political balance of power in Europe vanished leaving nothing to replace it, but also because Europe's industrial resources and economic organization were neither modern enough nor powerful enough to meet the competition of the United States. She suggests a single association or federation of nations which would include the United Kingdom, France, Italy, Belgium, Netherlands, Norway, Sweden, Denmark, Eire, Portugal, Luxembourg, and Western Germany, which would provide a free trade area from Scandinavia to the Pyrenees, and from the Elbe to Donegal. This area, which is so much larger and wealthier than any one of its components, would include all the basic economic resources and would, she maintains, be able more nearly to match the United States in productivity and trade possibilities. In other words, she claims that the substitution of supernationalism for national sovereignty is vital to the life of these countries.

Unfortunately, to the mass of people and to some "people in high places" the international exchange of goods is of no significance for the maintenance of a high standard of living. Many people feel that

---

[3] Barbara Ward, *The West at Bay* (New York: W. W. Norton & Co., Inc., 1948), pp. 76-79.

their own community possesses great enough productive power and capacity for their own needs. They do not feel impoverished by any lack of things which in their view they cannot themselves produce. They are horrified, perhaps, at the failure of industry to function swiftly and continuously, but many have the suspicion that international complications and entanglements might have been avoided and are in part to blame. In any event, the belief is widespread that a reorganization of the internal system of production is more important for the achievement of a high standard of living than is the maintenance or revival of international trade.

It is quite understandable, especially under modern conditions, that this should be the view of the great majority of modern nations. It is quite natural for a people to wish to produce at home everything that it is possible, within reason, to produce. The economic law of comparative advantage is not easily understood, the repercussions upon the domestic economy of international policies that cause international strain are not readily traced to their intricate and obscure causes. It is not to be wondered at that the practical man on the street turns aside from these difficult speculations and seizes firm hold of benefits that lie close at home. Politicians everywhere find it difficult to get votes for an international program but can easily insure an election on domestic slogans.[4]

Trade Barriers Restrict Production.—In the face of all the artificial trade barriers which have been erected, international trade goes on. The final result, however, of a continued policy of nationalistic protection must inevitably be a restriction of world trade to an exchange of those indispensable commodities that cannot be produced in the home country or, at least, that cannot be produced except at prohibitive cost. This would greatly curtail the operation of the principle of comparative advantage and would result in inefficient use of labor and other resources in each country. Such an unwise choice of production activities would necessarily reduce the total income rather than increase it.

Factors Affecting the Location of Industry.—Perhaps it may be well at this point to insert a statement concerning location of industry in general. In theory, the problem of location of industry is simple. The concerns that can produce goods most cheaply can undersell their rivals. These concerns will survive and their rivals will disappear. Goods generally cannot be produced at the same cost throughout a large area. Proximity to raw material, or to power, or to labor, or to the market—each of these things has an important bearing on

---

[4] Hansen, *op. cit.*, pp. 108-9.

costs. The relative cost of transporting raw materials and finished products is important; so also are taxes, site rent, accessibility to buyers and sellers, and technical considerations such as water supply and climate. Out of a complex such as this someone must decide in each case what industries have a chance of proving productive in each locality.

Certainly the market is one of the controlling factors in the location of industries. It appears to be the most important factor with those industries that are scattered widely, about in proportion to the population, such, for example, as bakeries, laundries, small machine shops, job printing, retail shops, and the like. It has far less effect, on the other hand, on the canning of vegetables, and practically none on the mining of diamonds. There is need for careful study of location factors as we contemplate a possible expansion of production, and yet without such expansion consumption cannot be increased.

In connection with future industrial developments it must be remembered that pioneer industries will be of less importance than formerly, at least in this country. This follows from the facts that population is increasing at a slower rate and that large accumulations of capital have already taken place to accommodate production needs. The new industries of the future will lie, perhaps, mainly in those lines of production referred to in Chapter 15, which are already being undertaken but in which the output is clearly too small to permit people to have all they want for consumption, and in new industries which have not yet been thought of, or for which the technical details have not been worked out to a practical point.

Personal Specialization

Individuals Tend to Do What Each Can Do Best.—The Principle of Comparative Advantage applies to people as well as to geographic areas. The individual should select that job for which he is best fitted or which offers the best opportunities in the form of getting the job and advancement. A simple example will illustrate this point.

When a young physician opens his office to begin his first practice he has an abundance of time upon his hands. Because his practice is light and income is small, he probably will handle all the record-keeping and correspondence himself, take care of his own instruments, answer his own telephone, and act as his laboratory technician. In time, however, if he is a competent physician, and has the proper manner, and is located in a city of appreciable size, he will have more practice than he can handle alone and attend to his records and correspondence besides. At this point, he will hire a secretary who will do his typing, answer phone calls, make his appointments for him, and the like. It will be of advantage for him to do this because in the extra time released to him he will be able to look after enough additional patients to more than pay the salary of this secretary. This is possible, of course, because physicians are much better paid for their time than are secretaries. Furthermore, the chances are that a properly trained secretary will keep his records and write his letters in less time and better than he can. Thus there is a saving both ways. Now if his practice grows still more, he may employ a nurse to help him look after his patients during office calls, and take care of his instruments and supplies. As a next step, he may take in a young physician as a partner and let him handle the routine, time-consuming cases. He now devotes his time to handling only the important or difficult cases. He is now a full-fledged city physician! Each step in his progress to this end, unless taken prematurely, has been to his economic advantage. Each step has released more of his time for the doing of more important things. Each step has increased his *net income*, because it has increased his *gross income* more than his expenses. Each is a step toward greater specialization.[5]

As suggested by this illustration, each person tends to do those things which he can do to best advantage. But this does not mean that tasks are always performed by those who can do them best; in fact, quite the contrary is the case! In the example of specialization by persons given above, the secretary did the record-keeping better than her employer-physician could have done it. However, many a small-scale businessman in the country could do a better job of book-keeping than his bookkeeper. Many a manager could do a better job of supervising the details of operation of his plant than do his foremen. Many a store operator could do a better job of selling than many of the salesmen. But if the businessman kept his own books, he would have little time left for matters of general policy, and if the store manager spent his time waiting upon customers no one would be left as competent as he to do the buying.

Not Everyone Does What He Can Do Best.—Many a person in the world today is not doing the thing for which he is best fitted or best trained, but instead, something else which no one else can do so well as he, even though he is not especially apt at doing it. There was

-----

[5] The material in this paragraph is adapted from John D. Black, *Production Economics* (New York: Henry Holt & Co., Inc., 1926) pp. 129-36.

other work to do and no one else was especially fitted for it, and so he stepped in and did it. A case in point is that of a coach building up a football team. He may have a man who would make an excellent tackle, but he is well supplied with tackle material and is short of material for the fullback position. So he takes his most promising tackle out of the line and makes a fullback of him because the young man will make a better fullback than any other available man. The individual man may not show up as brilliantly in consequence, but the team as a whole will win more games. Hence, although in general the individual is usually found doing the task for which he is best fitted, there are many occasions when it is a task for which he is only fairly well fitted, but for which no one better fitted is available. There is a tendency, it is true, for the individual to do the thing he can do best. But it is only a tendency, and one which is frequently offset by countertendencies.

A Well-Chosen Occupation Makes Life Worth While.—The wise individual choice of occupation is of importance not only because it results in increased total product as well as increased exchange power, but also because

. . . approximately two thirds of the life span of the average man is devoted to gainful employment. Of these years half of the waking hours are commonly spent in active work, if vacations, illness and involuntary idleness are left out of consideration. In any community the satisfactions of life are dependent upon the character of the occupations in which the people are engaged. The nature of the daily tasks is the leading determinant of the real meaning and quality of living. The quality of the job goes far to set the tone, pitch, and tempo of leisure as well as of working hours. In an age of economic interdependence and specialized subdivision of labor the welfare of the community rests upon the maintenance of balance in the numbers in the different occupational groups.[6]

Job Opportunities Are Important.—It is important that individuals specialize in those occupations where there is employment—as we said above, they should choose those fields which are not overcrowded. There are common fallacies which have kept people from appreciating the importance of selecting a field where they will be at the least disadvantage. We must explode these fallacies! Individuals do not have equal opportunities; anybody *cannot* do anything if he tries hard enough; there is *not* one job and one job only for which

6 Ralph G. Hurlin and Meredith B. Givens, "Shifting Occupational Trends." By permission from *Recent Social Trends* by the Research Comm. on Social Trends, Inc. Copyright, 1933. McGraw-Hill Book Company, Inc., p. 268.

each person is perfectly suited, and the law of compensation is a fiction and doesn't work very well in the job-span of the individual. To select a job one should think in terms of job opportunities as well as in terms of one's own abilities.

Wise individual choice of an occupation depends, first of all, on available information about job opportunities. Such information often is not available in sufficient detail to be a sound guide. Some data are available, however, which are helpful in a general way. Figure 1 shows the percentage distribution of men and women according to what we may call the *level* of occupation for each census year from 1910 to 1950. From these data the following facts appear:

1. Semiskilled workers, clerical and sales jobholders, proprietors, managers and officials, service workers, and professional workers have increased relative to total employment.
2. Farmers, farm laborers, and unskilled workers have decreased relatively.
3. Skilled laborers have remained about a constant proportion of the total.
4. Clerical and sales jobs, service workers, semiskilled workers, and professional workers are the only fields in which women are present in important numbers.
5. The semiskilled class accounts for more men than any other with skilled labor a close second.

The increase in professional occupations and the decrease in unskilled workers relative to total employment indicate a rise in the general level of employment. The increase in the proportion of semiskilled workers, on the other hand, might be interpreted as an indication of mediocrity in employment opportunities. Fortunately, however, this has been accompanied by a decrease in hours of work so that a larger part of one's life is spent outside his job, which fact may compensate in part for the monotony and mediocrity of the work.

The broad classifications shown in Figure 1 are broken down into about 500 more detailed classes. Comparison of census data for various years would show which specific occupations have been increasing in numbers and in proportion to total employment, and also which have been decreasing. This matter is too detailed to be undertaken here for the multitude of occupations. Any individual may make the study rather easily for the few fields in which he is interested.

Some data also are available on the earnings rates for different occupations. Here again there is too much detail to justify presentation of the facts in a general text. Each individual can find informa-

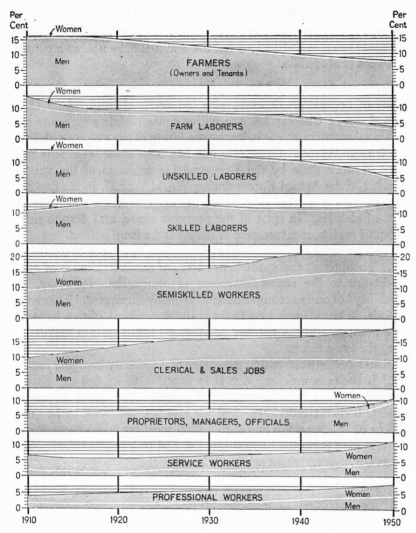

FIG. 1.—Job Opportunities Are Constantly Changing

See how the percentages of men and women doing different kinds of work have shifted in forty years. Source: Changing Times, *The Kiplinger Magazine*, March, 1951.

tion in such sources as the *Statistical Abstract, Census Reports,* the *Survey of Current Business,* and publications of the Bureau of Labor Statistics that will help him estimate the chance of gaining a satisfactory income from the occupations in which he is interested.

But to be able to determine the chances for employment in a growing occupation one should know something about the number of applicants for jobs in that field. Separate and unrelated studies of this type in certain fields have been made from time to time by private and governmental institutions but the findings have not, as a general rule, been made public.

Personal Ability Is Also Important.—Of course, wise individual choice of occupation depends, also, on one's abilities. As will be pointed out in Chapter 13, one major cause of labor turnover and individual maladjustment is inaccurate fitting of the worker's abilities to job requirements. Great progress has been made, especially as a result of work done by the Personnel Departments of the various branches of the Armed Forces during World War II, in the development of tests and other devices for the determination and measurement of abilities. In spite of the progress made, and despite many favorable results, measurement of ability is far from perfect.

Wise personal specialization involves, then, two types of consideration. The interest and aptitude or ability of the individual is of great importance to the successful choice of occupation. However, the "salability" of one's accomplishment is equally important. This latter depends, in turn, upon two factors: the desire that others have for one's product, and the number of other persons who are making or doing the same thing.

In an age of specialization the choice of a specialty is highly important. If the economic machine is to function to its full capacity, if economic income is to reach its full measure, the choice of special activity, both for individuals and for regions, will need to be made with care. Each person and each region must try to do those things that will give them the highest income, and to buy from those other persons or regions where prices are lowest.

PROJECT QUESTIONS

1. Make two lists, one of the things which you and your family use which were produced in your state; the other, the things your family uses which were not produced in your state.

2. What are the principal goods and services produced in your state that are sold to people in other states? Get the best estimate you can of the dollar value of these sales outside the state.

3. From the most recent data, find out what are the principal imports and exports of:

   a) The United States
   b) England

    c) Argentina
    d) Australia
    e) Indonesia

4. What goods are imported into the United States for which we have essentially no domestic production?

5. Select three or four occupations in which you feel you might be interested. Find out all you can about the increase or decrease in number of persons engaged in these occupations in the United States, and about the change in income received by those who earn their living from these occupations.

Chapter 6

MECHANICS OF EXCHANGE

Money Effects Exchange of Goods and Services

Many things have been done to facilitate the processes of specialization and exchange. Transportation systems that reach to the far corners of the world, communication devices that make possible conversation between individuals anywhere at any time, and long-distance transmission of power are significant examples. Among the mechanics of exchange, however, perhaps none is more important than the establishment, facilitation, and regulation of a monetary system by means of which exchanges may be carried out. Time was when goods were bartered directly. Although barter is a primitive method and is rarely used today as a method of exchanging goods and services, it is sometimes temporarily resorted to during crises. For example, during the great depression of the 1930's in certain sections of the United States people exchanged goods and services directly, and in isolated parts of the world where peoples are completely removed from trade with the outside world, one may find barter used today. To improve on barter in the exchange of goods, various clumsy media of exchange were tried. Large stones, pieces of iron, tobacco, beads, and salt are examples of commodities used but found to be unsatisfactory. It is a far cry from those cumbersome units to paper money in convenient denominations, personal bank checks, and drafts or bills of exchange that may be handled quickly and easily. Trade has been freed and assisted by the introduction of a workable monetary unit and medium of exchange.

The Pecuniary Unit Is a Calculating Unit.—The monetary unit, technically called a pecuniary unit, is a language device used to express the value of goods and services exchanged. It does not necessarily circulate in the form of currency; in fact, it may not be coined at all. It is a calculating unit. The word "pecuniary" derives from the Latin word for money, *pecunia,* which in turn came from the Latin word for cattle, *pecus.* In very early days, cattle were used as a measure of value; to calculate the exchange value of cloth and corn each was first expressed in terms of their individual exchange value with a cow. Cattle were not used as a media of exchange, of course, but merely as a means of measuring the exchange value of goods to be traded. It thus became customary to call whatever was accepted as a measure of value, the pecuniary unit. Today, in the United States, the pecuniary unit is money and the standard which fixes the value for that money is the gold dollar.

The Standard of Value Is a Measuring Stick.—Money is a very broad term; it includes a great many kinds. Not all forms of money serve as a standard of value, for only what a country or an economy designates as standard money performs that function. There is in most modern countries a large number of circulating media, some of which may be properly called money and some of which are actually money substitutes. Both money and money substitutes, however, serve as the medium of exchange.

"Standard money is that form of money in which all other forms of money are redeemable." Gold is the standard money in the United States. The gold dollar, if it were coined (which it is not), would contain 13.7 grains of pure gold.[1] Certain other forms of money (gold certificates, United States notes or greenbacks, and Federal Reserve notes) are finally redeemable in standard money. In the United States, that should mean that this money is redeemable in gold dollars. However, since the gold dollar is not now being coined this cannot be done. We are, therefore, on a limited gold standard because although gold money does not circulate, gold bullion is available for industrial purposes and for export.

No one questions the gold value of "convertible" paper money because the government accepts it at face value which means at the value of the gold behind that paper. Our money is still "tied to the gold standard." The gold dollar is still the standard of value even though it does not circulate and currency is not freely interchangeable with gold.

The story of how gold became the standard of value in the United States is a long and interesting one. At one time, 1792, we even had a double or bimetallic standard, with both silver and gold used as bases for determining the value of money in the ratio of 15 units of silver to one unit of gold. After a long political struggle between silver and gold supporters, the gold dollar was finally adopted as the unit of value in 1873. Silver-tongued William Jennings Bryan, call-

---

[1] The gold dollar was devalued under the Gold Reserve Act of 1934 by reducing its weight to 59.06 per cent of its former weight, i.e., from 23.22 to 13.7 grains of pure gold. Conversely, the price of one ounce of gold was increased from $20.67 to $35.00.

ing this the "crime of 1873," accused Congress of crucifying silver on a cross of gold. For years following the formal adoption of the scarcer metal, gold, as the monetary standard, silver supporters have periodically advocated either the substitution of silver for gold or the adoption of both metals as the standard of value. In fact, there are members of Congress (usually representatives from the "silver states") who still argue in favor of silver as the official standard. But since 1873, the gold dollar has been (and largely because of its scarcity probably will remain) the monetary standard.

The great weakness of bimetallism lies in the fact that when two metals are used as the official standard, both freely coined and both legal tender, one of which is scarcer and therefore of higher value than the other, the natural tendency is for individuals to use the cheaper money and to hoard the more valuable. Sir Thomas Gresham first observed this tendency in 1560 in England and the monetary principle that cheap money drives more valuable money out of circulation is called Gresham's Law. The bimetallists argue, however, that the dearer money would never entirely disappear from circulation because of the workings of the compensatory principle of bimetallism. For example, if the mint ratio or official coinage ratio of gold and silver were sixteen-to-one the effect would be for the market ratio to rise, say to sixteen and one half to one. Naturally, gold would be sold abroad, hoarded, or sold in the commercial market at home, and the demand for silver as standard money for payment in domestic trade would increase. But the increase in supply of gold in foreign and other markets would lower its price, whereas the increase in domestic money demand for silver would increase its price and thereby gradually re-establish the former ratio. As soon as this happened, the "flight of gold" from the money market would stop.

The weakness in this "compensatory principle" argument of the supporters of bimetallism is that to raise or lower prices of gold or silver effectively, very large amounts must be shifted. That is, the monetary demand of the two metals must be large enough to have the desired price-raising effect in order to bring the market ratio in line with the mint ratio. It is perhaps true, as the bimetallists claim, that if all countries in the world would operate on a bimetallic standard with the same mint ratio, a bimetallic standard would work. But it seems unrealistic to consider such a situation, inasmuch as all countries cannot agree on much less complicated matters.

Kinds of Money.—In any mature economy, with its complex and highly specialized socioeconomic organization, there is need for many kinds of money. In the United States there are two main types, government money (issued by the United States Government) and bank money (issued by the United States banks, as authorized by law). There are two kinds of government money, namely, specie and paper money. All bank money is paper. The following is a classification of United States money:

I. Government Money or "lawful money."
   A. Coins or specie.
      1. Gold (not coined at present).
      2. Silver subsidiary coins: 10 cents, 25 cents, 50 cents, and $1.00.
      3. Minor coins: 5 cents and 1 cent.
   B. Paper Money. Government paper money is an unusual feature of modern monetary systems. In other countries paper money is used only by central banks.
      1. Gold Certificate. 1882 (has orange seal).
      Is representative paper money because it is backed, dollar for dollar, by specie.
      Not being issued at present.
      2. Silver Certificate. Bland-Allison Act of 1878 (has blue seal). 100 per cent silver reserve.
      Legally, representative money but so long as market value of silver is less than coined value they are in fact credit money.
      3. United States Note or Greenback. (Has red seal.)
      First issued during the Civil War to meet expenses of federal government.
II. Bank Money.
   A. National Bank Note. 1864.
   Retired, and for all practical purposes not in circulation.
   B. Federal Reserve Note. 1913. (Has green seal.)
   Backed by 40 per cent gold or gold certificates and 60 per cent eligible paper.
   C. Federal Reserve Bank Note. 1913.
   Issued to retire national bank notes.
   Retired in 1935, and for all practical purposes not in circulation.
   D. Treasury Note of 1890.
   A few still outstanding but they are gradually being retired.

It will be noted that, in actuality, the only types of paper money in circulation are the silver certificates, United States notes, and Federal Reserve notes.

Weaknesses of Our Monetary System.—Gold satisfies most of the requirements of a standard of value, but it is not a perfect standard. The value of gold fluctuates. Like the King's Horses, it marches up the street and back down again. It lacks stability. But it satisfies more of the requirements of a standard of value than any other commodity discovered so far. It has made it possible for us to establish a monetary system which satisfactorily fulfils required functions.

But even though our present system works fairly satisfactorily, it is not perfect. One of the crying needs is for a money to measure income adequately, and none has been found which does this job. It can be said that money is an inadequate and inexact measure of income for at least three reasons. In the first place there are many satisfactions that we receive without any monetary payment. In the second place it frequently is difficult to distinguish "consumption goods" from "production goods." These two reasons have been discussed in connection with the definitions of income and consumption in Chapter 3, so need no further elaboration here.

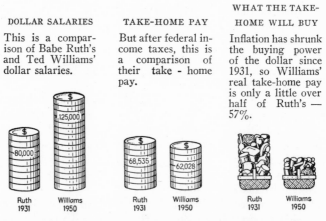

DOLLAR SALARIES

This is a comparison of Babe Ruth's and Ted Williams' dollar salaries.

TAKE-HOME PAY

But after federal income taxes, this is a comparison of their take-home pay.

WHAT THE TAKE-HOME WILL BUY

Inflation has shrunk the buying power of the dollar since 1931, so Williams' real take-home pay is only a little over half of Ruth's — 57%.

If Ted Williams were to have as much buying power in 1950 as Babe Ruth had in 1931, he would have to be paid $327,451.

Fig. 2.—Purchasing Power of Salaries

Source: *Clippings of Note,* No. 26, The Foundation for Economic Education, Inc., Irvington, N. Y.

The third difficulty with money as a measure of income lies in the fact that the value of the dollar is not constant. By this we mean that a given number of dollars will not always buy the same bill of goods. (See Figure 2.) The converse of this is that the general level of prices is constantly changing. This fact makes difficult any direct comparison of monetary income at different moments of time. We cannot tell whether we live better than or not so well as our grandfathers did just by comparing our dollar expenditures with theirs.

The Index Number as a Measuring Technique.—A good many years ago a monk, who had the responsibility for making a fixed money revenue cover the expenses of his monastery, undertook to

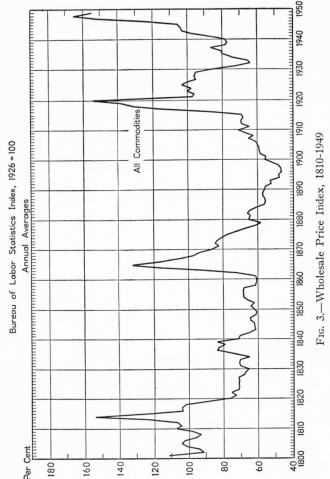

FIG. 3.—Wholesale Price Index, 1810-1949

Sources: Data up to 1929—*Historical Statistics of the United States, 1789-1945*, U. S. Department of Commerce, Bureau of the Census (Washington, D. C., 1949), pp. 233-34. 1929-50—*Federal Reserve Bulletin*, December, 1950.

work out a method of estimating the year-to-year changes in the value of money. He did this by noting the changes in the prices of each of the commodities and services which he had to buy and then averaging these changes. In making this average, the change in each item was given a weight equal to the ratio of the expenditure on that item to the total budget. We call the resulting figure an index of prices; it generally is reported in percentage terms, some year or period being taken arbitrarily as 100 with other years shown as percentages thereof.

Since this method of figuring the change in the value or purchasing power of money was first thought of, many index numbers have been calculated. Figure 3 shows graphically one such index of wholesale prices in the United States for a long period of time. The figures are quoted as percentages of the average prices prevailing during the year 1926, which is called the base year. In recent years the Bureau of Labor Statistics has calculated and published several monthly indexes of prices. These indexes measure price changes from week to week, month to month, and year to year, in a representative list of important commodities. The *Survey of Current Business,* published monthly by the Department of Commerce, contains the leading price and purchasing power indexes for the United States and some for foreign countries. The *Federal Reserve Bulletin,* published by the Board of the Federal Reserve Bank, contains useful indexes of retail sales, income (both national and personal disposable), and others.[2]

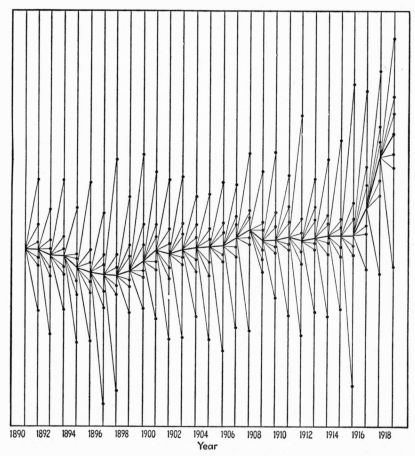

Fig. 4.—Summary of Yearly Changes in Wholesale Prices, United States, 1891-1918. Source: Vaile, Roland S. and Canoyer, Helen G., *Income and Consumption* (Henry Holt & Co., 1938), p. 46.

[2] National and disposable income will be explained in Chapter 12.

Many of these indexes will be referred to in this book. This is by no means a complete listing of the indexes prepared and made available by different private and government agencies in the United States. It will, however, illustrate the type of change measurable by means of the index number technique and where to go for such indexes.

An index number, then, measures the average percentage change of something (prices, births, deaths, income, cost of living, etc.) from one point of time or place to another. A price index, for example, usually measures average percentage change in prices from one year to another although price indexes may have to do with comparing price changes between parts of the United States or world or between days, weeks, or months.

Figure 4 illustrates the relative stability of a price index number. The index number of wholesale prices is composed of a great diversity of price fluctuations. The index number (being an average) lies in the center and is represented by the heavy line. The erratic movements of its component parts are represented by the light lines radiating from one central point for each year. It is important to note that an index number may be constructed to measure the average percentage change of almost anything. We shall, for simplicity's sake, limit ourselves to consideration of an index number of prices. Moreover, although there have been some refinements in the technique of weighting and averaging individual items in the making of index numbers since the good monk used the device, this is not a book on statistics and we shall not, therefore, stop to consider them. We need only to become familiar with the basic elements of index number construction in order that we may understand and properly interpret them.

How to Construct an Index Number of Prices. Although any index number of prices would be composed of prices of many commodities (Figure 5 shows some typical price movements that would be combined to form a price index number), we shall select two commodities, namely, A and B, for purposes of explanation. All procedures used in this simple example would be used with any number of commodities and for a series of years as well as for only two.

EXAMPLE

		1940					1946	
1	2	3	4	5	6	7	8	9
			Rela-tives	Weighted Rela-tives			Rela-tives	Weighted Rela-tives
Commodities	Weights	Prices	tives	tives	Weights	Prices	tives	tives
A (in bushels)	1	$1.80	100	100	1	$2.43	135	135
B (in pounds)	2	.15	100	200	2	.36	240	480
Totals	3			3| 300	3			3| 615
				100				205

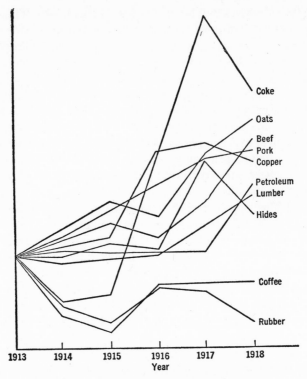

Coke

Oats

Beef
Pork
Copper

Petroleum
Lumber

Hides

Coffee

Rubber

| 1913 | 1914 | 1915 | 1916 | 1917 | 1918 |

Year

FIG. 5.—Individual Prices, Dispersing from 1913

This chart shows the wide dispersion of price movements of ten commodities between 1913 and 1918. In the figure the price of each commodity is shown as 100 in 1913; the prices in the subsequent years are then shown at their existing level relative to that position. If you will imagine the movements of price in this small group of commodities multiplied by the number of commodities on the markets of the world you will have a picture of the extreme complexity of price movements which must be averaged to form a price index. Source: Irving Fisher, *The Making of Index Numbers* (Boston, Houghton Mifflin Co., 1927), p. 12.

We assume in the example on page 61 that we wish to find out how food prices changed *on the average* in 1946 *as compared with* what they were in 1940 and that the price movement of commodities A and B is representative of the prices of all common foods. (This latter assumption, as we said above, is for simplicity's sake. In reality, we would include many more food prices in order to determine how all food prices changed during this period.) We further assume that we have studied market transactions of food items and have found that B is twice as important as A in terms of total amount bought.

To compare prices in 1946 with prices in 1940 we assign the value of 100 to the prices of commodities in 1940—the year against which we wish to compare another year. We then convert the prices in 1946 into comparable values (compute price relatives or relationships) by dividing each 1946 price by its corresponding 1940 price and then multiplying the quotient by 100, i.e., $2.43 ÷ $1.80 × 100. After all (here, only two) price relatives have been computed, each relative is multiplied by its corresponding weight in columns 2 and 6. We then add the weighted price relatives (in columns 5 and 9) for each year and divide by the sum of the weights. The resulting quotients are the index numbers for 1940 and 1946. It is clear that prices for the commodities studied rose, *on the average,* 105 per cent in 1946 compared with 1940, although the price of A rose only 35 per cent while the price of B rose 140 per cent.

The importance of accurate choice of weights should be noted. By interchanging weights in the above example, i.e., two for A and one for B, the index number becomes 170, which says that prices (on the average) rose only 70 per cent from 1940 to 1946 instead of 105 per cent. By giving greater weight to Commodity A, the price of which increased less than did that of Commodity B, the average price increase was smaller than it was when greater weight was given to Commodity B. It is desirable to assign weights representing varying degrees of importance to the items composing index numbers. If this is not done each commodity will be given a weight or importance depending upon the size of its price, or upon some other chance factor, rather than a proportionate weight depending upon its importance. Great care must be exercised in the selection of weights, for their value depends on the extent to which they truly represent the importance of the items being studied.

Uses of Index Numbers. As stated earlier, we are more concerned with the uses to which the indices may be put and the need for care in the selection of the best index for a specific purpose than in the intricacies of index number construction. One of the important uses of index numbers has already been mentioned, namely estimating the extent to which a fixed money income will permit the maintenance of a customary standard of living. An index constructed for this purpose is called a cost-of-living index. It must be constructed to reflect the changes in the prices of all the items that are included in the accepted standard of living, and each item must be weighted in accordance with its importance in the standard. Wage adjustments are sometimes made in accordance with changes in the cost-of-living index for wage-earners' families.

Another use to which index numbers are put is to compare the power of one group of commodities to exchange for other commodities. For example, a comparison may be made between the price movements of farm products and those of the things farmers must buy. Such comparisons show the changes in the purchasing power of farmers' crops and are an indication of rural prosperity.

A third purpose for index numbers of the sort we are discussing is to estimate real changes in the production or sale of goods when physical measurements are not available, or when commodities are to be combined for which no common physical measure exists. It is difficult, for example, to get any direct measurement of the change in production of wheat, eggs, butter, and potatoes in a general farming area—or of shoes, hats, and cotton cloth in an industrial area—but an approximation can be arrived at by adjusting the sales value of all the items by an index of the change in prices. Perhaps some simple illustrations will make these several uses clearer.

a) If a carpenter received $1,200 in wages in 1929 and only $1,100 in 1931, he might feel that his income had been reduced. If in fact, however, the relevant cost-of-living index had gone down from 100 in 1929 to 87 in 1931, his real income would actually have increased. The calculation would be as follows:

$$\frac{1200}{100} \times 100 = \$1,200 \qquad \frac{1100}{87} \times 100 = \$1,264$$

In other words, the smaller money income would actually purchase more goods and services in 1931 than the larger income did in 1929, by $64 worth.

b) If a farmer's cash income was $1,000 in 1929 and only $600 in 1931, the reduction would seem very great, but if the prices of things farmers buy had fallen from an index of 100 to 80, the loss would not be so serious as at first appears; the $600 in 1931 would then be worth as much to him as $750 would have been in 1929; that is, there would have been a reduction of only 25 per cent instead of the apparent 40 per cent in purchasing power. The method of calculation is the same as in the previous example.

c) If the value of goods produced by a group of factories decreased from $6 million to $4 million between two years, one might assume that the output had been greatly curtailed. But if the selling price per unit had fallen at the same time from an index of 100 to an index of 60, the physical output would have actually increased. The calculation in this case includes two steps:

$$(1) \quad \frac{\$6 \text{ million}}{100} \times 100 = \$6 \text{ million} \qquad \frac{\$4 \text{ million}}{60} \times 100 = \$6.67 \text{ million}$$

That is, the amount produced in the second year would have been worth $6.67 million in terms of the price prevailing in the first year.

This is an increase in value of output of $670 thousand and shows an increase in physical output when price remains unchanged.

(2) But price dropped 40 per cent from the first to the second year. If the value the first year is counted as 100, then the relative adjusted value the second year would be $\dfrac{6.67}{6} \times 100 = 111$. In other words, the physical output would have had to be increased 11 per cent to give the $4 million sales at the reduced prices prevailing in the second year.

These cases suggest some of the many ways in which index numbers make possible a more accurate interpretation of monetary measurements of income than could be made from the original dollar figures.

Banks and Their Uses

From 85 per cent to 90 per cent of the dollar volume of transactions in the United States is done by means of checks or bank drafts. Our interests have become so widespread, so world-inclusive, our livelihood has become so completely divorced from our immediate productive activity, our faith in our institutions is so great that we cannot and do not carry on daily transactions with just "money." When our banks closed for several days in March, 1933, the extent to which we depend on the banking system was made startlingly clear. Most people were greatly inconvenienced even though that crisis was but a short three days long. With no ready access to savings deposits, no opportunity to use checks, drafts, and other "bank money" the process of living was greatly limited even though many large mercantile institutions stepped into the breach in many ways, such as cashing personal checks and loaning small amounts of money on the basis of the customer's charge account record. This could be done because the banks were closed but a short time. The banking system is a very important facilitating factor in the processes of specialization and exchange. In fact, without such a system it would be impossible to operate our complicated arrangements for the interchange of goods and services including our warehouses, railroads, grain exchanges, and telegraph lines.

There are several kinds of banks in the United States. With most of them the average person has few direct dealings, but it is important to know about them. The form of bank organization in the United States is different from that found in other countries and is more complicated. This is because the United States, growing from thirteen colonies, is now composed of forty-eight states with an over-all federal government—each state having the right to issue bank charters. Fortunately, there has been a tendency for state legislatures to pass similar bank laws. But even today, we do not have a uniform system of banking; there are important differences between the laws (and thus the scope of operation permitted under them) of the states and national government and of those and the Federal Reserve System.

How Our Banking System Developed.—A brief look at the historical development of our banking system will go a long way toward explaining its present organization. As our country grew and slowly changed from a group of separate and highly independent colonies into a United States with a central government, as our economic interests and needs grew and expanded beyond community and then state boundaries, the struggle between state and national bank interests was long and bitter. Twice before the Civil War an attempt was made to establish a national banking system which was to be a sound and constructive system replacing the scattered and unorganized state and private banks. The third attempt succeeded with the passage in 1863 of the National Banking Act, under the guise of a war measure. It did provide for better banks but it did not result in a coordinated, smoothly functioning banking system because it failed to provide for a central bank to guide, strengthen, and control individual banks. This was not accomplished until the Federal Reserve System was set up by the Federal Reserve Act, which was passed in December of 1913.

It was hoped that the Federal Reserve System would cure the ills of the national bank system: (1) decentralization of banking, (2) immobility of bank reserves, (3) inelasticity of currency and credit, and (4) clumsy and therefore slow exchange of credit instruments between banks. Although these weak spots were not immediately or completely strengthened by the new system, considerable improvement was made. In addition, it established a central bank, a bankers' bank which was to provide, at the same time, more flexibility and regulation. As it exists today, the Federal Reserve System is the product of adaptation to changing needs. In 1933 and again in 1935, Congress passed laws designed to improve the efficiency of this central banking control.

How the Federal Reserve System Works.—The idea behind the Federal Reserve System is to use the monetary reserves of one community to meet a shortage of funds in another. For purposes of administering the system the country is divided into the twelve districts shown in Figure 6.

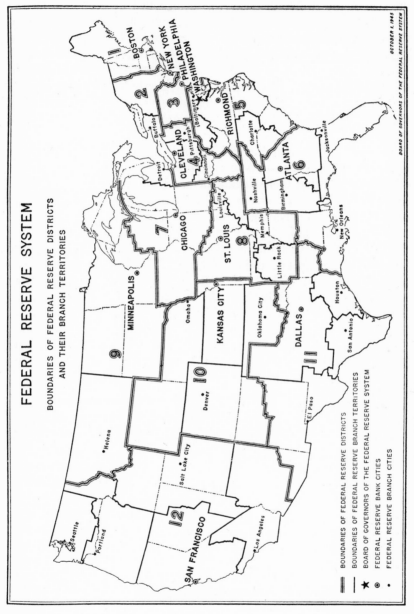

FIG. 6.—The Twelve Federal Reserve Districts

The district boundaries do not always follow state lines because the size of the twelve districts was determined by economic factors such as existing financial, mercantile, and industrial needs, transportation and communication facilities, and amount of business done in the region. Thus the second district is made up of only two states, New York and New Jersey, whereas the twelfth district embraces six and three-fourths states. The New York area is by far the most important of any in our country in terms of domestic and foreign trade; therefore its financial needs are the greatest even though it covers a small area.[3]

In each district is a Federal Reserve Bank. These banks differ essentially from other banks in that profits are not the object of their operations and that their stockholders, which are the member banks of the Federal Reserve System, do not have the powers and privileges of stockholders in privately owned corporations.

All national banks in each district are required to buy stock in the Federal Reserve Bank, and banks set up by state laws may also buy stock if they meet certain conditions. The Federal Reserve System at the end of 1949 had 6,892 member banks which was somewhat less than one half of all banks in the United States, but these member banks held more than three fourths of the country's bank deposits. Thus progress has been made toward centralizing banking functions. The number of banks (not including the twelve Federal Reserve Banks) in the United States at the end of 1949 and the amount of their deposits are shown in Table 1.

TABLE 1

NUMBER OF BANKS AND AMOUNT OF DEPOSITS
UNITED STATES, DECEMBER 1, 1949

Kind	Number	Deposits (Millions of dollars)	
		Demand	Time
Member Bank	6,892	82,628	29,160
Nonmember Bank	7,795	13,528	26,441
Total	14,687	96,156	55,601

Source: *Federal Reserve Bulletin,* August, 1950.

[3] Paragraphs on the Federal Reserve System are abstracted from *The Federal Reserve System, Its Purposes and Functions,* a publication of the Federal Reserve Board, 1939.

Demand deposits are checking accounts and the closest equivalent to money. The data show that member banks on the average have greater deposits than nonmember banks and that a larger percentage are demand deposits. The reports of the Federal Reserve Board also show that nearly three fourths of the member banks are national as opposed to state banks.

RESERVE BALANCES MAKE A SAFER BANKING SYSTEM. Member banks are required to maintain reserve accounts with their Reserve Bank. This is a credit control factor and may result in a somewhat safer banking system for depositors. Member banks are constantly drawing on these reserves and replenishing them in day-to-day transactions. Reserve balances must be kept at an average level, determined in relation to their deposits, but these deposits constantly change. A Board of Governors of the Federal Reserve System, consisting of seven members appointed by the President of the United States, has offices in Washington, D. C. The Board supervises the workings of the Federal Reserve System and, among other things, has full authority over changes in reserve requirements. In 1950 the Board required that $15½ billion member-bank reserves be held by the twelve Federal Reserve Banks. Actual reserves were nearly $1 billion in excess of this requirement. Furthermore it is important to know that this excess may readily be increased by the sale by member banks of government securities and eligible paper [4] to Federal Reserve Banks or merely by having the Board of Governors lower the reserve requirements. Large excess reserves make credit conditions easy and interest rates low, whereas small excess reserves result in tight credit conditions and high interest rates.

FEDERAL RESERVE BANKS REDUCE "IMMOBILITY OF RESERVES." Another way Federal Reserve Banks help member banks is by loaning money to them. A member bank can take paper which it gets when it loans money to you and me or a business firm when we are safe risks and sell this paper, i.e., promissory note, to the Federal Reserve Bank. This is called rediscounting. Rediscounting enlarges the loan capacity of a member bank. Instead of tying up the money loaned to John Jones for the entire time of the loan, the bank may, on the basis of Jones' promise to repay the money borrowed, rediscount the Jones promissory note and loan money to George Smith; and on the basis of Smith's promissory note, to Sam Jones and so on

---

[4] Eligible paper includes notes, drafts, and bills of exchange arising out of agricultural, commercial, and industrial transactions.

up to the legal safety limits set by the Board. This pooling of reserves greatly enlarges the member bank's loanable funds.

THE FEDERAL RESERVE SYSTEM PROVIDES ELASTIC CREDIT. The Federal Reserve System influences the amount of credit in use. Whenever banks loan money too freely, that is, beyond the point of safety as determined by bank reserves, or whenever credit is scarce and interest rates are so high that borrowing is held at a minimum, the Federal Reserve System may act. One way of handling such situations is to change the rediscount rate—that is, the rate of interest paid by member banks when they borrow from Federal Reserve Banks. When there is a growing demand for credit and borrowing is heavy, an increase in the rediscount rate (an increase in the interest rate charged banks who borrow from the Federal Reserve Bank) will discourage banks from making more loans. Similarly, when it seems wise to encourage the use of credit, a lowering of the rediscount rate will cause banks to increase the amount of loans made.

There are other ways by which the Federal Reserve System may regulate the amount of "money" in use, such as changing the reserve requirements of member banks. Because the Federal Reserve System can increase and decrease the quantity as well as the quality of our country's "money," it is often said that we have a managed currency.

THE FEDERAL RESERVE SYSTEM PROVIDES ELASTIC CURRENCY. The Federal Reserve Banks also issue currency, an important part of the currency circulation today. Federal Reserve Notes are issued in denominations from five dollars to ten thousand dollars. These are made safe by the fact that each Federal Reserve Bank must maintain a 100 per cent cover against its notes in circulation. At least 25 per cent of this reserve must be in gold certificates. The rest may be in commercial paper, Government securities, or gold certificates. Through the Federal Reserve System, our currency is made much more elastic than it was under any of the former bank systems; that is, the quantity in circulation can be increased when the need is great and, which is even more important, decreased when the need no longer exists.

Member banks get currency from Federal Reserve Banks much as you get money from your own bank. When you need money, you draw a check on the bank where you have an account, and cash it. When you haven't enough money to cover what you need you borrow it. In the same way, when a member bank needs money to pay out to its customers, it either draws on its account with or borrows from the Federal Reserve Bank. On the other hand, when a member bank

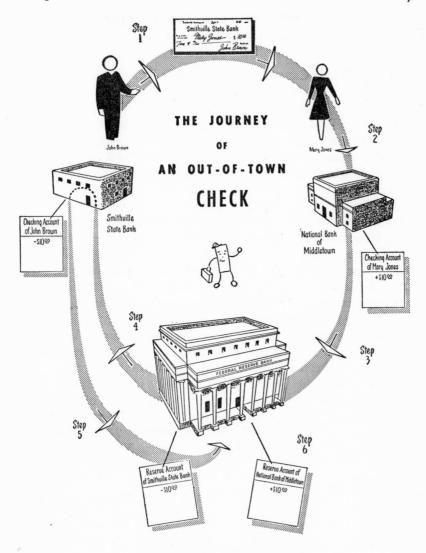

KEY TO THE PICTOGRAPH

STEP 1—John Brown sends his check for $10, drawn on the Smithville State Bank, to Mary Jones in Middletown.

STEP 2—Mary Jones deposits the check in the National Bank of Middletown, where her account is credited $10.

STEP 3—The National Bank of Middletown sends the check to the Federal Reserve bank.

STEP 4—The Federal Reserve bank sends the check to the Smithville State Bank, where John Brown's checking account is charged $10.

STEP 5—The Smithville State Bank authorizes the Reserve bank to charge its reserve account $10.

STEP 6—The Federal Reserve bank credits the reserve account of the National Bank of Middletown, completing the transaction.

FIG. 7.—The Journey of an Out-of-Town Check

Source: 1949 Annual Report of the Federal Reserve Bank of Minneapolis, p. 11.

has more money than it needs, it turns that money over to the Reserve Bank, receiving credit, or pays off loans previously made to it by the Reserve Bank.

EXCHANGE OF CREDIT INSTRUMENTS IS EXPEDITED BY THE FEDERAL RESERVE SYSTEM. It was stated above that about 90 per cent of all business transactions are paid for by check. Here again, the Federal Reserve Banks give valuable service not only to member banks but also through them to many nonmember banks, and to those individuals who use checks in place of money. Federal Reserve Banks serve as clearing houses for the collection of checks. This has reduced both the average time needed for check collection and the expense of such collection. This procedure has, for all practical purposes, done away with the payment of money balances arising out of check collections because most settlements can now be taken care of merely by making the necessary entries in the books of the Federal Reserve Banks—each member bank being charged or credited with the checks drawn against it. Figure 7 graphically explains how this is done.

Closely connected with this service is the speeding up of the transfer of funds from one part of the country to another. This is done daily by telegraph through the Interdistrict Settlement Fund, which is a part of the Federal Reserve System. Each Federal Reserve Bank is required to keep a minimum balance of $1,000,000 in the fund which is held in the United States Treasury in Washington, D. C. This money isn't frozen there because it counts as part of the Reserve bank's legal reserves and often the amount in the Interdistrict Settlement Fund is much greater than the minimum of $12,000,000.

To illustrate how the Interdistrict Settlement Fund works, assume that John Brown and Mary Jones (in Figure 7) live in different Federal Reserve districts—in the Seventh and the Ninth. Two Federal Reserve Banks get into the picture. The Federal Reserve Bank in Minneapolis (the Ninth) sends the check drawn on the Seventh district bank to Chicago. The Chicago Federal Reserve Bank sends John Brown's check to his home town bank, which pays the Chicago Reserve Bank. Payment by the Chicago Federal Reserve Bank to the Minneapolis Federal Reserve Bank is made without sending money, by using the Interdistrict Settlement Fund. The Reserve Bank of Chicago instructs the fund managers to reduce its share of the fund and add to the share belonging to the Reserve Bank of Minneapolis. It is a speedy, simple, and safe operation.

Checks and other credit instruments collected through the fund are not sent to Washington—interdistrict settlements are made daily simply by a book entry changing the total of the balance held by each reserve bank. At the close of each day the manager of the Inter-district Settlement Fund notifies the Reserve Banks of the change in their balance in the fund, and they make the necessary adjustments on their books. Thus, through this fund, money can be freely and quickly moved from one part of the country to another.

The Federal Reserve System has centralized reserves, provides an elastic currency, and speeds up the handling of credit instruments. It is not a perfect banking system, but it works the best of any which our country has yet tried. Today it is confronted with monetary problems very different from those it was set up to solve in 1914. Then, the monetary problem was one of scarcity and rigid limitation on expansion of money and credit; today, the problem is over-abundance of money and credit and great resistance to planned con-traction. Doubtless we shall continue to experiment both with the form and the operation of the system in the hope of adapting it still better to our needs.

CONSUMER CREDIT AND HOW IT FACILITATES EXCHANGE OF GOODS AND SERVICES

There are two ways of buying—paying cash and using credit. As we progressed from the barter economy, the first step was to pay for goods and services by using money. The use of credit and credit instruments is another step. Today, credit plays a leading role in the exchange of goods and services. We live in a credit era. We pointed out above that one of the functions of a good monetary system is to make it possible for people to buy goods at one time and to pay for them at a later time—in other words to make possible the use of credit. Literally, credit means faith or trust, but modern usage has perverted this literal meaning. Today credit is thought of merely as an advance of goods or services or claims to goods or services in anticipation of payment at a later date. Of course, credit may be based on faith or trust today, but more frequently it is based on' security or written instruments.

Types of Credit.—There are three principal types of credit in use today, namely, producer, public, and consumer credit. The main distinctions between these three types of credit arise from differences in motivation or needs rather than from differences in the uses to which credit is put. It may be well to describe very briefly the three types of credit before discussing consumer credit in detail.

Producer credit is motivated by anticipation of business profits. It fluctuates as changing conditions affect the calculations or the expectations of the business community with respect to anticipated future income or profits. Public credit on the other hand is motivated by a variety of forces—some political, others sociological, and still others economic. It is reflected in the fiscal policies of government agencies.

Consumer credit is motivated by the desire for satisfactions from the present use of goods and services. The quantity of consumer credit traditionally fluctuates with the business cycle. Fluctuations in consumer credit reflect pretty largely the influence of changes or anticipated changes in incomes, and the effect of such changes upon the consumer's estimate of the difficulty of future payment and upon the credit grantor's appraisal of the difficulty of collection. The classical economists contended that consumer credit was not productive because it destroyed or dissipated wealth. The conclusion of economists on this point has changed, however, and consumer credit is considered today as a desirable economic tool. Like any good tool, however, it must be used with discretion if the results are to be good.

Growth of Consumer Credit.—The beginning of consumer credit may be said to coincide with the beginnings of modern organization of business enterprise. It evolved and changed over time. As early as 1800, when the household had become predominantly a consumption unit and not a producing unit, there were some sections of the United States where consumer credit was being granted by merchants, physicians, and pawnbrokers.[5] However, the merchant was the predominant source of consumer credit until the Civil War. The types of consumer credit available at that time were similar to those types used today, namely, term credit found generally in the wholesale trade and used for high-priced goods; open book or charge account credit used in the retail trade on cheaper goods and largely in the agricultural area; and instalment credit. It is interesting to note, however, that instalment credit had been used as early as 1807. In that year a furniture store by the name of Cowperthwaite and Sons in New York City began to sell furniture on instalment terms. But it was not until the latter part of the nineteenth century that consumer credit, largely in the form of instalment credit, expanded progressively on three fronts: geographically, to additional fields of merchandising,

---

[5] For a more detailed discussion of the growth of consumer credit see Rolf Nugent, *Consumer Credit and Economic Stability* (New York: Russell Sage Foundation, 1939).

and to lower income classes and poorer credit risks. In general, then, up to the Civil War, consumer credit was granted almost entirely as an institutional by-product of some other activity. Following the end of the Civil War, a number of agencies developed whose primary purpose was the granting of an increasing amount of consumer credit.

The amount of consumer credit outstanding grew continuously until 1923 and doubled during the period 1923 to 1929. The most rapid growth was in the new specialized agencies which used instalment techniques. Behind this disproportionate growth of instalment credit, as compared with open book credit, was the increase in consumer's expenditures for durable goods. The automobile, electric washing machine, and electric vacuum cleaner had been introduced and perfected during the period immediately preceding World War I. Also, the war itself had been accompanied by a substantial increase in real wages which brought these much-desired goods within the budgetary reach of a larger part of the population. In addition, during the 1920's these new types of consumer durable goods became available on easier payment terms. However, this expansion of consumer credit up to 1929 was dominated by the growth of credit sales of the automobile.

The expansion of consumer credit came to an end in the early part of 1929. The decline in the sales of durable goods, led by the drop in automobile sales, threw instalment credit into a liquidation which continued until the spring of 1933. At that time, some types of consumer credit, particularly automobile financing, reversed their downward trend and led the expansion. Once initiated, this expansion continued slowly at first and then rapidly until April of 1937. The termination of expansion in the spring of 1937 was far less abrupt than it had been in 1929—partly because the decline in credit sales of durable goods occurred more gradually and partly because the return of liquidations of individual instalment contracts was reduced by longer periods of repayment. Once initiated, however, the deflation increased more rapidly than it had following the break in 1929 because there were no important consumers' goods with unexploited markets, such as the automobile had provided in earlier periods, to reverse the trend. Nor was there any continuing growth of cash-lending agencies to cushion the decline. The rate of liquidation was slowed up at this time by large-scale public spending in 1938 but gradual liquidations continued until the spring of 1939, at which time fear of war and preparation for war became the spark plug of an expanding economy and a renewed increase in the use of consumer credit.

Relation of Volume of Consumer Credit to Business Activity.
—We see, then, that prior to World War II the volume of consumer credit moved with the swing in business activity—upward in times of rising business activity and downward in periods of falling business activity. At the high point in 1929, the amount of consumer credit outstanding was over 7.5 billion dollars—the highest that our economy had experienced up to that time. In the summer of 1933, the volume of consumer credit had dropped to 3.5 billion dollars or less than one half of the 1929 maximum. The volume then rose uninterruptedly, with the exception of a precipitous but short-lived decline in 1938, to over 10 billion dollars in the fall of 1941.

At this point, the "typical relationship" between consumer credit and business activity disappeared. The diversion of production from civilian goods to war goods and the passage of Regulation W [6] brought about a rapid liquidation of consumer credit, particularly instalment credit. As production soared to new heights and our national income amounted to what then seemed a fantastic 100 billion dollars, the volume of consumer credit, instead of expanding as it had done previously, steadily declined from $10 billion in 1941 to less than $5 billion by the middle of 1944. By VJ Day it stood at $5.5 billion.

Since VJ Day, the amount of consumer credit outstanding has increased sharply. It will be seen in Figure 8 that strongly different rates of growth have occurred in the various types of consumer credit. Charge account credit showed the largest growth in the immediate postwar years, but instalment credit expanded as more durable goods came onto the market and credit regulations were lifted. In December 1950 consumer credit stood at $20 billion. Although this is the largest dollar total of outstanding consumer credit ever permitted in the United States, it is only 10 per cent of personal disposable income which is less than the relationship which existed during the period between 1936 and 1941, and is the same as during 1929 and 1936. The chart of consumer credit related to personal income, on page 78, shows this clearly.

Cyclical fluctuations of business activity, with the resultant rapid and extreme fluctuations in individual incomes, give us a dramatic demonstration of the dynamic character of our economic life and of the economic uncertainty in which we live. The latter sometimes has tragic effects on many individuals. Cyclical fluctuations have many causes, or at least there are many things which directly affect their

---

[6] Wartime control placed on consumer credit.

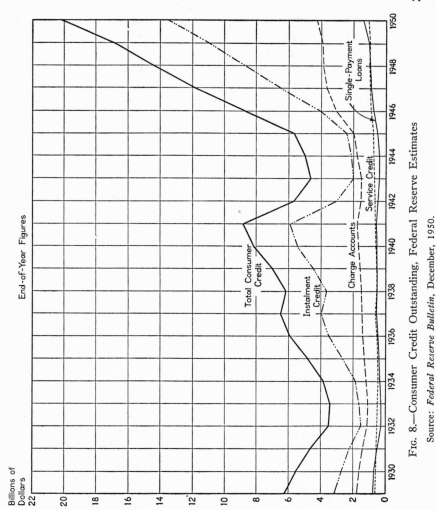

FIG. 8.—Consumer Credit Outstanding, Federal Reserve Estimates

Source: *Federal Reserve Bulletin*, December, 1950.

severity. Included among these things are the sudden decisions of businessmen to change the rate and volume of their expansion of capital plants, thus affecting employment and the flow of personal income in the construction and equipment-producing industries. This affects the amount of money in consumers' hands which is available for spending, and certainly the amount of consumer spending affects business activity. Anything which changes the ratio between money in consumers' hands and the flow of consumer goods tends to have an effect on prices, volume of production and employment, further flow of income, and thus, inevitably, on industrial fluctuations.

Contraction or expansion of consumer credit directly affects the spendable money in the hands of consumers. Thus to the extent of the changes, consumer credit affects industrial fluctuations. As used throughout the period from the Civil War to the second World War,

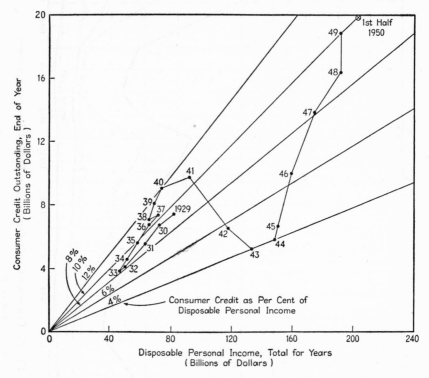

Fig. 9.—Consumer Credit Related to Disposable Personal Income

Data plotted for first half of 1950 are as follows: consumer credit outstanding, June, 1950; disposable personal income, first two quarters of 1950; seasonally adjusted, at annual rate. Source of data: consumer credit, Board of Governors of the Federal Reserve System; disposable personal income, U. S. Department of Commerce, Office of Business Economics. From *Survey of Current Business,* October, 1950, p. 13.

consumer credit has tended to increase the magnitude of the fluctuations. This followed from the fact that credit was expanded when business already was good, thus encouraging businessmen to expand their operations still further. As a result, industries were curtailed and consumer credit was reduced, thus still further reducing the flow of spendable funds to consumers.

Consumer credit is only one of several things which contribute to industrial fluctuations. In Chapter 14 it is pointed out that sales promotion also contributes to such fluctuations. Certainly the expansion and contraction of producer credit are very important factors, for much of the building of capital plant during prosperous years has been financed by borrowed funds, resulting in an increase in bank loans and bank money. A major part of these funds goes directly to wage-earners without there being any corresponding flow of consumer goods until after the plants are completed. Producer credit doubtless is more important in its influence on business cycles than is consumer credit, but swings of several billions of dollars in two or three years, as were mentioned in previous paragraphs, cannot be overlooked as important influences.

Government use of public credit sometimes has been timed in the attempt to reduce industrial fluctuations. The "pump-priming" efforts of the middle 1930's illustrate the method. Public works were undertaken all over the country. Employees and suppliers were paid money income out of expanded government credit. Thus the flow of consumer income was increased without a direct and immediate increase in the appearance of consumer goods. This caused prices to rise which, in turn, persuaded businessmen that they could afford to resume or increase the production of consumer goods. In other words, employment on public works to some extent took the place of employment on private capital plants and equipment as it had existed in the 1920's. The public works program was "too little and too late" to do the whole job of recovery promptly, but at least it worked in the right direction. Also, government has undertaken to reduce both consumer and producer credit during periods of high expenditure on war matériel. This attempt to lower the extreme peak of inflationary boom is a step in the right direction. We should point out again, however, that firmer control of producer and consumer credit in the 1920's (or any similar time in the future) would have lessened the boom and the subsequent need for digging out from the depths of depression. The old adage well applies to this situation: "An ounce of prevention is worth a pound of cure."

Project Questions

1. For a class project, visit the Federal Reserve Bank in your district (or local bank if the Federal Reserve Bank is not convenient) and be shown as many of the transactions as possible.

2. Obtain a copy of the *Survey of Current Business* and find how many different index numbers are reported in it. What do they attempt to measure in addition to price?

3. How does the Bureau of Labor Statistics decide what items to include in their Consumers' Price Index? How does the Bureau decide on the weights to be given to each item?

4. What is a bill of exchange and how does it work?

Chapter 7

MARKETS AND MARKETING

MARKETS AND MARKETING FACILITATE EXCHANGE OF GOODS AND SERVICES

In any economy regulated by specialization-exchange-cooperation, markets and marketing must play an important part. Nowadays, nearly everything from which consumers draw satisfactions is sold at least once before it is consumed. Some things are sold many times over, with more or less important changes in form each time they are handled. (See Figure 10.) You may purchase a pair of shoes today from a retailer, but some time earlier these shoes were sold by a wholesaler, or perhaps by the manufacturer, to the retailer. Still earlier, leather was sold by a tanner to the shoe manufacturer, hides were sold by a packer to the tanner, cattle were sold by a farmer to the packer. A similar list of transactions takes place with every commodity; with some the series is more complicated than the one just outlined, while with others it is more direct. Markets and marketing are as important in facilitating the exchange of goods and services from the producer to the consumer as is money, the banking system, or credit.

The Marketing System Serves the Consumer.—Marketing is a marvel of achievement. In Chapter 5 some of the complexities and the advantages of regional specialization were pointed out. Now let us think a little more about this matter. Picture an average family in a small South Dakota town. Much of the furniture in their home may have been ordered by mail from a description in a catalog, and it probably was manufactured in Grand Rapids, Michigan, St. Louis, Missouri, or in some other equally distant place. The members of the family have oranges for breakfast from California or Florida. Their clothes were made perhaps in Chicago, New York, or St. Louis. Even the flour they use may have been milled in Minneapolis from wheat actually grown on their cousin's farm five miles away. The magazines they read, their television set, their automobile and the gasoline to make it go, all come to them from somewhere else. The

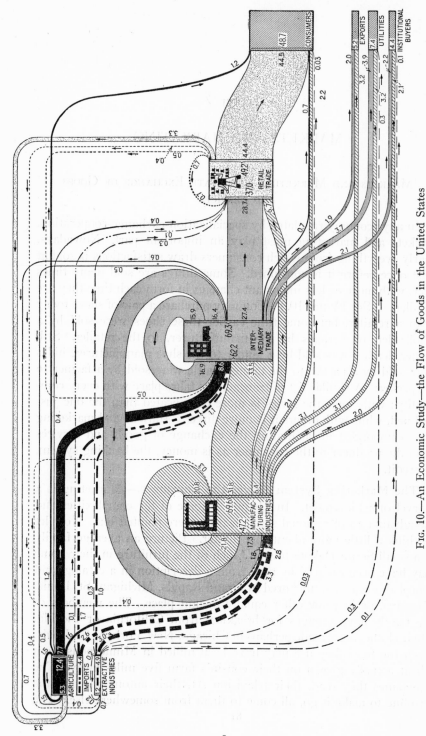

Fig. 10.—An Economic Study—the Flow of Goods in the United States Source: The Twentieth Century Fund, *Does Distribution Cost Too Much?*

Or how 130,000,000 Americans "take in one another's washing."

rubber in their automobile tires comes from Malaya, and their coffee from South America. The average consumer in South Dakota or any other state takes for granted the fact that the goods of the world are his. His breakfast, his home, his clothing, and almost everything else he uses in just "living" reach him through the processes known collectively as marketing or distribution.

DEFINITION OF MARKETING

All those activities necessary in transferring goods and services and in effecting a change in their ownership from the time they leave the hands of the producer until they reach the hands of the ultimate consumer are included in the term *marketing*. Economic theory states that all activities which create utilities, i.e., form, time, place, and ownership utilities, are a part of production. Thus any activity which makes a good or service wanted more than it was before is a productive activity. In this sense, marketing is a part of production. But, because marketing has to do mainly with creating time, place, and ownership utilities, we shall use the term *production* in a narrower sense—that is, as creating mainly form utility—the changing of the physical properties of a good or service in such a way that its want-satisfying power is increased.

Because marketing embraces those activities which have to do with the time when and place where goods and services are marketed and with the transfer of title of those goods and services, it is charged with many specific functions. As our economy became more complex with increasing separation of the producer from the consumer, the performance of these marketing functions became vital to the economic health of the country. It has become increasingly necessary to find out what the consumer wants, and when and where he wants it; to inform the consumer of what is being produced, and when and where it can be obtained; to see to it that goods produced in one part of the country are made available to those who want them in other areas, in as good condition as possible and at a cost which will make them sell.

This is the role of marketing, and it is an important one. Moreover, its importance will continue to grow as the quantity of goods produced continues to increase and as the production process becomes more and more mechanized. As this happens, marketing not only must handle more goods and a greater variety in terms of brands, styles, sizes, and other differentiating characteristics, but also many of the jobs formerly performed at the production stage are transferred to the marketing stage. All this not only increases its importance but its relative cost, as well.

Channels of Distribution.—The average consumer (ultimate consumer) has little opportunity to know about the different channels or methods of distribution. The oldest and simplest channel is the one in which the consumer buys goods directly from the producer, with no middlemen between them. This channel is still used to sell a very small proportion of goods and services today. Contrary to the opinions of many people, this channel is not the least costly method of distribution. As a matter of fact, it is often a very costly one. Today, the slogan "cheapest because direct from the maker to you" is not always true.

Another relatively simple distribution channel is from the producer directly to the retailer and then to the consumer. The retailer is a middleman because he comes between the producer and the consumer, performing distribution functions for both. This method is used today by large chain-store companies and by certain large independent stores such as department stores.

Still a third major channel of distribution has developed. Here goods pass from the producer (manufacturer) to various types of middlemen and then to the consumer. The number of middlemen, i.e., jobber, broker, commission merchant, etc., used depends on the characteristics of the commodity and the market area. This is an important method to the small retailer who, as we shall see later in this chapter, is a significant factor in retailing in the United States.

Marketing Functions Cannot Be Eliminated.—The aim of the distribution system is to transfer all goods and services which the consumer wants from the producer to the consumer as efficiently as possible. If fewer middlemen are used in this marketing process it does not follow that any of the functions or tasks of marketing are eliminated. It merely means that someone else, i.e., the manufacturer or the retailer, performs those functions instead of one of the wholesaling middlemen. For example, when a large department store like Marshall Field buys directly from a manufacturer, the functions of seeking out the goods, storage, packaging, advertising, risk-taking, transportation, financing, standardization, grading, and perhaps some others, must be performed by either or both of them. Nor is the more direct channel of distribution necessarily a less costly one than the more indirect one in which several types of middlemen are used. It is important to remember that although men and institutions may be added to or subtracted from the distribution system, functions cannot be left out without a loss of satisfaction to the consumer.

In some ways the most important marketing function is forecasting the demand, so that the many activities of production will be undertaken in the right amount. When this is not well done there is a lack of balance between production and the willingness or the ability to purchase the goods. This general statement calls for a definition of market demand. When there is a demand for goods and services, people not only want these goods and services but they stand ready to buy them at a certain price. Market demand occurs, of course, at several different levels, that is, the buyers who furnish the demand have different reasons for wanting the products. The market demand for raw materials such as tobacco leaf, crude rubber, iron ore, cotton, wheat, and electricity is called *derived demand*. It exists only because of the expectation that the final or ultimate consumer will want the finished products that can be made from these raw materials. The market demand for goods and services such as shoes, dresses, houses, bread, and electric light globes which are ready for ultimate consumption is called *direct demand*. The market price of the raw materials is a reflection of that part of the consumer price for the finished good which is not absorbed by the costs of processing. This market price or value may be imputed even to those materials that are not actually sold, but are used in integrated industries.

Marketing Costs—Are They Too High?—To the average consumer, what goes on before a can of corn is put on the retailer's shelf is a combination of mystery and inefficiency. Most consumers do not understand why the price paid to the farmer for a dozen eggs is sometimes about one half the price charged his city cousin at the corner grocery store. It is commonly believed that distribution cost, which is the spread between the price paid the farmer or other producer and the retail price, is "too high." Such criticism grows among producers during periods of falling prices and among consumers during periods of rising prices. Perhaps it will be worth while to take a consumer good—bread, for example—and "revolve the consumers' dollar backward" to see just who does get its various parts.

The consumers' dollar spent for baker's bread is divided into many parts as it travels backwards from the retail outlet to the various producers. The figures in Table 2 show approximately how much of it is retained by each institution or operation in the whole process.

This tabulation shows the total marketing costs at 44 per cent of the consumers' dollar. This is a larger percentage than for many other

TABLE 2

THE CONSUMERS' DOLLAR FOR BREAD

	Primary Production cents	Marketing cents
Retailer retains		20.0
Baker's selling and delivery		16.0
Manufacture of bread (including materials other than wheat)	25.0	
Transportation of flour		3.3
Manufacture of flour	1.0	
Storage and marketing of wheat		2.0
Transportation of wheat		2.7
Wheat grower receives	30.0	
	56.0	44.0

products, which is due less to the high cost of marketing, per se, than to the low cost of materials and manufacturing. It appears, for example, that the price of *bread* could not fall very much even if it cost nothing to market *wheat,* since the present cost is so small a part of the total. Even though marketing costs are high when stated as a percentage of consumers' price, bread remains a moderate-priced food.

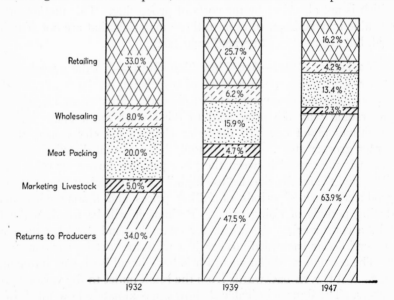

FIG. 11.—Distribution of Consumers' Meat Dollar

Packer's share of consumer's meat dollar decreased from 20.0 per cent in 1932 to 13.4 per cent in 1947; returns to producers increased from 34.0 to 63.9 per cent. Source: Bureau of Agricultural Economics, U. S. Department of Agriculture, *Farm-to-Retail Margins for Livestock and Meat.*

We said above that criticism by consumers of the spread between the price received by the producer and that paid by the consumer grows during periods of rising prices. Let us see what actually happens to the percentage of the consumers' dollar going to distribution or marketing when prices rise. The data on meat in Figure 11 and Table 3 show that when prices are low a relatively larger share of the consumers' meat dollar goes for marketing (although even then it was but 46 per cent) than when prices are high (22.7 per cent in 1947). Thus it appears that marketing charges are more stable than other costs resulting, in this case at least, in a smaller percentage of the consumers' dollar going to distribution than to producers when prices rise.

TABLE 3

DISTRIBUTION OF CONSUMERS' MEAT DOLLAR

	Percentage		
	1932	1939	1947
* Retail distribution	33.0	25.7	16.2
* Wholesale distribution	8.0	6.2	4.2
Meat packing	20.0	15.9	13.4
* Marketing of livestock	5.0	4.7	2.3
Total marketing margin ..	66.0	52.5	36.1
Returns to producers	34.0	47.5	63.9
Total	100.0	100.0	100.0

* Marketing
Source: Bureau of Agricultural Economics, U. S. Department of Agriculture.

But there are misconceptions which creep into any discussion of marketing costs when "spread" is used only in terms of percentages. Suppose the retail price of a certain food is $1, of which 55 cents (55 per cent) is the farmer's share and 45 cents (45 per cent) is the cost of distribution or the spread. Now suppose that the farm price declines 10 cents and that this is passed on to the consumer with a retail price reduction of 10 cents. The new retail price would be 90 cents, the farmer's share would be 45 cents and the spread would be unchanged at 45 cents. Now what happens to the spread in percentage terms? It increases from 45 per cent to 50 per cent but not because distribution costs more in money. This is an example of the misleading effect of relying on percentages.

It is not correct to assume that because marketing or distribution costs a larger proportion of the consumers' dollar than does production it is necessarily inefficient or that distributors make huge profits. The Twentieth Century Fund studied the costs of distribution and estimated that on the whole distribution costs took 51 per cent of the consumers' dollar as compared with 49 per cent for production costs. To conclude, then, that distribution costs are too high is to oversimplify a very complex situation. Undoubtedly some marketing techniques can be improved with resulting cost reduction. But we pointed out above the main reason why marketing cost as a percentage of retail price or the consumers' dollar is higher than production cost. Not only is this true, but there are also many reasons why the marketing cost percentage should be and probably will be higher.

Before concluding that marketing costs too much, we might ask the question, "Who gets the 'too much'?" Each of us knows proprietors of retail stores who are not getting rich. Clerking in retail stores is notoriously a low- to moderate-income job. The earnings of railroads have not been enough to increase stock values as rapidly as in many manufacturing firms. Consequently if marketing does cost too much, it is a result of general inefficiency in doing the necessary tasks rather than of high earnings for any particular group.

There are some obvious inefficiencies in marketing. These may be divided into three major groups which we may call economic inefficiencies, engineering inefficiencies, and customer inefficiencies. The first of these is illustrated by the lack of balance that occurs all too often between supply and demand. Manufacturers misjudge the market and produce so much of specific things that they must use intensive efforts to sell them. Or retailers overbuy and must sell at prices below those originally planned. In consequence they must have high margins on other goods if they are to cover all their costs. It sometimes is said that markdowns are the most costly part of retailing.

Engineering inefficiency is illustrated by the lack of use of power and other laborsaving devices—by unnecessary cross hauling of many items, by the operation of units, especially in the retail field, that are too small to be efficiently managed. This latter is almost inevitable as long as there is complete freedom to enter the retailing field.

Customer inefficiency is illustrated by the abuse of the returned-goods privilege and by insistence on having seasonally produced goods all year round, thus making necessary long-distance transportation, cold storage, and similar costly services.

When we come right down to it, much—perhaps most—of the so-called inefficiency of marketing must be laid at the door of the customers. We want stores conveniently located. We want a large inventory in which to shop. We want prompt delivery service and the opportunity to return goods. So long as we want these things enough to pay someone to do them, marketing will be expensive. When we are willing to do all our buying from automatic vending machines which furnish standardized products, the costs of marketing can be reduced. As consumers we have not yet taken full advantage of the lower-cost, lower-price stores largely because we behave like human beings rather than like perfectly integrated machines.

DEFINITION OF A MARKET

The term *market,* used in connection with this complicated process, has several different meanings. Sometimes it is used to designate the place where the sale is made—i.e., a retail store or a wholesale house; sometimes it is used in reference to the area in which a particular supply of a commodity generally is sold, such as the urban market for whole milk furnished by the Twin Cities Milk Producers' Association. Both of these uses involve a geographical concept of the term "market." A particular organization that carries out the marketing process may also be called a market. We may say that a market is highly organized or relatively unorganized depending upon the degree of regulation and regularity connected with transactions in it. In this connection, the word refers to the structure of the market.

For some commodities, such as highly perishable food products, the market structure is extremely simple whereas for a finished product such as an automobile it is very complicated. As already pointed out, goods may be sold many times before they reach the ultimate consumer. At each of these points of sale there is a salesman, a store, a broker's office, or some agency that makes it possible for the buyer and the seller to get together and transact their business. In some cases buyers and sellers meet casually and conduct their business in whatever way pleases them. A good example of this very simply organized market is the roadside vegetable stand during certain seasons of the year. In other cases like grain exchanges, central cattle markets, and wholesale fruit auctions, elaborate formal rules govern the conditions of trading.

When a business is integrated, that is, when the same people or closely affiliated corporations conduct several business processes, there is no necessity of any sale between the various steps. For example, the Ford Motor Company owns iron mines, steel plants, glass factories, and other industries supplying part of the raw materials from which it manufactures Ford automobiles. By integration, by bringing together under one ownership and management the various factories and plants, the Ford Company has reduced the number of purchases and sales of materials used to manufacture the finished automobile. Another example of integration is the retail chain system, such as the Great Atlantic and Pacific Tea Company, the J. C. Penney Company, Woolworths, and Kresges. These retail chains have in a few cases gone into the manufacture of certain products sold over the counter. Examples are Kroger's bakery goods and Kresge's pottery. They have taken over and integrated the marketing processes from the producing level to the retail level.

Perhaps the most basic "market," and the one which developed as our economy broadened and became more closely knit together, is the complex set of forces that results in a certain price being paid by the consumers for a particular share of goods. These forces include all the items that make up the cost of the goods, such as the rent and overhead in the factory, the necessary remuneration to the farmer or miner for raw materials, and the transportation charges to move both raw materials and finished goods from where they are produced to where they will be consumed. These cost items set a limit below which prices will not fall without a resulting reduction in the supply of goods. These market forces include, also, the various elements of demand which comprise the second blade in a pair of scissors—supply and demand. The desires of individuals and their purchasing power set an upper limit above which price cannot go.

All these forces, both on the supply and on the demand side, which act together to result in a price or prices of a commodity, comprise the third concept of the term "market." Thus, it is customary to refer to the world market for wheat, meaning that all forces of demand and supply affect the price of wheat quoted on the large grain exchanges in Liverpool, New York, Chicago, and Minneapolis, and thus all those forces comprise the market for that commodity. We said above that this use of the term is, today, probably the most basic of the three concepts in a price-controlled society such as ours is generally said to be. For further discussion of the effect of price on consumption, see Chapter 14.

To the ultimate consumer, however, the most realistic concept of "market" is the first one, namely, the place where the sale is made. Furthermore, most consumers deal almost entirely in the retail market. Let us examine some of the characteristics of this final stage in the marketing process.

The Retail Market

Retailing Is Big Business and Small Business.—There are about 1,770,000 retail stores in the United States today. This is roughly 40 per cent of the total number of business enterprises in operation. Retailing is at the same time "big business" and "small business." Although retail sales in 1948 totaled over 130 billion dollars, some stores sold as little as $15 a day whereas a few had daily sales of nearly one million dollars a day; in fact, Macy's advertised that it was selling above a million a day in December, 1950. Despite the tremendous annual sales of retail stores, most of them are small. Table 4 shows that in 1948 the average store employed only 3.9 persons and sold $73,470 worth of merchandise a year. The trend in number of stores, dollar sales, and number of employees is clear in Figure 12. There seems to be a slight movement in the direction of fewer but larger stores, measured in terms of either sales or employees per store.

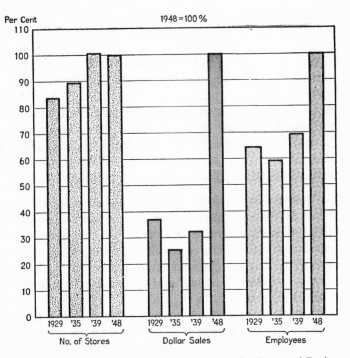

Fig. 12.—Trends in Retail Trade as Shown by the Census of Business

Source: Alderson & Sessions, *Cost and Profit Outlook*, June, 1950.

TABLE 4

RETAILERS AND SALES, 1929-48

	1929	1933	1935	1939	1948
Number of retailers	1,543,158	1,526,119	1,653,961	1,770,355	1,769,540
Total sales (000 omitted) .	$49,114,653	$25,037,225	$33,161,276	$42,041,790	$130,520,548
Average sales per store ..	$31,827	$16,406	$20,050	$23,748	$73,470
Average employees per store	*	*	2.4	2.7	3.9

* Accurate census data not available.

It takes many types of retail stores to serve all kinds of consumers. These stores may be classified according to geographic location, type of commodity handled, type of organization, number of employees, and total sales. Let us examine the retail market in terms of several of these classifications.

Retail Distribution by Type of Commodity Handled.—Of the total amount of money consumers spend at retail, about one fourth is spent for food. Figure 13 shows that retail purchases in other lines were much smaller although the automotive group and filling stations together represent nearly one fifth of the total, which is greater than the purchases of apparel or home furnishings. This measure of consumer preference will be referred to again in Chapter 9.

Not only do food stores make the largest percentage of all retail sales, but they are the most numerous. Twenty-eight per cent of all retail stores were reported by the Bureau of the Census to be food stores; about 20 per cent were eating and drinking places and roughly 11 per cent were gasoline service stations. All other kinds of retail stores were a smaller proportion of the total number of stores.

Retail Stores Classified by Ownership.—Another classification of retail stores depends upon whether they are owned as individual, independent units, or as groups of stores. Usually, groups of stores are operated under considerable centralization of policy control and of management. It has become common practice to speak of groups of four or more stores as "chains," and to consider three or less stores together with single units as "independents." This also is the official position of the Bureau of the Census. Table 5 shows the relative importance of these two classes of stores during a twenty-year period.

Perhaps the most striking thing disclosed by these data is the small change in percentage of total retail sales made by the two classes of

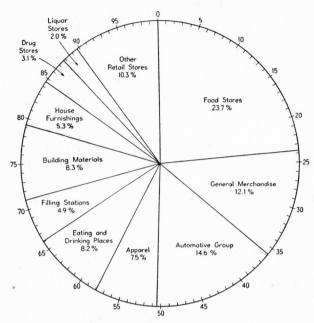

Fig. 13.—Retail Distribution—Sales of Each Group of Stores in Proportion to Sales of All Stores in the United States, 1948

Source: W. N. Peach and W. Krause, *Basic Data on the American Economy* (Chicago: Richard D. Irwin, Inc., 1950-51), Chart 6.

stores. The persistence of independently owned stores, despite their smaller average size, appears to be an interesting and significant illustration of the desire for personal independence in our economic life. It also strongly suggests that economies of large-scale operation are less important in many lines of retailing than they are in some lines of manufacturing. Retailing, farming, and some of the service enterprises may well be thought of as the main strongholds for small business enterprise in this country today.

Consumers vote with dollars as well as with ballots. They have consistently expressed their preference for the independent store by spending there such a large proportion of their money. Comparative price studies indicate that they have patronized small independent stores in spite of somewhat higher prices. Here is a place where the consumer must—and apparently does—make a choice between low costs and prices on the one hand, and convenience, special services, friendship with the proprietor, and other psychological or sociological considerations on the other hand.

TABLE 5
Retail Stores Classified by Ownership

A. Percentage of Stores			
	1929 [1]	1939 [1]	1948
Independent Units [2]	89.5	92.0	94.0
Chains [3]	9.8	6.6	6.0

B. Percentage of Sales			
Independent Units	77.5	74.7	77.2
Chains	20.2	21.7	22.8

C. Average Dollar Sales Per Store (000 omitted)			
Independent Units	27.6	19.3	66.2
Chains	66.0	74.0	283.0

[1] In 1929 and 1939, 1 or 2 per cent of retail firms were not placed in either of these classes. These firms did 3 or 4 per cent of total retail trade. The largest of these groups was the mail-order houses which in 1939 did about 1.3 per cent of all retailing. Others in 1939 included cooperative stores with .5 per cent and house-to-house selling with .4 per cent of retail trade. This breakdown is not available at present for 1948, but there is no reason to believe that these minor groups have shown any important change in relative position.

[2] Defined to include three or less stores under one ownership.

[3] Defined to include four or more stores under one ownership.

Many retail stores are too small to provide much of an income for their proprietors. If we generalize very broadly we can say that retail margins in small stores cannot average over 25 per cent of sales. The expenses other than labor will absorb about one third of this margin. Thus about 17 per cent of sales is all the labor income that a store can furnish and even this figure may be too high to be entirely realistic. A total labor income of $2,000 a year from a store operated as a family enterprise would require minimum sales of at least $12,000. In 1948 there were at least 300,000 retail stores with sales less than this minimum or about one out of every six retail stores. This 16 per cent of all stores made only about 1.5 per cent of all retail sales. This is, however, about as much as was done by all mail-order houses and more than all house-to-house selling. Small stores remain an important fragment of American business even if they do not produce millionaires.

While the independent unit store remains easily the most important form of retailing, it is not equally important in all lines of retailing. In nearly every line of retailing, however, the independent stores appear to have held their own in the decade between 1939 and 1948. Data on these two points are given in Table 6. Perhaps chain-store systems will show a new burst of growth in subsequent years, but the census data seem to show that they reached approximately their present relative position before 1929.

TABLE 6

RATIOS OF INDEPENDENT SALES TO TOTAL SALES

1939, 1948

Field	1939	1948	Field	1939	1948
Variety	13.2	17.1	Drugstore	79.2	77.3
Shoes	41.2	52.4	Lumber, building material	79.6	81.2
Liquor Stores (packaged goods)	54.1	69.8	Candy, nut, confectionery	82.0	71.2
			Family clothing	82.1	70.3
Accessory-tire-battery	54.9	66.5	Radio, household appliance	84.1	81.7
Dairy products, milk dealers	56.5	67.0	Furniture	85.3	88.4
			Restaurant	85.7	88.9
Combination grocery-meat	61.3	59.1	Filling station	88.4	93.0
Grocery	67.0	79.3	Jewelry	89.0	89.0
Women's ready-to-wear	68.8	70.8	Hardware, implement	95.5	90.7
Cigar store and stand	72.2	85.7	Florists	96.9	97.7
Newsdealers	72.5	75.0	Motor-vehicle (new)	97.3	98.4
Men's and Boy's clothing, etc.	77.4	83.4			

Source: U. S. Census of Business: 1939, *Retail Trade, by Types of Operation,* U. S. Census of Business: 1948, *Retail Trade, Single Units and Multiunits.*

Chain stores really are not a modern idea. As early as 200 B.C. a type of operation similar to our present chain-store system was in use. Some of today's great and well-known chain stores were started almost one hundred years ago. For example, The Great Atlantic and Pacific Tea Company was started in 1858 and others slowly followed. The greatest development of the chain system did not occur, however, until after World War I. At no time since the 1920's has this type of retailing increased at such a rapid rate. Perhaps there is little likelihood that it will ever again experience such growth. Because of its unique characteristics and limitations, the chain store predominates in a few fields. Table 7 shows, for a representative pre-World War II year, the business fields in which chain-store merchandising predominated.

In the main, the success of chain stores has been due to their ability to undersell competitors and to improve retail practices. These factors are largely the result of the advantages of size and standardization and of offering few if any services, which make possible a relatively low operating cost, a relatively low cost of merchandise, and a

TABLE 7

PERCENTAGE OF SALES BY CHAIN STORES, 1939

Kind of Business	Number of Chain Stores	Per cent of Chain Stores to Total	Per cent of Chain Sales to Total
Department Stores	2,672	65.6	30.0
Variety Stores	6,372	37.6	86.8
Men's and Boys' Clothing, Furnishings, and Hats	1,816	8.4	22.2
Family Clothing	1,082	10.8	17.8
Women's Ready-to-Wear Specialties	2,880	11.2	26.1
Shoes	5,721	27.9	49.7
Furniture	784	3.9	14.6
Household Appliance	1,214	10.9	18.3
Radio	169	2.4	10.2
Grocery	20,093	9.0	32.4
Combination Grocery and Meat	20,257	10.8	38.4
Restaurant	5,087	3.0	13.9
Cigar	1,533	8.3	27.1
Motor Vehicle	327	1.0	2.7
Filling Stations	10,291	4.3	10.2
Drug	3,240	8.2	27.1
Hardware	440	1.5	4.0
Jewelry	540	3.7	10.5

* Source: U. S. Census of Business, 1939: *U. S. Summary.*

policy of large volume at a low-profit margin. It is important to note that these advantages are not the sole property of chain systems. Rather, they can be found in any type of retail operation which has the same characteristics. For example, the Macy department store in New York City is a very large, independently owned store which experiences many of the same advantages in the retail market as do the chain systems. Certainly the consumer is frequently able to buy merchandise for less in the chain store than from merchants who do not possess these operating advantages or who offer more services.

Conclusion.—Markets and marketing are used in the United States as a principal means of balancing demand and supply. In the process, each commodity presents some special problems. As a result, marketing methods differ among the many commodities. This makes for an extremely complex system of distribution which, in spite of its complexity, operates with amazing smoothness. It brings to a consumer in South Dakota products from all over the world, and furnishes food to the millions of people in New York City where none of the raw materials are produced. It does this and other miracles of distribution with reasonably acceptable timing and at reasonable costs.

PROJECT QUESTIONS

1. Give a detailed and specific description of some firm or organization which is engaged in marketing. The information may be obtained either from reading or from experience and interviews. Show how this organization helps in the general problem of balancing production and consumption.

2. This exercise illustrates the fiction of one market price. The object is to have the class get, on the same day and for the same products, prices from chain and independently owned stores of the cash-and-carry and credit-and-delivery types. It is well to avoid possible "sales days" such as Friday and Saturday. Divide the class into groups—the number of groups needed will depend on the division of the market that is desired.

Choose nationally advertised brands of well-known products such as Palmolive Soap, Campbell's Tomato Soup, and Mazola Oil. It is important that the size of the can and the product be uniformly adhered to. For example, if a 10½ ounce can of Campbell's Tomato Soup is used for the survey, no student should get the price for chicken soup or for a can of Campbell's Tomato Soup of different size.

When the prices are reported and tabulated in class the wide disparity of market price is readily and startlingly illustrated. To prepare this exercise each member of the class will find it necessary to spend some time in the market, investigating prices of various commodities.

DIRECTIONS: Each student is to go to two grocery stores, one a cash-and-carry store and the other a credit-and-delivery store. From each of these two stores he is to get the prices *as listed on Monday* for each of the following commodities:

1. A quart can of Mazola Oil
2. A No. 1 can (10½ ounces) of Campbell's Tomato Soup
3. One hand-size cake of Palmolive Soap
4. A No. 2 can of Dole's Pineapple Juice

Be careful to get regular prices and not special sales prices. Also, get prices for the particular *brand* and *size* of the commodity in each case.

To hand in, write the prices opposite each commodity, classifying the prices by store.   A sample form is suggested below.

Commodity	Cash-and-Carry Store Name and Address	Price	Credit-and-Delivery Store Name and Address	Price
Mazola Oil	....	.xx	....	.xx
Campbell's Tomato Soup .	....	.xx	....	.xx
Palmolive Soap	....	.xx	....	.xx
Dole's Pineapple Juice	....	.xx	....	.xx

3.   Refer to the Retail section of the 1948 Census of Business.   How many retail stores are reported by size (size measured in terms of sales) ? What percentage of the total retail sales was made by stores with annual sales less than $25,000? $50,000? $100,000?

4.   Make a list of the retail stores within a mile radius of your home.

5.   In spite of the fact that wholesale prices are lower than retail prices, in many cities *total* sales at wholesale are greater than those at retail. Explain this.

6.   About how many door-to-door salesmen have come to your home during the last year?   What articles were sold?

7.   Visit various market places, such as auctions, commodity or security exchanges, public markets, department stores, mail-order houses, supermarkets, drive-in markets.   Each has points of special interest.

8.   Many textbooks treat department stores and chain-store systems as though they are separate and distinct types of retail units.   Discuss the error involved in such a classification.

Chapter 8

PRESENT-DAY CONSUMPTION: SOME GENERAL PROBLEMS

Consumption Limited by Production.—The possibility of consuming goods and services is dependent, first of all, upon the existence or production of the things to be consumed. This point has been made several times in preceding chapters, but it is of such basic importance to any discussion of consumption that frequent mention of it is appropriate. Moreover, the United States is a rich country in terms of natural resources. We are an uncommonly wealthy and "favored" nation which, as was explained in Chapter 5, gives us a great advantage both in domestic consumption and in international trade.

A few illustrations will be enough to show the importance of the United States in world production. Let us examine the data in Figures 14-18. It is clear that the United States is the world's largest producer of important minerals and other basic materials used in industry. For example, approximately 35 per cent of all the coal, 50 per cent of all the pig iron, 54 per cent of all the crude petroleum, and 46 per cent of all the steel ingot output is produced by the United States. No other country produces a comparable proportion of the world output of any of these products. Though our wealth is not inexhaustible, we are nevertheless probably more nearly able to live on our own natural resources than any other country in the world. Apparently, then, our production levels are determined, not by our supplies of natural resources, capital goods, and labor so much as by the intelligence, integrity, and industry with which we utilize our resources. We shall, then, examine present-day consumption in terms of national totals (Chapter 9), and in terms of individual and family consumption (Chapter 10).

How We Measure Consumption and Production.—The production and consumption of a country, region, or family are measured, as a general rule, in terms of dollar values, although this is admittedly only an approximate measurement. In so far as possible, consumption will be described in physical units, although this means of meas-

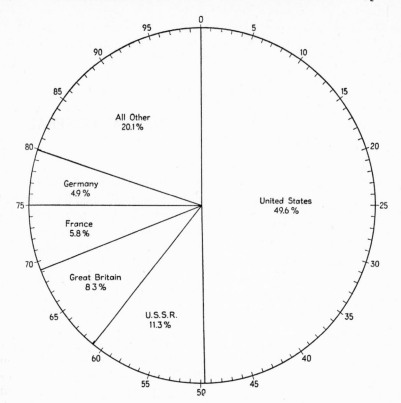

Fig. 14.—Production of Pig Iron in World and Leading Countries, 1948

Source: W. N. Peach and W. Krause, *Basic Data of the American Economy* (Chicago: Richard D. Irwin, Inc., 1950-51), p. 84.

urement has serious drawbacks, one of which is noncomparability. For example, adding dozens of oranges, bushels of potatoes, pairs of shoes, houses, and automobiles results in a meaningless total. This is particularly true when analyzing personal consumption patterns. In such cases, and in others where it seems more helpful to do so, an attempt will be made to represent physical consumption by using the index number technique described in Chapter 6.

It should be pointed out that annual data on income produced do not give an accurate account of consumption in that year even after adjustments have been made for changes in population and in price level, as suggested in Chapters 3 and 6. In the first place, both producer and consumer goods are included in the data on total production, and the proportions between the two are constantly changing. In the second place, durable consumer goods are used for many years so that changes in their *annual* production either may have little effect on their use, or such effect as the changes do have may be delayed for one or more years.

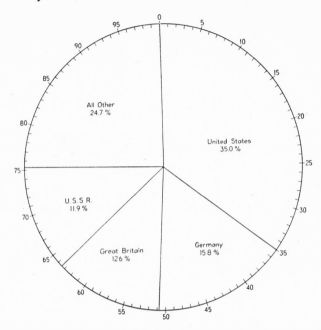

Fig. 15.—Production of Coal in World and Leading Countries, 1949

Source: W. N. Peach and W. Krause, *Basic Data of the American Economy* (Chicago: Richard D. Irwin, Inc., 1950-51), p. 82.

Influence of Time.—The year is a convenient and meaningful unit of time for many purposes, but for other purposes it is arbitrary and ill-suited. When agriculture is the dominant industry there is a natural reason for considering the year as a unit because most crops are grown but once a year. Even in a strongly agrarian society, however, annual production and consumption do not coincide.

In the case of manufacturing industries there frequently is no close relationship between production programs and the year as a unit of time. The construction and outfitting of a plant may take one half, one and one half, two, two and three fourths, or any other fraction or multiple of a year, just as "naturally" as a single year. Moreover, when a new plant is being built some of the forces of production are engaged in the enterprise, and no consumer goods are emerging from it at the moment. When the plant is completed, on the other hand, labor is released, additional construction materials are not required,

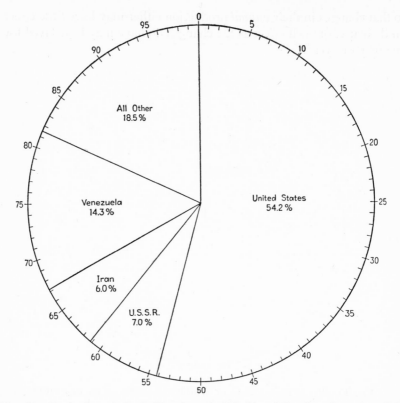

Fig. 16.—Production of Crude Petroleum in World and Leading Countries, 1949

Source: W. N. Peach and W. Krause, *Basic Data of the American Economy* (Chicago: Richard D. Irwin, Inc., 1950-51), p. 86.

some of the forces of production are used to operate the new plant, and consumer goods begin to flow from it. Several years may elapse before it is necessary to reproduce any important part of the plant, although consumer goods are being produced in it continuously.

The same general phenomena may occur in the production of durable consumer goods. Perhaps the most striking illustration is found in the housing industry. Figure 19 shows the marked changes in annual construction of housing in the United States. These changes do not always mean, of course, that people lived in poorer houses or consumed less of housing accommodations each year that construction declined. Doubtless the annual consumption of housing has been much more uniform than construction during the period depicted. Automobiles furnish another illustration. In each of the years 1932 and 1933 only 30 per cent as many new automobiles were purchased

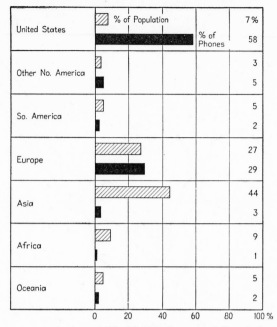

Fɪɢ. 17.—Distribution of World Telephones and Population, 1949
Source: The Cleveland Trust Co.

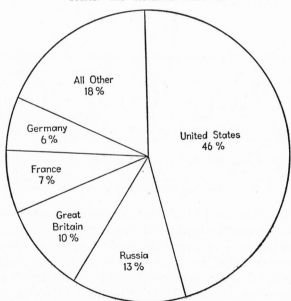

Fɪɢ. 18.—World Steel Ingot Output, 1949
Source: The Cleveland Trust Co.

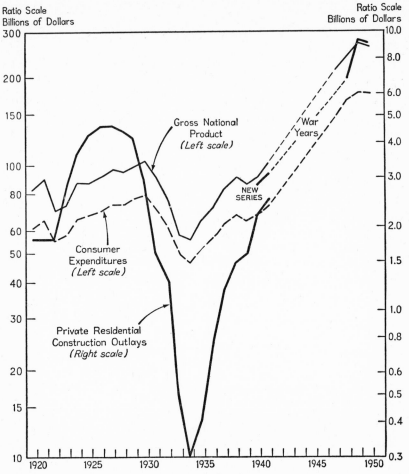

Ratio Scale
Billions of Dollars

Ratio Scale
Billions of Dollars

Fig. 19.—Housing Outlays, Consumer Spending, and National Product

Note: Most series prior to 1929 not comparable with later data.
Sources: Department of Commerce and Council of Economic Advisers

Private housing outlays have fluctuated much more widely than national output or consumer expenditures. Source: *The Economic Report of the President, January, 1950*, p. 92.

in the United States as in 1929, but the consumer purchase of gasoline was almost exactly the same during those depression years as in 1929. In other words, although the production and purchase of automobiles were curtailed greatly during the depression, their use was not. A similar comparison cannot be made for the 1940's because of the shortage of gasoline and its rationing during the war years.

Thus in any one year consumption may be either greater or smaller than production because of changes in the proportions of consumer and producer goods that are made, or because of changes in the rate of production of durable consumer goods. In the long run, however, consumption is set by total production.

Consumption May Be Less Than Production.—While consumption cannot for a long period be greater than production, there are circumstances that cause it generally to total less than production. For example, expenditures for military and naval armaments constitute an important element in the total volume of industrial production in the world, but they do not swell the total consumption of individuals, at least as we ordinarily think of consumption. The labor and material resources that are devoted to armaments might otherwise have been turned to the production of food, clothing, recreational facilities, or other typical forms of consumer goods and services. In Table 8 the movement of War and Navy departments' expenditures are compared to the value of all manufacturing production in the United States from 1926 to 1950 inclusive. The marked relative increase in War and Navy department expenditures and resulting

TABLE 8

COMPARISON OF MILITARY EXPENDITURES WITH MANUFACTURING PRODUCTION
1926-50

Year	Military Expenditures (War and Navy Depts.) (in millions of dollars)	Manufacturing Sales (in millions of dollars)	Per cent of Military to Manufactures
1926-29	722	64,160	1.1
1942-45	65,250	150,000	43.5
1949-50	40,000	227,000	17.6

Source: Data adapted from *Statistical Abstract of the United States 1944-45;* and *The Economic Report of the President, 1951.*

armaments manufacture is strikingly apparent. While United States manufactures more than doubled between the late 1920's and the middle 1940's, war and navy expenditures increased about 160 times. Moreover, the relative increase in military expenditures to value of manufactured goods has increased even during peacetime periods. In the late 1920's our military expenditures were only about 1 per cent as great as the sales of manufactured goods, whereas in the late 1940's they were almost 18 per cent as great. Since consumption is limited by production, this diversion of activity towards the making of armaments reduces consumption, as ordinarily considered. During World War II years the tremendous necessary stepup in production of war goods resulted in a sharp decrease in the production of certain consumer goods. Most of the decrease in manufactures was in durable goods, the decline in the use of which was less notable because of the available stock already in consumer hands.

There are other forms of production that do not result in consumption as we ordinarily conceive it. Protection against crime is, perhaps, the outstanding illustration. Police, penitentiaries, and court systems seem to be necessary to the orderly conduct of any commonwealth, but they do not add directly to the goods and services that increase the satisfaction of the consumer. All regulation by government agencies falls into this category: the persons who do the regulating receive part of the total income, but the only way in which they produce any of that income is indirectly, by making it possible for others to produce more than they could without protection or regulation.

Perhaps the illustration of armaments is only a special case of producer goods, although it seems to have some very real points of difference. When labor and material are used in construction of capital plant, it is expected that the flow of consumer goods will be increased later. It is by no means certain, on the other hand, that the production of armaments will have a similar result. Of course, machine guns and battleships finally are consumed in the sense that they are used up, but certainly the majority of people get no satisfaction out of the consumption.

The Relation Between Production and Consumption of Durable and Nondurable Goods.—However we may classify this special case, there is convincing statistical evidence that the fluctuations in business activity, from prosperity to depression and back again, are characterized by great, wave-like variations in the production of durable goods. Since durable goods may be made to last for long periods, their replacement may be postponed when business prospects are not too bright. On the other hand, it is frequently impossible to postpone buying such goods as food, clothing, gasoline, tobacco, soap, and so on. The volume of production of nondurable goods does not fluctuate greatly between good periods and hard times and, consequently, employment in the nondurable goods industries is relatively stable.

In Table 9 the changes in the estimated physical volume of manufactures in the United States are analyzed according to three classifications of commodities. Figure 20 graphically and perhaps, for our purposes, more clearly calls attention to the differences in the changes of output. Each of these commodity classifications permits some understanding of the effect of durability and use on the fluctuations

TABLE 9

CHANGES IN PHYSICAL VOLUME OF MANUFACTURING PRODUCTION 1926-48
(1935-39 = 100)

Year	Durable Goods	Nondurable Goods	Capital Equipment
1926	114	79	102
1927	107	83	99
1928	117	85	106
1929	132	93	130
1930	98	84	100
1931	67	79	66
1932	41	70	43
1933	54	79	50
1934	65	81	69
1935	83	90	83
1936	108	100	105
1937	122	106	126
1938	78	95	82
1939	109	109	104
1940	139	115	136
1941	201	142	221
1942	279	158	340
1943	360	176	443
1944	353	171	439
1945	274	166	343
1946	192	165	
1947	220	172	
1948	225	177	

Source: *Statistical Abstract of the United States, 1949*, p. 928.

in production. It must be emphasized, however, that the consumption of durable consumer goods probably was much more nearly constant during the period than was their production; also, the use of capital equipment might have been more constant than the production.

During the three worst years of the depressed 1930's, 1931-1933, the production of nondurable goods averaged almost 13 per cent below the three years 1927-1929 inclusive. That 13 per cent reduction doubtless had a serious effect on the consumption of many individuals, to whom such a cut means the difference between being fed and being hungry, being warm and being cold. The combined production of capital equipment and durable goods, in contrast, averaged about 54 per cent lower in 1931-1933 than in 1927-1929. If this drastic reduction had been immediately and fully reflected in curtailment of consumption, the painful effect would have been almost unbearable. If, for example, 54 per cent of the population had been forced to live

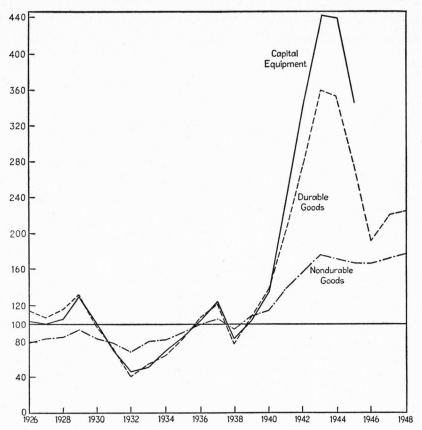

Fig. 20.—Index Numbers of Manufacturing Output—Capital Equipment, Semi-durable, and Durable Goods, 1926-45

Source: *Statistical Abstract of the United States, various volumes.*

without houses or all jammed in with others, a very serious situation would have resulted. Fortunately, as we have already pointed out, the replacement of durable goods may be postponed. Hence, it may well be that no more serious curtailment of the use of durable goods occurred during this period than of that reported for nondurable goods. In fact, the curtailment may have been even less severe in the consumption of very durable things like housing—although many families did double up in cramped quarters—than in the consumption of clothing.

In quite another way, however, the fluctuations in the production of durable goods are very important. When production is reduced, employees are put on part time or discharged, plants stand idle, and the flow of money income in the form of wages and profits is interrupted. This affects the purchasing power of some individuals in both the wage-earning and the property-owning classes. Consumption programs are necessarily modified as a result.

That much of the fluctuation in employment occurs in the durable goods industries is emphasized by the data presented in Table 10. Here indices represent the total employment of all industries manufacturing goods from 1929 to 1948 inclusive, classified into two groups. The total number employed has fluctuated during the period from a low point of about 6,797,000 to a high point of about 15,286,000. Although only about one third of the employment normally occurs in the durable goods industries, fully three quarters of the fluctuation is there.

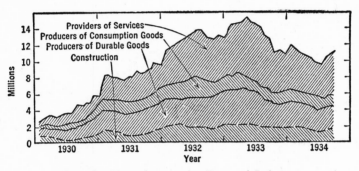

FIG. 21.—Unemployment by Types of Industry

Total unemployment is represented by the distance from the base line to the top curve. The area between the base line and the broken line represents the unemployment in just the construction industries. The second irregular area between the first and second lines represents that part of total unemployment which existed in the other durable goods industries and is the second largest area. The third area between the second and third curves represents unemployment in the consumption goods industries while the fourth and uppermost area, which is the largest area, shows that the largest share of total unemployment was in service industries such as wholesale and retail, trade, transportation, communication, professions, public positions, and domestic work. Source: The Cleveland Trust Co., *Business Bulletin*, October 15, 1934.

Fluctuations in employment are accompanied, of course, by fluctuations in unemployment. Hence, if employment is more unstable in durable goods industries than in nondurable ones, it follows that unemployment is a greater problem in the former than in the latter. Data showing the lines of industry which contributed the most to unemployment during the 1930's, a period of largest unemployment to date, are presented graphically in Figure 21. It is again evident that consumption-goods industries are much more stable than are other lines. All the data that have been examined on this point lead to the general conclusion that the total consumption of physical goods is a fairly stable matter, far more stable, certainly, than the broad indices of industrial fluctuations might lead us to suppose.

TABLE 10

INDICES OF MONTHLY EMPLOYMENT OF
WAGE-EARNERS FOR DURABLE AND NONDURABLE GOODS GROUPS
OF MANUFACTURING INDUSTRIES

1939 = 100

| Year | Factories | |
	Durable Goods	Nondurable Goods
1929	117.7	97.0
1930	97.1	88.7
1931	75.1	80.6
1932	58.5	72.5
1933	63.8	81.1
1934	80.2	90.1
1935	88.4	93.6
1936	100.6	97.9
1937	115.6	103.2
1938	87.4	93.8
1939	100.0	100.0
1940	115.5	101.3
1941	153.8	115.0
1942	193.8	122.7
1943	241.7	127.4
1944	235.6	122.7
1945	192.5	119.7
1946 *	162.5	128.3
1947	183.8	136.5
1948	186.6	138.9

* January-June Average
Source: *Statistical Abstract of the United States, 1946*, p. 156 (data up to 1942) ; *ibid., 1949*, p. 201 (data 1942-48).

PROJECT QUESTIONS

1. Compare the fluctuations in production of perishable goods with those of durable goods. Show if the differences in consumption are similar to those in production; and if not, why?

2. Are there any highly seasonal industries in your community or state? Can you suggest a way to smooth out this seasonality or reduce its seriousness?

3. List as many cases of production as you can find which do not result directly in consumption. Give as much information as you can about their importance, measured in money terms. Some of this information will be found in the federal budget, as expenditure data. but not all of it.

Chapter 9

PRESENT-DAY CONSUMPTION: NATIONAL CONSUMPTION

Consumption in Terms of Total Expenditures

It is by no means easy to show what total consumption consists of. Data from various sources may be utilized, however, to give some general impression concerning the kinds and quantities of goods and services that we have actually used in the United States. Such national consumption totals are useful because they point up the end products of our economic activity—that is, ultimate consumption goods as distinct from intermediate and producers' goods. They show us how our national purchasing power—in terms of the consumer—is divided among all the various consumption demands.

Total personal expenditures of the nearly one hundred fifty million people living in the United States in 1949 were 178.5 billions of dollars. Let us see how this money was spent. (See Table 11.)

Food Consumption

Measured in Money Terms.—Consumers spend more money for food than for any other item. In 1929, almost 20 billion dollars or 25 per cent of all money spent in the United States went for food. In 1949, partially because of price increases and partially because of the higher income level, expenditures for food rose to about $59 billion, which was 33 per cent of total consumer expenditures. The chart (Figure 22) shows this increase in the physical and money importance of food since 1909.

Measured in Physical Terms.—The 58.8 billion dollars spent on food by United States civilians in 1949, which was 33 per cent of total consumer expenditures, bought a somewhat different assortment of food items as well as more of certain ones than before the war. For example, we consumed 375 eggs per person in 1949, which was more than 25 per cent greater than the prewar (1935-39) average, and this 1949 consumption was lower than it had been in the earlier

TABLE 11

CONSUMER EXPENDITURES IN THE UNITED STATES BY MAJOR CATEGORIES,
ANNUALLY, 1929-48

(Billions of Dollars)

Period	Total expenditures	Durable Goods			Nondurable Goods				Services		
		Total	Automobiles and parts	Other	Total	Food	Clothing	Other	Total	Housing	Other
1929	78.8	9.4	3.2	6.1	37.7	19.7	9.2	8.9	31.7	11.4	20.2
1930	70.8	7.3	2.2	5.1	34.1	18.1	7.9	8.1	29.5	11.0	18.5
1931	61.2	5.6	1.6	4.0	29.0	14.8	6.8	7.4	26.6	10.2	16.4
1932	49.2	3.7	.9	2.8	22.7	11.4	5.0	6.4	22.8	9.0	13.8
1933	46.3	3.5	1.0	2.5	22.3	11.5	4.6	6.2	20.6	7.8	12.7
1934	51.9	4.3	1.4	2.9	26.7	14.3	5.6	6.9	20.9	7.5	13.4
1935	56.2	5.2	1.9	3.3	29.4	16.3	5.9	7.2	21.7	7.6	14.1
1936	62.5	6.4	2.3	4.1	32.9	18.5	6.5	7.9	23.3	7.9	15.4
1937	67.1	7.0	2.4	4.6	35.2	20.0	6.7	8.6	24.9	8.4	16.5
1938	64.5	5.8	1.6	4.1	34.0	19.0	6.6	8.4	24.7	8.7	16.0
1939	67.5	6.7	2.1	4.6	35.3	19.3	7.0	8.9	25.5	8.9	16.5
1940	72.1	7.9	2.7	5.2	37.6	20.7	7.4	9.5	26.6	9.2	17.4
1941	82.3	9.8	3.3	6.4	44.0	24.4	8.8	10.8	28.5	9.9	18.7
1942	91.2	7.1	.7	6.4	52.9	30.5	11.0	11.4	31.2	10.6	20.6
1943	102.2	6.8	.8	6.0	61.0	35.3	13.7	11.9	34.4	11.1	23.3
1944	111.6	7.1	.9	6.2	67.1	38.9	15.3	12.9	37.4	11.7	25.7
1945	123.1	8.5	1.1	7.4	74.9	43.0	17.1	14.8	39.7	12.2	27.5
1946	147.8	16.5	4.4	12.1	86.8	51.0	18.6	17.1	44.5	13.1	31.4
1947	166.9	22.0	7.2	14.8	96.2	57.8	19.1	19.3	48.8	14.5	34.2
1948	178.8	23.5	8.2	15.3	102.2	61.1	20.0	21.1	53.1	15.9	37.2
1949	178.5	24.8	10.4	14.4	97.7	58.8	18.4	20.5	56.0	17.0	39.0

Source: *The Economic Report of the President,* Transmitted to the Congress
January 1950, p. 150.

1940's. Civilian per-capita consumption of fruits (fresh and processed) was about 210 pounds; of meat, the total of 146 pounds was 18 pounds above the 1935-39 average rate. We produced 402 million bushels of potatoes, and civilian per-capita consumption of this staple food was almost 112 pounds. We consumed 484 million bushels of wheat (194 pounds per person) and 321 million bushels of corn (50 pounds grain equivalent of corn products per person).

Measured in Terms of Diets.—Comparison of quantities of food consumed in one period with that of another does not tell the whole story. It is not sufficient to point out that more food is being consumed today than formerly and that different foods are consumed in

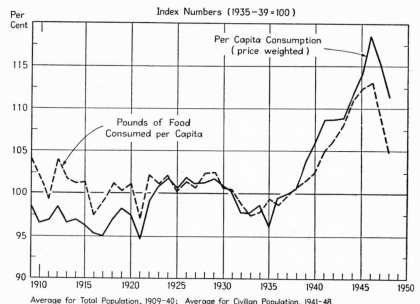

FIG. 22.—Consumption of Food per Capita, United States, 1909-48

Source: U. S. Department of Agriculture, Bureau of Agricultural Economics, *Consumption of Food in the U. S., 1909-1948*, Misc. Pub. No. 691 (Washington, D. C., August, 1949), p. 104.

varying amounts. We must also know what has happened to diets in the United States. Of course, the adequacy of diets depends on how national food supplies are divided among different groups, as well as on the total quantity of food available. A nationwide dietary survey made in 1936 by the United States Department of Agriculture showed that only one fourth of the families in the United States had diets that were considered by dietary experts to be good; more than one third had fair diets; and one third had poor diets—a poor diet being defined as providing less than minimum requirements of one or more nutrients. Riboflavin was the nutrient in which most of the diets were low, and calcium, ascorbic acid, and thiamine were next in order of deficiency.

However, there has been some improvement in dietary balance. Diets were considerably better in 1945 than they had been in 1936. This was brought out in a nationwide dietary study in the spring of 1942, followed by spot studies in later years.[1] Among other encour-

---

[1] See, for example, the U.S.D.A. Bureau of Human Nutrition and Home Economics study in 1945 in a Georgia county and one in Ohio.

aging things, it was found that the proportion of diets low in riboflavin, calcium, thiamine, and ascorbic acid had been markedly
reduced. However, the studies show that many families still have
poor diets.

Per-capita quantities of most nutrients in the civilian food supply
have been increasing and in 1946 reached the highest level on record.
Compared with 1936, there was available per person 28 per cent
more calcium, 40 per cent more riboflavin, and 51 per cent more
thiamine. The following table shows the progress made toward more
adequate diets for Americans.

TABLE 12

NUTRIENTS AVAILABLE FOR CIVILIAN CONSUMPTION PER CAPITA PER DAY,
1935-39 AVERAGE, 1936, AND 1949;
PERCENTAGE COMPARISONS OF 1950 WITH 1935-39 AND 1949

Nutrient	Unit	1936 † Quantity	Average * 1935-39	1949 †	1950 as a Percentage of	
					1935-39 †	1949 †
Food Energy	Cal	3,270	3,240	3,240	100	100
Protein	gm	90	89	93	106	101
Vitamin A Value	I.U.	7,800	8,100	8,500	106	101
Calcium	gm	.88	.92	1.04	112	99
Ascorbic Acid ...	mg	108	114	120	104	98
Iron	mg	13.8	14.0	16.9	121	101
Niacin	mg	15.6	15.5	19.2	127	103
Riboflavin	mg	1.84	1.88	2.35	125	100
Thiamine	mg	1.52	1.55	2.03	133	101

* *National Food Situation, April-June, 1950,* United States Department of Agriculture, p. 5.
† *How Families Use Their Incomes,* Misc. Pub. No. 653, United States Department of Agriculture, p. 20.

Measured in Terms of Retail Sales.—Another way of showing
what kinds and quantities of goods and services are used in the
United States is to examine retail sales. In Chapter 7 we saw that
sales of all retail establishments for 1948 totaled slightly over 130
billion dollars. In other words, consumers spent about 73 per cent
of their dollars in the retail market in 1948, as against about 60 per
cent in 1929, 1939, or 1941. The distribution of these expenditures
among the various types of retail stores (see page 93) shows that
sales through food stores were about 24 per cent of total retail sales.
But food is regularly bought in stores other than "food stores," such
as eating and drinking establishments, drugstores, general merchandise, and general stores. Moreover, soft drinks, candy bars, and
other kinds of food are sold in small amounts by various types of

retail outlets such as filling stations, theaters, hotels, railroad stations, airports, and bowling alleys. It is impossible to obtain accurate census data on total sales of various commodities, such as food, because of the way the data are reported. The best we can do is to estimate the total food purchases at retail. If to the percentage sold by food stores we add that of eating and drinking establishments and assume that a small percentage of the sales of drug, general merchandise, general stores, filling stations, and other miscellaneous types are food sales and should also be added, we find that over 35 per cent of total retail sales were food sales. Judged by historical standards and in real or quantity terms, consumers used a greater proportion of their retail dollar and total expenditures to buy food during the post-World War II period than they did during the preceding years.

HOUSING CONSUMPTION

Measured in Money Terms.—The second largest item of consumer expenditure in 1949 was shelter, embracing both housing and household operation. Included in this item is money spent on fuel, water, gas, and electricity to maintain and operate the household. If the consumer is a tenant, it includes the rent he pays for the use of the housing unit. If he owns his unit the cost of such things as insurance, taxes, and upkeep is used as equivalent to rent. This total amount paid by consumers in the United States in 1949 was 17 per cent of total personal consumption expenditures. Housing alone, exclusive of household operation, absorbed about 9.5 per cent of total consumption expenditures.

The cost of housing, as separated from household operation, consists basically of five items. These are: (a) depreciation, (b) maintenance, (c) taxes, (d) interest, and (e) insurance. Under urban conditions these five items are likely to result in an annual cost of about 10 per cent of the cost of the dwelling. From the standpoint of cost it makes little difference whether one owns or rents a housing unit provided the owner counts interest on his investment as a cost, and also counts his own labor in repairing and maintenance. In general, the family owning its own home actually has higher housing costs than do those who rent because it insists on better, and better kept up, homes.

The expense of housing is less variable than many other expenditures. This is because real estate taxes, the interest rates on mortgages, insurance costs, and some items of maintenance change slowly. As a result, the share of consumer expenditures used for housing is relatively high during periods of low national income, and lower during periods of national prosperity. This is shown by the averages for the depression years in the 1930's and the prosperous years of both the 1920's and the 1940's.

TABLE 13

HOUSING COSTS AS A PERCENTAGE
OF CONSUMER EXPENDITURES, FIVE-YEAR AVERAGES

Years	Percentage
1920-24	15.0
1925-29	14.9
1930-34	16.4
1935-39	13.3
1940-44	11.5
1945-49	9.2

Had it not been for rent control during the 1940's, the percentages doubtless would have been larger, but probably not so large as in 1930-34.

Housing is one of the most durable of consumer goods. In Europe there are many dwellings still in use that were built two hundred or

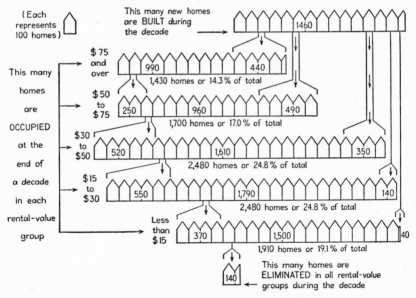

FIG. 23.—How New Construction and Depreciation Change a City's Housing Supply During a Decade

Estimated change and distribution per 10,000 homes in various rental value groups. Source: *Journal of Marketing*, April, 1944, p. 376.

even three hundred years ago. Even in New England there are some excellent houses that were built as early as 1800. The combination of physical depreciation and obsolescence, however, tends to limit the useful life of most dwellings in this country to something under one hundred years. The very durability of houses makes it possible to accelerate or delay the rate at which new houses are built, but Figure 23 shows what may be expected to happen to a city's housing supply in a normal decade.

Health Requirements for Housing.—Health authorities believe that the quality of housing has an important bearing on health. One carefully prepared statement emphasizes this belief and illustrates what health authorities believe the standards should be.

A. Fundamental physiological needs:

1. Maintenance of a thermal environment which will avoid undue heat loss from the human body.—This calls for reasonable nonconductivity of walls, ceiling, and floor, and an appropriate means of supplying the amount of artificial heat in the winter which local climate demands.

2. Maintenance of a thermal environment which will permit adequate heat loss from the human body.—This converse requirement is for keeping cool in summer. Adequate ventilation, specifically cross-ventilation, is the method advised.

3. Reasonably pure air for breathing purposes.—This means not only fresh air, but air containing a minimum of dust and smoke, and free from noxious fumes. The replacement of stale air by fresh is made possible by sufficient window space in relation to floor space. Freedom from smoke, dust, and fumes depends on neighborhood conditions outside the house.

4. Adequate daylight illumination.—Again we meet window area in relation to floor area and room depth. But adequate daylight illumination also depends on the open space outside—on the distance of the nearest building in relation to its height above the window admitting the daylight.

5. Direct sunlight.—This is a matter of orientation (placement of buildings with regard to the points of the compass) and also of outside open space in relation to height of buildings. To permit the entrance of direct sunlight through street-floor windows in the temperate zone during the winter requires roughly that the width of such open space should equal the height of the obstructing building. Sunlight is the greatest of germicides. Its ultraviolet rays help to prevent rickets in young children. Its stimulating and cheering effect on morale would qualify it for listing as a psychological need.

6. Adequate artificial illumination.—Badly placed lights result in glare. Inadequate lights produce eye strain. School children need good light for their home work, the housewife needs it for cooking and dishwashing, all members of the family for reading, writing, or sewing.

7. Protection against excessive noise.—It is only recently that noise has been recognized as something more than an annoyance. Careful scientific studies have shown the damage it can do to the human nervous system. The child in the noisy tenement may sleep, but does not rest completely. Street noises or boiler-shop noises age the arteries prematurely. We are again on the border line of the psychological.

8. Provision of adequate space for exercise and for the play of children.— This is a requirement of far-reaching importance. No one disputes that play is necessary for the normal development of children, or that play requires space, which should be available both indoors and out. That older persons also derive great benefit from an adjacent bit of outdoors is hardly questionable.

B. Fundamental psychological needs:

9. Provision of adequate privacy for the individual.—Room overcrowding and the elementary decencies come in here. The current English legal standards as to "person-per-room density" are commended—not more than two persons occupying one sleeping room with children under 10 counting as half-persons and infants under one not counted. The question is raised whether the age for separation of the sexes should not be lower than 10 years. Entirely apart from decency, all human beings need some opportunity to be alone from time to time. A goldfish bowl is not an ideal home even for goldfish.

10. Provision of opportunities for normal family life.—On the other hand, there can be no real family life without the opportunity to be together. Mealtime is a natural meeting time. But being together at meals implies sufficient space and sufficient furniture. Many low-income families do not have enough chairs or a large enough table for all the family to sit down to a meal at once, nor space enough to contain the chairs and table if they owned them. Similarly, being together for leisure time activities requires something more than enough cubage to prevent asphyxiation. And well-rounded family life cannot exist without space enough for occasional hospitality to outside friends.

11. Opportunities for normal community life.—This implies living in a normal, which is to say a socially wholesome neighborhood, with educational and recreational opportunities for all members of the family.

12. Facilities for the performance of household tasks without undue physical or mental fatigue.—We have been accustomed to think of conveniences and labor savers as nice if you can afford them, but a bit of a luxury. Our grandmothers did not have them, so we can do without. So we can if we have to. But it is time we learned to think of them in terms of health. Excessive hours, unnecessary fatigue, unnecessary nervous strain, are just as bad for the housewife as for the factory worker. If the housewife is also a mother, the interest of society in her welfare is even greater.

13. Facilities for maintenance of cleanliness of the dwelling and of the person.—Presumably cleanliness of clothing and household linen is intended to be included. It is interesting that this item would come here rather than

under protection against contagion. Twenty gallons of water per day per person, hot and cold, and a bathtub or shower for each family are stipulated.

14. Possibility of reasonable aesthetic satisfaction in the home and its surroundings.—There is much in this item which hooks up with mental health and successful family life, which obviously should be attainable at all income levels.

15. Concordance with prevailing social standards of the local community.— This is the only one of the 30 points on which the commentator entertains doubts. It sounds too much like "keeping up with the Joneses."

C. Protection against contagion:

16. Provision of a water supply of safe, sanitary quality, available to the dwelling.

17. Protection of the water supply system against pollution within the dwelling.

18. Toilet facilities of such a character as to minimize the danger of transmitting disease.—A private toilet for every family is the first requirement, with sewer connection where sewers exist.

19. Protection against sewage contamination of the interior surfaces of the dwelling.

20. No unsanitary conditions in the vicinity of the dwelling.—These include conditions on the premises, as uncovered garbage or overflowing cesspool. They may also include neighborhood conditions over which the householder has no control.

21. Exclusion of vermin which may play a part in the transmission of disease.—Screening keeps out flies and mosquitoes. Solid construction and tight joints are required to make a house ratproof. Freedom from bedbugs requires continued vigilance.

22. Provision for keeping milk and other food undecomposed.—It is noteworthy that the means by which the objective is obtained are not stipulated. If a ventilated larder serves the purpose in a cold climate during the winter months, well and good. But it will not be safe in summer.

23. Sufficient space in sleeping rooms to minimize contact infection.—Experience in barracks and institutions has shown the danger of contagion by mouth spray where beds are not at least three feet apart. A sleeping room should have a minimum of 50 square feet floor space per occupant. Double-decker beds are disapproved.

D. Protection against accidents:

24. Use of such building materials and construction methods as will minimize the danger of structural collapse.

25. Control of conditions likely to cause fires or promote their spread.

26. Adequate facilities for escape in case of fire.

27. Protection from electrical shocks or burns.

28. Protection from gas poisoning.

29. Protection against falls and other mechanical injuries in the home.

30. Protection of the neighborhood against the hazards of automobile traffic.—This is another instance of the impossibility of really good home conditions without good neighborhood conditions. Automobile traffic should be routed around, not through, a residential area. The Radburn superblock, with its interior park safe for children and other pedestrians, is one solution of this problem. If urban life is to endure, it must find a way to recapture some of the nerve-relaxing security of the countryside.

Out of the fullness of living, which is health, comes the joy of living. Out of it also comes efficiency—whether in school, factory, office, or home. The individual has a right to his health and joy in life. The Nation has need of his efficiency.

"What is prudence in the conduct of every private family, can scarce be folly in that of a great kingdom." So wrote Adam Smith, father of orthodox economics, in *The Wealth of Nations*.

Every prudent private family seeks a home conducive to the mental and physical health of all its members, but especially of its children. It can scarce be folly for the Commonwealth to pursue the same objective.[2]

The Supply of Housing and Its Condition.—In 1940 there were 37.3 million dwelling units in the United States. The average number of persons per occupied unit was 3.8, a number which had been decreasing regularly since 1900. Corresponding figures for the earlier decades are:

1930—4.1   1910—4.5
1920—4.3   1900—4.7

This change is just about the same as the reduction in average size of family during the same period. During the war years home building was greatly reduced, but since 1946 it has been very active, with over a million units built in 1949 and again in 1950. Later census figures will probably show a further small decrease in the average number of persons per unit.

The condition of housing in this country never has been completely satisfactory. The 1940 Census figures showed over 18 per cent of the dwelling units in need of major repair. For rural farm dwellings this percentage was 34, a figure which recent farm prosperity perhaps has reduced. The figures in Table 14 from the 1940 Census are illustrative of some other important housing conditions. Unfortunately there is much evidence that poor housing is a continuing phenomenon.

Apparently radios are more important to us than any of the other items in this list.

---

[2] Edith Elmer Wood, *Housing Facts and Principles* (Washington: Federal Works Agency, U. S. Housing Authority. 1939), pp. 28-34.

TABLE 14
AMERICAN HOUSING IN 1940

	Total	Urban	Rural Farm
Per cent without private bath	43.8	22.5	88.2
Per cent without flush toilet	40.3	17.0	88.8
Per cent without running water	30.1	6.5	82.2
Per cent without electric lighting	21.3	4.2	68.7
Per cent without gas or electric cooking ..	45.8	11.9	93.5
Per cent without radio	11.2	8.1	39.8

These data strongly suggest the desirability of, if not the acute need for, considerable improvement in housing construction during the next few decades. To this end home construction will need to be maintained at a higher rate than the average for the first half of the century. The annual housing development from 1900 to 1939 was as follows:

```
New units added ............ 464,000
Converted units added ....... 26,000
Units demolished ............         42,000
                                      _____
Net additions ........... 448,000
```

The figure for net additions may be compared to the increase in families at the rate of 435,000 per year, showing that we were just about holding our own.

During the 1940's a large number of temporary housing units were constructed. These included the veterans' villages of Quonset huts, trailer camps used as all-year residences, and so on. These types of housing definitely are substandard for anything except temporary use, when measured against the health requirements given above. Many individuals and groups hope they will be replaced within a very few years by more adequate structures.

If we are to raise housing standards materially within the next twenty years, we shall need to provide upwards of a million new units a year. About half a million will be required to replace minimum demolition and to provide for the increase in total number of families. Improvement in the housing of the third of our population which is estimated to be poorly housed at present can come only from building in excess of half a million units a year. This is not an impossible goal, for it was approximated for four years, 1923-26, and again in 1949-50. Moreover, public housing projects and government aid in financing make it easier to reach this level than ever before. It must be pointed out, however, that individual families pay the costs of housing and unless they are able and willing to pay for better housing they are not likely to get it. The money spent for automobiles, television sets, cosmetics, and liquor is not available for improved housing, but a differently balanced budget might provide real improvement. This possibility is referred to again in Chapter 17.

CONSUMPTION OF CLOTHING

Measured in Money Terms.—Another large field of consumption expenditures is that of clothing. Historically it ranks second both in terms of dollars and the proportion of total money spent by individuals on the major categories of consumption. In 1949 clothing cost consumers 18½ billion dollars (See Table 11) which was roughly 10 per cent of their total expenditures. This was about 2 billions less than was spent on clothing in 1948, even though clothing prices on the average increased somewhat. Undoubtedly this drop in clothing purchases was largely influenced by the growing availability of durable goods such as automobiles which had been either scarce or nonexistent during World War II and for several years thereafter. Consumer needs were only beginning to be noticeably satisfied in some lines in 1950.

Changes in Type and Amount of Textiles.—There has been an interesting shift in the types of textiles consumed by Americans. Outstanding have been the advances made by rayon and nylon. In 1929 the United States used 59,100,000 pounds of raw silk for clothing and 48,500,000 pounds of rayon. In 1939, only 8,900,000 pounds of raw silk was used whereas the use of rayon had jumped to 285,700,000 pounds.[3] The use of nylon has risen from 8,000,000 pounds in 1940, when large-scale production of it was first started, to an annual rate of 27,000,000 pounds in 1944.[4] The substitution of silk, rayon, and nylon for cottons, linens, woolens, and worsted goods for clothing represents a long-term trend. Table 15 presents indexes of physical volume of production for various materials from 1899 to 1937. The more than doubled production of silk, rayon, and knit goods (especially knit hosiery and outerwear) shows the striking changes which took place in these materials.

---

[3] James Stokley, *Science Remakes Our World* (New York: Ives Washburn, Inc., 1946), p. 50.
[4] J. Frederic Dewhurst and Associates, *America's Needs and Resources* (New York: The Twentieth Century Fund, Inc., 1947), p. 779.

TABLE 15

INDEXES OF THE PHYSICAL VOLUME OF PRODUCTION OF TEXTILE
PRODUCTS, 1899-1937

(1929 = 100)

Year	Cotton Goods	Woolen and Worsted Goods			Silk and Rayon Goods	Knit Goods	Linen Goods
		Total	Woolen Goods	Worsted Goods			
1899	49	71			22	19	137
1904	54	86			30	24	
1909	68	103	78	123	40	33	200
1914	73	102	83	118	49	45	192
1919	78	98	92	104	64	55	86
1921	70	93	80	105	58	59	72
1923	93	120	115	130	73	75	125
1925	93	108	112	106	86	77	117
1927	104	103	105	103	92	83	120
1929	100	100	100	100	100	100	100
1931	78	81	70	88	92	92	68
1933	87	87			84	100	72
1935	78	116			133	111	73
1937	99	114			135	116	77

Source: J. Frederic Dewhurst and Associates, *America's Needs and Resources*, p. 122.

Importance of the Clothing Industry.—Because these goods are used for other purposes as well as for clothing, it is impossible to obtain a precise measure of the importance of industries furnishing clothing materials alone. From the same bolt, for example, yard goods may be sold by the retailer for clothes, draperies, or other house furnishings. However, it is safe to assume that by far the major portions of textiles are eventually used for clothing. Thus it is possible to get some idea of the importance of the clothing field by comparing it with other industries in terms of number of establishments producing and selling the product, number of wage-earners employed, and the money spent for the product.

Long-Run Change to Simpler and More Functional Styles.— Another interesting long-run change which has taken place in the amount and kind of clothing worn by American civilian consumers is the persistent move toward simpler and more functional types and styles. This, of course, has not been limited to clothing but is evident in practically all the other areas of consumption as well. Such changes appear to take place first in clothing and later, if they persist, in other commodity lines. What we wear always reflects our socioeconomic way of life. The emancipation of women, the almost universal adoption of the automobile, prohibition, and war—together and separately —have had a revolutionary effect upon American clothing.

One example will illustrate this point. Before prohibition Americans, formally dressed, "dined out" in large, elaborately decorated and sumptuously appointed dining rooms, usually in hotels. The prohibition era changed all this. Small, dimly lighted rooms, secretly located and patronized by an intimate clientele and serving food and liquor, mushroomed into operation. Patrons dressed to suit the simple surroundings. This informality survived the repeal of prohibition. Smaller, less formal restaurants replaced most of the large and dignified dining rooms. Simple, informal clothing, more appropriate to such surroundings, became fashionable. And finally, evening clothes became less extreme in line and proportions. This trend toward informality was not only supported but actually reinforced by the tight economic situation which characterized the depressed 1930's. It was strengthened by the general use of the private automobile, in which long billowy skirts and silk top hats are a hazard. Until our mode of living changes to a less active, less casual and less independent one, this emphasis on the functional in all areas of consumption can be expected to continue.

Consumption of Recreation

Problems of Accurate Measurement.—"Recreation is an area of human activity that is difficult to define and harder still to measure." [5] Certainly, the point where work leaves off and play begins is often an illusory one. The reader, no doubt, has helped a friend build a dock at his lake home or spent a beautiful autumn day taking apart an old car, incidentally hoping to assemble it in better operating condition, or refinished a valued and loved piece of furniture or done any one of a host of things which he enjoyed doing but the doing of which took time, energy, and money and the result of which was a much wanted and needed end-product. Such recreational activities, though often productive and usually important in the life of the average person, result in nothing that is sold and therefore contribute no economic value. Consequently, their omission from expenditure data does not make them less accurate nor weaken their usefulness. However, there are certain other activities such as illegal gambling which conceivably belong in the broad area of recreation, and which unquestionably are

---

[5] *Ibid.*, p. 273.

of considerable economic importance, but which cannot be measured in dollars and cents.

We can reduce the difficulties of measurement if we concern ourselves only with legitimate and legal recreational activities. Their economic significance can be measured in terms of their use or consumption of goods or services. But there still is much overlapping with other areas of consumption. For example, how much money spent on the family automobile is for transportation only and how much for pure recreation; how much of the money spent on food and liquor is recreation; and what proportion of housing and household operation expenditures is for entertaining in the home or for personal enjoyment? Certainly, varying proportions of consumer expenditures in many areas should be included in any accurate figure for recreation.

Because of the difficulties of measurement there is considerable variation among the reported expenditure data on recreation. Recent

TABLE 16

CONSUMPTION EXPENDITURES FOR RECREATION
1925-49

Year	Amount (in millions)	Percentage of:	
		National Income	Total Consumption Expenditures
1925	$2,812	3.8	4.0
1927	3,110	4.1	4.2
1929	4,327	4.6	4.7
1930	3,986		
1931	3,298	5.3	4.6
1933	2,199	4.5	4.1
1935	2,625	4.1	4.1
1937	3,374	4.1	4.5
1939	3,446	4.2	4.5
1940	3,740	4.2	4.6
1941	4,225	3.9	4.7
1942	4,732		
1943	4,884	4.7	5.2
1944	5,550	3.3	5.4
1945	6,314	3.5	5.6
1946	8,928	4.7	7.2
1947	9,800	5.4	6.6
1948	10,068	4.4	5.5
1949	12,000	5.5	6.7

Source: *Survey of Current Business,* July, 1947, p. 43; July, 1949, p. S-8; Oct., 1950, p. S-8. Office of Business Economics, United States Department of Commerce. Does not include an estimate on vacation travel.

reports from the Department of Commerce estimate that consumption expenditures for recreation are over $10 billion annually. This is the sixth largest of the twelve commodity classifications on which consumers spend their money and is over 5 per cent of total personal expenditures. Table 16 shows the gradual but consistently growing importance of recreation as a field of consumption during this second quarter of the twentieth century.

Changes in Preferences for Types of Recreation.—Not only do consumers spend more on recreation than they did thirty years ago but they also seem to have changed their preferences for certain types of recreation. Shifts in consumer preference for kinds of recreation are fairly rapid and almost always unpredictable. Even though total recreation expenditures have almost trebled since 1925, for a substantial number of items considerably less money is now being spent than formerly, although for a much larger number expenditures are larger. To illustrate the nature of these shifts let us compare recreational expenditures for specific items in 1941 with 1929. See Table 17.

There were decreases in expenditures for ten items ranging from 1 per cent to 66 per cent. This was less than half the number of items for which expenditures increased during the twelve-year period. The largest declines as well as the largest increases were in nonparticipant classes of recreation but the decreases on the whole were much less startling than were the increases. The greatest decline of 66 per cent in theater and opera admission is sizable, to be sure, but represents no sudden withdrawal of consumer preference. It was merely a continuation of a long-time trend; a trend due to a number of factors, some technical and some economic.

At the other extreme are the dramatic increases in fairly new and attention-getting areas; increases of almost 1000 per cent in money spent on gambling machines, nearly 700 per cent in entrance fees to horse and dog races, and almost 400 per cent for admissions to professional football games. These very large increases certainly indicate a great preference by the consumer for recreational activities with which betting money is usually associated. These are forms of commercial recreation and are, in general, considered by the consumer to be luxuries. Expenditures for such items are therefore highly responsive to changes in consumer tastes, to changes in consumer income, and to skilful promotional efforts.

To look at only the increases and decreases in expenditure for items of recreation is to see but half the picture. Although 31 per cent less money was spent for radios and phonographs in 1941 than in 1929,

yet the 1941 expenditure of $656 million was the second largest sum
spent on any item of recreation that year. It far surpassed the
$82½ million spent on gambling machines, the $78 million spent on
horse and dog racing and the $3½ million paid for admissions to pro-
fessional football games. In fact, a smaller sum of money was spent

TABLE 17

INCREASES AND DECREASES IN CONSUMER RECREATIONAL EXPENDITURES, 1929-41

Class	Expenditures 1929 1941 (in millions)		Increase, 1929-41 Amount Per Cent	
Gambling machines	$ 7.6	$ 82.5	$ 74.9	985.5
Horse and dog racing	10.2	77.9	67.7	663.7
Professional football	0.7	3.3	2.6	371.4
Stamps, coins	2.3	8.8	6.5	282.6
Sightseeing buses and guides	0.8	1.7	0.9	112.5
College football	22.5	38.7	16.2	72.0
Book rental and repairs	2.5	3.9	1.4	56.0
Photography	73.0	111.9	38.9	53.3
Billiards, pool and bowling	57.6	87.3	29.7	51.6
Luncheon clubs	6.3	9.2	2.9	46.0
Professional hockey	2.8	4.0	1.2	42.9
School fraternities	13.5	19.0	5.5	40.7
Wheel goods, durable toys, sports equipment	177.8	223.8	46.0	25.9
Magazines and newspapers	511.4	636.5	125.1	24.5
Amusement devices and parks	16.1	19.9	3.8	23.6
Professional baseball	17.0	20.9	3.9	22.9
Dancing, riding, shooting, skating and swimming	29.8	34.9	5.1	17.1
Pet purchases and veterinary care	26.6	29.2	2.6	9.8
Boats	22.3	24.3	2.0	9.0
Sports supplies, nondurable toys	317.4	345.3	27.9	8.8
Entertainments—nonprofit organizations	32.7	35.0	2.3	7.0
Motion pictures	720.1	755.7	35.6	4.9
		Decrease, 1929-41		
Camp fees	30.7	30.4	0.3	1.0
Boat and bicycle rental, storage and repair	9.1	8.6	0.5	5.5
Pianos and other musical instruments	107.5	99.9	7.6	7.1
Books	308.4	260.3	48.1	15.6
Fraternal, patriotic and women's organiza- tions	133.7	101.7	32.0	23.9
Golf fees and instruction	91.1	64.1	27.0	29.6
Radios and phonographs	933.1	645.9	287.2	30.8
Private flying operations	8.7	5.8	2.9	33.3
Athletic and social clubs—dues and fees	148.0	73.5	74.5	50.3
Theater and opera	91.4	31.2	60.2	65.9

Source: J. Frederic Dewhurst and Associates, *America's Needs and Resources*,
p. 284.

in 1941 for each of these three items which enjoyed such sharp increases in consumer preference than was spent for many others—even for those which suffered a decline in preference such as books, pianos, and other musical instruments.

A further illustration of the changing nature of consumer preference is to be found in the radio and phonograph item. In 1929, nearly 25 per cent of all recreational expenditures went for radios and phonographs, whereas in 1941 they represented only 17 per cent. About that time, however, a combination of factors caused renewed interest in the radio-phonograph combination. Attention to and appreciation of music had been developed among great numbers of people by radio listening. Furthermore, technical improvements, not the least of which was the automatic record changer, improved the appeal of the radio-phonograph and restored a market which had reached a point of near-saturation. In the last several years the development and use of television have added an additional appeal and, as technical difficulties are overcome and improvements made, we shall undoubtedly see widespread use of this latest of radio adaptations.

Government expenditure, federal, state, and local, is important in the growth of several of those fields of recreation for which expenditures increased between 1929 and 1941. To illustrate just how important a factor government support is, let us take the field of participant recreation as a case in point. The percentage of recreation expenditures devoted to all forms of participant recreation increased fourfold from 1909 to 1941. Government support was moderate before World War I, but in the years following this war an enlarged government-supported recreation program was undertaken. Between 1930 and 1940, with the aid of WPA funds, there was an especially rapid growth in the recreational facilities made available by the government. In 1941, $203 million was spent by government on this expanded program, a sum more than three times greater than the pre-1914 figure. Of this 1941 expenditure, 84 per cent was spent by local governments, 10 per cent by the federal government, and 6 per cent by the states. This money was spent for such things as municipal parks, baseball diamonds, bathing beaches, outdoor playgrounds, and paid recreation leaders. Because we do not normally or easily count that portion of our taxes which is spent for such facilities, and because the use of them is usually free, money devoted in this way to the encouragement of recreation is not included in reported expenditures for recreation.

Recreation is an important item of consumption expenditure, yet we do not have complete and accurate data on how much is spent on

rest and relaxation. Those estimates which are available indicate
that it has grown rapidly during this century and ranks sixth among
the twelve commodity classifications for which the consumer spends
his money. Although the consumer always needs rest, relaxation,
and play, those activities by which he satisfies his needs change over
the years—sometimes slowly and sometimes rapidly but almost always
in an unpredictable way. The principal usefulness of the data presented above is in illustrating this point. We are not so much interested in the precise amount of money spent at any one time on specific

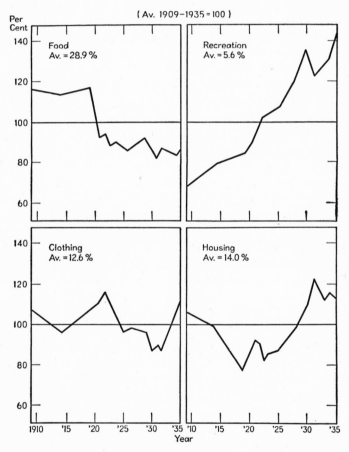

FIG. 24.—Changes in National Expenditure for Four Purposes, United States,
1910-35

　　The four charts show the percentage of the national income which was spent for four
purposes for the years 1910 through 1935 compared to the average expenditures for the
period which is represented by 100. Source: The Cleveland Trust Co., *Business Bulletin,*
October 15, 1937.

types of recreation as in the over-all pattern of growth and the changes in consumer preference for major kinds of recreation.

Conclusion.—We have pointed out in this chapter that the volume of consumption cannot be visualized directly from data expressed in money terms; physical units must be used to help us understand how much or how little we consume and what changes have occurred. Shifts or changes in consumption of certain types of commodities which have occurred during recent years have been pointed out, shifts which are not always pleasing to moralists and others who are primarily concerned with the general welfare. That food and clothing should have suffered a greater decrease in consumption during the depression of the 1930's than did cigarettes and gasoline (See Figure 24) is considered by some to have been a sign of a degenerating race. It appears to have been the result, however, of a democratic choice on the part of all the people as to how they would spend their money income—a voting with dollars, so to speak, for the most popular commodities. To be sure, the voting was influenced by advertising and other forms of commercial publicity, but in the last analysis it was voluntary and democratic. It had become clear as early as the winter of 1934-35, for example, that the vigorous production and sales efforts of the automobile industry were among the most important single factors in the early stages of recovery from the depression. There were many who believed that the country needed new housing far more than it needed new automobiles, but the people thought otherwise, and they put their money or their names on the line for automobiles. And in a price-regulated democracy, that sort of vote always will determine the national pattern of consumption.

Project Questions

1. Find as much information as you can about consumption in any other country or countries. The comparison will be more realistic if made in terms of the diets, housing facilities, clothing, and recreation. This project can be made as extensive as the teacher desires.

2. Find a list of dietary requirements for an adult male office worker in terms of calories, proteins, and fats. If possible, consider also the requirements for vitamins and minerals. Then make out a series of menus for a week that would give the required nutrients at a reasonable or low cost.

3. Make a survey of the community or area within a large city in which you live with respect to the adequacy of the housing facilities. You may be able to get some facts from a City Planning Commission or other city office that keeps records concerning housing, or you may have to make the survey personally. Consider the points given in the chapter concerning housing standards in this exercise.

4. Choose any item of clothing for either men or women and then find out all you can about the changes in style and material that have been used with this item during the past fifty or one hundred years. Wherever possible, give dates for the innovation, peak of popularity, and decline of each particular style.

Chapter 10

PRESENT-DAY CONSUMPTION: PERSONAL CONSUMPTION

INTRODUCTION

Since the ideal of plenty is as illusive as the proverbial pot of gold, individuals are constantly confronted by the necessity of choosing what they will consume and what they will go without. The basis for these choices is, generally, the satisfaction that each individual believes he personally will get from the various possible consumption alternatives. We may assume that consumers generally seek to receive the maximum of satisfaction or utility for every expenditure of money or of labor. We may assume that consumers will act as intelligently as their judgment and the available information permit in respect to the goods they buy; that is, they will consider the known facts relating to the market, to the best of their ability they will compare goods and prices, and they will make those purchases that they anticipate will give them the greatest satisfaction.

Consumers may have very different ideas, however, as to what each one individually wants or believes will give him satisfaction. The desires of people that find expression in the market place differ markedly from group to group, from individual to individual, and even with the same individual from time to time. In this chapter we shall examine some of the most important variations in personal consumption. The various causes of these differences in consumption patterns will be discussed in Chapters 12, 13, and 14.

CONSUMPTION PATTERNS RELATED TO INCOME LEVEL

One of the most important of the factors determining consumption is amount of income and its distribution. In Chapter 12 we shall inquire into the amount and the distribution of income in the United States. Here we are interested in the extent to which the amount of income one has affects how much and what is bought.

The first statistical study of the relationship existing between the amount of income and the proportionate expenditures for groups of consumption goods was made by Ernest Engel. In 1857 he formulated his famous "laws of consumption" as the outgrowth of his analysis of expenditures in Belgium and France of families whose incomes ranged from $300 to $1000. Briefly stated they are:

1. As the income of a family increases, a smaller percentage is spent for food.
2. As the income of a family increases, the percentage of expenditure for clothing remains approximately the same.
3. With all the incomes investigated, the percentage of expenditures for rent, fuels, and light remains approximately the same.
4. As the income increases in amount, a constantly increasing percentage is spent for education, health, recreation, amusement, etc.

Many detailed studies of family expenditures, called cost-of-living studies, by income classes have been made since Engel directed attention to the relationship between amount of income and the proportion spent on different groups of consumption goods. From the collected data it is possible to discover the relative importance of major commodity groups to twentieth-century consumers. As was Engel's practice, the importance of commodities at each income level is measured in terms of percentage of total consumption expenditures.

Several of these studies have been adjusted so that they may be combined, and generalizations drawn from them, with reasonable assurance of accuracy. In this compilation we arrive at the average percentage of family expenditures that is typical for various major commodity groups at each income level. The estimates, which are shown in Table 18, are presented in terms sufficiently general so that they can serve, in a general way, as useful guides to consumers even when considerable change takes place in the level and pattern of income and prices.

Although ninety-odd years have passed since Engel's pioneer study of consumption patterns, although consumer income and price levels have risen, and despite many changes in other factors affecting consumption such as custom, leisure, etc., the data in Table 18 clearly show that, in general, the proportion of money spent on major groups of commodities varies from one income level to the other pretty much the same as it did in the middle 1800's. It is possible in the light of recent studies, however, to restate Engel's laws. We refer to specific income levels in our restatement, but they are not to be understood as precise and unchanging division points. On the contrary, these income limits represent the *approximate* points at which consumption expenditures increase or decrease as a percentage of total expen-

TABLE 18

PERCENTAGE OF AMERICAN FAMILY EXPENDITURES FOR MAJOR CATEGORIES OF CONSUMPTION BY INCOME LEVEL IN TERMS OF 1948 INCOMES

Income Level	Food	Clothing	Housing	Household		Automobile	Transportation other than automobile	Medical Care	Recreation	Tobacco	Personal Care	Education
				Furnishings	Operation							
Under $1,000	40.0	7.6	23.2	1.5	6.4	5.0	1.3	4.0	1.0	0.5	1.7	.1
$1,000-$1,999	38.3	8.8	20.4	1.8	8.2	6.3	1.7	4.6	1.8	2.0	2.1	.4
$2,000-$2,999	36.2	10.2	18.3	3.5	7.8	6.4	1.6	4.3	2.7	2.0	2.2	.5
$3,000-$3,999	33.0	10.3	17.4	3.9	7.9	8.0	1.7	4.9	3.4	2.0	2.1	.6
$4,000-$4,999	30.8	11.4	17.5	4.3	7.8	9.4	1.5	4.5	3.5	1.7	2.0	.5
$5,000-$5,999	27.8	11.6	14.7	5.0	8.1	11.2	1.3	4.9	4.8	1.7	2.0	.9
$6,000-$7,499	28.0	13.1	14.3	5.9	7.0	10.5	1.6	4.2	5.1	1.5	1.9	.9
$7,500-$9,999	25.2	14.6	13.0	4.6	7.2	14.4	1.6	4.3	4.8	1.3	1.3	.9
$10,000 and over	19.7	13.7	18.8	3.7	10.9	12.6	5.3	4.9	5.5	1.0	1.7	2.8

ditures. Within this limitation the "refined" laws are stated in terms of 1948 levels of income. These data can be converted into similarly approximate figures for any year merely by multiplying or dividing each income level by the change in average disposable income. The restatements of Engel's laws are as follows:

1. The percentage spent for food decreases very slowly up to yearly incomes of $1,000-$1,300, then decreases sharply up to $3,000, and finally decreases steadily but at a constantly declining rate up to $20,000.

2. The percentage spent for clothing increases slowly up to yearly incomes of $2,000, remains about constant from $2,000 to $4,000, increases from $4,000 to $10,000, and decreases thereafter.

3. The percentage spent for home maintenance increases sharply for incomes of $1,000 to $2,000, declines irregularly up to $10,000, and thereafter rises abruptly.

4. Automobiles are, of course, new since Engel's day. The percentage spent on personal automobile use is shown to increase regularly with increasing income until at the $10,000 level it is nearly three times as high as at the $1,000 level and is substantially equal to the percentage spent on clothing. The only classification on which a greater percentage is spent at the $10,000 level is food.

5. The percentages spent for education, health, and recreation rise more or less steadily throughout. For education, as income goes above $10,000, the percentage increases sharply whereas the increase for recreation is more moderate. The percentage spent for health (medical care) is the most constant throughout the entire range of income levels of any of the commodity categories.

Certain additional observations may be made on the patterns of expenditure of various income groups. First, $10,000 seems to be the dividing line (which changes as the general income level changes) below which marked adjustments in the proportionate utilization of income are usually made and above which the percentage of total income spent for any consumption goods, with a few exceptions, varies but slightly. Second, the changes in income below this dividing line will necessarily result in important readjustment in consumption patterns. Third, for the very low income group choice is restricted to bare necessities, and the market for sundries is negligible for this group. Fourth, the percentage of expenditure on broad commodity groups for all people of the same income class is similar. Fifth, low income groups accumulate practically no savings from current income for further use. This last point will be referred to again in this chapter and in detail in Chapters 14 and 17.

CONSUMPTION PATTERNS RELATED TO INCOME CHANGE

When the Incomes of Specific Families Change.—Not only do families with different incomes have different consumption patterns in a given year, but also when the income of a particular family changes, its proportionate expenditures are modified. By way of illustration, let us note the results of a study at the University of Minnesota, which was made in February, 1935. An inquiry was made of the families of three hundred freshmen concerning the changes that had taken place in their incomes and expenditures, the year 1934 being compared with the year 1932. Of the total number, 57 per cent had suffered a decrease in income and 43 per cent had enjoyed an increase. The following percentages of all the families with *increased income* reported that their expenditures had increased in the certain specific ways: (1) payments of debts, 42 per cent; (2) education, recreation, and similar expenditures, 48 per cent; (3) purchase of durable goods, such as automobiles, 34 per cent; (4) purchase of food and other necessities, 28 per cent; and (5) purchase of more expensive clothing, 17 per cent. Similarly, the following percentage of all the families with *decreased income* reported that their expenditures had decreased at specific points: (1) purchase of durable goods such as automobiles, 62 per cent; (2) purchase of clothing, 60 per cent; (3) rent or home upkeep, 40 per cent; (4) education, recreation, and similar expenditures, 36 per cent; (5) payment of debts, 29 per cent; and (6) purchase of food, 22 per cent. These figures are of interest in showing how individuals tend to modify their consumption when their income changes. When income increases under ordinary circumstances the consumption of some goods increases much more than that of others; only 28 per cent of the families with increased income purchased more food and only 17 per cent purchased more expensive clothing. When income falls, relatively few families reduce their expenditure for food, which means that this field absorbs an increased percentage of income. In other words, the changes in consumption patterns of these particular groups of families following a change in their incomes were in accord with the generalizations presented above.

These data are not to be interpreted too narrowly. In the first place there is some variation among families within each income class, variations based on such things as differences in age, taste, and environment. Moreover, the averages given will change somewhat with each change in the general level of prices. Still further, inventions and other changes in the arts and sciences frequently have important effects on production and consumption of particular goods. Nevertheless, the general relationships among the several groups of expenditures that have just been described have been found so consistently throughout the past ninety years that they must be the result of deep and lasting influences. These influences appear to affect both the cost of goods and services and the desire for the particular satisfactions that they bring to people.

When the Income Level Changes.—A comparison of consumer expenditure data in Tables 19 and 20 for two widely separated periods —1935-36 and 1948—shows, in general, differences in percentage distribution of expenditures in the direction pointed out by Engel almost one hundred years ago.

During the period 1935-36 to 1948, personal income per capita increased two and a half times. If we relate income levels in Tables 19 and 20 which are comparable in terms of consumer income (i.e., compare 1935-36 income classes with those in 1948 which are approximately two and a half times higher), we find that in general the percentages of total expenditures spent for each commodity category are very similar. Thus even though consumers received more money in 1948 than they did in 1935-36 they spent it in much the same way.

Some general observations may be made concerning the similarities of and differences between these two sets of data. This comparison is fruitful despite the fact that the two studies are different in certain respects. For example, the 1948 study covered only urban families in an industrial area of higher than average income level. Nevertheless, rough comparisons can be made and do give us an idea of over-all trends in consumption patterns.

1. In general, the proportion of consumption expenditures going for food decreased, for clothing remained about the same, and recreation increased, which agrees with the trends pointed out by Engel.

2. Housing, which includes rent or its equivalent, took a smaller share of what consumers spent for living in 1948 than it did in 1935-36. Rent controls, of course, were largely responsible for that. Moreover, property taxes in most areas of the United States remained at about the 1935-36 level. In addition, as was suggested in the discussion of housing in Chapter 9, the cost of building a house rose more slowly than did income during this period.

3. The cost of operating the house was a much smaller proportion of total expenditures in 1948 than in 1935-36 largely because utility rates, i.e., gas, water, and electricity, remained about the same in dollar terms during this period.

TABLE 19

AVERAGE PERCENTAGE EXPENDITURE OF AMERICAN FAMILIES AND INDIVIDUALS FOR MAIN CATEGORIES OF CONSUMPTION, BY INCOME LEVEL, 1935-36*

	Income Classes	Total Expenditures (in dollars)	Food	Clothing	Housing	Household		Automobile	Other Transportation	Medical Care	Recreation	Education	Personal Care	Reading	Tobacco
						Operations	Furnishings								
1.	Under $500	420	44.5	7.6	22.4	9.5	1.4	2.1	2.1	3.8	0.9	0.2	2.1	1.2	1.7
2.	$500-$749	673	42.3	9.2	20.0	10.0	1.6	3.0	2.1	3.6	1.9	0.5	2.2	1.2	1.9
	$750-$999	886	40.4	9.5	19.4	10.0	2.2	4.2	1.9	3.7	2.2	0.6	2.1	1.2	2.1
3.	$1,000-$1,249	1099	37.8	9.6	18.9	10.4	2.7	5.7	1.7	3.9	2.6	0.6	2.1	1.2	2.2
	$1,250-$1,499	1285	36.3	10.0	18.4	10.2	2.8	6.5	1.7	4.2	2.9	0.7	2.1	1.2	2.2
	$1,500-$1,749	1480	34.4	10.1	18.4	10.1	3.1	7.3	1.6	4.5	3.2	0.7	2.1	1.1	2.1
4.	$1,750-$1,999	1652	32.6	10.2	18.5	10.2	3.4	8.6	1.6	4.5	3.3	0.8	2.1	1.1	2.1
5.	$2,000-$2,499	1925	31.2	10.8	18.3	10.1	3.3	9.7	1.6	4.6	3.6	0.9	2.1	1.1	2.0
6.	$2,500-$2,999	2269	29.8	11.2	18.0	10.8	3.3	10.2	1.3	4.7	3.8	1.2	2.1	1.0	1.9
7.	$3,000-$3,999	2681	28.0	11.7	18.2	11.0	3.4	10.3	1.8	4.9	4.1	1.3	2.0	1.0	1.8
8.	$4,000-$4,999	3219	25.9	12.6	18.1	11.4	3.0	11.3	1.4	5.0	4.4	1.6	2.0	1.0	1.6
	$5,000-$9,999	4369	23.0	12.6	18.5	12.3	3.2	11.5	1.4	5.7	4.9	1.7	2.0	1.0	1.4
9.	$10,000-$14,999	6060	19.7	13.5	20.6	11.5	3.3	11.1	2.2	4.2	5.8	3.3	1.7	0.9	1.3
	$15,000-$19,999	8937	19.3	13.6	17.7	11.9	2.7	10.4	4.3	5.0	5.6	5.2	1.6	0.7	1.1
	$20,000 and Over	14,799	15.2	14.2	20.0	13.1	2.7	12.1	3.0	6.1	6.4	2.9	1.6	0.8	0.8

* Rows are numbered for comparison with Table 20 on the basis of roughly equivalent purchasing power.
Source: National Resources Commission, *Consumer Expenditures in the United States*, p. 84.

TABLE 20

AVERAGE PERCENTAGE EXPENDITURE OF DETROIT FAMILIES FOR MAIN
CATEGORIES OF CONSUMPTION, BY INCOME LEVEL, 1948

Income Classes (after Taxes)	Total Expenditures (Average) (in dollars)	Food	Cloth-ing	Hous-ing	Opera-tions	Furnish-ings	Auto-mobile	Other Trans-porta-tion	Medical Care	Recrea-tion	Educa-tion	Personal Care	Read-ing	Tobacco	Surplus
1. Under $1,000	1834	35.0	7.5	24.0	3.4	1.6	8.8	0.5	3.4	1.5	0	1.3	1.0	0.3	0
2. $1,000-$1,999	2232	32.4	7.8	21.4	4.8	1.6	11.9	1.3	6.5	1.3	0.04	2.0	1.0	2.0	0
3. $2,000-$2,999	3022	34.6	10.9	17.8	3.2	5.1	7.1	1.9	4.5	2.7	0.2	2.1	1.0	1.7	0
4. $3,000-$3,999	3743	31.5	10.8	15.4	3.6	5.3	8.1	2.3	5.8	3.7	0.4	2.0	1.0	1.9	0
5. $4,000-$4,999	4665	30.4	12.0	16.7	3.5	5.4	9.2	1.4	4.5	3.5	0.2	2.0	0.9	1.5	0
6. $5,000-$5,999	5915	26.8	12.0	11.5	3.5	6.7	12.3	1.4	5.1	5.9	0.6	2.0	0.9	1.5	0
7. $6,000-$7,499	6928	28.0	14.6	10.4	3.0	8.4	10.8	1.5	3.5	6.1	0.6	1.8	0.7	1.3	0.2
8. $7,500-$9,999	8889	24.6	16.6	7.9	3.0	6.3	17.6	1.9	3.7	5.2	0.6	1.6	0.6	1.1	0
9. $10,000 and Over	15,830	20.2	13.9	17.3	5.6	6.6	8.5	0.6	3.5	4.6	0.8	1.4	0.7	0.7	50.5

Source: Bureau of Labor Statistics, *Consumer Spending: Denver, Detroit, and Houston, 1948.*

4. Consumers in upper income groups spent a higher percentage on clothing in 1948 than in 1935-36, and those at the lowest levels spent a smaller percentage on this category. Considerably higher prices for quality items and some scarcity resulting from the war dislocations undoubtedly contributed to this change. Moreover, in 1948, former servicemen were able to economize, if necessary, by wearing out government-issue clothing.

5. Private expenditure on education, always a small proportion of total expenditure, took a noticeably smaller proportion in 1948 than it did in 1935-36. In the earlier period the high-income families which traditionally send their children to private schools and colleges spent as much as 5 per cent on education. In 1948 at no income level did the percentage reach 1 per cent of total consumer expenditures. No doubt federal GI grants for education purposes had a lot to do with this decrease.

6. A majority of the 1948 families spent more than they received as income. For them it meant going into debt or using up their "war savings." The increase in consumer credit, especially instalment credit, probably was important in this situation. (See Chapter 17 for further discussion of consumer credit.)

7. On the whole, consumers in 1948 spent a smaller proportion on reading materials than they did in 1935-36. Magazine, newspaper, and book prices did not decrease during this period. On the contrary, many magazines and newspapers and practically all books cost more in 1948 than they did in the earlier year. The growing popularity of the radio and radio-phonograph (see Chapter 9) no doubt was at the expense of leisure-time reading.

The importance of the differences in expenditure by income classes is made more apparent when compared with the percentage distribution of families by income classes. It is estimated that in 1949 there were 39.1 million families in the United States. They were divided into income classes as follows:

FAMILY INCOME	PER CENT OF FAMILIES
Under $1000	12.0
$1000-$1999	14.8
$2000-$2999	20.8
$3000-$3999	20.0
$4000-$4999	12.0
$5000-$5999	7.9
$6000-$6999	4.9
$7000-$9999	5.1
$10,000 and Over	2.5

Relation of Changes in Consumer Expenditure to Business Fluctuations.—A study of the "sensitivity" of demand for various kinds of consumption goods and services to changes in income over the period of extreme cyclical variations from 1929 to 1941 further substantiates the general tendencies recognized by Engel. Louis J. Paradiso of the Bureau of Foreign and Domestic Commerce made a study of the sensitivity of 174 items of consumption expenditure to changes in consumer income [1] over this period of 1929 to 1941. He found that the 174 items could be classified into three "income-elasticity [2] groups" according to the "percentage increase in consumer expenditure for a specified commodity or service which is associated with a given percentage increase in disposable income, [3] all other factors affecting expenditure assumed to remain constant." [4] For consumption expenditure as a whole, a change of 8 per cent accompanied a 10 per cent change in disposable income from 1929 to 1941. Those expenditure items that rose or fell less than 8 per cent with a 10 per cent change (rise or fall) in disposable income he classified as "insensitive"; those which changed more than 8 per cent but less than 12 per cent with a 10 per cent rise or fall of disposable income were classified as "somewhat sensitive"; and those which changed more than 12 per cent with a 10 per cent change in disposable income were classified as "sensitive."

Although about 15 per cent of the total consumption expenditures were highly sensitive to income changes, housing expenditures were not sensitive, and less than 1 per cent of the sensitive items were in the food, religion, and welfare groups, 2 per cent in the medical care and death group, and only 6 per cent were in the clothing and personal care group. In contrast, the highly sensitive class was composed of 60 per cent of the household equipment and operation items, almost 43 per cent of consumer transportation items, and 37 per cent of the recreation items. These findings are in general agreement with Engel's study and the more recent ones described above. A smaller proportion of an increase in income is spent on food than on durable household equipment. And, in general, a large group of expenditures is relatively stable in relation to changes in income while some fluctuate widely.

---

[1] Disposable income of individuals was used as a measure of the broad changes in economic activity.

[2] For the definition of this term see Chapter 14.

[3] See Chapter 12, pp. 167-68 for an explanation of "disposable income."

[4] Louis J. Paradiso, "Classification of Consumer Expenditures by Income-Elasticity," *Survey of Current Business,* January, 1945, p. 7.

Let us relate Paradiso's findings to the change in the composition of the family expenditure between 1909 and 1941, a period during which there was a fourfold increase in consumer income.

The data in Table 21 show that, with one exception, the largest increases in the percentage of family income spent for consumption were in the groups of items classified by Paradiso as "sensitive." These include household equipment and operation, personal transportation, and recreation. The exception is the medical care and insurance group, which shows a substantial increase in the thirty-year period. Expenditures on this commodity group were about twice as important in 1941 as in 1909. Part of the explanation undoubtedly is that the increase was in terms of those items in this group which

TABLE 21

PERCENTAGE OF FAMILY INCOME SPENT ON NINE GROUPS OF
COMMODITIES, 1909 AND 1941

Group of Commodities	1909	1941
Food, Liquor, and Tobacco	34.4	31.5
Clothing, Accessories, and Personal Care	15.2	14.3
Housing and Utilities	23.8	16.6
Household Equipment and Operation	9.9	12.8
Consumer Transportation	5.6	10.7
Medical Care, Insurance, and Death Expense	3.8	6.4
Recreation	3.0	4.7
Private Education	1.4	1.5
Religion and Social Welfare	2.9	1.5

Source: J. Frederic Dewhurst and Associates, *America's Needs and Resources,* pp. 352-53.

Paradiso found to be sensitive to income change. They were net payments to mutual accident and sick benefit associations and to group hospitalization and health associations and practical nurses and mid-wives. But part of the explanation is probably due to a factor which applies in a greater or lesser degree to all items. During a longer period of time, social and cultural changes occur which may either counteract or reinforce the effect of income change. As was stated by the Council of Economic Advisors to the President, it might be that "services such as education, health, and recreation are an area of economic development yet in relative infancy. The expansion of these services may involve varying patterns of private and public spending." [5] The period 1909-41 saw an increased emphasis by

[5] *The Economic Report of the President, Together with the Annual Economic Review by the Council of Economic Advisors* (Washington: Government Printing Office, January, 1950), p. 96.

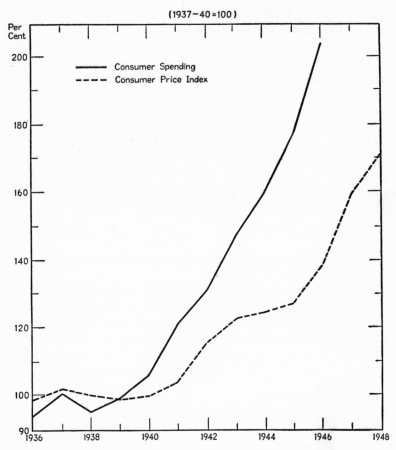

FIG. 25.—Change in Spending Per Person by All Consumers in the United States, and Consumer Price Index for Moderate-Income Families in Large Cities, 1936-46

Source: Derived from data of U. S. Department of Commerce and U. S. Bureau of Labor Statistics; U. S. Department of Agriculture, Misc. Pub. No. 653, p. 4.

both public and private agencies on all aspects of health. This naturally resulted in an upward trend in expenditures on this group of services quite apart from any relationship to income. It is to be hoped that a similar upward trend in consumption expenditures for education will take place in the coming years.

Although the general long-run trend of consumer expenditures has been upwards, it has been especially noticeable since 1940. Spending went up faster than prices as Figure 25 shows. This indicates that the general level of living rose during this period. Of course, price increases differed from one type of consumer goods to another and from one region to another, and therefore all families were not affected equally. The price of food, for example, went up more than the prices of some other consumer goods. Thus large families for whom food takes a larger percentage of income than for others, low-income families for whom food always occupies a very large share of the budget, and city families who raise a small (if any) amount of the food they consume were especially affected by the price rise.

Even though the number of dollars that families and individuals spend for living may change a great deal over a period of years, and even though the precise distribution of that money may change as between the classes of consumer goods, nevertheless we have seen above that *at any one time* there are general patterns of family and individual spending and that these patterns of consumer expenditure do not change very much.

GEOGRAPHIC DIFFERENCES IN PATTERNS OF CONSUMPTION

Not only do expenditures vary by income group but they also vary as between geographical regions. In the light of the above discussion, it is not surprising to find sizable differences between the consumption of farm families in the North and in the South. The data in Figure 26 show a disparity between the two regions for each

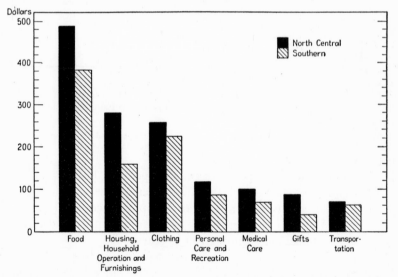

FIG. 26.—Spending for Family Living by Farm Families in North Central and Southern Regions, 1945.

Source: U. S. Department of Agriculture, *How Families Use Their Incomes*, Misc. Pub. No. 653, p. 18.

commodity category. This is partly due to the lower income in the South than in the North, but in large part it is due to different climatic and topographic and other conditions. For example, the farmer in the North Central region must have warmer clothing and more durable housing, which are expensive, to protect him from the cold winters than does the farmer in the South. The food consumption, both in terms of amount and type, and the amount of medical care required are also likely to be greater in regions of severe climatic fluctuations. The reader will have no difficulty in finding other examples.

Moreover, differences in personal consumption between regions exist even when families have the same income. Many factors other than money income influence the expenditure patterns of consumers. The opportunity for spending, social pressures, educational and occupational opportunities, and climatic requirements differ between regions. Consumers' expenditure patterns often are affected to a greater extent by these factors than by the amount of their income.

OCCUPATION AFFECTS PATTERNS OF CONSUMPTION

An additional important factor which causes consumption patterns or levels of living to differ is occupation. In Table 22 the reader, by comparing the percentage distribution of expenditures of wage-earners and university professors, will note the appreciable differences for food, housing, clothing, and miscellaneous items.

TABLE 22

PERCENTAGE DISTRIBUTION OF EXPENDITURES AMONG THE MAJOR BUDGET ITEMS, FOR
UNIVERSITY PROFESSORS AND FOR WAGE-EARNERS

Items	Wage-Earners	University Professors
Food	38.2	25.6
Clothing	16.6	13.5
Housing	13.4	25.0
Fuel and light	5.3	4.5
Furniture and furnishings	5.2	5.1
Miscellaneous	21.3	26.3
	100.0	100.0

The proportion of total expenditures going for food among faculty members was over 13 points lower than among the wage-earners, but the proportion spent for housing by wage-earners was 12 points less than among faculty members. The fuel and light, furniture and furnishings, were similar, but the proportion spent for clothing was 3 points greater among wage-earners, while the miscellaneous item was 5 points greater for the faculty group. The demands of academic life are different from those of industry and commerce, and this difference exhibits itself, as we have seen, through different levels of living. This is, of course, but one illustration of the effect of occupation on social customs and consumption patterns.

TYPE OF COMMUNITY AFFECTS PATTERNS OF CONSUMPTION

What we consume and how much is likewise affected to some extent by the type of community in which people work and live. An analysis of a study of consumer purchases gives a general picture of the character of the expenditures of American farm and city families.[6] Tables 23 and 24 present the Survey's data for major commodity classifications.

TABLE 23

AVERAGE INCOME AND EXPENDITURE—URBAN

	All Families		Upper Half		Lower Half	
	Dollars	Per Cent	Dollars	Per Cent	Dollars	Per Cent
Average Income	1,487	100	2,244	100	731	100
Savings or Deficit ...	43	2.9	201	9.0	—114	—11.4
Total Expenditures ..	1,444		2,043		845	
Food	460	30.8	597	26.5	323	44.2
Clothing	141	9.5	216	9.6	66	9.0
Housing, Household Operation, Furnishings and Equipment	449	30.0	611	27.2	288	39.0
Automobile	111	7.5	189	8.4	33	4.5
Other Transportation	20	1.3	27	1.2	13	1.8
Personal and Medical Care	100	6.7	145	6.5	56	7.7
Amusement, Recreation Equipment.	45	3.0	73	3.2	17	2.3
Tobacco	29	1.9	39	1.7	18	2.5
Reading	15	1.0	21	.9	9	1.3
Education	12	.8	20	.9	3	.4
Gifts, Taxes, etc. ..	56	3.8	96	4.2	16	2.2
Miscellaneous Items	6	.4	9	.4	3	.4

[6] "Selective Spending in Rural America" (An Analysis of the U. S. Consumer Purchases Survey Conducted by the Bureau of Home Economics and the Bureau of Labor Statistics). Commercial Research Division, The Curtis Publishing Co., No. G-1, p. 32.

TABLE 24

AVERAGE INCOME AND EXPENDITURE—RURAL

	All Families		Upper Half		Lower Half	
	Dollars	Per Cent	Dollars	Per Cent	Dollars	Per Cent
Average Income	1,141	100	1,797	100	484	100
Savings or Deficit ..	117	10.2	324	18.0	—91	—18.7
Total Expenditures .	1,024		1,473		575	
Food	390	34.0	513	28.5	267	54.5
Clothing	96	8.7	144	8.0	49	10.1
Housing, Household Operation, Furnishings and Equipment	271	24.0	395	21.6	148	30.5
Automobile	95	6.4	161	9.0	30	6.2
Other Transportation	4	.3	5	.3	2	.4
Personal and Medical Care	68	6.0	99	5.5	36	7.4
Amusement, Recreation Equipment.	25	2.2	42	2.3	8	1.6
Tobacco	17	1.5	22	1.2	12	2.5
Reading	9	.8	13	.7	4	.8
Education	9	.8	15	.8	3	.6
Gifts, Taxes, etc. ..	34	3.0	55	3.0	12	2.5
Miscellaneous Items	6	.5	9	.5	4	.8

In general, the upper-half rural families spend about as much as the upper-half urban families and in every case, except for housing and transportation other than automobile, spend more than the lower-half city families. In terms of total expenditures the two groups are amazingly similar, except for money spent on the home. The urban group spent 30 per cent of their income on this category whereas the farm group spent only 24 per cent. Offsetting this difference, the farm group saved 10 per cent of its income while the city group saved only 3 per cent.

However, farm and nonfarm consumption patterns have become more similar in recent years. Higher farm income and increasing mechanization of farm work inside as well as outside the home have made farm and city ways of living more alike. To be sure, social pressures remain quite different, but it is clear from the tables given above that, as income of the farm population more nearly equals urban income, the differences in consumption patterns become smaller.

Conclusion

Whenever the social system is controlled in large part by the ability of people to sell their goods and their services, the dominant influence on how much and what people consume is the money income received by them. But there are other factors which have an important effect on consumption patterns, such as geographic location, type of community, and occupation.

The consumption patterns or scale of living of families differs greatly between the different income groups. At each income level, however, there are fairly definite patterns of consumption or use of money income. The amount of money income required to maintain any particular scale of living varies from year to year, and sometimes violently so, because of price changes. When the change in the general price level is noted it is possible, however, to estimate the money income required for a particular scale of living in any year.

The "laws of consumption" formulated by Ernest Engel over ninety years ago seem still to hold. They show that food and other necessities take a smaller percentage of money income as the size of the income increases. Perhaps it may be said, therefore, that a test of economic civilization is the share of total income devoted to food; as that share decreases, the economic status of the family or community increases.

Project Questions

1. Keep an expenditure diary for at least a month (a longer period is preferable) and a diary of consumption. The latter will include items that actually are used up such as the eggs eaten, the shoes worn out and discarded, gasoline used in the automobile, cigarettes smoked. Estimate the depreciation (wear and tear) on the commodities used but not used up and include a money estimate in the consumption diary. Note the difference between the two diaries.

2. What experience has your family had concerning the change in consumption expenditures that have accompanied any changes in family income? Have these consumption changes followed the general patterns described in the text?

3. Assume that your family has just received an unexpected sum of $1,000 for the purchase of some durable commodity. Rank your family's choices in the expenditure of this money.

4. For what commodity expenditure are differences in income the most noticeable? (See data in text.)

Chapter 11

FACTORS WHICH AFFECT OUR NATIONAL CAPACITY TO CONSUME

WE ARE RELATIVELY RICH BECAUSE WE PRODUCE SO MUCH

This section of our study well might be titled "Why we in America are so rich." For we are rich in material things relative to the people in any other part of the world. On the average we eat more food and more healthful food, wear better clothes, drive automobiles many more miles, listen more frequently to radios or see television programs, take longer vacations, live in better houses, talk further and more frequently by telephone, print and buy more books, magazines, and newspapers, go longer to school, smoke more cigarettes, and drink more whiskey than the people of any other country.

As already pointed out, income may be thought of in its relation either to production or to consumption. Over a reasonably long period of time, the production of goods and services must, of course, set an upper limit to the ability to consume. That is, we cannot consume more than we produce without reducing the existing stock until finally all stocks are brought to zero. So far as tangible goods and services are concerned, therefore, production may serve as a measure of capacity to consume, although some adjustment may be necessary between specific periods of time.

INDUSTRIAL ORIGINS OF PRODUCTION

It will be recalled that national income has been defined as "the net value of commodities and services produced by the nation's economic system." These commodities and services are of many sorts and they have varied industrial origin. They all result from the application of human labor (physical and mental) to natural resources. They each may be placed in one of several classifications based upon the type of industry that gives rise to each. One commonly accepted classification of industrial origins is comprised of the following ten classes:

149

1. Agriculture
2. Mining
3. Manufacturing
4. Construction
5. Transportation and other public utilities
6. Trade
7. Finance
8. Government
9. Personal and professional services
10. Miscellaneous

Each of these classes might be subdivided, of course, into many subclasses. Agriculture, for example, includes such diverse productive enterprises as wheat farming, cattle fattening, and the raising of tomatoes in hothouses; manufacturing includes the making of paper flowers and of railroad locomotives; construction embraces both houses and harbors; and so we might go through each of the groups, supplying almost endless detail.

Production within each of these industrial groups contributes to our ability to consume. Table 25 shows the percentage of the total national income that originates in each of the ten industrial classes. This is, of course, a measure of the relative value or importance contributed by each group. Manufacturing contributes the largest percentage to the total income, an amount averaging about 27 per cent. That is to say, the value that is added to raw materials in the manufacturing and processing industries is about one fourth of the total value created annually in the United States and, correspondingly, the change in form of commodities represents one fourth of the ability of the people to consume or to receive satisfactions. The raw materials produced in the agricultural and mining industries represent about one tenth of the total. The services performed directly by governmental agencies (police, fire protection, highways, schools, welfare activities, forest management, and a host of other things) are a growing portion, now equaling from 10 to 15 per cent of the total. Wholesale and retail trade represents between 15 and 18 per cent, the service group (doctors, lawyers, barbers, housemaids, and so on) accounts for 10 per cent, while the transportation-communication group and the financial group of services each also equal about 10 per cent.

The listing shows both the relative importance of production in the several groups and something of the relative value of things made available for consumption. It is interesting to note, for example, that we make available for consumption annually about three times the value of personal and professional services that we do of the products of the construction industries. In terms of value, trade is 50 per cent more important to us as a nation than the products of agriculture and eight times as important as the products of mines. At least these comparisons appear to be true when we measure our relative consumption by the amount that we pay in money and effort for the products of different occupations.

TABLE 25

PERCENTAGE OF NATIONAL INCOME BY INDUSTRIAL ORIGIN

Origin	1929	1934	1939	1944	1949	Average
Manufacture	25.3	22.5	24.8	32.8	29.0	26.9
Trade	15.0	16.2	16.8	13.7	19.7	16.3
Government	5.9	12.9	11.8	18.6	10.0	11.9
Finance	15.1	12.1	11.3	7.1	8.2	10.8
Services	11.6	12.5	11.1	7.2	9.5	10.4
Agriculture	9.2	7.4	8.5	8.1	8.0	8.3
Transportation	7.6	6.9	6.3	6.1	5.5	6.5
Communication and Public Utilities ...	3.3	4.5	4.0	2.2	3.0	3.4
Construction	4.3	2.1	3.1	2.4	4.8	3.3
Mining	2.4	2.4	2.2	1.6	2.0	2.1
Rest of World * ..	.1	.1	.1	.1	.2	.1

* I.e., foreign investment.
Source: *Statistical Abstract of the United States, 1950.*

There have been some notable changes recently in the relationships among the industrial groups. The personal and professional services are becoming a larger proportion of the total; so are government services. Material production in mining and agriculture is becoming a smaller proportion. Perhaps these changes are the result of increasing efficiency of production of material goods relative to production of services. In part, the change in importance of governmental services is accounted for by an increase in the number of things done by government instead of by private industry. These relationships will be considered in more detail when we come to discuss the patterns of consumption.

The facts concerning the relative importance of each different line of activity in our complete program of consumption are significant for many considerations. For example, the opportunity for employment in the different lines will be roughly proportioned to the income produced in each. This, in turn, will suggest the relative number of persons who should be given opportunity and encouragement to train for each line of activity, and thus we can plan more wisely the educational facilities that should be provided.

As another illustration, we may consider the significance of the fact that the value produced by the processes of manufacture appears to be more than triple that produced in agriculture. It would seem to follow that a 10 per cent reduction in the value added by manufacture would have three times as much effect on national income and ability to consume as would a 10 per cent reduction in the value of farm products. This suggests that the slogan "as the farmer prospers, so prospers the nation," while true to a degree, is really less completely true than the slogan "as manufacturing labor prospers, so prospers the nation." This has its bearing, in turn, on public policies of control and aid for agriculture and industry.

Who Gets Our Money Income?

Total income may be divided, also, among the various classes of claimants or recipients. It already has been said, but bears repeating, that production of income results from the application of labor to various natural and man-made resources. Income is paid out to individuals and groups in return for their labor and for the use of whatever resources they may own. And, of course, income thus paid out becomes purchasing power. It is informing to note, therefore, the proportions of total income that have been paid out for labor, on the one hand, and for ownership, on the other.

Table 26 presents the estimates of the Department of Commerce covering the division of income. From this table it will be noted that the reported compensation of employees has been approximately 65 per cent of the total income in the five years shown. In order to get a measure of total labor income or payment for personal service it is necessary to add to this figure of 65 per cent an undetermined part of the income of unincorporated enterprises. This classification includes both the personal earnings and the return on ownership of many small operators whose accounting makes no distinction between the two sources of income. Nearly all farmers, many retail shopkeepers, some professional men, and a few in all lines of endeavor fall in this group. Probably at least two thirds of this income is reward for personal effort. On this assumption, personal efforts account for a little over 75 per cent of total income, while property rights represent a little less than 25 per cent. In other words, direct personal effort is over three times as important in total as a source of income as is ownership of all forms of property. This is an important point for consideration in connection with the continuous controversy between "capital" and "labor" over the division of income. It is significant, also, in showing that "labor" has over three fourths of the total capacity to consume in the United States. This point is discussed in greater detail in Chapter 12.

TABLE 26

PERCENTAGE DISTRIBUTION OF NATIONAL INCOME BY TYPES OF PAYMENT

Types	1929	1934	1939	1944	1949	Average
Compensation of Employees ..	58.3	70.1	66.0	66.0	64.8	65.0
Income of Unincorporated Enterprises:						
Nonfarm	9.4	8.8	9.5	9.3	9.6	9.3
Farm	6.5	4.8	6.1	6.4	6.2	6.0
Rental Income of Persons ...	6.6	4.1	4.8	3.5	3.4	4.5
Corporate Profits	11.7	2.3	7.9	13.1	13.7	9.8
Net Interest	7.5	9.8	5.8	1.7	2.2	5.4
Total Income Paid Out	100.0	100.0	100.0	100.0	100.0	100.0

PRODUCTION PER WORKER IS HIGH

In most, perhaps in every, industrial class we in America produce more per worker employed than is the case elsewhere. In agriculture, for example, less than 20 per cent of our labor force is required to produce all our food supply while in Japan over 40 per cent and in China about 80 per cent of the labor force is engaged in food production. This means, together with our better dietary plane, that our farmers produce about two and a half times as much food per worker as do farmers in Japan and five times as much as the farmers in China. This is not because our farmers work harder or are intrinsically more efficient. When either Japanese or Chinese start farming in California, for example, they frequently produce more per person than do the American farmers with whom they are competing. This, in fact, is an important cause of friction and of prejudice against Orientals on our Pacific Coast. Our farmers produce more per worker than farmers do abroad mainly because of two factors, namely, more acres of land per worker, and more equipment (such as tractors) per worker.

Our larger production per worker is not limited to agriculture. Our coal miners produce about twice as much coal per miner as the

English miners and over three times as much as the Japanese. In many manufacturing lines our value added [1] per worker is greater than elsewhere. This is not universally true, however. Before World War II the cotton textile factory with the greatest physical output per worker was in Japan, and our merchant seamen long have had difficulty competing against those of England, Norway, or Japan. This latter is partly because of our more stringent and thus costly maritime regulations.

WHY PRODUCTION IS HIGH

Several factors, singly or more frequently in combination, account for our greater production per worker. And remember, this greater production means greater income and greater ability to consume. Among these factors the following surely are important:

Plentiful Natural Resources Per Capita.—For example, the cropland harvested *per farm* in the United States in 1944 was about 60 acres; in Minnesota it was nearly 100 acres; in China and Japan it was less than 3 acres. It has been estimated that an agrarian reorganization that would increase the average size of farms in China to 12 acres would increase by 50 per cent the physical volume of production per worker. Even then the average would be considerably below that in the United States.

Our agricultural advantage is not limited to our greater acreage of farm land per farmer. We also have such a wide range of soil and climatic conditions that each major crop may be grown under nearly ideal conditions. This permits the gaining of optimum benefit from regional specialization and the principle of comparative advantage referred to in Chapter 5.

We also have greater per-capita supplies of some other raw materials than do most countries. Our fuel resources—coal, gas, and oil —are plentiful. Iron ore and copper have been available in large deposits, relatively easy to work. While we lack good sources of tungsten, tin, and some other minerals, we are in total much richer per capita in minerals than is the world as a whole.

Restraints on Population Growth.—During the nineteenth century, economists generally assumed that as any country matured population would increase so rapidly that the per-capita supply of

---

[1] This term refers to the difference between the sales value of the product and the cost of all raw materials, containers, fuel, and power. Therefore it may be thought of as the product of the labor and machinery used directly in the process.

natural resources would decrease. As a result it was assumed that per-capita production and ability to consume would fall. These assumptions provide the reason for calling economics "the dismal science."

Actually there is little in the history of this country to date that bears out the assumptions. Of course we started only a couple of centuries ago to fill an almost unsettled continent with people. During these two hundred years we have found increasing sources of many raw materials. Petroleum conspicuously illustrates the point. Since the early discovery of oil in Pennsylvania new fields have been found that are far greater in extent than anyone had imagined. Doubtless, some day our ratio of oil resources to population will fall and we shall be forced to develop other forms of fuel, but perhaps our technologists will by then have discovered other equally inexpensive sources of power. This we have been able to do so far with the result that our per-capita production has gone up rather than down.

Another circumstance that has prevented a decline in per-capita production has been the reduction of the rate of population growth. This reduction has resulted from two forces, namely, decline both in immigration and in birth rate. Data on population growth and immigration are given in Table 27. Data on births and deaths are given in Table 28.

These data show the great importance of immigration to the total increase of population in this country. This was especially large in the decades ending in 1890, 1910, and 1920. After World War I many individuals believed that the rush of people from Europe to the United States soon would result in a reduction of per-capita production and so Congress passed the Immigration Restriction Act in 1926. The effect on immigration in the 1930's and 1940's is easily seen in the data.

From 1915 to 1935 the birth rate per 1,000 population fell continuously. While the death rate also fell it did not go down as rapidly and so the excess of births over deaths fell from 11.0 per 1,000 in 1915 to 6.0 twenty years later. During the prosperous and wartime years of the 1940's this trend was reversed. Whether this reversal is to be temporary or of longer duration still remains to be seen, but it seems likely that the downward trend may soon be re-established. Unless we can continue to increase our per-capita production and ability to consume we probably shall continue to grow slowly. Certainly it is in keeping with the modern trend of mores and of education in this country and in western Europe to restrain population growth so that per-capita ability to consume will not be impaired.

More Man-Made Capital Per Worker.—We have done much in this country to strengthen the arms of men in the performance of their daily tasks.

1. INSTALLED HORSEPOWER. For example, at the outbreak of World War II we had about six and a quarter installed horsepower for every worker in our manufacturing industries. This was at least 50 per cent more than in any other country and nearly two and a half times as much as in Japan. Consequently, the value added by our manufacturing processes resulted partly from the efforts of the direct

TABLE 27

POPULATION GROWTH AND IMMIGRATION

Decade Ending in	Population Increase		Immigration	
	in Millions	in Per Cent	in Millions	Percentage of Pop. Increase
1850	6.1	35.9	1.7	28.0
1860	8.2	35.6	2.6	31.6
1870	8.3	26.6	2.3	27.8
1880	10.3	26.0	2.8	27.0
1890	12.8	25.5	5.2	40.6
1900	13.0	20.7	3.7	28.5
1910	16.0	21.0	8.8	55.0
1920	13.7	14.9	5.8	42.3
1930	17.0	16.1	4.1	24.0
1940	8.9	7.2	0.5	5.6
1950	18.9	14.3	0.7	3.2

Source: *Statistical Abstract of the United States, 1950.*

TABLE 28

BIRTHS AND DEATHS

Rates per 1,000 of Population

Year	Births	Deaths	Excess of Births over Deaths
1915	25.0	14.0	11.0
1920	23.7	13.1	10.6
1925	21.3	11.7	9.6
1930	18.9	11.3	7.6
1935	16.9	10.9	6.0
1940	17.9	10.7	7.2
1945	19.6	10.6	9.6
1947	25.8	10.1	15.7

Source: *Statistical Abstract of the United States, 1949.*

employees and partly from the energy supplied by the installed horse-power. As an accompanying result, of course, the income derived from manufacturing was distributed partly to the owners and employees in each factory and partly to the owners and employees of the firms which furnished the power. In spite of the need for thus broadening the distribution of income, the use of power energy greatly increased the total output of consumer goods and services and, consequently, the average income distributed to all workers.

2. MECHANIZATION OF INDUSTRY. We not only have supplied power to workers, but we have also been ingenious in adapting machinery run by power to the jobs of making many forms of consumer goods. Some of these machines, like the cotton gin and sewing machine, were first invented in this country. Others, like our lathes and printing presses, were adapted from inventions elsewhere. Whatever the original source, today our industries are highly mechanized. Perhaps our inherent laziness, combined with an equally inherent desire for more gadgets to consume, is responsible for our ready adoption of the many laborsaving devices in industry. In any event, they have resulted in a substantial increase in our ability to produce and to consume.

3. TRANSPORTATION FACILITIES. Throughout the economic development of the United States much emphasis has been placed upon the provision of adequate low-cost transportation. This has added to the forces already mentioned to make possible a high degree of regional specialization. Agriculture illustrates this with our distinct wheat, cotton, citrus fruit, and other belts or areas. Similarly, manufacturing has tended to concentrate in limited areas from which products are given national and even international distribution. This permits individual firms to take full advantage both of the economies of specific locations and of the economies of large-scale production. Low-cost communication via mail, telegraph, and telephone has also contributed to these developments.

Economies of Scale.—Americans appear to like big things. Perhaps this is due in part to our environment which includes big mountains and rivers, the largest trees in the world, vast expanses of open farm land and of forests. We have big railroad locomotives for long-distance freight hauling, we use enormous equipment in our open-pit copper and iron ore mines, we have built huge dams to regulate river flow and provide for production of electric power as well as irrigation.

We also have organized big companies to own and operate big factories. These have permitted us to gain the advantages of large-scale production. These advantages are of several kinds. In the first place, products are standardized and are produced in volume. This makes unnecessary the costs of frequent re-planning or of special work on individual units. Second, the fact of standardization makes it worth while to make special laborsaving machines to do things that otherwise would need to be done by hand. This is economical only when the special machines can be used for shaping a great many similar units. Third, a large concern can finance much research out of a small charge against each unit produced. This leads to progress both in technology and in fitting the product to the market demands. In many ways, large firms are able to take advantage of specialization through using the best abilities of individuals and by developing these abilities through practice.

Democratic Institutions.—In listing the factors which favorably affect our volume of production we cannot omit the free and democratic institutions that make the framework of our political economy. Within this framework individuals are given great freedom to do whatever they believe will give them the greatest income and ultimate satisfaction. This, in turn, has fostered experimentation, the discard of unprofitable activities, and progress into more and more productive action.

Some specific tenets in our political economy have contributed very directly to our productivity. For example, almost from the beginning we have had a national policy of giving tariff protection to new industries. This permitted favorable competition against the older industrial countries in Europe. Perhaps in many cases the protection has been continued longer than was necessary to give the new industry a fair start. In some cases we have probably raised consumer prices as a result. Almost certainly it would be in the interest of world economy if we discontinued the policy of protective tariffs. But it is equally certain that part of the rapid and successful growth of industry in this country is due to our early tariff policy.

Another institutional device that has contributed to our growth of productivity is our patent policy. Under this policy individuals and firms have been encouraged to seek new and better ways of doing things, for they knew that they could avoid direct competition for twenty years. Thus they could hold for themselves the major gains from their new devices for at least half of the active life of the average individual. This period of protection is longer than granted in many other countries.

Ambitious and Aggressive People.—Important among the influences leading to our high level of production is the fact that so many of our people are ambitious and aggressive. It has been said truly that the most important product of New England, for example, has been the large number of social and industrial leaders born there. The same might be said, perhaps, of many other parts of the country. Certainly it seems to be true that our people are characterized to an unusual degree by the spirit of industrial conquest. This stems in part, no doubt, from their personal heritage; only those willing to break with tradition and possessing enthusiasm for a cause came to our shores. Add to this the effect of a stimulating climate, frontiers to be developed, a progressive system of nearly universal education, democratic institutions, and the tremendous urge supplied by commercial advertising, and almost inevitably a high level of production resulted.

Our environment, as a whole, has tended to develop ambition, imagination, willingness to experiment with new ideas, and a quickness to adapt the ideas of others to our particular circumstances. At least two other characteristics seem typical of the rank and file of Americans and have contributed to our national progress. We are jealous individuals: that is, we do not want anyone else to have things which we do not have; we want to "keep up with the Joneses," whoever and wherever they may be. And we are egotistical: we are sure we can do anything anyone else can do and perhaps do it a little quicker, less expensively, or better in some other respect.

These, then, are the natural, historical, political, and human forces that have led to our high plane of per-capita production relative to the rest of the world.

WHY CONSUMPTION IS NOT STILL GREATER

We should be remiss, however, if we did not remind ourselves at this point to ask a question different from the one with which this chapter commenced. We need to inquire not only why we are so rich, but also why we are so poor. Each of us still has many unfilled desires. There are slums in our cities; some areas are peopled with "poor white trash"; many of us do not even have enough to eat, to say nothing about enough automobiles, television sets, vacation trips, formal education, or shoes.

Limited by Production.—We have said that consumption is limited by the volume of production. If we do not have all we want to consume as a national group, it is because we do not produce enough in total. Harder work, or better (i.e., more efficient) organization and work, or both, are essential if we are to increase our ability to consume.

Not Limited by Supply of Resources.—Apparently our production is not held to its present general level by our supply of natural resources, capital goods, and labor. At least, the Brookings Institution has made a careful and elaborate study of America's capacity to produce which leads to this conclusion.[2] This study shows that in the peak pre-World War II year, 1929, and in the prosperous period, 1925-29, the capital plant of the country was actually utilized only to between 70 and 85 per cent of its practical capacity. This is a composite estimate, including all types of capital plants such as farms, factories, stores, railroads, power plants, and the like.

The same study indicates that there was sufficient unutilized labor supply to bring the estimated plant capacity into full use. This unused supply of labor was not distributed, however, in precisely the way to bring about such a result. Many minor shifts would be required throughout industry and, as a major shift, perhaps a million workers would need to be moved into the mining and manufacturing industries from agriculture and trade. Admitting the possibility of such shifts, however, the production of the country could have been raised by, perhaps, 20 per cent just by keeping our unemployed people and machines busy.

The Tragedy of Waste.—Some individuals long have believed that we could—and should—do better. Stuart Chase, for example, in his book *The Tragedy of Waste,* written in 1925, estimated that about 50 per cent of all our manpower was being wasted. His estimate of wasted manpower went about as follows:

> 20 per cent wasted on production of useless or harmful things;
>> This item involves an ethical evaluation.
> 15 per cent wasted on unemployment;
>> This was due in part to illness and in part to the failure of our economic machine to function smoothly.
> 10 per cent wasted through inefficiency in production;
>> This is largely a matter of engineering efficiency.
> 5 per cent wasted in distribution of goods;
>> This is partly engineering and partly social waste.

---

[2] E. G. Nourse *et al., America's Capacity to Produce* (Washington: Brookings Institution, 1934).

When Herbert Hoover was Secretary of Commerce after World War I he instituted an elaborate study of waste in industry which reported almost as startling amounts of waste as had been estimated by Chase. The committee which made this study was composed almost entirely of private businessmen and engineers. The findings led to some improvement both in the methods of attacking waste and in its actual reduction. Many other studies, both public and private, have since been made.

One of the very useful institutional developments resulting from governmental interest in waste was the increased cooperation between industry and government in the trade practices conference procedure under the leadership of the Department of Commerce. Surveys of many industries have been undertaken and recommendations have been brought to large manufacturers and to trade associations through the conferences. The reports often include specific recommendations to reduce the number of types and sizes of products in a line, and to adopt interchangeable parts whenever feasible. Among the fairly early accomplishments of the trade practice conferences the following reductions in varieties and sizes may be mentioned:

Blanket Sizes	from	78	to	12
Metal Lath	"	125	"	24
Hotel Chinaware	"	700	"	160
Files and Rasps	"	1351	"	496
Spades, Shovels, Scoops	"	4460	"	384

Fairly substantial savings have resulted from these decisions. Even more substantial improvements in production have resulted from the direct initiative of businessmen. Better-engineered plant layout and flow of material through factories are important illustrations of these improvements.

Competition, however, continues to result in the desire to differentiate products so as to obtain patronage from more customers. Sometimes the product differences really are important to consumers, sometimes they are not. Thus not all the improved methods of production have actually been put into effect. This is a difficult area for judgment which is considered in more detail in Chapter 14.

Private enterprise has contributed greatly to the elimination of waste. One of the main merits of the private-enterprise system, perhaps, is that it continually urges producers to utilize resources more efficiently in order to gain or hold customers. Better products at lower prices tend to be the result. Then, too, whenever labor receives a wage increase, management and ownership look for laborsaving methods. Ruthlessly the struggle for material progress goes on through rivalry under our system of political economy.

We have reached towards the goals suggested by Chase. At the beginning of World War II the question had been asked: "Can we hope to have both guns and butter?" and many were inclined to answer in the negative. On the whole, however, in spite of the men and material devoted directly to war, we lived during the war years better than ever before. Those years combined the inducements of patriotism, social pressure, high wages, and some measure of actual coercion. As yet we have not been able to do as well in peacetime, although our postwar level of production per capita is higher than at any time before the war.

We Could Use Better Industrial Leadership.—Perhaps it may be suggested, therefore, that what we have need of is neither man-power nor natural resources, but brain power that will permit us to use efficiently the available supplies of the other two. And it may be pointed out, also, that perhaps Mr. Chase has omitted from his list the most devastating of all forms of waste, namely, the production of the right things, but at the wrong time or in the wrong amount. Whenever manpower and natural resources are combined into products which no one with purchasing power will buy, then the effort might as well have been spent in beating tom-toms or in chasing any will-o'-the-wisp that strikes the fancy. And when business leaders think they have made such a mistake, their immediate reaction is to retrench, dismiss their employees, cancel their orders for raw materials, and upset the established flow of income. If our business leaders had enough wisdom and insight or if marketing research were developed sufficiently to forecast both the kind and the quantity of things that people will be willing and able to buy at prices that will cover costs, we might be able to keep our plants operating at full capacity. Then our consumption would be limited only by the stage of our technical ability in production. Unfortunately such inspired leadership does not exist. One of the purposes of education, surely, is to aid in its development.

If we could double the effectiveness of our manpower, what would be the effect on consumption? Obviously, as will be pointed out in more detail later, we should not double the present production of everything, but we should develop our increases only in certain lines. Food would need comparatively little increase in total amount. Clothing output would hardly need to be doubled. Since these two items combine into 40 or 50 per cent of the expenditures for consumption of the masses in this country, the labor saved through efficient production in these lines would permit much more than doubling in some others—improved housing construction, for example, or educational and recreational facilities. The details of an enlarged program of consumption are discussed in much more detail in the chapters on consumption patterns.

PROJECT QUESTIONS

1. How is installed horsepower used in your community? Find as many instances as you can of both private and public installations. Also, get as much information as you can concerning the amount of electrical or steam power used by different industries.

2. Choose any industry, preferably a manufacturing industry, in which you are interested. Examine the data given in either Poor's or Moody's *Manual of Industrials* and find the figures on net profit as a percentage of net worth for individual firms in this industry. Compare these net profit percentages for the large and the small companies in the industry. What do you conclude concerning economies of scale in this industry?

3. What evidences can you find of waste in your community? Are these wastes connected with manufacturing, distribution, or consumption? Measure the amount of waste as accurately as you can against the best standard you can find.

Chapter 12

MONEY INCOME AFFECTS PERSONAL CONSUMPTION

MANY FACTORS INFLUENCE CONSUMPTION

We in the United States are richer than most other peoples, yet we are poorer than we wish. In the previous chapter we discussed some of the reasons for each of these conditions in respect of *national* income. In this chapter we consider how the *individual* fares; what portion, that is, each of us gets from the national total, and why our portion is as large or as small as it is.

Our total national consumption is limited by our total production, and our total purchases are limited by our total money income. Within these limits we do not all live alike. Some men manage large corporations, others teach school, still others dig ditches, paint pictures, write detective stories, play professional baseball, or wash dishes. Some use their leisure time in world cruises, others play golf, others hunt and fish, while some are so fatigued and depressed by their daily tasks that they seem to have neither time nor energy for any enjoyment of leisure. Some spend much money on clothes, others on automobiles, others on books, while some give liberally to welfare institutions and still others seem to have no income beyond that needed for the barest necessities.

The causes of these variations, that is the factors that limit and influence our individual choices concerning both the way in which we make our income and the way in which we spend it, are deeply imbedded in our individual inheritance and environment. Some of the causes are physiological, some are psychological, and some are economic in origin and nature. Frequently two or more basically different factors combine to influence our choices. By way of illustration, the blonde desires colors in her wardrobe or her lipstick different from the brunette; the introvert enjoys forms of recreation different from the extrovert's; he who inherits a million dollars at age twenty-one has a program of consumption entirely different from the one who continues through life to dig ditches for the wage of the common laborer. Residents of California or Florida wear clothing different from that of those who live in Boston or Minneapolis. The surgeon whose income is $25,000 a year lives very differently from either the common laborer whose income is less than $2,000 or the farmer whose cash income is $1,500. Perhaps the difference in money income is the most important single factor producing different modes of living. Many other things are of some importance, however, including tastes and abilities, customs, regional environment, and others soon to be discussed.

The most obvious as well as the most important factor influencing or even determining individual consumption is money income. Since this is true we shall first examine the facts of income distribution, the relations of these facts to consumption, and attempt to explain the pattern of income distribution. The following two chapters deal with other factors influencing consumption patterns.

MEASUREMENT OF PRODUCTION AND CONSUMPTION IS DIFFICULT

The possibility of consuming goods and services is dependent, first of all, upon the existence or production of the things to be consumed. The total production of the world, nation, or region generally is measured in terms of dollar values, although this is admittedly only an approximate measurement. (See Chapter 6.)

It is impossible to compare directly the physical productivity of different occupations. For example, there is no physical basis for combining the counsel of a lawyer with the product of a ditch digger or that of a potato grower. Of course, we might make a list of the many things produced in the United States: that is, so many bathtubs, toy whistles, spark plugs, houses, nitric acid, beauty facials, and ice-cream cones. But a numerical total of such a list would be practically meaningless. Another method of estimating production might be to measure the national product by weight, i.e., tons or pounds; or by volume, i.e., cubic feet or yards. Such a figure would not be much more useful than the first one because it badly misrepresents the importance of certain goods we produce and consume. For example, coal weighs so much more than rayon and is so much bulkier that it would appear to be of greater value in our economy than we know by experience it actually is. Moreover, such measure as weight or volume could not represent the value of services produced. Thus the most meaningful measure of the total output of a nation is the money value of goods and services produced. This total is called the gross national product.

Money Values of Production and Consumption

Gross National Product.—The gross national product concept is a relatively new one in the United States. The need for some such measure of the goods and services produced arose in 1941 when the nation's rearmament program grew ever larger month by month. Before Congress and the Administration could form a policy for guidance during that uncertain period it was necessary to know the facts of total demand (of government and private consumers) and total production. Consequently a measure of total production was developed. Very simply stated, the gross national product is the technical name of the dollar value of all that is produced in the United States during a period of time. It may be defined as the aggregate value of the current production of goods and services flowing to the government, to consumers, and to business.

National Income.—For some purposes we are more directly concerned with national income statistics than with gross product statistics. To be sure, we appreciate the limiting nature of total production. But it is the income resulting from production of goods and services, and the distribution of that income to the respective recipient groups, which consumption economists find more useful.

National income has been defined in Chapter 3. Although the national income is created in the production of the national product, yet the former is smaller than the latter. Why? The relationship of the two can be clearly seen in Table 29.

TABLE 29

RELATIONSHIP OF NATIONAL INCOME TO NATIONAL PRODUCT

Factors			Amounts 1949 (in $ billions)
Gross national product			255.6
Less: Capital consumption allowances	18.8		
Business taxes and related liabilities	22.0	40.8	
Statistical discrepancies		1.9	38.9
			216.7
Plus: Subsidies less current surplus of government enterprises			.1
Equals national income			216.8

Disposable Personal Income.—Not all the national income is available for individuals to spend as they choose. For example, a portion of it appears in the government tax collections, expenditures, and resulting government services. Some adjustments also result from the operation of corporations. The relationship between national income and the income available for consumers to spend is shown in the following table, the portion available for spending being called *disposable personal income.*

TABLE 30

DISPOSABLE PERSONAL INCOME

Factors		1949 in $ billions
National income		216.8
Less: Corporate profits and inventory adjustments	29.9	
Contributions for social insurance	5.7	
Excess of wage accruals over disbursements	.0	
	35.6	35.6
		181.2
Plus: Government transfer payments	11.6	
Interest paid by government	4.7	
Dividends	7.8	
Business transfer payments	.7	
	24.8	24.8
Personal income		206.0
Less: federal, state and local taxes		18.7
Equals disposable personal income		187.3

Estimates of total disposable personal income are given in Table 31 for the years 1929 to 1949 inclusive. The items are first shown in current dollars for each year. Next, they are converted into dollar values with the average 1935-39 consumer purchasing power by dividing the original figures by the Consumers' Price Index of the United States Department of Commerce. Finally, each of these values is converted into a per-capita figure by dividing by the estimated population for the year. Thus the final column gives the average per-capita personal income after taxes in terms of its 1935-39 purchasing power. Variations in the first column of per-capita figures measure approximately the year-to-year differences in the average disposable money income of consumers, while the second column of per-capita figures measures the variations in real income or purchasing power available for consumption.

TABLE 31

DISPOSABLE PERSONAL INCOME, TOTAL AND PER CAPITA, 1929-49

Year	Total National Income		Per-Capita Income	
	Current Dollars (in millions)	1935-39 Dollars (in millions)	Current Dollars	1935-39 Dollars
1929	82,484	67,300	677	553
1930	73,688	61,600	597	500
1931	62,977	57,900	507	464
1932	47,819	49,000	384	393
1933	45,165	49,000	360	390
1934	51,635	54,000	408	427
1935	57,973	59,000	455	464
1936	66,095	66,700	515	520
1937	71,055	69,300	552	538
1938	65,465	65,000	504	501
1939	70,167	70,700	537	541
1940	75,743	75,700	574	573
1941	92,015	87,400	690	655
1942	116,740	100,000	866	744
1943	132,441	107,000	970	774
1944	146,957	117,000	1060	845
1945	151,060	117,500	1080	844
1946	158,916	114,000	1120	808
1947	169,494	106,000	1175	735
1948	177,446	103,500	1210	708
1949	178,832	105,800	1200	710

The drop in per-capita disposable income from $677 in 1929 to $360 in 1933 was a result of the tragic depression of the 1930's. This was followed by considerable recovery through 1937, a short recession in 1938, and further recovery through 1941. Then came the prosperity of the war years.

Fluctuations in purchasing power have been unpleasantly large, especially when they were downward, but not nearly so large as those in money income. In the postwar years the purchasing power has leveled off, at least temporarily, some 15 per cent below the war years, but 25 per cent above the close of the prosperous 1920's. Even after all taxes were paid we had an amazingly high ability to purchase goods and services. And yet it was not enough to satisfy our intense, and perhaps overly nervous desire for things to use and do. Higher taxes will reduce our disposable income somewhat so that it is impossible to predict with any degree of certainty what it will be in subsequent years.

SOURCE OF MONEY INCOME

Work Is More Important Than Ownership.—Income originates in the efforts of individuals working with natural resources and man-made capital. The money value of the products resulting from these efforts is distributed among the several kinds of workers and the owners of the natural resources and capital. In recent years in the United States, as pointed out in Chapter 11, about two thirds of the national income has been distributed in the form of wages and salaries, about one sixth has gone to independent proprietors of farms, stores, and other small business enterprises in return for their personal efforts and the use of their capital, while about one sixth has gone in direct payment for the use of property. Since some of the income distributed to proprietors is in return for their personal services, at least 75 per cent of money income is distributed to individuals in exchange for their work.

This fact has important social implications. For example, even if half of the money recently distributed to individuals in exchange for the use of their property had been added to wages and salaries, the latter would have been increased by not more than 10 per cent. This strongly suggests that any increase in the personal income of wage-earners must come from increases in production more than from a different distribution of income between labor and capital.

There Are Regional Differences.—There are some interesting regional differences in the proportional distribution of money income among different types of claimants. In North Dakota, for example, only 46 per cent went directly to wages and salaries in 1949 and only 7.6 per cent directly to property, while 39 per cent went to independent proprietors. Much of the latter went, of course, to farmers. In the District of Columbia, in contrast, 78 per cent went directly to wages and salaries and only 5.9 per cent to proprietors.

Contrasts like these are due to differences in the socioeconomic structure. In North Dakota independent farming is a dominant industry and consequently much of the income goes directly to the farm proprietors. In clerical Washington there are relatively few independent proprietors and many workers on wages and salaries. These illustrations are sufficient, perhaps, to show what large differences there are in the way income is earned and distributed.

Manufacturing and Trade Are Very Important.—In Chapter 11, total money income was classified also to show its industrial origin. It will be recalled that the largest share comes from manufacturing, with the combination of trade and transportation not far behind. These lines of activity originate over half of our gross national product. In fact, the employees in these lines receive in wages and salaries nearly half of our total personal disposable income.

DISTRIBUTION OF MONEY INCOME BY SIZE

Individual Incomes Differ Widely.—It has been estimated that in 1948 the upper 10 per cent of family incomes were about three and one half times as large on the average as the average for all families. In contrast, the 10 per cent of families with the lowest incomes received only about one tenth as much as the average of all families, or one thirtieth as much as the average for the upper 10 per cent. The largest family incomes were many times as high as the average for the upper 10 per cent. Moreover, the upper half of the families received about 75 per cent of the income while the lower half received only 25 per cent, or one third as much as the upper. Data for several selected years are given in Table 32.

TABLE 32

SHARE OF MONEY INCOME RECEIVED BY EACH TENTH OF THE FAMILIES
(OR SPENDING UNITS) IN THE UNITED STATES

	1910	1918	1929	1937	1948	Lowest family income in each group in 1948
	%	%	%	%	%	
Top 10 per cent	34	34	39	34	32	$6,000
" 20 " "	46	47	51	48	46	4,500
" 30 " "	56	57	61	60	58	3,750
" 40 " "	65	66	70	70	68	3,200
" 50 " "	73	73	78	79	77	2,840
" 60 " "	80	81	84	86	84	2,400
" 70 " "	86	88	90	92	90	2,000
" 80 " "	92	93	95	96	95	1,500
" 90 " "	97	98	98	99	99	800
" 100 " "	100	100	100	100	100	*

* Not available.

As already reported, the average income has varied with the years. For example, it is estimated by the Department of Commerce to have been about $680 in 1929, $368 in 1933, and $1,330 in 1949. Similarly, the lowest income in each decil of total families will have varied. Consequently the proportion of families with over $5,000 income has increased since 1935 from about 2 per cent to over 12 per cent. It is to be noted, however, that the proportion of total income going to each 10 per cent of families arranged by size of family income has varied only slightly.

Two obvious conclusions are to be drawn from these data, namely:

1. Individual family incomes differ in any one year over a very wide range.
2. The general pattern of income distribution has changed very little in the past 40 years.

In other words, the rich and the poor are with us always, and as groups they continue to receive about the same proportion of total income.

Purchasing Power Is Increasing

With the passage of time, the average wage-earner appears to be getting a higher real wage.   This is a phenomenon different from that of wage differences among individuals at a moment of time.   The increased productivity of an hour's work is illustrated by the estimates in Table 33.

TABLE 33

Time Which the Average Wage-Earner in Industry Must Work to Buy Specified Products

Product	1939	1947	1947/1939 Percentage
Pair of men's street shoes	4 hrs., 57 min.	4 hrs., 50 min.	97
Ford automobile	166⅞—8-hr. days	155—8-hr. days	93
1 movie admission	25 min.	22 min.	88
1 quart of milk	11 min	9 min.	82
1 pound of bread	8 min.	6 min.	75
1 gallon of standard gasoline	18 min.	12 min.	67
24 oz. package of granulated soap	28 min.	12 min.	61
Electric iron	9 hrs., 21 min.	5 hrs., 56 min.	60
2-quart aluminum saucepan	1 hr., 20 min.	44 min.	55

Thus, regardless of unequal distribution of income, the average wage-earner today should be able to buy and consume somewhat more than previously, provided he works as long a day.

It appears also that we in the United States produce more efficiently than do the people in other parts of the world.   Consequently we can consume more or work shorter hours.   Doubtless we do both. The July 1950 issue of the *United Nations World* contained an article on "The Cost of Staying Alive," from which the figures in Table 34 are drawn.

TABLE 34

MINUTES OF WORKING TIME REQUIRED TO EARN ENOUGH TO BUY CERTAIN FOODS

Country	1 lb. beef	1 doz. ·eggs	1 lb. sugar	1 lb. flour	1 lb. butter	5 items total
United States	29	27	4	4	22	96
Australia	22	53	6	4	34	119
England	38	57	10	5	34	144
Sweden	33	55	9	8	58	163
Italy	136	112	46	22	222	538
U.S.S.R.	254	158	141	52	542	1147

These five food items are common staples in the American diet. Assuming the estimates to be even reasonably accurate, it is apparent that we have much more time left for the production of other things than do the people of the other countries cited. Moreover, it generally is believed that Sweden and Australia are the countries that most nearly approach our level of consumption.

CAUSES OF INEQUALITY OF INCOME

Both Ability and Opportunity Are Important.—The causes of inequalities of income are as old as Methuselah and as uncontrollable as the Mississippi. Basically, they are of two sorts: those associated with differences in the capabilities of individuals and those associated with the differences in opportunities that are presented to individuals. Of course, there is much interplay between the two. An opportunity to use specific abilities generally results in the development of those abilities, while a lack of opportunity tends to retard development. Moreover, where an individual finds no chance to do those things he greatly enjoys, a feeling of general frustration may occur with a more or less complete breakdown of ambition and morale. But when the urge to express and develop a particular ability is strong enough, the individual frequently can make the opportunity. Differences in ability and their effect on income are discussed in Chapter 13.

Opportunities Are Not Equal.—Equal opportunity for all individuals is sometimes supposed to be a sacred guarantee in a democracy; in reality, such equality never has been even closely approached. For one thing, the operation of our laws and customs concerning inheritance prevents equality of opportunity. Because of inheritance practices, the children of rich parents may receive a large income from ownership of property towards the acquiring of which they, them-

selves, never did anything. In fact, the differences in opportunity
that result from the income level of parents begin to appear long
before the specific act of inheritance. Differences in early training, in
general standards and scales of living, in physical and cultural environment, occur from the very beginning of the individual's life. It
is not certain that the advantages associated with the differences in
family income are always in one direction; sometimes sons of wealthy
parents become ne'er-do-wells, while many from modest homes suc-
ceed in every sense of the term. It is certain, however, that the
opportunities presented to children differ greatly among the various
income classes.

Combinations Affect Individual Incomes.—There are other
ways in which our laws and customs have permitted or caused inequality of opportunity among individuals. For example, the right of
individuals to combine their shares in the ownership of property in a
partnership or corporation has permitted certain persons so to pool
their financial strength that they have held an advantage, at least
temporarily, over their competitors, or their employees, or their customers. To be sure, the opportunity to combine for business or economic purposes is open to all. Labor unions might, and sometimes
do, bring to people as workers the same sort of strength in numbers
that corporations bring to people as owners. Perhaps consumers'
cooperative organizations can, and sometimes do, bring the same sort
of advantage to people as consumers. In reality, at least until recently, people appear to have taken advantage of the chance to pool
their ownership rights much more frequently and effectively than they
have to pool their strength as laborers or as consumers. Consequently, equality of opportunity for bargaining has not existed because those who have not possessed property rights have also lacked
the power given by combination. Recently some labor unions have
used the method of pooling their strength so effectively as to seem to
have an unfair advantage over both owners and consumers. The
much-debated Taft-Hartley Labor Law was passed, in part, in an
effort to equalize the bargaining position of ownership and labor
groups.

Value of Product as the Distributor of Income.—Basically, production is the source of individual income just as it is of national
income. The most important single reason for the differences among
individual incomes, therefore, is the difference in individual productivity. It is highly desirable that this point be understood, for it has
many important implications and ramifications.

One ramification, for example, is found in the present-day policy of some labor unions. These unions demand and obtain a uniform hourly rate of pay for all their members. This leads in some cases to the establishment of "standard tasks" such as the number of bricks to be laid in a day. Such standards tend to prevent the able worker from utilizing his ability to the full and receiving a money income above that of the less able worker. There are some persuasive arguments in favor of a policy of "standard tasks," else it would not be adopted so often. Whenever it is adopted it illustrates the inescapable relation between production and income.

In fields where no such limitation exists individual incomes may differ greatly. The surgeon who performs two major operations a day may get double the income of the surgeon who performs only one; the farmer who grows 100 bushels of potatoes gets more than the one who grows only 50 bushels; the insurance salesman earns more when he sells $200,000 of insurance than when he sells only $100,000. Within each single line of work, differences in individual productivity mainly account for differences in individual income.

Different Jobs Offer Different Rewards.—The most striking differences among individual incomes occur, perhaps, between occupations or lines of work. While some lawyers or doctors have much larger incomes than others in the same profession, the general level of income in those professions is above that for teachers. Corporation managers generally receive more than mechanics, and mechanics more than janitors working for the same firms. The explanation of these differences among lines of work also lies in productivity, a statement which calls for a discussion of the determination and measurement of productivity, or value, among unlike products.

The General Law of the Market.—No one will pay more for anything than he believes it is worth to him, in the light of such factors as his available purchasing power and the alternative chances to spend money. What any individual believes a specific thing is worth to him may be a matter either of how he believes it will increase his ability to produce in the future and thus to increase his income, or of satisfaction obtained directly from using or consuming the item. The former is, of course, derived demand while the latter is direct demand.

Also, no one will pay more for anything than he needs to, even though he might be willing to pay much more if necessary. What he needs to pay is determined by what everyone jointly is willing to pay for the entire amount offered for sale. In free markets, prices of things gravitate as closely as human knowledge and judgment permit towards the point where the entire supply is bought and the least anxious actual buyer feels satisfied with his purchase. This tendency is referred to as the marginal determination of price or the determination of price at the margin; that is, when prices are determined in free markets it is expected that every unit of supply, including the last or marginal unit, will be bought.

This general law of the market applies to the purchase and sale of goods and to the distribution of income among individuals. Thus the fee of a brain surgeon is high partly because the operation he performs is expected to result in great satisfaction to the person on whom it is performed and partly because the number of surgeons competent to perform it is very small. The reason the salaries of corporation managers are so much higher than the wages of common or semiskilled laborers employed by the same firms is that there are large numbers of persons competent and available at the low wage to do the common tasks. If one of them demands a higher wage he may be replaced by someone else without loss of company production. In the case of the manager, in contrast, the supply of competent and available individuals is small. Moreover, a poor manager may lessen the productivity of the firm much more than will a single poor workman. Consequently the directors of the corporation are both willing and forced to pay high salaries to managers in order to get and keep the desired number of competent individuals.

The Number of Large Incomes from Personal Services Is Not Large.—Actually, the number of managers or others who are paid a large amount for their personal services is relatively small. Some data on this point were discussed in Chapter 11 but, for emphasis, an estimate is given here, in Table 35, of the ways in which we earned our livings in 1950.

It will be noted that the great majority of us are engaged in what may be called semiskilled occupations. It will be recalled from the earlier discussion that in recent years the proportion of professional and managerial workers has increased somewhat, but it still is small. The proportion of skilled workers and artisans has decreased, and so has that of unskilled laborers. The proportion of semiskilled has increased. Some of the social implications of these facts have already been suggested.

Property Ownership Is a Cause of Inequality of Income.—We have been speaking as though payment for personal services accounted

TABLE 35

WHAT WE DO FOR A LIVING—APRIL 1950

Major Occupation	Per Cent of Employed Persons
Machine operatives, mechanics, etc.	20.3
Clerical workers	13.1
Craftsmen, foremen, etc.	12.8
Farmers	11.9
Proprietors, managers, etc.	10.9
Service workers (exc. domestic service)	8.1
Professional and semiprofessional	7.6
Salespersons	6.6
Laborers	5.4
Domestic service	3.3
	100.0

Source: Estimates by Dun and Bradstreet.

for the entire distribution of income. Of course this is not true since, as pointed out earlier in another connection, some income is distributed to the owners of property in payment for its use. A little less than a quarter of our total income is distributed to individuals in payment for the use of property. Details already have been given, and it need only be said here that the amount paid for the use of property is determined in essentially the same way as in the case of payment for personal services. As will be pointed out in greater detail in Chapter 17, personal savings and ownership of property are concentrated in a small proportion of our total families. Consequently, the income from ownership goes to relatively few persons and thus is a major cause of inequality of income.

One further point deserves emphasis in connection with this general problem. Certainly one of the reasons for permitting combinations in the ownership of property is found in the economy or increase in production that accompanies the use of large amounts of capital in a single undertaking. Frequently the most efficient use of capital occurs only when the power of ownership of many individuals is brought together in one plant and under one management. Buildings, machines, and similar items of capital equipment frequently are not physically divisible into units that are as small as are the units of labor, i.e., the single person. This matter also was discussed in Chapter 11, under "Economies of Scale." Suffice it to say here that if the present forms of combination of ownership were to be discarded some other method would need to be devised to permit the use of large units of capital equipment, lest many of the advantages of machine production be lost.

Consumer Credit Modifies Consumption Temporarily.—We have said that income limits the ability to consume. For short periods of time this is not entirely correct. Changes in consumer credit temporarily will either increase or decrease the ability to purchase and consume. When credit is expanding, purchases may exceed income; when it is contracting, purchases must be less than current income in order that present debts may be reduced. Over longer periods of time, however, changes in consumer credit cannot increase purchasing power, for consumer credit is not expandable continuously. Consumer credit was discussed more fully in Chapter 6.

INCREASING PRODUCTION MORE IMPORTANT THAN CHANGING DISTRIBUTION OF INCOME

There are some persons who do not like the present distribution of income among individuals and who propose various methods and degrees of redistribution. Some have advocated an equal distribution to each person. Had this been the situation from 1920 to 1929, everyone would have received $615 per year or about $2,500 per family. A few years ago a proposal called the Townsend Plan, for aiding old people, was given wide publicity. This plan provided, among other things, that $2,400 be given each year to everyone over 60 years of age. Had this been done in 1935 the total income produced that year would have provided $2,400 for each person over 60 years of age all right, but would have left only enough to give each individual under 60 a mere $211, or about $850 per family.

At this point in our discussion we are not ready, perhaps, either to support or to condemn any scheme for the redistribution of income. It should be clear from the figures that have been presented in this chapter, however, that unless total income is greatly increased no pattern of distribution of it will permit Americans to enjoy the scale of living that they would like.

PROJECT QUESTIONS

1. What are the five largest personal salaries that you can discover, either in your own community or in published information? Why are they so large? How important are they, relative to the total sales of the firm which is paying the salary?

2. Obtain a copy of a recent issue of the *Survey of Current Business*. What data do you find there concerning gross national production, national income, and disposable personal income? Look particularly at the most recent July issue of the *Survey of Current Business* and see what data are given there that are not given in the other monthly issues.

3. Obtain an issue of the *Statistical Abstract of the United States*. Turn to the section on manufacturing and then examine any industry in which you are interested. Note the value added by manufacture in dollar terms and in per cent of sales. Then note the wages paid in dollars, in per cent of sales, and in per cent of value added. Make such comments as occur to you concerning these several figures.

4. Find in your library any published farm management studies. Usually these are issued by State Agricultural Experiment Stations. See what you can determine from the publication concerning the division of the farm's net income between labor income and return to ownership.

5. Consideration of the national income alone is likely to have a weak appeal to the average person. After all, it is pretty difficult to comprehend a fabulous sum of $173,000,000,000. Likewise, its distribution is not very meaningful. Some supplementary data on the present distribution of income of the families in your particular community would mean more to you and it would no doubt aid in your appreciation of the national figure. Of course, accurate income data for families and individuals are difficult to obtain, but your local civic and business organizations should have estimates of local income and its distribution which you could use. It is important to call attention to the weakness of any such income data.

Chapter 13

PERSONAL CHARACTERISTICS THAT AFFECT THE INDIVIDUAL'S PATTERN OF CONSUMPTION

Introduction

Many things besides individual or family income affect consumption both in total amount and in pattern. Some of these are inherent in the individual; they result from his physical, emotional, or mental nature. Others are environmental; they result from the actions of other people, from the natural resources that are available to the individual, or from the institutions (social, political, economic) that have been developed in the community in which the individual lives. Several of the most important of these things are discussed in this chapter and the next.

Personal characteristics affect consumption. Individual ability, ambition, attitudes, and habits will influence both the size of the money income of the individual and the things for which he spends it. So also will the health of the person, his age and occupation, and the composition of the family of which he is a member. The customs or mores of the community in which one lives are important determinants of consumption patterns. These personal and community influences are discussed in this chapter as one group of things which affect consumption.

A second group of factors contains items which are, perhaps, neither more nor less important, but which are more directly economic in their nature. The decisions and actions of suppliers, for example, regarding sales promotion, quality of goods, and prices help to determine both the use of resources (including employment patterns) and the expenditure of money income. The uncertainties and risks that are inherent in our roundabout production affect the patterns both of production and subsequent consumption. The decision of individuals to save part of their money income, and the way in which the savings are used, affect both present and future consumption. Improvements in production techniques have been accompanied by less hours of work per week, with accompanying increases in leisure.

Each of this second group of influences is discussed briefly in the following chapter. It is the authors' hope that although the discussion in each of these chapters is brief it is adequate to suggest and illustrate the manner in which each factor exerts its influence and something of the interplay of them all on our consumption patterns.

ABILITIES

People Are Different.—People differ greatly in abilities. Some college students are great football players, others are sprinters, others play tennis, others seem to have no athletic ability; some dance well while others are just plain clumsy; some have photographic memories of great accuracy, others can memorize only after many repetitions; some have very high I.Q.'s, others lower ones.

During the years 1931 to 1936 the Employment Stabilization Research Institute of the University of Minnesota conducted many case studies of men and women workers, employed and unemployed alike. One of the groups that was observed was composed of some 300 "casual" workers in the city of Duluth. These were men who had held no regular job for some years prior to 1931, but who had worked irregularly in seasonal industries or at odd jobs. More than three fourths of them had never been married and most of them were classed as "homeless men" lodged in central quarters by the community. In terms of measured abilities and education these men represented an inferior section of the working population. Tests were given them in seven fields to show their physical and mental abilities and in only two of these tests were they able to perform as well as the average of the population. Because of a combination of poor abilities, poor physical condition, advanced age, and meager background, about one third of these men could not, even under the most favorable conditions imaginable, be fully self-supporting in any ordinary type of work. Persons with similar limitations are present, of course, in every community.[1]

There are distinct differences in abilities among other groups of workers. Figures 27 and 28 are taken from the summary of the tests made by the Employment Stabilization Research Institute to illustrate some of these differences.[2] Garage mechanics were found to be superior to men office clerks in mechanical assembly tests, but inferior in number tests and in finger dexterity. Retail saleswomen, as a

---

[1] D. G. Paterson, J. G. Darley, and R. M. Elliott, *Men, Women, and Jobs* (Minneapolis: University of Minnesota Press, 1936), pp. 23-25.
[2] *Ibid.*, pp. 44-45.

class, were found to be inferior in all the tests to women office clerks. These "occupational ability patterns" give a pretty good picture of the traits that characterize steadily employed workers in different jobs. Similar measurements have been made—or may be made—of the characteristics of workers in many different occupations or jobs. It has been found, in fact, that the "ability" patterns for many jobs are well enough known to permit reasonably accurate forecasts of an individual's chances for success from his performance in certain prescribed tests.

Differences in Ability Affect Incomes.—The presence or lack of specific abilities has a direct bearing upon income. In the first place, competitive industry is attempting constantly, through trial and error, to use individuals where they will be most effective and to weed out

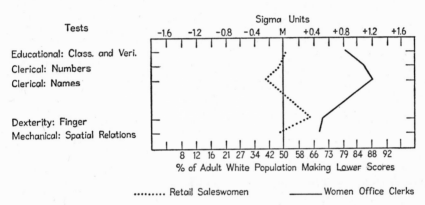

FIG. 27.—Occupational Test Scores Made by Women Clerical Workers and Department Store Saleswomen

Source: D. G. Paterson, J. G. Darley, and R. M. Elliott, *Men, Women, and Jobs* (Minneapolis: University of Minnesota Press, 1936), p. 45.

the inefficient from each specific job. Sometimes this process brings tremendous hardship to the individual, but in the long run it must result in increasing the total output of society. Data gathered by the Employment Stabilization Research Institute show that industry did tend to eliminate the less efficient people first during the period of increasing unemployment in the 1930's. Figure 29 shows the average test scores of women clerical workers who lost their jobs early in the depression, compared with the scores of those who lost their jobs later and those who were continuously employed.[3] Apparently

---

[3] *Ibid.,* p. 41.

employers were able, in general, to single out the individuals with relatively low ability and to dismiss them early in the period of retrenchment. This has a very pertinent bearing on such matters as civil service, permanence of tenure, and seniority rights for employees.

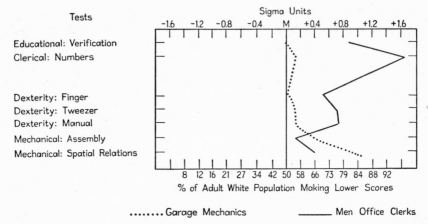

FIG. 28.—Occupational Test Scores Made by Men Clerical Workers and Auto Mechanics

Source: D. G. Paterson, J. G. Darley, and R. M. Elliott, *Men, Women, and Jobs* (Minneapolis: University of Minnesota Press, 1936), p. 44.

Specific abilities affect income in ways other than through mere employment and unemployment. The true geniuses in any of the arts —the Menuhins, the Rachmaninoffs, the Whistlers, the Sinclair Lewises—are rare. Their works are scarce and cannot be reproduced at will, and if people want what they alone can give, the price for their services is high. Inventors, captains of finance, great surgeons, are scarce and, sometimes, society is willing to pay handsomely for what they alone can do. The situation that faces the individual in his attempt to market his abilities is similar to other cases of sale: if the ability is scarce relative to the desires of others for what it will produce, the price the individual can charge for his services is high. If the ability of the individual is common relative to the demand for that type of ability, the price or wage will be low. It has already been pointed out that income affects consumption, so it follows that as abilities result in differences in income, they also modify consumption.

Abilities Affect Consumption.—Abilities also affect the *patterns of consumption,* even within each income group. Persons with musical ability are likely to spend more on musical training, concerts, and the like than do those who lack such ability. Those who lack discriminating intelligence are likely to reduce their total consumption through careless purchasing and lack of planning. The specific abilities to redesign and make over dresses may reduce the family expen-

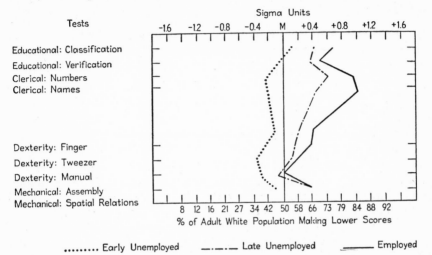

.... Early Unemployed   _.._.._ Late Unemployed   _____ Employed

FIG. 29.—Occupational Test Scores Made by Early Unemployed, Late Unemployed, and Employed Women in Clerical Positions

Source: D. G. Paterson, J. G. Darley, and R. M. Elliott, *Men, Women, and Jobs* (Minneapolis: University of Minnesota Press, 1936), p. 41.

diture on clothing. In these and many other ways specific abilities affect the details of the individual's consumption program.

ATTITUDES

The Desire for Wealth and Income Is Strong.—Consumption will vary among the individuals in any social group or among social groups as a result of the differences in attitudes of individuals toward many questions, and quite in addition to the effects exercised by income and ability. It is sometimes said that the desire for wealth or income is *the* economic motive, beside which all others are unimportant. Perhaps this is true for enough individuals so that it is largely true for people en masse, but certainly there are other motives which strongly influence some individuals. Much of the discussion of economics has been predicated upon the assumption of a hedonistic philosophy or psychology : that people generally do those things which give them the greatest pleasure and cost them the least pain. Perhaps they do, but it must be pointed out that there is no precise measurement of either pleasure or pain and, furthermore, that our voluntary acts frequently do not appear to be entirely so regulated. Missionaries, for example, have gone through terrific hardships because of an "ideal," and soldiers go "into the jaws of death" as a patriotic duty.

Personal Philosophy Affects Consumption.—Doubtless there are many shades or degrees of philosophy and psychology that affect the individual patterns of consumption. The optimist, with his bowl full of Wheaties in front of him, asks politely, "Please pass the cream," while the pessimist, in contrast, laments, "There isn't any milk left in that pitcher, is there?" The stoic consumes the food placed before him without any sign of like or dislike, while the epicurean tastes critically, consumes only that which pleases the palate, and suffers acutely over anything that is not right. Some people insist on remaining on farms, while others are happy only in the midst of crowds. Some take vacations in the north woods where they may "suffer together" from mosquito bites, campfire smoke in the eyes, and muscles weary from canoeing, while others luxuriate on the beach at Miami, and still others attend the latest shows on Broadway and shop in the crowded New York stores.

Perhaps there is little that can be said with definiteness about the "right" or "wrong" of these different philosophies or tastes. There are those who believe that individual selfishness should be curbed in the interest of general welfare, but it might be difficult to find objective or positive proof for such a belief. Many of the classical writers in the field of political economy had in mind some special problems in general welfare and the means by which organized government might be used to solve these problems. Their suggested solutions always carried certain assumptions, however, concerning what was socially desirable. Common among the assumptions that have been held from time to time are the following:

1. It is desirable to have an increasing population in a country.
2. It is desirable to have an increasing per-capita consumption of material goods.
3. General prosperity is dependent upon prosperity in agriculture.
4. Wage-earners should have an increasing share of total product.
5. Monopoly profits are, prima facie, bad.

Whether we care to accept any of or all these assumptions, or what others we should add to the list, is pretty much a matter of individual attitude. Let us illustrate. We decided, for example, in the middle 1920's not to permit the rapid rise of the population of this country through immigration and passed the immigration restriction law, to the discomfiture of some persons in other lands. The Keynesian economists have been arguing in recent years that the only way to keep a free-enterprise economy going is through the continuous introduction of new industries, leading to new and increased consumption. In contrast, the late Mahatma Gandhi believed that in the increase of production and consumption of unnecessary things lay the basis for many of the really serious troubles with world economy. We have referred in Chapter 11 to the fact that the prosperity of manufacturing appears to be more important to our economy than the prosperity of agriculture, admittedly important though that may be. Certainly it seems that wage-earners should have all of produced income except the amount necessary to cause individuals to continue to save and invest, but not so much that private investment will dry up. Monopoly *profits* are thought to be bad whenever they are greater relative to investment than are those earned in more nearly competitive situations, but public utilities are permitted to operate as monopolies so that we may get the benefits of their efficient use of resources; their prices and profits, of course, are controlled by public agencies. So we seem to find no absolutely right or wrong answers to questions of public policy such as these. Generalizations do not seem to apply and each case needs careful consideration on its own merits. Our individual attitudes and where we stand in the socioeconomic scale will influence our individual answers. Even when we individually want to do the best thing for the commonwealth there is, perhaps, no way to put objective meaning into the phrase "the greatest good for the greatest number," even if we wanted to. Consequently, the procedures in our economic life remain very much in the field of art rather than that of science.

HABITS

"A habit is a way of living that has been learned; the doing of the same thing always in the same way under the same conditions—it is a stereotyped form of response." [4]

Consumption is regulated to a considerable degree by the fact that people tend, both individually and en masse, to react habitually in the

---

[4] Knight Dunlap, *Habits, Their Making and Unmaking* (New York: Liveright Publishing Corp., 1949), p. 1.

same way to the same stimuli. By and large, the consumer prefers to use the commodity with which he is familiar and which he sees his compatriots using. Moreover, many of our everyday actions are the direct result of habit. William James pointed out that "There is no more miserable human being than one in whom nothing is habitual but indecision, and for whom the lighting of every cigar, the drinking of every cup, the time of rising and going to bed every day, and the beginning of every bit of work are subject to express volitional deliberation." Thus persons raised in poverty acquire habits of economy which follow them through life, whereas the children of the wealthy find it extremely difficult to live frugally if ever they need to do so. We conclude therefore with Mr. Wyand that "Habit determines the choice made, but is in turn the product of the relationship existing between the consumer and the conditions under which he lives." [5] It then follows that the determinants of habitual choices are in reality the "other factors" which we are discussing in this chapter.

HEALTH

The state of one's mental and physical health has a marked effect on one's buying habits. To most depressed individuals, all activities and commodities lose much of their appeal. On the other hand, the happy person tends to buy impulsively, has a variety of interests and will, therefore, buy a wider range of products and, perhaps, more of each. Similarly, those who are physically ill or who suffer from any of various neuroses are either not able to indulge their interests or think they cannot. They retain little interest in buying ordinary goods but spend large sums for medicine, medical services, and in travel in search of relief.

Our consumption habits clearly express our physical and mental health. Although relatively few people are chronic invalids either of the physical or mental type still there are few who do not suffer from minor illnesses and still fewer who have a perfectly balanced mental life. The total effect of illness is undoubtedly very large. For example, the best available estimates show 360,000,000 days lost annually by workmen in the United States as the direct result of illness, much of which loss could be prevented with reasonable care and foresight. The loss of produced income that accompanies this loss of working time clearly must have its effect on total consumption.

---

[5] C. S. Wyand, *Economics of Consumption* (New York: The Macmillan Co., 1937), p. 196.

SIZE AND AGE OF THE FAMILY AND THE INDIVIDUALS

Large Families Require Much Food.—Consumption patterns are affected to some extent by the structure of the family. As the family increases in number the goods required to satisfy physical necessities increase. In any income group the larger expenditures for food and clothing necessary for large families tend to reduce expenditures for other items. These general tendencies are illustrated in Table 36. It may be pointed out that while the data in the table refer directly to the 1930's, the changes due to size of family are believed to be essentially the same at one time as another. After all, more people eat more food, and while some accommodation is made by changes in diet, large families generally spend more for food than do small ones with the same income. The authors believe that many of the data used in this book are equally timeless and illustrate long-lasting relationships. Others of course show marked tendency to change with the passing of time.

TABLE 36

AVERAGE EXPENDITURES FOR ONE YEAR FOR FAMILIES OF THREE DIFFERENT SIZES
(SAMPLE CONTROLLED FOR INCOME). EMPLOYED WAGE-EARNERS AND CLERICAL
WORKERS: NEW YORK CITY, 1934, 1936

(in percentages)

Expenditure Groups	Mean Expenditures, Family Consisting of		
	Husband and Wife Only	Husband, Wife, and 1 Child	Husband, Wife, and 4 Children
Food	35.2	38.2	41.9
Housing	23.8	23.8	23.8
Home Operation..	9.4	8.8	9.5
Recreation	7.7	6.9	5.9
Personal Care ...	2.1	2.0	1.9
Medical Care	4.0	4.0	3.7
Transportation ...	7.3	4.7	4.0
Clothing	10.5	11.6	9.3

Source: Faith Williams, "Methods of Measuring Variations in Family Expenditures," *J. Am. Stat. Assn.,* March, 1937, p. 40.

Miss Williams points out that "These figures show the increases in expenditures for food and housing with increases in family size are obviously not large enough to provide food and housing for the large families at the same level as for the smaller ones; average expenditures for personal care and medical care per family decrease slightly but the average expenditures for these items per person decrease markedly with increase in family size. Expenditures *per family* for recreation and for transportation decrease greatly with the addition of children, but not so rapidly as average expenditures *per person* for medical care." [6]

Children Are Different from Adults.—Not only does the size of the family affect the buying habits of the family but the degree of family maturity affects what will be purchased as well as the amount of those purchases. Families with small children will spend less money on clothing than adult families in the same income class. The data in Table 37 illustrate how the age composition of the family affects what is purchased.

TABLE 37

DISTRIBUTION OF $1,500 INCOME AMONG THE PRINCIPAL GROUPS OF GOODS AND SERVICES: FIGURES ADJUSTED FOR SIZE OF FAMILY

(in percentages)

Kinds of Goods and Services	Preschool 66 Families	Grade School 92 Families	High School 58 Families	All Adults 51 Families
All	100.0	100.0	100.0	100.0
Food	34.4	37.4	37.9	30.0
Clothing	11.2	11.7	16.2	16.5
Rent	16.7	16.2	13.6	13.3
Furnishings	3.9	4.8	2.5	4.8
Home Operation	16.8	15.3	14.6	13.7
Maintenance of Health	6.1	4.6	3.3	4.5
Advancement of Goods	3.8	4.1	6.6	9.2
Personal Goods	3.6	3.1	3.2	4.3
Insurance, Life and Health	3.5	2.8	2.1	3.3

Source: *The Life Cycle of the Farm Family,* Wisconsin Research Bulletin 121, p. 34. Figures have been adjusted on basis of the average size for all the families i.e., 4.4 persons. Therefore the average cost of family living for each state is for a theoretical family composed of 4.4 persons.

Preschool family, children under 6 years of age; Grade-school family, children 6-13 years of age; high school family, children 14-18 years of age; all-adult family, children 19 years of age and over.

Furthermore, the age and physiological structure of each individual have decided influence on consumption. We are all familiar in general with the gamut of wants which are the function of age. Children want marbles, dolls, bicycles; youth demands cigarettes, lipsticks,

---

[6] Faith Williams, "Methods of Measuring Variation in Family Expenditures," *J. Am. Stat. Assn.,* March, 1937, p. 43.

flashy clothing, fast automobiles, swing music; middle age gives up tennis for bridge; old age puts comfort ahead of either fashion or speed. Perhaps it is true that children nowadays become sophisticated at an earlier age than they did one hundred years ago and that people do not grow old so soon as they once did, but the differences between the social age groups are still distinctly evident in their consumption patterns.

Similarly, physiological characteristics of the individual exercise an important influence on his purchasing habits. The person who conforms to the measurements most common among his fellows can buy shoes and clothing at prices considerably lower than those the unusually large, small, or deformed person must pay. Due to the economies of large-scale production, the price of the "ordinary size" is less than that of the "special order."

Custom

Custom Is a Group Phenomenon.—The phenomenon of custom somewhat resembles habit, and is almost equally responsible for consumption patterns. It may be defined as "the repetition of acts or ways of doing solely because they are practices of the others now living, and probably of many generations gone before. It differs from habit in that in habit the repetition is always by the same person after himself, whereas in custom the repetition is always after others." [7] Most of the details of daily life are regulated by custom. In Sumner's comparison of cases of food taboos there are illustrations of the degree to which food preferences are influenced by custom.[8] We do not eat dog flesh but some North American Indians preferred it, while the Banziris in the French Congo solemnize the eating of dog's flesh with rituals. Negroes in the French Congo have a perfect horror of the idea of drinking milk whereas Americans believe it the most nutritious food for infants. And other things besides our food preferences are influenced by custom. Women travelers in Japan are shocked at the failure of some Japanese workmen to wear clothing and are totally unconscious that their own dinner costumes shock Orientals.[9] Thus we see that custom plays an important part in influencing what we buy.

---

[7] R. M. McIver, *Society, Its Structure and Changes* (New York: Rinehart & Co., Inc., 1931), p. 288.

[8] W. G. Sumner, *Folkways* (Boston: Ginn & Co., 1907), pp. 28-29.

[9] W. E. Atkins, ed., *Economic Behavior* (Boston: Houghton Mifflin Co., 1931), Vol. II, p. 5.

Custom Is a Tyrant.—Social pressure may affect the individual's consumption in much the same way as does custom, if it does not in fact produce custom. As a member of a society the individual may try to consume a greater quantity and a greater variety of goods than does his neighbor. Keeping up with the Joneses or ahead of them explains much wasteful consumption. Last year's car, although in excellent condition, is traded in for a new one, and living rooms are constantly being refurnished with the "modern" pieces of the particular decade. Women's fashions are subject to sudden and extravagant change due in the main to this desire on the part of adults to imitate.[10] Many garments which are essentially as good as they were when they were new become obsolete and either require major alterations or are not wearable and must be discarded. For example, Figure 30 shows the frequent change in the lengths of women's skirts during the period from 1923 through 1932. The knee-length skirt, which reached its peak of popularity at the close of 1928, was completely replaced one year later by a skirt sufficiently longer to render the knee-length skirt obsolete. The variation in skirt length did not end in 1931, but is a continuous style phenomenon. Fashions may be either short-lived or long-lived; if they are very short-lived they are spoken of as fads; if they persist for a long time they become customs.

Habits and Customs Reflect the Stage of Civilization.—Habits and customs often result from, and tend to reflect, the stage in the development of civilization to which a particular people have come at a particular time. By way of illustration, it could not be customary to listen to the radio until the physical scientists had discovered certain practical methods of transmitting and receiving sound; the stylish horse and carriage was not replaced on Fifth Avenue by the automobile until the internal combustion engine had been satisfactorily attached to a wheeled vehicle; legend has it that the custom of eating roast meat arose in China only after someone discovered by accident the excellent flavor of a pig roasted quite accidentally by fire that destroyed a home from which the pig was unable to escape; even the custom of the daily milk delivery had to await the domestication of the cow. Changes in "the state of the arts" are occurring constantly and these changes frequently affect the habits and customs of people, thus modifying their consumption.

---

[10] A distinction should be made between "style" and "fashion." Style is a characteristic or distinctive mode or method of expression in the field of some art, while fashion is the prevailing style at any one time.

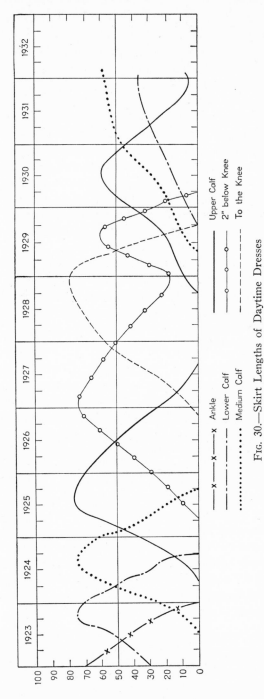

Fig. 30.—Skirt Lengths of Daytime Dresses

Source: Paul Cherrington, *The Commercial Problems of the Woolen and Worsted Industries* (The Textile Foundation, Inc., 1932), p. 67.

Consumers' Reactions to Quality

Consumers Often Are Disappointed.—People tend to spend their money incomes so as to get about the same degree of satisfaction out of each dollar's purchase. This is no easy thing to do. One reason it is not easy lies in the fact that consumers frequently are poor judges of the quality of things they buy and, consequently, they anticipate satisfactions from the purchased commodities that are quite different from those actually realized. Sometimes as consumers we are agreeably surprised, but more frequently we are disappointed for we have anticipated better quality than we have received. Whenever this is true, any of several things may happen to our consumption. We may, for example, be so disappointed with a particular commodity that we avoid buying that type of thing in the future. On the other hand, we may still desire the particular satisfaction so keenly that we immediately purchase again, with greater care in the selection of quality. Whether we do either of these two things, or react in some different way, our future program of purchase and consumption is different than it would have been if the original commodity had come up to anticipation.

What We Want Cannot Be Measured.—Many specific qualities of merchandise are not subject to exact measurement. The amount of style in a dress, for example, or flavor in a peach, or beauty in a painting is a matter about which complete agreement seems impossible. Moreover, several specific qualities are usually important in the choice between purchases. Comfort, appearance, and durability are each important in shoes, for example, but there is neither a good way to measure any of these qualities nor is there any sure way to combine the three into a measure of satisfaction to be derived from shoes. Consequently consumption patterns of individuals always will appear somewhat whimsical to others, and they will contain no little element of surprise and disappointment. Government has done some policing in the field of intangible qualities. It has attempted to prevent misrepresentation, the calling of inferior commodities by names customarily used for better goods, the copying of the appearance of high-quality merchandise in a low-quality line, and the like. Here, however, the consumer must, unfortunately, still beware.

Custom Affects Quality Standards.—The fact that specific qualities are combined in a single commodity influences consumption. At a particular time it may be fashionable, for example, to dress in cloth of the finest quality even at the expense of variety and numbers in dresses. At another time, in contrast, the popular idea may be to have many different dresses even though the durability and the appearance of each are somewhat inferior. Thus custom and fashion interplay with quality to influence consumption.

Conclusion

Personal characteristics and reactions are in a very real sense the most important determinants of consumption. After all, it is individuals who do the consuming. Production—the use of resources—is directed and patterned by what those in charge of industries believe will be consumed. People are open to persuasion, of course, but only within certain limits.

People are what they are partly because they were born that way. But only partly, for they are also creatures of their environments. No one knows exactly the relative importance of the two. Certain it is that they interplay on each other to make us what we are. In this chapter we have discussed some things that may be in considerable part the result of our choice of parents, although not entirely. In the next chapter we consider some of the influences that are more completely the result of contemporary forces.

Project Questions

1. How important to yourself and to society do you consider good health? Make a list, with brief comments on each, of several individuals who have made important contributions to our cultural life in spite of notably poor health. What influence should these cases have on our attitude concerning health, as a social asset?

2. For what commodities can you personally judge quality? How do you do so objectively?

3. To emphasize the lack of agreement between income and apparent ability, prepare one or more short biographical sketches of well-known persons who have foregone money rewards in the interest of a burning cause. For example, Jane Addams, the Curies, Pasteur, Schubert, and Thoreau are but a few of a long list. It may be useful to have members of the class select representatives of three groups: the artists and scientists who work for the joy of the work, the humanitarians, and those who work for prestige.

Chapter 14

ECONOMIC AND INSTITUTIONAL FACTORS
THAT AFFECT CONSUMPTION

SALES PROMOTION

Sales Promotion Is a Powerful Influence.—Sales promotion on the part both of manufacturers and of merchants has exerted a powerful influence on consumption. Advertising is, of course, the most conspicuous form of sales promotion, but personal salesmanship, artistry in product and package design, store displays, special merchandising "deals," and other sales techniques also are important in directing consumer purchases. In total, these other techniques are much more important and much more costly than advertising.

Sales promotion is used for many purposes. Sometimes the effort is to introduce new and revolutionary commodities such as television sets. Or it may be to induce new or greater uses for old commodities; the gasoline companies, for example, urge the taking of vacation automobile trips so that more gasoline will be used. Much sales promotion merely urges the use of one specific product to do the same old thing: Dreft rather than Tide or Ivory Flakes; Chesterfields instead of Camels; Studebakers rather than Fords. Each of these uses of sales promotion modifies consumption patterns, but the first two types lead to changes that seem much more important or significant than those induced by the third type.

There are many cases where advertising appears to have created a demand for a product. Two classical examples are raisins and cranberries. In 1914 the per-capita consumption of raisins was 1.66 pounds. After an intensive "eat more raisins" campaign the per-capita consumption was increased to 3.41 pounds by 1919. Cranberry consumption showed a similar increase in response to advertising at about the same time.

Examples are not difficult to find where advertising has "sold" a new use for a well-known product. It required a strong educational campaign to persuade consumers to use Listerine to stop dandruff, or lemons for garnishment and for a rinse after shampooing, or Scotch tape to remove lint from fabrics; but each of these was successfully accomplished.

Advertising is more effective, however, in causing shifts among brands of a commodity already in use than in causing people to do new things. It has not been successful in making people continue to wear stiff collars and play mah-jong, but it has helped to make more people buy Chesterfields, Camels, or Lucky Strikes than Viceroys, Wings, or Twenty Grands. Of 140 separate advertisements appearing in a typical issue of the *Saturday Evening Post* only five were designed to increase total consumption of the commodity involved. In fact, more than 96 per cent of the total advertising space was devoted to taking the existing market from one brand and giving it to another.

Advertising, Quality, and Consumer Indifference.—Consumers' buying habits often are effectively influenced by advertisers' claims of quality and performance. Nystrom points out that consumers have increasingly bought ready-made goods on the basis of brands and advertised statements instead of on the basis of careful, old-fashioned methods of shopping and testing for quality.[1] While Nystrom made this point nearly twenty years ago it seems still to be true.

The advertisers are aware that sales increase with the use of claims for their goods based on quality, especially if such claims can be stated dramatically. "Because it pays best we are coming to quality and performance-promise of the merchandise." Macy's advertises "tested drugs." Gimbel's slogan is "Gimbel's Tells the Truth." Some other slogans in this vein are: "When Better Automobiles are Built, Buick Will Build Them"; "Best by Test"; "U. S. Tires Are Good Tires"; "Cleans Teeth the Right Way"; "More People Ride on Goodyear Tires Than on Any Other Kind."

While consumers can be influenced by claims of quality, they often do not know how to test or measure it. Several authorities say that many consumers show a surprising indifference to the matter of finding out the quality of the things they buy. They purchase "bargains" without having the least idea whether or not the quality has been reduced even more than the price. They are easily satisfied by the glowing recommendations of salesmen and advertisements.

Probably there are many reasons for this paradox of the consumer's interest in quality, as shown by his response to claims and the apparent indifference shown by his failure to find out more about

---

[1] Paul H. Nystrom, "The Causes of the Present Decline in Quality," *Advertising and Selling,* June 22, 1933, p. 19.

it. Some of these reasons seem obvious. It takes time and hard mental effort to discover the appropriate questions to ask about quality. Accurate and complete answers to intelligent questions often are hard to get even after the right questions are framed and asked. Perhaps sometimes shoppers believe either that what was good enough for Dad and Mother is still good enough—or one's own experience and intuition may seem a sufficient, albeit actually a whimsical and biased guide. Whatever the reasons, unsupported claims remain a rampant and successful form of sales promotion.

Salesmen versus Self-Service.—In some fields salesmen influence consumer choices more than do any other factors. An illustration came to the attention of one of the authors a few years ago when a small chain of grocery stores set out to increase its sale of bulk coffee, freshly ground for each customer at the time of purchase. In three months they changed the percentage of coffee sales made in this way from about five to over eighty. At the same time total coffee sales increased 12 per cent. Perhaps this is an unusual case, but it supports the assumption that the salesman may be very important. Certainly in connection with commodities for which style, design, color, or taste is important, the persuasion of salespersons may be the deciding factor in consumer choice.

For some types of commodities, however, salesmen may do little to influence consumption. The development of self-service stores, especially in grocery retailing, is the most conspicuous case in point. Automatic vending machines have been used satisfactorily for the sale of some lines of goods including cigarettes, matches, postage stamps, paper drinking cups, handkerchiefs, toothbrushes, toothpaste, shaving cream, sanitary napkins, and other varieties of notions, toilet goods, and druggists' preparations. The principle of automatic selling has been applied to sales in other fields such as gasoline, soft drinks, some grocery products, perfume, milk in school lunchrooms, shoe polishing, photometers, and the Automat lunchrooms. Development of self-service merchandising appears, however, to be limited and highly selective. Its use in the sale of higher priced and unstandardized, unpacked merchandise appears to be unsatisfactory. This is true because with many goods consumers want to compare different styles and colors and because they want the help of the salesperson or of a friend in reaching their choice.

Social Gain or Loss from Sales Promotion.—A lot of effort—and money—goes into sales promotion. Expenditures on advertising alone are estimated to total at least five billion dollars, or over $100 per year for each family in the United States.

There is much discussion pro and con of the economic and social desirability of this intensive effort. On the one side it is argued that successful sales promotion permits large-scale production and the accompanying economies of scale. Moreover, new and better devices are made known quickly to consumers. Desire to possess new things is stimulated and this leads to ambition, greater effort to earn a money wage, and hence to greater total production. On the other side it is argued that consumers are misled as to quality, urged to spend beyond their means, befuddled as to the relative values of such things as whiskey and milk, and influenced to make Things into Gods.

It is difficult to balance these conflicting viewpoints realistically. However, at least two things may be pointed out: first, when we recall that the cost of our radio and television programs and about half of the cost of our newspapers and magazines are paid for by commercial advertising, the $2 per family per week spent for advertising may not seem too much; and second, consumers must remain wakefully skeptical of advertising claims and especially of both the accuracy and the pertinence of their evidence.

The intensity of sales promotion fluctuates directly with the general cycle of business; that is, when business is good and sales are high advertising is at its peak, and when a slump starts advertising is likely to be one of the first things curtailed. This tendency has the inevitable effect of increasing the magnitude of industrial fluctuations since the intense sales effort in prosperous periods increases sales above the level they otherwise would reach, and the reduction in sales effort permits sales to drop further than they otherwise would.

This cyclical fluctuation in sales promotion intensifies the business cycle in yet another way. The high sales record associated with strong sales promotion gives businessmen a false feeling of prosperity and causes them to forecast still greater sales in the future. Consequently they contract for expansion of plants and equipment. Later, when the new capacity is coming into use, some businessmen seem to believe that too many firms have expanded their capacity at the same time and that sales cannot be increased rapidly enough to absorb the entire output profitably. As a result, the construction of new plant and equipment is curtailed sharply and employees in these heavy industries become unemployed. This checks the flow of income to individuals and tends to start the downward spiral to depressions. Expansion and contraction of credit and of savings may contribute to this same tendency, as discussed respectively in Chapters 6 and 17.

These forces, combined, may be sufficient to result in a serious industrial depression which will have tragic effects on many individual consumers.

The consumption of oranges increased greatly under intensive sales promotion. The resulting change in diet doubtless was good for us. Advertising certainly merits credit for part of the increased consumption. But the purchase of head lettuce increased during the same years at about the same rate without any important amount of advertising. Perhaps the central heating of homes in replacement of stoves and fireplaces, our gradual change to less strenuous occupations, the general publicity from medical authorities concerning the need for fruit and vegetables in the diet, and emphasis on streamlining the female figure had a lot to do with both cases of increase. Perhaps, too, the advertising of oranges helped sell lettuce and tomato juice because of the belief that benefits from them were about the same.

It is said that much product improvement has resulted from the increased sales caused by advertising. Automobile tires often are cited as a case in point. Forty years ago tires rarely lasted five thousand miles—now they are still good at fifty thousand. To be sure, roads are much better now, but speeds are much higher. Tires are greatly improved, all right, but the improvement has come with time and learning how to do the job. Not all the improvements have been initiated by the companies doing the most advertising and having the greatest sales. Probably advertising helped the improvement along, but how much no one can say.

Advertising lets us know when and where new things are available. But in the cases of some important innovations the public has stayed pretty well ahead of the advertiser. Twenty-five or thirty years ago every boy had a crystal radio set of his own making—and advertising had nothing to do with his having it. Today every small boy whose home does not include a television set visits the neighbors, and it takes no advertising to get him to do so. So be a little skeptical of the advertising enthusiast. Of course advertising attracts our attention, holds it sometimes, and gets us to do many things. But some things we would do anyhow and they even may be the more important ones.

Advertising has misrepresented some products, to the disadvantage of consumers. During the 1930's, particularly, there was a flood of books and articles attacking advertising on this ground. Books like *Your Money's Worth* and *One Hundred Million Guinea Pigs* were best sellers for a time. Doubtless they exaggerated the importance of the misrepresentation. Moreover, the worst hoaxes never have been advertised because their perpetrators did not want that much publicity. In general it is true that unbranded, unadvertised goods are less uniform in quality than branded goods, but perhaps there is not so much difference as the advertisers claim.

Advertising has helped firms grow large, a fact which seems to have both good and bad aspects. Large firms can produce economically. But in some lines the largest firms seem no more efficient than the medium-sized ones. It seems to have been unnecessary to grow so big in order to get all the economies of scale.[2] And bigness has developed problems of human relations and monopoly that are not entirely beneficial to society.

In the long run, advertising cannot increase the profitability with which specific resources are used. When a business grows as a result of advertising, the aggregate income should increase. But more capital resources are in use, and the *rate* of return will be improved only up to the point where an existing plant or supply of capital resource is utilized to its full economic capacity. The adding of units of capital increases the total net income, but not necessarily the rate relative to the capital. The orange growers in California make no more per acre than they did forty or more years ago, but the increased demand absorbs the crop from many more acres. International Shoe Company and United States Steel actually show lower rates of return on invested capital than do some smaller shoe and steel companies.

When an industry reaches the point now held by the cigarette industry, all the millions spent for advertising fail to increase the total sales. They were up about 1 per cent in 1949 and another 1 per cent in 1950, which is just the rate of increase in population. Moreover, the relative position of the various companies does not change very much, although the two largest advertisers seem to have lost just a little during the past two years, perhaps because of the quality rather than the quantity of competitive advertising. Advertising is apparently necessary to keep people smoking their favorite brand, but that seems to be about all it accomplishes at present.

So it is hard to give a net evaluation of advertising. Your authors believe it to have been somewhat less useful than its enthusiastic champions make it out, but much less injurious than many of its critics rate it. We believe that the controversies over it have been given more attention than they merit. Certainly, advertising has aided business firms to sell goods and to make a profit. It has made purchasing easier for many persons by telling when and where goods

---

2 The concept "economy of scale" was discussed in Chapter 11.

are available and at what prices. It has given some useful information concerning products. Some of the information has been misleading and some of it is not pertinent to the consumer's needs. But after all, advertising men and women are human beings like you and me, with just about the same ethical standards of social responsibility. Perhaps they even watch their step a little closer than some of us because what they say is said publicly and is clearly subject to review both by consumers and by government agencies. If advertising ever were to disappear from the American scene we are pretty sure that it would be missed not only by business but by consumers as well.

Finally, perhaps it is fair to say that sales promotion is an important element in the dynamics of American life. Desires are aroused and stimulated by advertising. These aroused desires lead to continual change both in production and consumption. The wastes due to obsolescence are hastened and increased. But so is the general tempo of living. Certainly the pressure that is generated by sales promotion, leading us to strive for larger money incomes with which to buy things, seldom leaves a dull moment in the active and dynamic life of the average American. It may be a wasteful system, but it is a dynamic and an interesting one.

PRICES

Price Is a Directing Force.—Prices are strong forces in directing human behavior. The price which one hopes to get for his services often will determine his choice of occupation. Anticipated prices of different crops are important to the farmer's consideration of what crops to plant. The difference between the price of flax on the one hand and the prices of linseed oil and meal made from the flax on the other hand will determine whether or not a firm can operate with profit in the crushing of flax. Prices offered by different buyers will determine whether a certain type of lumber is prepared for and used in the production of furniture, yachts, houses, or bonfires. The decision depends largely on what someone will pay in connection with the particular use.

Prices influence not only production, but consumption as well. The relative prices at which things can be bought have much to do with the relative quantities of different things that are consumed. As prices of specific things change, relative to each other, consumption patterns also change. At present we are not concerned with the forces that have caused the change in relative prices, although that is a field of major importance, but we are concerned with the effect on consumption of the change in price.

It has been said that the greatest single urge to human activity is the desire to obtain goods to satisfy our wants. Ordinarily it is the power of a good to satisfy a want, rather than the good itself, that the consumer is after. We really are not interested in an automobile per se, but in the ability to go places or the thrill of speeding; we are not interested in owning cloth or even garments per se, but in the warmth, comfort, and distinction that well-designed clothes can give; when we buy tea we are not interested in ugly, shriveled leaves that color water a sickly brown, but we are interested, perhaps, in a Sunday evening spent before a cozy fire with charming friends whose pleasure and comfort are enhanced by the warmth and sprightliness of the brew. Only misers are interested in mere possession of the goods themselves.

Many goods have more than one use, more than one way, that is, in which they can satisfy a want. A piece of wood, for example, may be useful as fuel in a fireplace; the same piece of wood might have been fashioned into a canoe paddle, a table top, or a picture frame and thus have had its usefulness greatly extended in time. It also would have served very different purposes.

The Law of Demand.—Whenever economic goods are scarce—that is, when the supply of them is inadequate to permit *all* people to have them for *all* their possible uses, they are rationed to the highest bidders. Generally they go to the persons who put them to their most valuable uses first—that is, they are used where they will satisfy the most intense desires, or at least those desires the satisfying of which calls forth the greatest purchasing power in exchange. When people bid intensively for a good its price rises and the satisfaction derived from it becomes smaller relative to the price paid. If the price continues to rise, the satisfaction derived from the purchase of a particular good finally becomes less than that to be obtained from expending the same amount of purchasing power on other things. In such circumstances, a smaller quantity will be purchased, for purchasing power is used by each person so that each unit of it buys about the same degree of satisfaction. Consequently, when the price of one commodity or service rises in relationship to other prices there is a reduction in the quantity purchased and consumed. This tendency for the consumption of any economic good to increase when its price falls and to decrease when its price rises is sometimes spoken of as the Law of Demand.

Elasticity of Demand.—The consumption of some goods is affected much more violently by changes in price than is that of other goods. For example, it has been discovered through experience that the consumption of staple commodities that are in constant, customary use is but slightly changed by moderate changes in price. This is the case with many common food products, medium-priced clothing, and so on. Price concessions in these lines may change patronage from one store to another, or from one week to an earlier one, but they are not likely to increase total sales very much. In contrast, the consumption of novelties, style goods, and high-priced items like automobiles may be markedly changed by a change in price.

The degree of change in consumption that accompanies a change in price of a particular commodity is spoken of as the *elasticity of demand* for the product. If the percentage change in quantity purchased is greater than the percentage change in price, the demand is said to be elastic; if the quantity change is small relative to the price change, the demand is called an inelastic one. However, if the percentage changes are the same in both price and quantity, i.e., unit elasticity, the same total amount of money will be paid for the commodity regardless of price; if the demand is *elastic,* total purchases in money terms will increase as the price falls, and vice versa. If the demand is *inelastic,* total purchases in money terms will decrease as the price falls, and vice versa.

It follows that increasing the physical quantity of things with an inelastic demand benefits the consumer in two ways, while decreasing the physical quantity inflicts double injury upon the consumer. For example, if in a free market the total quantity of milk offered for sale is increased, consumers can buy it at a lower price per quart—enough lower in fact so that their total expenditure for milk is lessened. Thus they will have more milk to drink and more money left for other things. If in contrast the supply of milk is reduced, the consumers must pay enough more per quart so that their total expenditure is increased even though they have less milk to drink. Consequently, cost-reducing improvements are especially welcome for such commodities, while restrictions upon output are particularly obnoxious.

If a product may be sold in either of two markets, in one of which the demand is inelastic while in the other it is elastic, the amount of the product offered in the market with an inelastic demand may be restricted to the advantage of the seller. Milk, for example, appears to be such a product; the demand for milk for whole milk consumption is relatively inelastic, while the demand for milk to convert into butter and other dairy products is relatively elastic.

For purposes of illustration, we might assume that dairy farmers in a particular area have 2,000 units of milk to sell and that if they offer half the supply for each of the two uses, both will bring the same price; that is, in each market 1,000 units would sell for $4.00 per unit, or a total revenue of $8,000. Now if the amount offered as whole milk could be restricted to 900 units, the price might rise as shown in Figure 31 to $5.00 a unit or a total value of $4,500 in that part of the market. The remaining 1,100 units might then be sold in the dairy products market at $3.75 per unit, as shown in the figure, or $4,125. The total sales in the two markets now would be $8,625. Thus, if the supply offered in each market can be controlled, the total revenue can be raised by restricting the amount offered in the market with the inelastic demand. The consumers in this market suffer the higher price. Milk and some other commodities with alternative uses are, in fact, often controlled in this manner.

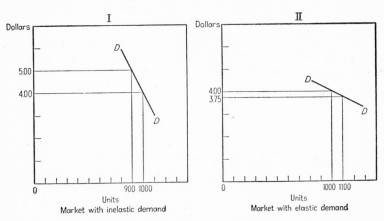

Fig. 31.—Alternative Uses for a Commodity and Their Effect on Total Value.

Income Elasticity of Demand.—It was pointed out in Chapter 10 that families with different incomes spend different portions of their total disposable income for specific groups of things such as food, recreation, or medical care. The corollary which also was pointed out is that as a family's money income increases, the pattern of its expenditures changes. The change in quantity bought that accompanies change in income rather than change in price is called *income elasticity of demand.* Experience shows that as income increases, purchase of groceries increases less than proportionally, clothing about proportionally, food in restaurants and most durable consumer goods more than proportionally.

This point is illustrated by the comparison of purchases from retail stores in the depression years of 1932 and 1933 with those in the prosperous year of 1941. Between these two years the total disposable money income of individuals in the United States approximately doubled from $45 billion to $90 billion. With this doubling of disposable income, total retail purchases a little more than doubled. Purchases from different types of retail stores, roughly representing different kinds of goods, varied sharply in the percentage of increase. The Department of Commerce has published data showing these comparisons (see Table 38).

TABLE 38

RETAIL PURCHASES, PERCENTAGE INCREASE, 1941 OVER 1932-33
(Increase in Disposable Income = 100%)

Purchase	Percentage Increase
Types of Good	
All Retailing	124
Nondurable Goods	100
Durable Goods	200
Types of Stores	
Variety	70
Drug	70
Shoe	75
Grocery	90
Department	100
Men's Clothing	100
Women's Apparel	110
Filling Stations	130
Household Appliances	170
Furniture	180
Farm Implements	190
Hardware	200
Eating Places	200
Jewelry	215
Auto Parts and Accessories	270
Motor Vehicles	310

Source: Calculated from data in the *Statistical Abstract of the United States, 1943*, p. 843.

These data strongly support the assumption that the demand for drugs, food, and the small things bought through variety stores is relatively insensitive to change in income. That is, during the depression the purchase of such things fell less than did that of many others, so with the return of high incomes in 1941 their purchases increased less than those of some other things. Purchases of clothing appear to have changed at approximately the same rate as income. Durable consumer goods, farm implements, and jewelry, in contrast, increased much more than did income. This is due in part to the fact that old items already on hand could be used during the years of low income. Very few new automobiles, for example, were bought during the depression years, but the amount of gasoline used in automobiles in 1932-33 was just about the same as in 1929. In the case of farm implements it is a common observation that purchases are made only when farm income is high unless the item is needed desperately. Moreover, many of the consumer durables are considered semi-luxuries, to be bought only when income is high and more than sufficient for the necessary things that change little in purchase despite changes in income.

UNCERTAINTY IS EVERYWHERE

Another factor that affects the individual's consumption is his feeling of uncertainty. The size of his income and its continuance are uncertain: if he is an employee he may lose his job, or be demoted; if he is a farmer, he may have a poor crop or a low price for his products, or his best cow may sicken and die; if he is a proprietor of a retail store a new competitor may move in next door and reduce his patronage. No matter who he is, he may die and leave his family without means of support. In addition, sudden and unforeseen drains on his income may occur at any time: sickness, serious damage to his automobile, or the loss of household belongings either through theft or fire may bring unexpected expenditures that brook no delay. Moreover, there are some expected events that will require large monetary outlays, provision for which must be planned and started well in advance. Such things as schooling for the children, a trip to Europe, the building of a larger home, or the replacement of durable goods like automobiles and furniture, frequently cannot be financed out of any one year's income. People who want to prepare for such emergencies must save part of their current income for the proverbial rainy day. In so doing they necessarily decrease their expenditure for current consumption.

THE PROPENSITY TO SAVE

Perhaps as individuals we differ as much in our habits and practices of saving as in any other item of behavior. Some save through the purchase of life insurance, others use savings banks, others invest in farms, small businesses, stocks and bonds of industrial firms, government bonds, or in other ways. Some place their savings in a variety of places to spread their risks. The wise use of different methods of saving is discussed in Chapter 17. Unfortunately, it is apparent that too many individuals and families have little or no savings of any sort.

Life insurance is in part a form of saving and often is purchased mainly for that purpose. Insurance is discussed in more detail in Chapter 17, and it is sufficient to say here that in 1949 over 193 million policies were in force in this country. The average size of these policies was $1,110, and in the aggregate they amounted to $1,425 for every man, woman, and child in the United States. This was nearly as much as the total national income for that year.[3]

We Save to Borrow.—In connection with this volume of insurance, $50 billion has already been accumulated by the insurance companies and this amount represents the present total cash or loan value of the policies; that is, savings of that amount have been accumulated by policyholders.[4] Against this amount, about $2.3 billion has already been withdrawn by borrowing; that is, individuals are making temporary use of the savings they have accumulated with the insurance companies. These borrowings have been used to meet emergencies of all sorts. In some cases, the policies were taken primarily to provide savings, while in other cases the borrowing was unexpected. If saving was the primary objective, the policies may be allowed to lapse after they have served their main purpose, while if protection was the primary objective, they will be continued because of the importance of the death benefits in the individual's general plan. In such cases the loans are likely to be repaid, although even if they are not they reduce the remaining death benefits by less than 4 per cent on the average. In individual cases, however, the loan on a policy may so reduce its death benefits and, consequently, so increase its cost as pure insurance as to cause it to be dropped. Individuals who have borrowed heavily on their policies will do well to consult an expert concerning the wisdom of making some change in their general program of insurance.

We Save in Many Ways.—Other methods of saving are also common in providing for the unforeseen social, economic, and physical uncertainties. By saving we do not mean hoarding money—that is, taking it out of circulation by placing it in the proverbial sock or

---

[3] Data used in this paragraph are from the *Insurance Yearbook for 1950.*
[4] *Ibid.*

by burying it, although we realize a certain amount of such "providing for emergencies" exists. We mean, rather, the placing of some
part of our current money income so that it may be used in some way
other than in satisfying our own individual desires. It is money
which may be reclaimed later, if we wish, for use in our program of
consumption.

Banks are among the outstanding institutions that provide the
individual with facilities for savings. As one of their many services,
and the only one that need concern us at the moment, banks act somewhat as money merchants, accepting deposits from those who want
to save, and extending loans to those who want temporarily to use
more money than they possess.[5] The data in Table 39 illustrate the

TABLE 39

SAVINGS AND OTHER TIME DEPOSITS AND DEPOSITORS IN
BANKS AND TRUST COMPANIES IN THE UNITED STATES

On or about June 30	Savings and Other Time Deposits in All Banks (in $ millions)	Savings and Other Time Depositors (thousands)
1926	24,692	46,762
1927	26,091	48,355
1928	28,413	53,188
1929	28,218	52,764
1930	28,479	52,729
1931	28,220	51,399
1932	24,281	44,352
1933	21,126	39,262
1934	21,868	39,562
1935	22,614	41,315
1936	23,464	42,397
1937	24,492	44,226
1938	24,626	44,543
1939	25,081	45,104
1940	25,750	45,791
1941	26,149	46,151
1942	25,487	45,417

Source: *Statistical Abstract of the United States, 1949,* p. 441.

number of savings and other time depositors in banks and trust
companies in the United States, together with the total savings and
other time deposits from 1926 to 1942.

The average size of these savings accounts was about $560 in
1949, but this is a misleading figure. Many of the accounts were for

---

[5] A more complete description of the services offered the consumer by banks
was given in Chapter 6.

business savings and were much larger than the average. Personal accounts, therefore, averaged smaller. In fact, it is estimated that at least half of the accounts open at the end of 1949 were for $100 or less. Thus this form of savings appears to be less important to individuals than life insurance.

Total Savings Seem Small.—There are other forms of savings that are used by many individuals. Investment in one's own business, or in stocks and bonds, or in a farm represents savings from which income is expected in the future. In fact, all private ownership of natural resources and of capital plant is the more-or-less direct result of past savings. It is a pertinent and somewhat disturbing fact, however, that in this richest country in the world half of the families appear to have no net savings. Many more than half of the nation's families would be unable to live at their normal rate of consumption for so long as a year if their current labor income were cut off. Thus in a very real sense we live from hand to mouth. This lack of reserve savings and the uncertainty of continued employment are the motivation behind our Social Security programs.

Saving Affects Consumption.—To the extent that the desire to guard against uncertainty diverts income into insurance, savings, and investments, and away from purchases of food, clothing, shelter, and so on, immediate-consumption patterns are affected. Moreover, future-consumption patterns are likewise modified. The extent and direction of this modification depend, in large part, upon the wisdom with which the original program for saving was conceived and carried out.

Personal savings, like consumption expenditures, vary with the general level of income. This tendency is illustrated by the data in Table 40.

TABLE 40

DISPOSABLE INCOME AND ITS USE

(in $ millions)

	1929	1932	1934	1939	1944	1949
Disposable Personal Income ...	82,484	47,819	51,635	70,167	146,957	187,444
Consumption Expenditures	78,761	49,208	51,882	67,466	111,550	178,832
Personal Savings	3,723	—1,389	—247	2,701	35,407	8,612

Source: Adapted from Survey of Current Business, July 1950, Table 3, p. 9.

During the depression years disposable income was insufficient to cover current consumption expenditures. During World War II

TABLE 41
LIFE EXPECTANCY IN THE UNITED STATES
(in years)

Age Attained	Life Expectancy *	Age Attained	Life Expectancy *	Age Attained	Life Expectancy *
0	63.62 †	42	29.35	84	4.56
1	65.76	43	28.53	85	4.31
2	65.10	44	27.71	86	4.08
3	64.28	45	26.90	87	3.86
4	63.40	46	26.10	88	3.66
5	62.49	47	25.30	89	3.47
6	61.57	48	24.52	90	3.30
7	60.65	49	23.74	91	3.14
8	59.71	50	22.98	92	2.99
9	58.77	51	22.22	93	2.86
10	57.82	52	21.48	94	2.73
11	56.87	53	20.74	95	2.61
12	55.92	54	20.02	96	2.50
13	54.98	55	19.31	97	2.40
14	54.04	56	18.60	98	2.31
15	53.10	57	17.92	99	2.21
16	52.17	58	17.24	100	2.13
17	51.26	59	16.57	101	2.04
18	50.34	60	15.91	102	1.96
19	49.44	61	15.27	103	1.88
20	48.54	62	14.63	104	1.80
21	47.64	63	14.01	105	1.72
22	46.75	64	13.40	106	1.64
23	45.86	65	12.80	107	1.56
24	44.98	66	12.21	108	1.48
25	44.09	67	11.64	109	1.41
26	43.21	68	11.08		
27	42.32	69	10.53		
28	41.44	70	10.00		
29	40.55	71	9.49		
30	39.67	72	9.00		
31	38.79	73	8.52		
32	37.91	74	8.06		
33	37.04	75	7.62		
34	36.17	76	7.20		
35	35.30	77	6.81		
36	34.44	78	6.43		
37	33.58	79	6.07		
38	32.72	80	5.73		
39	31.87	81	5.41		
40	31.03	82	5.11		
41	30.19	83	4.82		

* Average length of life remaining to each individual alive at each attained age.
† At birth.
Source: *Life Insurance Fact Book,* 1951, pp. 94, 95 (New York: Institute of Life Insurance).

current money income was high, but the prices of most consumer goods were held down by the OPA and durable consumer goods were not available for purchase. Consequently, savings were high. In the near-normal years of 1929 and 1949 the percentages of disposable personal income saved were 4.5 and 4.6 respectively. At that rate of saving, with 3 per cent compound interest added, it would take about seventeen years for a person to accumulate a year's income. During the typical span of working years, therefore, an individual who saved at the average rate of those normal years would accumulate only between two and three years' income. This certainly is not enough to permit early retirement, for even at age sixty-five the average life expectancy in the United States is about thirteen years (see Table 41). Nowadays many actually retire at age sixty-five or before, thus increasing the need for savings and the clamor for increases in publicly administered, compulsory old age allowances.

LEISURE AND TIME AS CONSUMPTION FACTORS

Leisure Is on the Increase.—Since 1890 there has been a considerable reduction in the daily hours of work of nearly all classes of labor in the United States. A reliable estimate suggests that the normal work week in American industry as a whole has probably decreased by twenty hours during the last fifty years. The decrease in average hours of labor per week that occurred between 1890 and

TABLE 42

AVERAGE HOURS OF LABOR PER WEEK IN ELEVEN INDUSTRIES, 1890-1928

Industry	Average Hours Per Week		Per Cent Decrease During Period
	1890	1928	
Bakeries	64.7	47.4	26.7
Boot & Shoe	59.5	49.1	17.5
Building	52.0	43.5	16.3
Cotton Goods	62.8	53.4	14.9
Foundry & Machine Shops	59.8	59.4	15.7
Blast Furnaces	84.6	59.8	29.3
Marble & Stone	54.7	44.0	19.6
Millwork	52.0	44.8	13.8
Book & Job Printing	56.4	44.3	21.5
Newspaper Printing	48.2	45.1	6.5
Woolen Goods	58.9	49.3	16.3

Lazare Teper, "Hours of Labor," *Studies in Historical and Political Science,* Vol. 50, No. 1. (Baltimore: The Johns Hopkins Press.)

1928 in eleven major industrial fields is estimated to have ranged from a minimum of 6.5 per cent to a maximum of 29.3 per cent (see Table 42). It is interesting to note that the eleven industries became much more uniform in their hours of employment during the period. In the twenty-odd years since 1928, the work week has been shortened still further and also made still more uniform among the various industries.

Leisure Affects Consumption.—The shortening of the work week has resulted in our having more leisure time. What we do with it directly affects our pattern of consumption. This growing margin of leisure, coupled with the ever-increasing variety of leisure-time facilities available at decreasing prices, is an important factor in the changing of consumption practices. People have more both of physical and mental energy as well as time to devote to leisure-time activities. This opens a field of consumption that merits careful planning both from the economic and from the philosophic or moral standpoints, for what we do as individuals with our leisure time will determine in large measure what sort of civilization we have. The competition for such leisure—and the money that is spent in enjoying it—is strong between tennis and "hot rods," beer parlors and libraries, gardening and golf, Beethoven and Roy Rogers, Coney Island and the Quetico wilderness, as well as a host of other urges and opportunities.

Time Is Relentless.—Time is, perhaps, the most relentless of all factors limiting consumption. Is there anyone who has not said, "I'm sorry, but I cannot take the time to do it, much as I'd like to." And "it" can be so many things! You cannot listen to two radio programs at once, you cannot study economics while watching television, you cannot go with Tom to the theater and with Jerry to the dance the same evening—or can you? Many circumstances will occur to you in which a choice must be made between two (or more) things you would like to do—but cannot, because to be done at all they must be done at the same time.

Not only does time limit consumption because things get in each other's way, but the total time in each day is limited to twenty-four hours. About sixteen of these hours are usually spent in working and sleeping, and the remaining eight hours set a rigid limit for the day's consumption. Usually it is difficult to do two or more things at the same time. Whenever you change your clothes or shave, or curl your hair, you reduce the time available for the consumption of other things. Generally, when you consume material things you reduce the time available for meditation, enjoyment of the sunset, and similar

things. The person who becomes greatly involved in the consumption of *things* has little time to do as the proverbial farmer who often
"sits on the fence and thinks, and sometimes just sits."

Life Is Short and Our Producing Span Is Still Shorter.—The
day is short and so is life itself. In our Western civilization we have
found no close approach to the beautiful timelessness that was found
at Shangri-La in *Lost Horizons*. When we have reached the common age of college students we can look forward only to about forty-
five more years, for that is the average length of life beyond the
eighteenth year. The average life expectancy as one reaches each age
level was shown in Table 41.

With regard to the length of life that remains, on the average, for
college students, it should be noted that nearly all economic production is accomplished in the middle forty-five years or less of each
individual's life. During these forty-five years each person must
produce not only what he consumes at the moment, but enough in
addition both for those who are below the producing age and for
those who are above it. It has been pointed out, in an earlier chapter,
that about 40 per cent of all the people in the United States are gainfully employed at some economic task. This means, of course, that
each employed person must produce enough economic goods to supply
2.5 persons, including himself. This ruthless necessity to produce
during the years from twenty to sixty-five limits rather strictly the
time which the individual may spend on anything else. Many of us
are too busy producing during those years to do much consuming beyond the biological necessities for life. For this reason, we emphasize
again the probability that those who do not find satisfaction in their
work are likely to lead barren lives.

Project Questions

1. Talk with your parents or with others of about that age, or perhaps even with your grandparents or others of that generation, for the
purpose of comparing the forms of recreation in which they engaged at
your age with those in which you engage. Which kinds of recreation
cost them the most? Which consumed more of the individual's personal
time? How do you account for any changes that have taken place?

2. What are the most important purposes that would lead an individual or a family to invest part of its money income? Assume a family of
husband and wife age thirty-five and children age nine and seven believe
they can save and invest about $500 a year. What program of invest-

ment would you recommend for them? Assume this to be in addition to an ordinary life insurance policy of $10,000.

3. What is the significance of the time element on elasticity of demand?

4. Prepare a list of ten specific risks that you have faced. In connection with each give the

a) Cause or origin
b) Effect
c) Method used to meet the risk
d) Improvements in methods of meeting the risk that you might employ another time
e) Further protection against this particular risk that might be given by government.

5. Prepare two lists of commodities, one composed of those commodities which you consume and for which you have an elastic demand; the other composed of those commodities which you consume and for which you have an inelastic demand.

Chapter 15

INCREASING NATIONAL REAL INCOME

What Production Is—A Reminder

National real income can be increased only by increasing production. Production includes any adaptation of environment or rearrangement of matter which results in an increase in human satisfaction or enjoyment. This statement applies, of course, to any field of human activity such as farming, mining, manufacturing, the showing of movies, horse racing, house painting, or what not.

The businessman defines production as any change that will command a price. Whenever any person or group is paid by someone else for baking bread, piloting an airplane, clerking in a store, or managing a factory, the payment is prima facie evidence of production. The converse also is true. No matter how much energy one may have exerted, or how much physical rearrangement of matter may have resulted, if no one is willing to pay for the result there is prima facie evidence that no production has occurred.

Of course we do some things for ourselves, the results of which give us personal satisfaction. Since these things are not exchanged for money they generally are not counted in the money estimates of either production or consumption, although they really contribute to both. Doing things for ourselves is not so common nor so large a part of total production as it once was. The work of the housewife still is highly important, but it does not include spinning and weaving or the making of clothes and butter to the same extent it did one hundred years ago. Undoubtedly, the transition from home to factory production has increased total national product per person, in spite of the fact that it has made necessary the development of complicated institutional arrangements for transporting and marketing the products of commercial industry.

Sometimes businessmen can increase their personal "production" in the sense of their money income by restricting their production in the physical sense. This is possible because, for some things, a small supply is desired so strongly that it will be bought for more total money than a large supply while, of course, the small supply costs less to produce. This possibility has been mentioned earlier, in the discussion of inelastic demand. It is illustrated and its implications are discussed more fully in the next chapter. Here we discuss only the possibilities of increasing total national real income, which presumably never can be done through decreasing physical supply.

Four Ways to Increase National Real Income

The possibilities of increasing national real income are found principally in connection with (1) the development of new industries, (2) an improvement in management practices, (3) technological developments, and (4) more effective specialization. Each of these areas of possibility is considered in the remainder of this chapter.

New Industries and Income.—The production and corresponding consumption of goods and services are changing constantly. New things appear while old ones disappear; some things become more important and others less. These changes are due, in the main, to the interplay of three important forces, namely:

1. Changes in the availability of raw materials. For example, the depletion of soil fertility, the opening of new irrigation projects, the exhaustion of mines and wells, the discovery of new mineral deposits, and the like would have an important effect.

2. Changes in the techniques of processing. Examples of this are the introduction of the electric blast furnace, the use of aluminum to lighten trains, the belt-line system of factory operation, new methods of extracting dyes from coal tar, improvements in the generation of electricity, and the like.

3. Changes in the ways in which people satisfy their desires Examples are the attendance at movies, listening to the radio, and watching television (principal forms of recreation which were unknown fifty years ago), the change in the type of swimming suits worn by different generations, and the return to popularity of the old square dances of the 1880's.

A Regional Example. The fact of change in production resulting from the interplay of these forces is evident everywhere. Perhaps a brief consideration of the economic developments in Minnesota will be sufficient to suggest some of the important ways in which these changes affect production and consumption within a particular region. It will be understood, of course, that the effects are not exactly the same in all regions.

Instability and change are clearly shown in the rise and fall of industries in Minnesota. For three quarters of a century Minnesota has been characterized by the pioneer development that is typical of young communities. Early in the history of the state two industries became dominant: lumbering and flour milling. Both were based on the productivity of the land and both were natural to a new country. As the state has matured, however, the prominence of these two industries has declined. Their rise and decline may be traced briefly to illustrate the ebb and flow that is inevitable until a community has matured. In fact, some such series of changes will probably continue indefinitely, although at a slower rate.

Since 1910 there has been essentially no increase in the total amount of land in farms. The intensity of land use has increased, however, ever since the turn of the century. Wheat, which was the primary crop for many years, has become of secondary importance. In the southern part of the state, particularly, corn has proved to be a more profitable crop and therefore has largely replaced wheat. Throughout the state, livestock industries have increased to major importance. This change in the relative importance of different types of agricultural products in the farmers' income is illustrated in Table 43.

TABLE 43

Gross Cash Sales from Minnesota Farms

(Expressed as percentages of total sales)

Year	Field Crops	Livestock	Livestock Products
1910	59.6	19.3	21.1
1915	50.2	28.9	20.9
1920	42.5	31.7	25.8
1925	34.4	36.0	29.6
1930	21.2	42.5	36.3
1944-48 (av.)	26.2	40.4	33.4

The development of the livestock industries which these figures show represents an intensification of agriculture. This intensification is reflected in the fact that the total agricultural income of the state has been increased by the change. In turn, this makes possible a greater consumption of goods and services by the farmers of Minnesota than was possible forty years ago, even though there has been no increase in the amount of land in use. In this particular case the effect of intensification has been felt in city industries as well as on the farm, for the increase in the number of persons gainfully employed in the butter and meat-packing industries is greater than the decrease in the number employed in flour milling. Even the decline in the lumbering industry has been offset in large part, so far as employment is concerned, by increases in employment in tourist resorts that occupy the districts formerly covered by commercial timber. Moreover, the harvesting of young forest trees for pulpwood is becoming a major industry in the state, furnishing the raw material for a growing volume of paper manufacturing. Thus, as changes occur in the industrial pattern of a region, more and more productive uses may well be found for the natural and human resources with a corresponding increase in the opportunity for consumption.

THE SEARCH CONTINUES. The search for new industries, the products of which will add to general well-being and enjoyment, is a continual one. A generation ago the automobile revolutionized our ideas concerning travel, sight-seeing, and outdoor living. The movies, radio, and now television came shortly afterwards as new forms of recreation and education. Aluminum and rayon are comparatively new raw materials that permit the fashioning of new types of merchandise. The chemical industries are continuously reporting new ways of refining or combining materials to make them more useful to consumers without increasing the human labor that must be expended on their preparation. Television and stratosphere flying are among the developments of the 1940's. Perhaps space ships, propelled by atomic energy and guided by radar, may be looked forward to with reasonable assurance during the next few decades. As science and industry combine to make these and other things possible, consumption will change and the lot of people as consumers will be improved. We cannot too strongly emphasize the fact, however, that these new developments and others like them will come only as the result of intelligent and painstaking effort on the part of many people. Moreover, with a few conspicuous exceptions, those individuals who put forth the most intensive and intelligent efforts in production will continue to have the purchasing power with which to obtain the lion's share of the new products and their enjoyment.

Management Practices and Income.—Improvement in the scale of living need not wait, however, upon the development of new industries. Any increase in the efficiency with which production is carried on in existing industries will add to the real income of the community. This will be true regardless of whether the improvement occurs in those industries that cater to local trade or in those that produce for interregional trade.

An increase in the output of the industries catering to local demand would add directly to the commodities and services available for consumption. If such an increase occurred through improved efficiency without increase in total cost, the enlarged output could be paid for with the same exchange that now commands the present output. That one change would enrich people in general—that is, would give them more things to consume—and no individual would be made poorer thereby.

Similarly, if the production of things for interregional trade were more efficiently performed, there would be more goods available to exchange for commodities and services which are not produced to advantage in the home community. There is enough diversified supply of natural and human resources in almost every region in America, so the ability to organize and manage industries is likely to be the most important limiting factor in the production of income.

SCIENTIFIC MANAGEMENT CAN HELP. The problem of increasing income seems clearly to involve, as one very important element, the application of scientific management to individual plants and then the extension of this application to matters of general industrial and regional control. The Employment Stabilization Research Institute, in its studies in Minnesota, found that neither individual concerns nor whole industries in that state were, on the whole, adequately and efficiently managed. In one of its publications the Institute suggested that many firms would do well to adopt the following program for the improvement of their plants.

1. Each plant should periodically consider its layout and the flow of materials in process; determine the operations necessary to be performed on each product; the order in which the operations should be performed; the location of each production center required in the processing, and the flow of materials in process.

2. Production centers, or points at which operations are performed, should be considered with respect to light, working conditions, receipt and disposal of materials, plant transportation systems, equipment used, and possible changes.

3. Control of materials should be considered with regard to the possibility of developing standard raw material requirements; the establishment of minimum and maximum inventories; and the control of the movement of materials in process.

4. Processes should be considered with regard to the suitability of the machinery and equipment that is being used and that which is available; the capacities of the worker; the means of testing applicants for these capacities; the "one best way" of performing the job; and the work content of each job.

5. By organizing unfilled orders and analyzing them, it becomes possible to re-plan their production. Knowledge of the workers and machines, and of

the requirements of unfilled orders, makes it possible to lay out a production program and to schedule its movement through the processes.

6. Each plant should install some means of knowing its costs, thus making it possible for whole industries to get on a comparative cost basis.

7. Markets should be analyzed to ascertain what changes are taking place and the condition of the market at any given time. Industries may thus measure the demand for their own products, and the compilation of data on the productive capacities of the industries will make it possible to plan production accordingly.

8. A clearance of information on wages and income will make it possible to measure the consumer demand in the region. The relation of demand for producer goods to supply will serve to forecast the possibilities and limitations to be placed upon the manufacturers of such goods.

9. Comparison of the local industrial situation with general business conditions and the condition of related industries that are national in scope will make it possible to adopt a course of action based upon these facts.

10. Classification of jobs and the requirements of each will make it possible to select the persons best able to do the work, to train people according to the demand for particular services, and to adjust the available labor supply to the requirements of industry.[1]

GROUP ACTION CAN BE A USEFUL SUPPLEMENT. However, group action in industrial management is needed to supplement individual action in plant management in order to achieve full development and stability. By group activity small manufacturers can secure results which they could not otherwise obtain, results which it is quite possible for a large plant to accomplish independently. A large unit may be able to develop a well-selected and well-trained labor force because it can carry a personnel department with the requisite skill to accomplish this purpose. A small plant cannot afford such a department, but a group of plants may be able to do so. A large plant may be able to afford a statistical department to collect, organize, and interpret market data and to develop other managerial devices. This would be quite impossible in a single small plant, but not in a group of small plants. A large firm can determine the basis upon which its operations should be expanded and contracted by collecting facts on trends and relating productive capacity to the market. Among a number of small plants no one of them can do this, but a group of plants acting as a unit may achieve a similar result.

Highly developed research is possible in a large plant and impossible in the small unit, but a group of small units may carry on such research through group organization. A large integrated plant may

---

[1] George Filipetti, *Scientific Management—An Aid to Industrial Control* (Minneapolis: University of Minnesota Press, 1933), pp. 51, 52.

readily measure the output required to meet previous sales; once it has estimated its probable future sales, it may adjust output to coincide with the estimate. A group of small plants combined in horizontal and vertical associations [2] can do likewise. Knowledge concerning the best methods in the various functional aspects of business may be available to large units because of their wide contacts; group activities may bring to members similar information, and in this case their adoption may be effected more easily and quickly in the small plants than in the large units.

Within the region are companies engaged in production for local consumption. These companies require an analysis of the total sales of each of their products for local consumption; the changes in consumptive power of the local area; a knowledge of the local productive power to fill these needs, and of outside forces likely to affect them. Companies selling over a wider area will need a clearance of information with the producers selling over that area, probably through the horizontal type of organization.[3]

Finally, group action can be achieved by trade associations, which should act as central agencies for the clearing of information. Data on trade, current data on production, stocks on hand, consumption, current price levels of essential commodities, statistics of active and idle plant capacity, and information on costs and profits for related industries would be collected. Such a system, regional or state-wide in scope, would supply valuable integrated statistics. A free enterprise system with rivalry among producers will work most efficiently when each rival has the fullest possible information concerning the industry and the market in which he operates.

The comments in the preceding paragraphs suggest methods by which the present economic system may be made to operate more efficiently and effectively. Because the consumer's income and consumption are limited by the results of the economic machine, its effective operation is of paramount importance to us as consumers.

Technological Improvements and Income.—Another way of increasing real income is through improvements in technology. Beginning with the industrial revolution, with its harnessing of steam power, the machine has increasingly displaced human labor, not only because much heavy work could be done by machines which men were

---

[2] A horizontal association is composed of firms all at the same industrial level, such as manufacturers or wholesalers. A vertical association has members from more than one level.

[3] Filipetti, *op. cit.*, pp. 54-55.

not strong enough to perform but also because machines could be speeded up to greater and more uniform production than could men.

One of our greatest increases in the ability to produce comes from our use of electrical power in industry. It has been estimated that in 1949 the electric power consumption by American industry amounted to 10,500 kilowatt hours per worker. This figure may be compared to 67 kilowatt hours of energy, which is the amount that an average man can expend on 240 eight-hour days of manual work. In other words, in 1949 every factory worker in the United States had the aid of electrical power equivalent on the average to the physical energy of 157 men. It is no wonder that we process more material than before we knew how to harness electricity.

EXPANSION OF MAN-MADE CAPITAL PLANT. Electricity is not the only aid to man's production. All other items of man-made capital plant assist in the making and distributing of things. The October 1950 issue of *Fortune* Magazine contained an item under the heading "The Expansion Frenzy," from which we quote as follows:

> The rate of spending on new plant and equipment in the third quarter [of 1950] was at a rate some 27 per cent higher than in the second, and the announced plans were little less than staggering. In the East, the Pennsylvania Railroad put in a $55-million order for 214 more diesels; the 360-mile railroad to tap Labrador's iron-ore reserves would probably be started this fall instead of 1952 as previously planned; Dow Chemical announced plans for a new polystyrene plant near New London, Connecticut; and Chance Vaught postponed indefinitely the projected sale of its $9-million plant at Stratford, Connecticut. In the textile-heavy South, Robbins, Deering-Milliken, and Duplan were building new rayon-weaving mills; du Pont was soon to begin construction of a fourth nylon plant, this one in North Carolina, plus expanding its Martinsville, West Virginia, unit; and ten "non-tire" rubber companies set up a joint subsidiary to re-open the $7-million government plant at Louisville. In the Midwest, Ford began work on its 700-car-a-day assembly plant in Kansas City, to cost between $25 and $30 million; and Chrysler started construction on its new Indianapolis transmission plant, slated to employ 5,000 workers when finished. "We're barreling along in a frenzy," said a Los Angeles contractor. "Business, if I may understate a situation, is excellent." [4]

OUR RELATIVE ADVANTAGE. It is evident that much is being added to the nation's capital plant right along, with which we may work to increase our total production. Each of these new plants will be modern, designed to take advantage of the latest in engineering

---

[4] By permission of *Fortune*.

know-how. Thus both the quantity and the quality of our capital plant are constantly being increased.

It would be difficult to exaggerate the advantage which we in this country have over others because of our greater supply of man-made capital with which to work. Perhaps nothing illustrates the difference better than the figures on installed horsepower per worker. Estimates published by the Department of Commerce show the following comparisons:

HORSEPOWER PER WORKER IN INDUSTRY

United States	4.86
Great Britain	2.56
Canada	2.17
Italy	2.14
France	1.78

These data refer only to industrial countries. India, China, Indonesia, and even the U.S.S.R. are much poorer in installed horsepower per worker than any of the countries in the list. Our horsepower per worker increased fourfold in the first thirty years of this century. Perhaps other countries of the world will catch up somewhat during the last half of the century, in which case world-wide production will increase greatly.

CHANGES IN AGRICULTURE. In some fields the increase in efficiency in this country has been greater than in other fields. For example, in agriculture great change has taken place in the amount of labor required for the production of field crops, but the change has been quite different with different crops. Table 44 presents data which show the decrease in the amount of man labor used to produce wheat, corn, or cotton.

It is interesting to note the large and continuing decrease in man hours of labor per 100 bushels of wheat where machinery has been substituted so extensively for man power. On the other hand, the decrease in hours of labor per bale of cotton started more slowly and has been less marked to date, largely because there has been slower introduction of machines in the production and harvesting of cotton.

Efficiency in agricultural production continues to increase. The Bureau of the Census reports that in 1940 there were 9.5 million persons engaged in agricultural production in the United States, while in 1948 there were only 7.4 million so employed. In spite of this sharp reduction of 21 per cent in farm labor, there was a 4 per cent increase in acreage planted and a slightly greater increase in total physical crop. In other words, American farmers and farm workers increased the average of their physical output by over 30 per cent in nine years.

TABLE 44

ESTIMATED MAN HOURS OF LABOR USED TO PRODUCE
100 BUSHELS OF WHEAT, 100 BUSHELS OF CORN, OR 1 BALE OF COTTON
IN SELECTED PERIODS

Years	Wheat	Corn	Cotton
1872-1882	129	180	304
1898-1902	86	147	285
1928-1932	49	104	235
1940-1944	43	86	190
1947-1948	33	66	172

MAN HOURS REQUIRED IN 1947-48 AS PERCENTAGE OF THOSE REQUIRED IN 1872-82

	25.6	36.6	55.5

Calculated from data in *Agricultural Statistics,* United States Department of Agriculture, various years.

WHAT THE 1920's DID FOR MANUFACTURING. Manufacturing shows a similar increase in the output of goods, relative to labor employed. Table 45 summarizes the changes that have taken place in output per worker in the manufacturing industries since the turn of the century. The data approximate the change in physical production per worker, as explained in Chapter 6.

TABLE 45

ALL MANUFACTURES IN THE UNITED STATES

Year	Number of Production Workers (millions)	Value Added by Manufacture		
		In Current Dollars (billions)	In 1926 Dollars (billions)	Per Wage-Earner in 1926 Dollars (thousands)
1899	4.5	4.6	8.8	19.5
1909	6.2	8.1	12.0	19.4
1919	8.4	23.8	17.2	20.5
1929	8.3	30.6	32.2	38.8
1939	7.8	24.5	31.7	40.5
1947	11.9	74.4	42.8	41.0

The increase in the value added by manufacture per wage-earner during the decade of the 1920's is phenomenal. A moderate rate of increase has continued since 1930. Perhaps the price index used to adjust the current dollar figures for changes in the price level has not compensated completely for the change in price. Even with a liberal allowance for error in this respect, however, the increase in accomplishment per worker would be large. This increase is largely the result of increased efficiency of operation of factories. It is associated with increases in the use of mechanical devices, electrical power, time and motion studies to eliminate unnecessary motions, and the like. In all probability, further significant improvements in manufacturing techniques will be accomplished in the next few decades. Certainly, as was pointed out in the section above, our engineers and experts in production management already know many ways in which efficiency can be increased. If and when these improved techniques are adopted, our national ability to consume will be materially increased.

Political Action and Efficiency.—Perhaps it should be emphasized at this point that the types of efficiency about which we have been speaking are not limited to any particular form of sociopolitical organization. That is to say, an increase in the use of mechanical power relative to human labor, or the saving of effort resulting from time and motion studies, or the economies of large-scale production, will have the same effect on the total capacity to consume in a communistic, a fascist, a democratic, or a monarchial society. These economies are the result of physical laws underlying engineering, and man-made laws have no direct effect upon them. The form of sociopolitical organization may, however, either encourage or discourage the application of these physical laws to specific situations in production. Most individuals in this country believe that the democratic, free-enterprise system in use in this country encourages their use to a greater extent than any other system of political economy tried so far.

Do We Want Efficiency? Even in this country, however, we sometimes use political laws to control the application of physical-engineering laws. In some cases we encourage, while in other cases we appear to discourage, development of full physical efficiency.

One illustration of the interrelationship between physical laws and political laws in our economic life may be cited from the chain-store field. There seems to be no question but that chain stores have, in general, been able to distribute groceries and some other commodities at retail more economically than the older types of retail institutions —that is, with less expenditure of human effort. In many states, however, the legislative bodies have tried to offset these physical-engineering advantages by special chain-store taxes or other antichain legislation, thus interfering with the full use of the efficient methods. Perhaps the advantage that is afforded to the independent merchants through such legislation is socially desirable since it permits this group of citizens to hold their existing places in the community, but it must be remembered that there is a direct cost to consumers in the form of higher prices.

Another illustration of this interplay between physical and political laws is found in the field of public utilities. In the cases of street railways and telephone systems, for example, there are undisputed engineering economies in monopoly operation—that is, a single concern operating a single system in an area can furnish the desired services with less expenditure of human effort than would be required to operate two competing systems. In these cases it has been customary for legislatures to grant exclusive franchise privileges to single operators in order that advantage might be taken of the resulting economies.

Our political action in these two illustrative cases appears to have been predicated on different attitudes towards the benefits to be derived from efficient operation. Without going into the relative merits of the two cases, we should nevertheless urge that as long as total national income is inadequate to meet the desires of people as consumers, careful attention should be given to the effect of any legislation on the efficiency of production.

The Effects Are Both Temporary and Permanent.—The repercussions of the increasing substitution of machine power for man power are of both temporary and permanent nature. It is the difference between these two types of effects, perhaps, that leads to some confusion in thinking about them and to some inconsistency in political action concerning them. The temporary effect almost always includes a measure of unemployment and maladjustment of both physical and human resources. Moreover, the history of technological change is full of sharp and violent oscillations which have been—and remain—hard to predict. Consequently, the first social reaction is likely to express itself in an effort to prevent the change. The more permanent effect, however, is almost certain to be an increase in total income, which is, of course, what people in general earnestly desire. It seems, therefore, that a moderation of the suddenness of technological change may be desirable, but that the coming of the change should not be unduly delayed.

What We Hope and What We Fear

The National Resources Committee carefully studied the relationships between technology, labor income, and consumption. As a result of this study the Committee published the following recommendations.[5] While these recommendations were made in a specific year (1937) they are really almost timeless.

1. The reports herewith presented reveal the imminence of a few very important inventions that may soon be widely used with resultant social influences of significance. Since these inventions may deeply affect planning it is recommended that a series of studies be undertaken by the planning agencies herein recommended or by existing planning boards, with the aid of such natural and social scientists as may be needed, on the following inventions; the mechanical cotton picker, air conditioning equipment, plastics, the photoelectric cell, artificial cotton and woolen-like fibers made from cellulose, synthetic rubber, prefabricated houses, television, facsimile transmission, the automobile trailer, gasoline produced from coal, steepflight aircraft planes, and tray agriculture.

2. A special case of the influence of invention is technological unemployment. It is recommended that a joint committee be formed from the Department of Labor, the Department of Commerce, the Department of Agriculture, Bureau of Mines, Interstate Commerce Commission, Social Security Board, and the Works Progress Administration with such other cooperation as may be needed, for the purposes of keeping abreast with technological developments and ascertaining and noting the occupations and industries which are likely to be affected by imminent technological changes and the extent to which these inventions are likely to result in unemployment. It is recommended that such information be made available through the appropriate departments to the industry and labor likely to be affected.

3. In view of the findings regarding the importance of technology and applied science, it is recommended that the Federal government develop appropriate agencies for continuous study of them; and more specifically that there be set up in the respective departments, science committees with the definite function of investigating and reporting at regular periods on the progress and trends of science and invention and the possible and economic effects flowing therefrom as they affect the work of the departments and of the agencies to whom they render service. Copies of such reports should be supplied to the National Resources Board and it is recommended that in so far as is feasible they be made available to the various city, county, and state planning boards, and to the public.

4. Since the patent laws have considerable influence on the rate of technological progress, it is recommended that the whole system be reviewed by a group of social scientists and economists. This review, unlike others dealing

---

[5] National Resources Committee, *The Technological Trends and National Policy,* (Washington, D. C.: Government Printing Office, 1937), pp. viii and ix.

with specific reforms, technical operations, scientific aspects, or ethical implications should be concerned with the articulation of the patenting process with
the fundamental processes of human progress and the types of economic systems. From such basic relationships the better adaptation of the system to
changing conditions can be worked out in the necessary detail.

5. It is recommended that the Science Committee of the National Resources
Committee, with the cooperation of other scientists that may be needed, make
an investigation of the adequacy of the reporting of inventions and of discoveries in applied science and advise on the feasibility (a) of more coverage,
(b) of selecting those more socially significant, and (c) of assembling of such
data in some central location or locations.

6. The most important general conclusion to be drawn from these studies
is the continuing growth of the already high and rapidly developing technology
in the social structure of the Nation, and hence the hazard of any planning
that does not take this fact into consideration. This pervasive interrelationship
so clearly manifest throughout the pages of this report points to one great need,
namely, a permanent over-all planning board. Such a board is needed to give
breadth of consideration to the variety of factors which affect specific plans.
This board would take its place in the governmental pattern as coordinator
for the many special planning boards, of which there are now 47 state boards,
400 county boards, and 1,100 city boards. The Technology Committee, therefore, makes to the National Resources Committee, as a major recommendation
of this report, the creation of a National Resources Board, as recommended
by the President's Committee on Administrative Management in their report
of January 8, 1937.

It is interesting to note how many of the innovations mentioned
in the first paragraph of the Committee report already have developed. Others now are on the horizon, perhaps including industrial
uses of atomic energy and some commercial control of rainfall. The
progression from one list of new industries to another is a significant
part of economic dynamics.

The precise form of attack on the problems listed by the Committee in 1937 has not been followed, but progress has been made on
many of them. The copyright and patent laws, for example, have
been reviewed and modified in somewhat the manner suggested in
paragraph four. One of the most significant developments since the
Committee report has been the organization of the Committee for
Economic Development (CED). This is a voluntary organization
of businessmen that has been undertaking a self-analysis of private
business policy, to the end that greater stability may be reached
through wiser planning of private enterprise. This organization co-
operates with the federal departments of Labor and Commerce to
give business management more complete information upon which to
base policy decisions.

It is clear the National Resources Committee feared, when it made this report, that technological improvements would be developed and put into use in the future, as in the past, in such a way that the income of many individuals would be adversely affected for a time. The world has long sought for a method by which such changes could be made without serious interference with established employment and flow of income. The problem is by no means easy to solve. If new inventions and processes are held out of use, progress in production is retarded; if they are put into use without careful planning by all related industries, unemployment and other maladjustments are likely to follow. Certainly the suggestions of the National Resources Committee would provide a better basis for anticipating changes and for doing something about their effects before they occur.

Intelligent adjustment to changing industrial conditions can only be made when full information concerning developments is at hand. The question will be raised in some quarters as to who should collect and interpret the necessary information. Some would desire that all such things be undertaken by governmental agencies, while others would feel that business organizations, such as trade associations, are better fitted for such tasks. Perhaps the location of the agency is much less important than the job; the important thing would seem to be an increase in general knowledge so that the risks of business uncertainty may be reduced to a minimum.

The Committee for Economic Development recently published a pamphlet under the title "How To Raise Real Wages." In it are suggested ten particularly promising ways of increasing output, and hence real wages. These ten methods are:

1. Stabilize the growth of industry and avoid serious business recessions.
2. Reduce seasonal unemployment.
3. Improve the quality of business births and reduce the infant mortality among business concerns.
4. Reform the tax system to make risk-taking more attractive.
5. Stimulate more rapid replacement of equipment.
6. Increase the imports of the United States relative to its exports.
7. Provide more employment opportunities for older people.
8. Improve the incentives for efficiency among the rank and file employees.
9. Develop regular methods of drawing upon the knowledge and training of the labor force.
10. Abolish make-work rules and featherbedding.

Of course, opinion will differ as to whether these are the only or even the best ways in which to increase total production and hence real wages.   Even when there is agreement on that matter, it will not be easy to put these recommendations into effect.   It is encouraging, however, that an important group of businessmen has made such a series of recommendations.   This is especially significant since several of the suggestions appear to involve improvement in the position and the share in total income on the part of the rank and file of employees.   This kind of thinking among business leaders well may be a harbinger of better human relations and greater cooperation throughout American industry, with a resulting increase in consumption possibilities.

Project Questions

1. Can you think of any items of legislation in control of our economic life that appear to be inconsistent with each other? Discuss the inconsistencies as they affect us as consumers.   Do these legislative acts appear to increase or decrease economic efficiency?   How would you define the term *economic efficiency?*

2. Take the list of suggestions in the chapter section titled "Scientific Management Can Help," and discuss them with the manager of some industrial plant in your community.   Write a brief report of his opinion concerning these suggestions and particularly include his statement concerning the extent to which each suggestion is being used in his plant.

3. See what you can find out about the existence and operation of trade associations in your community.   These may be either associations of retailers or of manufacturers.   Write a brief report on what you find.

4. Pick any commodity that was introduced into our American economy sometime between 1890 and 1940, such as automobile tires, telephones, radios, and electric refrigerators.   Find out all you can about the changes in the manner in which it is made.   Include in your study the materials from which it is made, the scale of production and purchase, the change in design, and any other technical developments on which you can get information.

Chapter 16

INCREASING THE INDIVIDUAL'S SHARE IN NATIONAL INCOME

INTRODUCTION

We Want Our Share.—One of the oldest and most intense human conflicts is over the question of who shall have how much of total income. Jealousy is a strong emotion, producing results which often are unfortunate and occasionally are tragic. Each of us is inclined to be envious of others who can afford better clothes, drive a more expensive automobile, take longer vacations, or live in a larger house. In other words, we want to be able to live as conspicuously as anyone else. We tend to resent the high salaries paid to certain corporation presidents. When the firm for which we work has a year of high profits we feel that more should have come to us in wages and less to the "wealthy owners" (even though the owners in the particular case really may not be wealthy). Not only do we want a greater supply of goods and services in total, but even more particularly we want our personal supply increased both absolutely and relatively.

Three Ways to Get Our Share.—In the present workaday world, individuals may increase their personal purchasing power—and through it their consumption—in any of three ways or combination of the three, namely:

1. By increasing their output of goods or services (production in the narrow sense).
2. By increasing the desire of other people for the particular wares which they would exchange (advertising and sales promotion—including "selling" one's self).
3. By making their particular wares relatively scarce (restrictive programs of all sorts).

Each of these will be discussed in the following pages.

Individuals Are Not Always Free.—The decision to influence the value of goods or services in any of these ways may rest either with individuals (rugged individualism), with nonpolitical groups (such as corporations, trade unions, or consumer cooperatives), or with political groups (such as state or federal legislatures, soviet officials, or administrators of a national agricultural program). There is continuous quarrel among the advocates of different ways of making these decisions. For example, certain governmental authorities recently have proposed that Coney Island should be changed radically in the interest of the general public, to which *The New Yorker* has replied :

Reluctantly we have to oppose Commissioner Moses' plan to turn Rockaway and Coney Island into decent replicas of Jones Beach. It is inspiring to think of cleanliness and order and a sort of young preparatory-school morality descending on those infested sands ; on the other hand, there are unfortunately many perturbed and disreputable spirits to whom minatory young men in blue coats and duck trousers, and archery butts, and little tables under gaily striped umbrellas, will be forever matters of suspicion and hatred. These men and women love shooting galleries and bars with sawdust on the floor and the jungle beat of nickel piano. It is their theory of American liberty that the beaches belong to the people to desecrate as they please, and they do not like to be whistled at when their conduct exceeds what seems to them an arbitrary propriety. Mr. Moses, we think, falls into the error of supposing that everybody likes the same things he does—that the standards of beauty and pleasure are universal. This is arrogant. It is arrogant for any man to imagine that he can landscape the human heart.[1]

We are not concerned at present with the rights and wrongs of this particular controversy—with the question, that is, as to whether Coney Island is to remain the Coney Island of tradition at the behest of those who like it as it is, or is to be changed to something else at the behest of someone else. We are interested to point out, however, that whenever there is departure from the test of the market place in the decision of such questions, the measurement of production becomes hazy if not entirely impossible. Perhaps if groups of individuals could be prevented from combining to control and to restrict the supply of their particular economic good (and thus increase their purchasing power at the expense of their customers) the ability to command a price would be a true and democratic measure of production. It is in the belief that this would be the case that many persons have urged the continuation of the competitive system. Within that system, however, have grown up large organizations, such as corporations, holding companies, trade unions, and financial institutions,

---

[1] By permission. Copyright 1937, The New Yorker Magazine, Inc.

which frequently and almost inevitably resort to the use of the third method of "increasing production"; that is, they restrict output at times in the attempt to affect favorably their share in purchasing-power income even though the total social product is reduced thereby. As we go on to consider the possibilities of increasing income for the individual and for the commonwealth, we need to keep clearly in mind the distinction between an increase in production measured in terms of goods and services for people to consume, on the one hand, and an increase in production measured in terms of the purchasing power of certain groups obtained through a planned scarcity of the things they sell, on the other hand.

Getting Rich by Reducing Output

Cooperation Important for Results.—Individuals occasionally have products which are so unique that personal income can be increased by withholding part of the supply. Famous paintings, rare books, jewels, and some antique furniture are the most usual cases. Such things are relatively unimportant in our total economy although a few individuals make a good living from trading in them.

When individuals combine in corporations or cooperatives, however, frequently there is opportunity to increase income by withholding supply. If a product may be sold in either of two markets, in one of which the demand is inelastic while in the other it is elastic, the amount of the product offered in each of the markets may be controlled to the advantage of the seller. Milk, as was pointed out in Chapter 14, appears to be such a product; the demand for milk for whole-milk consumption is relatively inelastic, while the demand for milk to convert into butter and other dairy products is relatively elastic. As a result it sometimes is possible to restrict the portion sold as whole milk and thus to increase the seller's revenue.

Labor Unions and the State Can Play This Game.—This restrictive behavior is not limited to industrial management. Labor unions sometimes use the same tactics, either by setting standards for a day's work or through limiting the number of members and of apprentices who may work at a certain trade.

Government agencies in this country have used restrictive devices in the attempt to increase the total incomes of special groups under at least two sets of circumstances. In the first place, when the supply of certain farm products has been so large that the total value in the open market is forced down, government has provided ways to hold part of the supply off the market.[2]   As a result of the restriction of the supply actually available for purchase, the price has risen so that total farm revenue from that crop has been considered satisfactory.   An effort is then made, though it is not always successful, to dispose of the withheld supply at some later date when supply-demand conditions appear to justify its release.

In the second place, government agencies sometimes conduct business directly under conditions of local monopoly.   Municipal liquor stores and electric light systems are illustrations.   Sometimes these governmental monopolies set prices which yield substantial profits above costs, with which many of the other expenses of the government may be paid.[3]

Right or Wrong?—Here again we are not concerned with the rights and wrongs of these devices.   Rather, we want to make it clear that particular groups within the economy can, and sometimes do, obtain an increase in income through restriction of output, and that the restriction may be carried out under different auspices.   Whatever the net value to society in individual cases, it seems impossible that the general welfare can be improved through long-continued restrictions arbitrarily imposed on parts of the economy—except, of course, when the restrictions are limited to those products which by common consent are considered injurious.

MORE PERSONAL PRODUCTION

The Direct Approach.—The most direct way for a person to increase his income relative to that of others is for him to increase his personal production.   This one can do by harder work, better planned effort, or by working on things that have greater value in exchange.   When one is his own boss, working on his own enterprise, his own ability and energy are the things that limit his production, and as his production increases he gets the direct benefit in exchange for himself.   When, on the other hand, one works as an employee for someone else and is paid by the hour or month, the benefit of his increased production goes directly to his employer.   One advantage of piece-work payment is the chance it gives for the

---

[2] See Chapter 20 for further discussion of this point.

[3] Government action sometimes leads to a particular use of resources and distribution of income to individuals through means other than high prices or restrictions of output. For example, federal subsidies have been granted to the merchant marine, and the postal service has been permitted to operate with a deficit. These and similar activities of government are referred to again in Chapter 20.

individual worker to make more by working harder, but many lines of employment are not adapted to this method of payment. Consequently, the individual frequently can get no more pay than the rank and file with whom he works. To some extent this destroys the incentive for the individual to do anything more than the average of his group and one of the things constantly being sought is some form of wage incentive that is effective in causing the rank and file to increase their output.

Better Machinery Helps.—The use of more and better machinery has resulted in increased output generally, but the increase is more conspicuous in some industries than in others. The use of machinery has, in many cases, also increased the skill needed to operate it. In bookkeeping, for example, the installation and use of IBM machines and systems will reduce the number of bookkeepers needed, but will increase—or at least greatly change—the skills required by those still employed. The present-day operation of an American farm, as another example, requires individuals who are skilled in the use of electric power, tractors, and many complicated machines operated by power. The need for technical competence in farming is more fully recognized than it was a generation ago. At the turn of the century the faculty members in agricultural schools were considered by most farmers to be theoretical incompetents, but the great increase in the use of the services of county agents and other specialists is evidence of their changed point of view. The same thing is seen in one form or another throughout industry: the man with developed skills and trained intellect is preferred over others. If a choice must be made, the trained intellect is given preference, for the particular skill can be developed on the job more easily than the general intellect.

Correct Specialization Is Important.—It was pointed out in Chapter 5 that proper personal specialization will lead to greater production, and in Chapter 13 mention was made of a case in which it seemed evident that employers were aware of who were their less able employees and that these became unemployed early in the depression of the 1930's. Clearly this is ample evidence that wise choice of occupation and sound training for it will be steppingstones to larger personal income as well as to greater personal satisfaction in a job well done.

Coordinating Individuals With Their Jobs.—Much effort must be directed towards the coordination between economic opportunities, testing of the individual's abilities, and his training.[4] One major cause of labor turnover and individual maladjustment is the square peg in a round hole. Anything which reduces turnover and maladjustment by accurately fitting the worker's abilities to job requirements, fitting square pegs into square holes, is net social as well as individual gain. Moreover, to gain the fullest efficiency, individuals must take advantage of the opportunities that are offered for testing, training, and placement.

CLEARANCE THROUGH GOVERNMENT AGENCIES. In this connection the operation of the clearance system of government placement agencies is especially important. All too often workers and jobs have been in different places. To meet this situation the development of an adequate yet simple method of clearance has been an important contribution of the Federal Employment Service.

Another governmental service that is of great assistance in this connection is the collection and prompt dissemination of detailed information on employment and unemployment by regions and specific industries. This information is sent out by press releases and the radio in much the same way as crop, market, and weather reports are now handled. This has made possible more intelligent decisions on the part both of employers and of employees.

SEASONALITY IS HARD TO DEAL WITH. Not the least important consideration concerning the desirability of particular jobs is their relative regularity or seasonality. In a recent survey of industry in Minneapolis, St. Paul, and Duluth it was found that 62 per cent of all employees were in seasonal industries. The amplitude of fluctuations [5] in the seasonal firms was 19 per cent in Minneapolis, 32 per cent in St. Paul, and 99 per cent in Duluth. Since different industries are affected in different seasons, a proportion of the working population is idle throughout the entire year. It may be, for example, that the dock workers in Duluth are idle during the winter months, while the lumber workers are actively engaged in timber cutting. The dock

---

[4] In this section the authors have drawn illustrations liberally from studies made in Minnesota. While these studies are dated and were made in a single state, their implications are believed to be of such wide application that their use in a general text seems fully justified. Moreover, this happens to be the region which we know best.

[5] The difference between the number employed in the maximum and the minimum months divided by the number employed in the minimum month gives the amplitude expressed as a percentage. The amplitude of 99 per cent found in Duluth shows that employment in the maximum month was almost double that in the minimum month.

workers and the lumbermen generally, however, are different individuals. Thus each group has only a part of a year's work although the total employment figures for the city may be fairly constant. Each industry tends to maintain a group of workers sufficient to carry it through the peak season, which creates a sort of floating reserve that is, in fact, a surplus of labor. This is one of the possible wastes of manpower referred to in Chapter 15. The wages paid in the seasonal industries are frequently insufficient to support a family throughout the year; consequently, the community must provide some form of relief during the off season. The existence of seasonal unemployment reduces the total volume of production that might be realized and thus limits our total capacity to consume as well as curtails the consumption of the families employed in the seasonal industries.

There are two ways in which seasonal unemployment may be reduced:

1. By stabilizing employment within each individual firm.
2. By shifting workers between firms with different seasonal peaks.

There are many cases in which stabilization by individual firms is impossible. Lake shipping, lumbering, harvesting, and canning, are illustrations. The habit consumers have of greatly increasing their purchases in some lines before and during the Christmas holidays makes it impossible for retailers to maintain a stable force throughout the year. Some manufacturers, perhaps, can do more than they have in evening employment through manufacturing for stock during dull sales seasons, but to do so increases their market risks.

An effective program of dovetailing employment requires:

1. A centralized system of employment exchanges.
2. A thorough job analysis in all seasonal industries.
3. A basic training program designed to enable workers to shift successfully from one firm or industry to another.

The Employment Stabilization Research Institute made some progress in these matters in Minnesota and similar work has been done elsewhere.

Testing and Training Are Essentials. An analysis of the training needs of adult workers was undertaken from the extensive case records of employed and unemployed individuals studied in the Occupational Analysis Clinic conducted at the University of Minnesota by the Employment Stabilization Research Institute. While this study referred mainly to depression conditions, its results have a bearing on seasonal unemployment as well. It was found that:

A surprisingly small number of individuals were found to be in need of retraining. This finding is in harmony with the fact that technological change plays a far less important role in causing unemployment during a depression than popular writers have claimed. Nevertheless a considerable number of the unemployed were judged to be in need of more training. Of a total of 1,186 adult workers not occupationally adjusted, the clinic staff recommended more training for 501 and retraining for only 23. Of the men who were advised to take more training, 169 were directed toward professional and business pursuits such as drafting, reporting, engineering, teaching; 126 were directed toward clerical types of work and 124 toward the skilled trades. Of the women, 51 were directed toward clerical work, 44 toward professional and business types of work, and only 10 toward skilled work (beauty parlor work and dressmaking).

The clinic aided many of the unemployed to undertake some form of training in an existing training agency. Careful records were kept regarding the training of 189 of the persons. In 126 cases the training was in harmony with the recommendations of the clinic staff, but in 63 cases the unemployed persons insisted on taking training that was not in harmony with the recommendations of the technical staff. An important difference between these two groups in the degree of success in the training courses was disclosed by the follow-up study. *More than three fourths of those who took the training recommended were successful and fewer than 6 per cent were unsuccessful. Of those who took a training course not recommended two thirds were unsuccessful in their courses and fewer than 5 per cent were successful.*[6]

While these findings refer directly to a particular area and time, they illustrate situations that are almost universal.

OCCUPATIONAL DIAGNOSIS IS AN IMPERFECT ART. In spite of these favorable results it must be admitted that occupational diagnosis is still an imperfect art. The cooperation of individuals and of labor groups with the best local agencies for making such diagnosis would seem to offer splendid opportunity for lessening both industrial and individual maladjustment. It is to be hoped, therefore, that research in this field will be continued and that there will gradually come into being a series of competently staffed employment agencies equipped to test, diagnose, and recommend lines of action for a large number of unemployed or maladjusted individuals. If the record of the occupational clinic at the University of Minnesota could be repeated throughout the country, our national income, as well as that of the particular individuals directly concerned, would be greatly increased.

---

[6] D. G. Paterson, J. G. Darley, and R. M. Elliott, *Men, Women, and Jobs* (Minneapolis: University of Minnesota Press, 1936), pp. 50-51.

The Place of Formal Education.—Wise choice of occupation and efficient performance after the choice are both dependent in considerable measure upon the educational regime through which a person passes. Basically, one principle of public education always has been to prepare an individual to perform better the many tasks set by the scale of consumption of society. The educational system should be geared, therefore, to the needs and abilities of individual students in their efforts to find their most useful place in society. There is much evidence, unfortunately, that our educational system is not so geared at present.

Since it is true that the workaday world requires the performance of many tasks, and that these tasks involve the use of different skills, techniques, and abilities, it follows that the ideal educational system should give different persons different training about in proportion to society's demand for the various occupations. Not everyone need go to a classical high school and still fewer have any occupational reason for attending a liberal arts college.[7] Perhaps, however, training in the mechanical arts, in homemaking, in taste and judgment in consumption, could be substituted, in part, for the present formal curriculum to the advantage both of the individual directly concerned and of society in general. In fact, of course, there have been important developments in this direction, but the opportunities are by no means fully met.

An indication of the lack of a wise attitude towards the desirability of certain types of education is found in a survey made by the Testing Bureau of the University of Minnesota. In this survey the occupational choices of high school senior boys and girls were tabulated for a five-year period in the early 1930's. About 40 per cent of the boys indicated a choice in the professions of medicine, engineering, law, and scientific research. The choices of the girls were equally centralized on teaching, commercial occupations, and nursing. Obviously, any such high proportion of engineers, doctors, and lawyers would far exceed society's demand for these types of services. It is equally true, although perhaps not so obvious, that far less than 40 per cent of high school senior boys have the peculiar combination of interests and abilities required for satisfactory performance in these professions.

If formal education is to serve its greatest usefulness with respect to occupational choice and performance, then parents and others responsible for children may need to take a somewhat different view of

---

[7] The authors do not intend to quarrel with those educational experts who advocate general education for citizenship at the college level to the extent that the commonwealth can afford and will support it.

its possibilities and its limitations.   In place of the present concept of identical opportunity for every student there might be substituted the concept of equally adequate opportunity for training in the field for which the individual is fitted, whether that field be the highest professional endeavor or the common run of workaday jobs of the world. The testing, advising, and guiding of students throughout their school career in accord with their abilities and accomplishments, on the one hand, and with the economic opportunities for employment, on the other, might well become an integral part of the educational system.[8]

The exact extent of increase of production and of capacity to consume that would follow wiser regional and individual specialization cannot be determined.   Probably not even an intelligent estimate can be made.   It seems perfectly clear, however, just from observations of the inefficiencies that surround us, that the opportunities for improvement in these directions are enormous.   These opportunities present one of the enticing new frontiers still open to wise and courageous leadership.

Making People Want What We Have

Sales Promotion Again.—One of the most amazing aspects of American business, and certainly the most dynamic, is the manner in which we persuade each other to buy our wares.[9]   The $5 billion spent annually on advertising causes many of us to spend money in ways that would not have occurred to us otherwise.   The slogan "with the sharpest edges ever honed" convinces many of us that Gillette Blue Blades are better than others.   As a result, the income of the Gillette Company is increased.

At times it seems as though we are led by our eyes and ears to do many things whether we want to or not.   Persons with things to sell become almost tyrannical in their bombardment of consumers with reasons for buying very specific merchandise.   The purpose of the bombardment, of course, is to make consumers think so well of the goods that sales may be made at prices yielding a good income to

---

[8] Perhaps it may be pointed out, in passing, that until governmental agencies more clearly define the field and more nearly solve the problems connected with public education—with which government long has been concerned—there is arrogance in the suggestion that new governmental agencies undertake new and important fields of endeavor on the assumption that such agencies can do the job better than can private individuals. The social progress that might be expected from sound and intelligent bureaucratic leadership in the fields of education and training is very great, but as yet the opportunities in the field have been only imperfectly realized.

[9] This matter of sales promotion was discussed in Chapter 14 but here we take another look at it for a different purpose and with somewhat different perspective.

the sellers. Successful sales promotion increases one's share of the total income.

Trivialities Sometimes Count.—One of the early advertising experts, Mr. Claude Hopkins, tells of many interesting instances that illustrate some of the ways in which consumers are persuaded to buy. The case of Palmolive shaving cream will serve as an example.[10]

> I sent out some research men to interview men by the hundreds. I asked them what they most desired in a shaving cream. Then I took those answers to V. C. Cassidy, chief chemist. I said: "These are the factors men want. They may get them in other shaving creams, but nobody yet has told them. Give me actual data on these results as applied to Palmolive shaving cream."
> Men wanted abundant lather. Cassidy proved that Palmolive multiplied itself 250 times. Men wanted quick action. The Palmolive chemists proved by tests that within one minute the beard absorbed 15 per cent of water, and that made the hairs wax-like for cutting. Men wanted enduring lather. Chemists proved that Palmolive maintained its creaminess for ten minutes on the face. . . . So we claimed for Palmolive, and rightly, bubbles that meet the requirements. Probably other shaving creams could meet the specifications. I have no idea that one man far excels some others in this line. But we were the first to give figures on results. . . . I am told that in 18 months Palmolive shaving cream dominated the field it entered.

In other words, many men were persuaded to change their brand of shaving cream for no better reason than that they had been told certain things about the new brand, things which probably were equally true of the brands they had been using. To the extent that this example is typical it appears that as consumers we cannot qualify as expert buyers, but merely as chance purchasers who are swayed by the most vivid or the most recent claims of superiority. This example from the experiences of Claude Hopkins is a generation old, but the same forces of persuasion are still in use.

> In a long string of newspapers all over the United States last fortnight the American Tobacco Company started a new campaign, . . . using the theme they adopted last fall—testimonials from tobacco experts, auctioneers, inspectors, etc., that they all smoked Lucky Strikes.
> In almost the same list of newspapers was a new series the R. J. Reynolds Tobacco Company was running . . . for Camels. Especially newsworthy for its copy theme, the Camel campaign played up a stable of tobacco planters . . . who asserted that each year the Reynolds people paid them the highest prices for the best part of their harvests, that they all smoked Camels.[11]

---

[10] Claude C. Hopkins, *My Life in Advertising* (New York: Harper & Bros., 1927), pp. 140-41.
[11] *Tide of Advertising and Marketing*, January 15, 1938, p. 13.

In 1950, these two companies still were paying for the use of these same nearly identical testimonials.   In that year Camels led the parade of cigarette sales with 97½ billion and Lucky Strikes were second with about 86 billion.[12] Apparently the managers of these companies are convinced that the measures they have adopted to encourage consumption of their particular brands are successful and if we are to judge by total sales, they appear to be right.   And so we must conclude that most of us fail to see anything odd or out of the way in the competing claims of superiority made by the two producers; if we take the testimony of the two groups of "experts" we must conclude that there are no important differences between the two brands, and yet many of us are persuaded by the testimony of these "experts" to buy one brand in preference to the other.

Successful Advertising Controls Dollars.—While it is true that as consumers we "vote with our dollars," it appears to be equally true that we are persuaded to "keep in office" some producers, not entirely because of the excellence of their products but because of the excellence of their propaganda.   If, in our capacity as our own purchasing agents, we could become more expert and hardboiled, we might make our meager incomes furnish us with a much larger total of consumption satisfactions.   On the other hand, even though we may be persuaded through sales promotion to do some silly things, on the whole we are led or cajoled towards living fuller lives.   As a result, the total national income, as we measure it, is increased.   And the successful advertisers increase their share of the larger total.

Our Share Through Bargaining

Wages Result from Bargaining.—Wage disputes are so common nowadays that everyone realizes they occur. In simple terms they are, of course, attempts on the part of organized labor to get a larger share of total income.   For the past hundred years or more wages generally have been determined much as have other prices, as a result of the interplay of supply and demand.   Persons seeking work have tended to take the highest-paid job for which they could qualify. Employers have paid no more than necessary to attract the number and quality of employees they wanted.   An upper limit to wages is set by the value of the product resulting from the labor.   Wages crystallize, therefore, somewhere between the upper limit of the value of product and lower limit of the next-best opportunity open to workers, often as the result of direct bargaining.

---

[12] *Business Week,* December 30, 1950, p. 53.

In this country, the willingness of individuals to shift from one employment to another, plus the opportunity to do so, have tended to keep the alternative opportunities somewhat similar in attractiveness and monetary reward. If one occupation offered much better wages than others, workers would desert the lower-paid jobs and flock towards the higher-paid ones. These changes in supply tend to equalize wage opportunities.

The pull of high wages was illustrated, for example, by the migration of many men and women from all over the country to the airplane and shipbuilding industries on the Pacific Coast during World War II. The earlier migration of immigrants from Europe to America, which has been such a conspicuous feature of our history, resulted in large part from the high wages said to be available here. As already pointed out, nowhere else in the world can one buy so much with the money income from so short a period of work.

Organized Labor Has an Influence.—Organized labor has exerted its influence with much success to keep labor's share of income high. Where peaceful bargaining has not brought about that result, strikes sometimes have been successful. At times industrial leaders have realized that sales of their products depended upon high purchasing power among the rank and file. The late Henry Ford early came to that conclusion and set the pace with his $5-day. (That now seems small, but when first paid by the Ford Motor Company it was considered almost revolutionary.)

The combined pressure of mobility, labor organization, and enlightened self-interest on the part of employers has resulted in a large share of total value going directly to personal service; as already pointed out, salaries, wages, and compensation of those who work for themselves amount to 75 or 80 per cent of national income. If the percentage went much higher there would be left little incentive to invest in capital plant and our steady increase in the amount of capital for labor to use might suffer seriously.

Labor Is Less Fortunate in Other Lands.—Labor is not so fortunate in all parts of the world. In Japan during the 1930's, for example, wage rates in most manufacturing industries were low and were a smaller part of total value produced than they are here. This was due in no small part to the fact that if individuals did not work in manufacturing, their alternative was in overcrowded agriculture. In this alternative the value of their product was very small. Consequently, they could be attracted into factory work with a wage considerably less than their value to their employer. This tended to keep the scale of living of the industrial workers low. Incidentally, it permitted Japanese manufacturers to set prices of their exports somewhat below those in other countries. One of the postwar developments in Japan has been that labor is encouraged to organize, so that pressure may be exerted toward raising wages to a level as high as the value of product will permit.

Conclusion.—No single individual can do much to increase his share of the total value of the product on which he works. Group effort usually is required if this is to be accomplished. In this country recent opinion seems to be that group pressure exerted by labor unions on behalf of members can become too severe. The Taft-Hartley labor law was passed in the attempt to effect a balance between labor and capital, with government as referee. The law is not perfect and will be modified, but the very fact that it has lasted as long as it has is evidence that some regulating authority is essential.

On the whole, the chances for a person to make a reasonably good living in this country are excellent. Personal ambition, intelligence, and diligent effort are the ingredients. The legal and institutional framework within which the individual may work is good. When the individual makes more products, designs them more nearly to the public taste, presents them persuasively to the public, stands ready to ride with the tide of opportunity, and will bargain wisely with others, he will achieve a pretty satisfactory scale of living.

PROJECT QUESTIONS

1. Write a brief essay on the comparative merits, from the standpoint of both the individual and society, of undertaking to increase one's personal income through restriction of output on the one hand and through sales promotion on the other hand.

2. Interview managers of factories in your area. Find out how much and what they produce for local consumption.

3. What changes in copyright and patent laws have been made since 1940? How important are these changes?

4. Go to your library and locate as many publications of CED as you can. Are any of them of specific help to the consumer?

5. Several current publications, including *Business Week, McCall's, Good Housekeeping,* and *Science Newsletter,* publish regularly lists of new products or commodities which have just been put on the market or are about to be offered. Prepare a list of such commodities and discuss the effect you believe their manufacture and marketing will have on employment and consumption.

Chapter 17

TOWARD MORE INTELLIGENT USE OF
PERSONAL INCOME

The Rationale of Consumers' Choices

Emotional and Rational Buying Motives.—The psychology of consumer purchasing may be classified in many ways. One interesting and useful division is into "rational" and "emotional" responses to the various stimuli that urge us to buy. Emotional buying motives include such things as emulation, satisfaction of appetites, pride in personal appearance, securing of pleasure or comfort. Rational buying motives, in contrast, are aroused by such appeals to reason as economy in purchase or use, durability, dependability, and so on. Emotional buying is likely to be done or at least to be modified on the spur of the moment as the direct result of some suggestion or stimulus, while rational buying is likely to occur only after reflection and a weighing of advantages against disadvantages. In rational buying the individual is likely to consider, for example, what he must go without in case he makes the particular purchase under consideration. In emotional buying, on the other hand, one is more likely to "act in haste and repent at leisure."

Advertising of consumer goods uses both emotional and rational appeals with some emphasis on the former. Apparently people with things to sell to the ultimate consumer consider it profitable to appeal to the emotions of their prospective buyers. Studies aimed at discovering the "why" in buying have found that people tend to act first and then justify their choice afterwards. A person feels an impulse to make a purchase and without stopping to think, he buys the article. Only afterwards does he ask himself why he behaved as he did.[1] It seems clear that if consumers wish to resist the bombardments of salesmanship, they must "think" as well as "feel" when they prepare to buy.

Women Are the Chief Family Purchasing Agents.—In our complex system of division of tasks, consumer purchasing has fallen

---

[1] Robert N. McMurry, "Finding the Why in Buying," *Management Review,* April, 1936.

largely to the women. While men earn about 80 per cent of the money income in the United States, women either do or greatly influence from 60 per cent to 70 per cent of the family purchasing. Thus, in a discussion of the way consumers go about buying and the forces which motivate and influence their choices, it is important to examine the characteristics of women which affect buying patterns. Many of these characteristics are not unique to women; rather, they are characteristics of the human being. Men might do the family shopping in much the same manner. Nevertheless, women as the chief family purchasing agents exhibit certain tendencies which account, in part, for the high costs of marketing. One way to reduce the price of some articles of merchandise, and thus to stretch family income, is to modify or control these characteristics.

Buyers Want Economy.—In the first place, women are concerned with economy in their buying; they insist on quality at a price. This causes them to shop among many stores, to request a large range of styles, colors, materials, and prices among which to choose. Whenever stock in stores becomes low, women shoppers are inclined not to buy at all except at greatly reduced prices, regardless of the intrinsic quality of the goods still in stock. This buying habit leads to heavy markdowns at the end of each season, which the merchant can grant without impairing his business only if he has obtained a large margin above cost on his earlier sales. It also leads to heavy inventories which are expensive to carry, and to a high cost of clerical help in showing the goods and in keeping the stock in order. If a way could be found to reduce the amount of shopping, the cost of operating retail stores could be reduced and the price of consumer goods could be lowered accordingly. Moreover, because of their concern for economy, it is hard for most women to resist a "bargain," even though they may have no immediate or specific use for the particular commodity. A curbing of the practice of "picking up bargains" might result in fuller consumption programs for many families without any change in their money income.

Women Buy by Sight, Touch, and Smell.—In the second place, women have a very acute sensory development. As a result, things must look, feel, and smell "right" if women are to purchase them. As an illustration we may cite the findings of a psychologist who asked two hundred and fifty housewives to pick the one of best quality out of four pairs of silk stockings which were identical except that three of them were faintly perfumed. The perfume was so faint that it was not consciously recognized as a reason for choice by any of the women. Since the stockings were identical, each pair should have received the same number of votes as being the best quality unless the scent played a part in subconsciously influencing the choices. The findings, which are summarized in Table 46, show that scent apparently did play an important part and that some scents are more influential than others.[2]

TABLE 46

EFFECT OF PERFUMERY ON CHOICE OF HOSIERY

Scent	Per Cent Judged to be Best Quality
"Natural"	8
Sachet	18
Fruity	24
Narcissus	50

Thus it appears that women permit the acuteness of their senses to guide their choices even when the particular sensory impression is not directly connected with the use or with any important characteristic of the merchandise. Perhaps men would have reacted in the same way to the same stimulation, but the psychologist who performed this particular experiment doubted that they would. The extent to which merchants and manufacturers have taken advantage of their women customers and have raised the prices of their goods as the result of arousing an immaterial sensory reaction is not clear, but the illustration just given may serve to put shoppers on their guard.

Buyers Are Ambitious and Sensitive.—In the third place, women are generally both ambitious and sensitive. These characteristics account in considerable measure for their continuous attempts to "keep up with the Joneses." If their dresses are not in the latest color and style they feel that other women will talk about them behind their backs. If they do not have some pieces of furniture in the newest mode, or if their car is not of the latest model, they are inclined to be uncomfortable or even jealous. Manufacturers and merchants have long realized this tendency and have flashed before their women customers constantly changing styles in many lines of consumer goods. This has resulted in crowded attics and in other evidences of goods discarded when still useful. Also, people—and especially women—

---

[2] Donald A. Laird, *What Makes People Buy* (New York: McGraw-Hill Publishing Co., 1935), p. 29.

are interested in change, per se; they become bored at seeing or doing the same things. Consequently it is not clear how much of the purchase of new styles is due to caring about what others will say or think, how much is due to boredom with the old, and how much is due to a real appreciation of the superior merits of the new.

Basic Changes Affect Buying Habits.—Complicating this already complex situation are the basic changes in our living. For example, a study of retail purchases of household fabrics during the five years beginning in 1929 showed the effect of economic and other conditions. The general trend was away from silk, wool, linen, and rayon fibers to cotton, mainly because consumers were looking for cheaper goods because they had less money to spend, but also to the increased variety and beauty of cotton fabrics. Furthermore, the popular demand for oilcloth which developed during this time was no doubt due to the fact that it is easier to keep clean and is cheaper and more colorful than many other fabric substitutes.[3] The question of what determines style change and the resultant effect on demand is similar to the unanswerable question of which comes first, the chicken or the egg. The reader is referred to the discussion in Chapter 9 of the factors which affect style change. These factors are basic and powerful, causing changes which are constantly reflected in the type and style of almost all things we buy, and intensify the effect of the capriciousness of the average buyer. There is not much that we as individuals can do, even if we wanted to, about these basic factors themselves. But if we could become less emotional in our buying, less sensitive and less easily bored, we could certainly reduce the influence of some of the factors, if not of all, on what and how we buy and achieve considerably more satisfaction in the expenditure of our personal money income.

Buymanship Can Be Improved.—Of course, carelessness in buying is limited neither to women nor to the particular characteristics we have mentioned. Perhaps, as we stated above, it is more in evidence with women than with men merely because they do a major part of all consumer buying, which is notoriously impulsive and whimsical, while men do a majority of industrial buying, which is more nearly rational and objective. In any case, however, a more careful selection of merchandise on the basis of its ability to satisfy specific wants unquestionably would increase the real income of many

---

[3] Henrietta M. Thompson and Ada C. Dowling, "Trends in Consumer Buying of Household Fabrics," *Journal of Home Economics,* June, 1935, p. 364.

families. Moreover, many women—although by no means all—have spare time that they might use to their own advantage and that of their families in becoming more expert as purchasing agents. To become truly expert in this field would require close attention to the ways in which members of a family want to obtain their satisfactions, on the one hand, and to the want-satisfying qualities of specific goods, on the other. It is a recognized fact that this is no simple task; its proper performance would require continuing adult training of a high order. But there is room for a vast amount of improvement in buymanship.

STANDARDIZATION AND PROFESSIONAL BUYERS. Other escapes from the bombardment of salesmanship might be found either in the standardization of merchandise or in the use of professional buyers. In connection with the first of these possibilities it seems certain that we do not want complete standardization of consumer goods in the sense of regimentation; we do not want, that is, everyone to wear uniforms, or to eat the same sequence of meals, or to drive exactly the same car. We might, on the other hand, welcome standardization in the sense of a guarantee of certain specific qualities attaching to every item of merchandise. The present status of standards for consumer goods and the possibility of further development of such standards are discussed later.

Professional buyers for a community already exist in a sense, for retailers maintain that they perform exactly that function. And they do, to a degree. One difficulty with our present system of retailing, however, is that the urge for profits leads to a certain advantage being taken of the ignorance of consumers; perhaps we should better say an *uncertain* advantage, for no one knows how much there is of misrepresentation and appeal to gullibility in the retail trade. Consumer ignorance is probably outstanding concerning the *quality* of things bought, and the so-called "expert buyers"—the retailers—give very little assistance. For example, at one time the New York Better Business Bureau assembled 90 suits and overcoats, removing all identifying labels and tags. They were then appraised by a large number of manufacturers and buyers from retail stores. The prices estimated by these experts, who could be expected to know much more about quality than the average consumer, ranged from 4 per cent below the quoted retail price to 40 per cent above.[4] Here indeed is a situation

---

[4] H. H. Shively, *The Nature of Unfair Methods of Competition in the Retail Field*, Ohio State University Studies, Bureau of Business Research Monographs, No. 10, February 1928, p. 29.

where the consumer needs help both by more realistic pricing and by better-trained merchandisers, particularly in the retail field. Perhaps retailers do not take full advantage of the ignorance of the consumer, but there is enough of this sort of thing done to lead some persons to suggest that consumers should combine and hire their own professional experts to test, recommend, or even to purchase goods for them.

CONSUMER COOPERATIVES. Consumer cooperative societies are one logical way, perhaps, through which consumers might get the services of better and more disinterested experts to select the retail stocks of merchandise. The use of such organizations to perform the retailing tasks would benefit consumers and enlarge their real incomes, provided they employed more disinterested and/or more competent buyers and salespersons than do the present retailers. (Consumer cooperatives will be discussed in some detail in Chapter 18.)

In this connection it is interesting to note that many retail stores long have conducted training courses for their employees, and that some of them have cooperated with universities in the attempt to improve the service offered to customers. Moreover, the government has made available, through the provisions of the George Dean Act, vocational training in the field of marketing as an extension of public education. This training is available both to young people who are still in the regular public school system and to persons already employed in the field of marketing. Perhaps this new emphasis on training will be a direct aid to consumers by supplying more expert advice in stores; at least, it may set a standard for employees that must be improved by any new form of retailing if consumers are to be benefited.

Even though consumer cooperative societies or some other form of organization could furnish better judgment in the selection and greater honesty in the representation of merchandise, it is not certain that the real income of the masses of people would increase more rapidly than under the present system of retailing. This is because, as someone has truly said, "the progress of civilization consists primarily in the multiplication of human wants. If you want a stagnant civilization you have only to destroy the influences that cause these wants to multiply." And intensive salesmanship in the effort to make individual profits for the seller certainly has been a strong force in the multiplication of human wants. Remove it, and the result is not certain. Perhaps consumer cooperatives can *lead* people to better living more effectively than the profit-seeking retailers can *drive* them. The results of such a movement, however, will depend in large measure upon the type of people to whom specific jobs in retailing are given. Consequently, if consumer cooperative societies should become common, the selection of personnel would be the matter of first concern to the consumer rather than, as at present, the selection of goods.

THE RETAILER CAN BE MORE HELPFUL. There is another way in which many persons feel that the present retailers give inadequate service. Consumers generally are not well informed concerning the quality of competing brands of merchandise, and it is felt that retailers sometimes mislead consumers rather than inform them correctly about quality. In the first place, many goods are so complex that the ordinary person does not even know what criteria to use in judging quality. Hosiery, for example, may be either sheer or durable. A particular retailer may emphasize the sheerness of hosiery without informing the prospective buyers of its lack of durability. Perhaps the consumers' own representatives in a consumer cooperative society may advise consumers more completely about the many different characteristics of their goods.

Some of the present retail stores have recognized the possibility of gaining and holding the good will of their customers by giving full information concerning goods. Several of these have established their own Bureau of Standards which in cooperation with the publicity or advertising department of the store issues a large amount of factual information on all sorts of merchandise. Some of the material is broadcast by radio, some is distributed to a wide mailing list in mimeograph form.

There are other cases of the same sort of effort to give sound buying information to consumers. As one other illustration, a recent book entitled *Food Buying Today* gives a great deal of information concerning the things to look for in purchasing food commodities. It undertakes to answer such questions as the following: What are "milk-fed" chickens? Is it to the advantage of the consumer to buy large-sized or small-sized prunes? What is the difference between canned tuna labeled "white meat" and tuna labeled "light meat"? Why are some shrimps canned in brine and some canned dry? How do cold storage eggs compare with fresh eggs? These are samples of the many questions asked and answered. The use of such materials as these, and others which will be discussed in Chapters 18 and 19, may well make the individual much more competent in his personal buying.

OTHER WAYS TO IMPROVE BUYING EFFICIENCY. There are still other ways in which individual consumers can improve the efficiency of their purchasing without waiting for any fundamental change in marketing institutions. To a growing extent, for example, we buy in very small quantities and this practice raises the cost of retail service. We insist on elaborate store furnishings, on attractive packages, on liberal return-goods privileges, on free delivery, and on delayed payment. Each of these elements adds something to the price we pay for goods.[5]

If a customer orders a 2-pound paper bag of sugar delivered and charged, the retailing costs are almost as much as though the order had been for a 100-pound sack. Consequently, as a percentage of the unit price, these costs on small-unit purchases are very much more than on large units, and the total costs of retailing 100 pounds of sugar in 2-pound lots is almost fifty times as great as in the single sale of a full sack. Perhaps this is an extreme case, but every merchant performs many transactions that approach it in wastefulness.

As another illustration, when a woman phones a department store that she wants to return some merchandise sent out previously on approval, at least a dozen entries must be made in the store's records. These entries include a pickup order issued to the delivery department, a change in the customer's charge account, an adjustment of the clerk's sales record and the inventory record of the department. Moreover, the commodity requires considerable rehandling, including the pickup itself, return of the article to the department, frequently remarking, and occasionally cleaning or repairing. Each of these things requires time and costs money. The total of the costs so incurred by a store is included, of course, in the total of prices charged for the merchandise that stays sold. If more accurate original selections could be made, the prices of goods could be lowered in accordance with the lessening of cost, and consumers' real income could thus be increased.

The savings that are possible to consumers through attention to details of the sort just illustrated appear to be very large in total. However, each individual case involves a balancing of money cost that might be saved against the trouble of buying in a different way.

---

[5] See the discussion of this point in Chapter 7.

PLANNED SPENDING

Why Plan What We Spend?—Intelligence in the use of money income may be greatly increased if individuals plan their consumption programs and allot certain limited amounts to specific expenditures. A plan made out in advance to regulate or control the distribution of expenditures among the many family uses is known as a budget. There is no magic in budgeting. A budget is not a substitute for money; it merely provides an opportunity for a more intelligent use of personal income. A well-planned budget helps the individual or family to get greater satisfaction from income received than might otherwise be possible. Chapter 10 contains a considerable discussion of family expenditures under differing conditions. These observations and experiences make it possible to set up approximate or "typical" budgets of expenditures for families under widely different conditions of income, location, age, and so on. Each family may want some personal adjustment in its budget because of some special circumstances, but general experience provides a useful starting point.

How to Set Up a Budget.—One very simple procedure in the use of budgets might be merely to have the weekly or monthly pay check converted into cash and then place the amounts previously determined into separate envelopes marked "food," "clothing," "housekeeping," and so on. This is a system that might be used by families with low incomes and without a checking account in a bank. Small balances in any of the envelopes at the end of a payroll period could be used for larger purchases in the next period, or they could be transferred either to a savings account or to one of the other envelopes. "Borrowing" between envelopes might be carried out occasionally, with memoranda of the transaction entered on the envelopes. A few months' use of this system should be sufficient to determine whether 40 per cent or 50 per cent of the income was needed for food; whether 20 per cent was used for rent; whether 10 per cent or 20 per cent could be used for clothing, and so on. Then the amount in each envelope would make the housewife and other members of the family consider each item in each general line of expenditure in the light of the total allowance for that line.

When the income is larger and checking accounts are used, some form of simple bookkeeping is necessary for a controlled family budget. There are numerous household account books that can be purchased at low price or obtained free at banks, credit unions, or government agencies. Most of these are easy to use. Generally they provide separate columns for each major division of the household budget in which expenditures may be entered daily.

Perhaps the principal economic problem of wise use of income from the individual or family point of view is the proper administration of income; that is, the proper distribution or budgeting of the income among its general uses. Budget-making appears to be especially helpful for a new family without experience to guide its expenditures, or for a family which moves to a new place, or for a family having had an appreciable increase or decrease in income. A plan of expenditures, or budget, does not necessarily have to be written although most people find it easier to follow a written than a mental guide.

Examples of Budget Forms.—There is no "right" or "wrong" budget. One can be made only roughly for, as we have pointed out earlier, the classification of items in a budget as well as the distribution of expenditure among those items necessarily varies with the precise situation in which the individual or family finds itself. There are, however, suggested classifications which may be used from which the individual or family may develop his or its particular budget. Figures 32 to 34 present sample budget classifications and forms. These are not suggested as the most desirable for any particular case, but as examples of forms that have been found useful by others.

Published Budgets Must Be Adjusted to the Individual's Needs.—From time to time, government agencies, educational institutions, and private agencies publish budgets which can be used as a yardstick or tool with which to measure present-day differences in living and to assist the individual or family in the preparation of individual budgets. The Bureau of Labor Statistics, for example, published in 1947 after a three-year study a budget which was "the estimated dollar cost required to maintain the family at a level of adequate living—to satisfy prevailing standards of what is necessary for health, efficiency, the nurture of children, social participation, and the maintenance of self-respect and the respect of others." It was set up to measure a modest but adequate standard of living. It purports to be a scientific measure of adequate living for various-size families using standards established by the American Public Health Association for housing, by the National Research Council for food, and by the Department of Labor, assisted by the Department of Agriculture and the Social Security Board, for other groups of expenditures.

THE WANAMAKER BUDGET GUIDE

Annual Income $ . . . .   Income Tax $ . . . .   Net Income $ . . . .

Estimated Expenditures

	Annual	*Monthly*	*Weekly*		*Annual*	*Monthly*	*Weekly*
SHELTER				MAINTENANCE, *Cont.*			
Rent or taxes				Gas			
Water				Electricity			
Insurance *				Telephone			
Repairs				Service			
Commutation				Laundry			
FOOD				Fees			
Milk				Insurance ‡			
Ice				Supplies			
Meat & Fish				Replacements			
Fruit & Veg.				SAVINGS			
Groceries				Pay'ts on Home			
Meals out				Savings Bank			
Kitchen Garden				Bldg. & Loan			
(credit supplies rec.)				Life Insurance			
Entertainment				Securities			
(where not elsewhere				New Equipment			
provided)				Thrift Clubs			
CLOTHING				Other Savings			
Clothes †				EXTENSION			
Cleaning				Advancement &			
Repairs				Recreation			
Accessories				Benevolences			
GENERAL				Gifts			
Automobile				Clubs, etc.			
Gardening				Educational			
Traveling				Reading matter			
Personal				Entertainment			
Carfare				Diversion			
Postage				HEALTH			
Stationery				Health Fund or Doctor			
Casual reading matter				Dentist			
Incidentals				Oculist			
Man's lunches				Hospital			
MAINTENANCE				Nurse			
(Running exp.)				Drug Store			
Fuel				Vacation Fund			
Oil				Insurance §			
				Fwd. from first column			
TOTAL				TOTAL			

* On house.   ‡ On household goods.
† Each member of family separately.   § Health and accident.

FIG. 32.—The Wanamaker Budget Guide

SUMMARY OF MONTHLY EXPENDITURES

Savings and Investment

Bank Account ________
Investments ________
Life Insurance ________
Total ________
Budget Suggested ________

Food

Meat and Fish ________
Fresh Fruit and Veg. ________
Groceries ________
Milk ________
Meals Out ________
Total ________
Budget Suggested ________

Shelter

Rent ________
Taxes ________
Fire Insurance ________
Upkeep and Repair ________
Total ________
Budget Suggested ________

Clothes

Wearing Apparel ________
Sewing Material ________
Total ________
Budget Suggested ________

Operating

Fuel, Light, Tel. ________
Renewal of Equipment and House Incidentals ________
Service ________
Misc. ________
Total ________
Budget Suggested ________

Advancement and Recreation

Education ________
Dentist and Doctor ________
Carfare ________
Personal Allowance ________
Clubs ________
Gifts ________
Total ________
Budget Suggested ________

(Fill these in when month is ended)

DAILY EXPENSE RECORD

	SAVINGS			FOOD					SHELTER				CLOTHES		OPERATING				ADVANCEMENT AND RECREATION						
	Bank Account	Invest-ments	Life Insur-ance	Meat and Fish	Fresh Fruit and Veg.	Gro-ceries	Milk	Meals Out	Rent	Taxes	Fire Insur-ance	Upkeep and Repair	Wearing Apparel	Sewing Mate-rial	Fuel, Light, Tel.	Renewal Equip. Incid.	Service	Misc.	Educa-tion	Dentist and Doctor	Car-fare	Personal Allow-ance	Clubs	Gifts	
1																									1
2																									2
3																									3
4																									4
5																									5
6																									6
7																									7
8																									8
9																									9
10																									10
11																									11
12																									12
13																									13
14																									14
15																									15
16																									16
17																									17
18																									18
19																									19
20																									20
21																									21
22																									22
23																									23
24																									24
25																									25
26																									26
27																									27
28																									28
29																									29
30																									30
31																									31
Total																									Total

Fig. 33.—Summary of Monthly Expenditures

Source: Savings Banks Association of the State of New York.

BUDGET CLASSIFICATION

(1) Food
(2) Housing
    Rent
    Taxes
    Fire insurance, etc.
(3) Operating
    Fuel
    Light and power
    Telephone
    Laundry done out
    Rent of safety-deposit box
    Fare on street car, etc.
(4) Furnishings and Equipment
    Furniture
    Bedding
    Flowers (cut and potted)
    Stoves
(5) Clothing
(6) Health

(7) Developmental
    Formal education
    Reading matter
    Public welfare
    Gifts outside of family
    Recreation
    Vacation and trips
    Vocation
(8) Personal
    Candy, tobacco, beauty parlor
    Barber shop, cosmetics
(9) Automobile
(10) Savings
    Emergency fund
    Savings account
    Insurance, life
    Payments on house
    Investments

FIG. 34.—Classification Used by U. S. Department of Agriculture
Source: Farmers Bulletin No. 1553.

Tables 47 and 48 give the hypothetical budget in terms of dollars and quantities for an urban family of four consisting of an employed father, a mother not employed, a boy aged thirteen, and a girl aged eight. This family lives in a five-room house having kitchen and bathroom and equipped with heat, hot and cold running water, electricity, and mechanical aids such as gas or electric cook stove, refrigerator, and washing machine. Such budgets are available for families of one, two, three, and five persons.

The budget in Table 47 shows that in June of 1947 a family of four should have been able to live adequately in a large city on $3,213. In that year, total national disposable income per family was $4,200 and personal consumption expenditure per family was $4,100 with personal saving per family at the extraordinarily low figure of $100.

If this budget is realistically set up, it should be very usable for a great many families. The median income in 1947 was roughly $3,200, which means that the median family could have followed this budget exactly. Fifty per cent of the families in the United States that year could have achieved a higher level of living whereas the other fifty per cent could not have lived this well.[6]

Budgeting has been tried by many persons who have not continued it. "The pages of abandoned budget books in this country, if gathered in one pile, would make a fire big enough to warm the cold feet

---

[6] See the discussion of consumption patterns by income level in Chapter 10.

TABLE 47

Cost of Urban Family Budget

(June 1947 Prices)

Items	Dollars	Per Cent
Total	3,213	100.0
Food	1,046	32.5
Food at home	926	28.8
Housing	707	22.0
Rent, heat, and utilities	593	18.4
House furnishings	82	2.6
Household operation	32	1.0
Clothing	432	13.5
Husband	140	4.4
Wife	126	3.9
Boy	86	2.7
Girl	80	2.5
Medical Care	161	5.0
Medical and dental services	119	3.7
Husband	26	.8
Wife	47	1.5
Boy	22	.7
Girl	24	.7
Hospital services	23	.7
Supplies and eyeglasses	19	.6
Transportation	253	7.9
Automobile owners	319	10.0
Non-automobile owners	92	2.9
Other Goods and Services	301	9.4
Reading and recreation	79	2.5
Personal care	60	1.9
Tobacco	36	1.1
Public school expenses	9	.3
Gifts and contributions	79	2.5
Miscellaneous	38	1.2
Total Cost of Goods and Services	2,900	90.3
Other Outlays	313	9.7

Source: "A New Concept of a Family Budget," Research Department, The Curtis Publishing Co., Release No. 138, April, 1948.

TABLE 48

QUANTITY OF ANNUAL PURCHASES FOR FAMILY OF FOUR

Item	Quantity per Family
Food	
Cereals, ready-to-eat	37.6 pounds
Coffee	36.2 "
Citrus juices, canned	14.3 "
Desserts, packaged	2.7 "
Flour	186.3 "
Milk, canned	67.0 "
Salad dressings	20.8 "
Shortening	58.8 "
Tea	3.7 "
Vegetables, canned	207.5 "
Personal Care	
Razor blades	7.7 pks of 5
Toilet soap	67.1 cakes
Toothpaste	10.2 3 oz. tubes
Cold cream	1 3½ oz. box
Face powder	1 2½ oz. box

	Number per 1000 Families
House furnishings	
Blankets	590
Iron	90
Mattress	210
Refrigerator	60
Rugs	810
Sheets	2160
Toaster	40
Towels, bath	3170
Washing machine	70
Vacuum cleaner	60

Source: "A New Concept of a Family Budget," Research Department, The Curtis Publishing Co., Release No. 138, April, 1948.

of all who tried it." Why? Because, for one important reason, the budget as originally planned did not fit the individual case. This lack of fit may have occurred either because the requirements of the par- ticular family were different from the "average" or "ideal" from which the budget was originally adopted (see Chapter 10), or because of some unexpected emergency expenditure.

To guard against disappointment in the use of a budget it will be helpful to include an item to act specifically as a shock absorber. Much consumer buying is impulsive, resulting in unwise purchases, and uncertainty affects consumption programs in many ways. Con- sequently, in any workable budget there must be a fund that permits adjustments and that will take care, for example, of a $15 Christmas gift which was planned to be only $10, or will allow for money lent and never repaid, and so on.[7]

Results of Planning One's Expenditures.—By planning expendi- tures a more intelligent use of income will surely result because:

1. The necessities will be provided since they will no doubt be con- sidered first. With their consideration may come a conscious- ness of expenditure habits which will result in deliberation as to preferences.
2. Purchases will be made more wisely since, having been planned for, advantage can be taken of seasonal reductions in price and time may be allowed for finding the particular article wanted.
3. Purchases will fit together better because they have been planned together.
4. "Leaks" will be uncovered and can be stopped.
5. Often an evaluation will be made by the person or family of its standards of consumption. By tying all parts of the spending together, a recognition of their relation is forced to the fore.
6. More "provisions for the future" may be made in accordance with a definite plan.[8]

It is well to remember that a wise use of individual income is not only desirable from the standpoint of the consumer but is also impera- tive for the well-being of the producer. Our modern economic system of industry is geared for a large-volume mass production and is de-

---

[7] For a helpful discussion of budgeting see *Personal Finance,* by Elvin F. Donald- son (New York: The Ronald Press Co., 1948).

[8] See S. Agnes Donham, *Spending the Family Income* (Boston: Little, Brown & Co., 1936), p. 22, for a discussion of these suggestions.

pendent for its functioning on a continuous large volume of consumption, not a spasmodic one. It is therefore important for both groups that everything be done to make possible a more efficient use of the consumer's dollar.

Wise Use of Insurance

Introduction.—Insurance is another tool which makes possible an increased use of personal money income. Insurance contains two elements which are found in different types of policies to a varying extent. One element is protection and the other is investment to meet future needs. As was pointed out in Chapter 14, there are uncertainties or risks which are insurable. Protection against money loss resulting from certain occurrences, but not against the risk itself, can be transferred from the individual, family, or business to an insurance company.[9] It was also stated in Chapter 14 that insurance permits saving or a form of investment for future requirements. We shall not duplicate that discussion here but, rather, call attention to the fact that both protection against sudden money loss from unforeseen occurrences and provision for systematic saving can result in a more intelligent use of money income.

Perhaps the warning in Chapter 14 should be repeated here, however, that when he is planning an insurance program the average person should consult a recognized expert in the field. Even though the ordinary person can learn much about insurance in a general way, he still cannot know *all* its intricacies and technicalities as the expert knows them. After all, that is his job. It is sensible to depend on competent, reliable insurance companies.

But the individual should know what kinds of insurance are available and the main purpose of each in order to lay out his general plan of insurance. He should first consider fully the protection to which he is entitled through the government (federal, state, and local), e.g., Workmen's Compensation, Social Security, etc. Second, he should plan his own insurance program to supplement all social insurance in order to:

1. Provide for his old age and for the support of his dependents if his job is not sufficiently covered by social insurance; and to provide additional sums for these purposes to give more than the minimum provided by law.

---

[9] See the discussion of Uncertainty in Chapter 14.

2. Provide for any losses and costs due to ill health and off-the-job accidents.

3. Protect his personal possessions.[10]

There are two kinds of insurance coverage which it would be useful to know about when deciding what insurance to buy: namely, personal insurance, and property and liability insurance. Only the most important points concerning each kind will be presented here.

Personal Insurance.—This kind of insurance involves the continuance of the individual's economic life. There are many types of personal insurance. It is sufficient here to list only the more ordinary kinds and to give the distinguishing characteristics of each.

LIFE INSURANCE. More life insurance was purchased in 1949 in the United States than in any previous year and more than twice the total annual purchase in the years just prior to World War II. This appears to be a continuation of a trend which has been apparent for some years, a trend which probably will continue. The following three types satisfy the life insurance needs of most persons.

1. ORDINARY LIFE INSURANCE

Such a policy requires that a person pay the same sum, called "premium," each year until his death, at which time the company pays his dependents (or anyone named as his beneficiary) the face value of the policy. The policy remains in force as long as the premiums are paid. Ordinary insurance has always been the most widely used type of life insurance. One reason for its popularity is its cost. It is next lowest in cost to term insurance and, experts insist, is the lowest-cost policy which has proved satisfactory for general use.

2. TERM INSURANCE

Here the individual pays premiums either for a definite period, i.e., five or ten years, or to a specific age, i.e., sixty, sixty-five, or seventy-five years. Often the latter form is called "protective insurance." If the person dies at any time during the period selected, the company pays the beneficiary the face value of the policy. In this case Term Insurance is like Ordinary Life. The difference becomes evident when the insured lives longer than the stated period, in which case he gets no further payment from the company.

This is the lowest-cost insurance and it may carry the privilege of conversion into another type of insurance without medical exami-

---

[10] For further material see *Buying Insurance*, Consumer Education Series, Unit 8, The Consumer Education Study, National Education Association, Washington, D. C., 1946.

nation. The shorter the term of the insurance, the smaller the premiums, thus lending itself well to short-time needs. It can be used, for example, to cover part of a man's insurance needs during the period when his family income is dependent mostly on his earnings and the expense of maintaining and educating his children is large, without the expense of extending the protection to later years when presumably his income would be larger and his expenses smaller. Of all the forms of insurance, however, it involves the least element of investment.

3. LIMITED-PAYMENT LIFE

This type is similar to ordinary life insurance in nearly all respects. The major difference is that premiums are paid for a limited number of years instead of for life. Like life insurance, the face of the policy is paid only at the death of the insured person. It differs from term policies in that, even if the person dies after all premiums have been paid, the face of the policy is paid. The premiums or rates are higher than those on ordinary life or term policies, thus this policy has higher investment value than an ordinary life policy, but it gives less protection to others per premium. Some forms of limited-payment policies are called participating policies and they become an endowment at the end of a certain number of years if the dividends are left with the company in order that they may accumulate interest which is used for the payment of the endowment.

RETIREMENT INSURANCE. Two types of retirement insurance are commonly used to provide income during retirement.

1. ENDOWMENT INSURANCE

This type of policy may be used by persons who need not only life insurance protection for others but also a definite sum of money or income at some later date. The person pays a certain fixed sum as premium each year for a limited period, usually twenty or thirty years, or to any specified age. If he dies during the contract time, the company pays the beneficiary the face value of the policy. If he lives to the end of the contract period, the company pays him the face value of the policy. The premiums are high but stop when the contract period is up. It is easy to see why this type of insurance, particularly the short-term policy, is considered to have the highest element of investment of any insurance policy. However, it provides low protection to one's beneficiaries for a given premium. It actually is a short-run savings plan with some protection to one's beneficiary. It is a particularly useful method of building up a cash fund for those who cannot discipline themselves to bank money regularly.

2. ANNUITY INSURANCE

This type of insurance provides a regular income from a given date until the end of an agreed-upon period. There are several types, such as life annuity, deferred life annuity, immediate life annuity, etc. The chief value of an annuity is regular income for one's self from a definite sum of money and not protection for one's dependents. People buy life insurance because they want to leave money for dependents in the event of their death; people buy life annuities because they want an assured income in old age.

CASUALTY INSURANCE. There are at least four types of casualty insurance available which pay the insured either for income lost due to an unforeseen event, or for extra expenses such as medical bills, or for both. Certainly a carefully thought out plan to cover the more probable happenings is an intelligent way to use one's personal income. The policies differ greatly, hence we shall not attempt to do more than describe them in a general way.

1. Accident Insurance (more often a combination health and accident policy)
2. Sickness Insurance
3. Disability Insurance

It has been said that doctors in the United States treat more persons in three days than the undertakers bury in a year. In addition, there are always many persons laid up by sickness or accident who do not see a doctor. Here is a hazard which can play havoc with one's budget or bank account.

Many, perhaps most, of the illnesses and accidents are minor, involving no great expense or loss of time. Often the worker's contract provides for a certain amount of "sick leave." Losses from such causes can be handled without much strain on the purse strings by the average individual or family. But the serious misfortune—the long illness, the major operation, the crippling accident—may run up staggering bills which would wipe out the average person's resources and even snow him under with huge debts; or the costs may be so great that the needed medical service cannot be bought and great tragedy results.

By means of insurance, such costs may be spread evenly over the years. An adequate program should provide for income during the period of enforced idleness and provide for money expenses incurred as a result of the illness or other disabling occurrence. There are many reasons why insurance companies will not sell policies giving unlimited coverage today. It is important, therefore, to examine the policies of several reputable companies before making a decision in order to get the most adequate coverage possible. It is customary for companies to limit the amount they will pay under a policy—either the sum or the number of weeks of payment. Most companies reserve the right to cancel the policy or to refuse to renew it to persons who suffer frequent accidents or illnesses. Moreover, it becomes increasingly difficult to obtain such policies as one grows older, and they are usually cancelled before the age when long illnesses are most likely to occur.

Property and Liability Insurance.—More families in the United States have the protection of property insurance than of life insurance. Everything we own is subject to some risk. In planning one's property insurance program one must be discriminating and insure first things first. Each person must analyze his own situation, calculate his risks, determine the cost of covering each risk by insurance, and choose accordingly. The important thing to consider is not how likely this is to happen, but how serious it would be if it did happen. A good rule to follow is to insure against any happening which would result in a serious financial loss or completely exhaust one's resources. Of course, there may be psychological reasons why one may choose to insure against minor happenings, and such policies are available. But few individuals can or will insure against every possibility of loss.

There are many forms of property insurance available today—too many to be described or even listed here. Moreover, this type of insurance is not so intimately a part of programs of investment and saving as is life insurance and thus does not justify detailed discussion in this section. We call attention to it because protection against sudden and great drains on one's income and savings is, of course, an important way to get greater use of personal money income. It seems appropriate to call attention to the most common types only.

Liability insurance covers your duty to others. Because this type of insurance, in general, is closely associated with the ownership of property, it will be included in this section.

The main forms of property and liability insurance which need to be described here are:

FIRE INSURANCE. This is one of the main forms of property insurance with which the average citizen should be familiar. Straight fire insurance will pay the insured person for any loss of property value from fire or smoke and water damage resulting when extinguishing the fire. For an additional sum one may get protection

covering such destructive happenings as windstorms, cyclones, tornadoes, hailstorms, explosions, falling aircraft, etc. Also, it is possible
to buy a specific policy covering any one occurrence. For example,
there are certain geographical sections of the United States where
tornadoes are fairly common and very damaging. In such areas, it
is good planning to carry tornado insurance. Again, farmers in most
sections of our country have found insurance against windstorms and
hailstorms very important protection.

THEFT, BURGLARY, AND ROBBERY INSURANCE. These policies
provide reimbursement when someone steals your possessions. The
main difference between the three types of insurance lies in how the
stealing takes place. Theft insurance covers goods stolen by persons
who enter your home, car, or other property without using force.
Burglary insurance implies a forced entrance whereas robbery insurance covers a situation where goods are stolen in the presence and
with the knowledge of persons in charge, but who are restrained from
preventing the act. Some of these policies are very broad, covering
"mysterious" disappearance; that is, no proof of theft, burglary, or
robbery need be given. It is also possible to buy policies which cover
a specific location, i.e., your own home, or any or all locations in
which the property happens to be stolen. Persons who travel a great
deal find this latter type of insurance very useful.

AUTOMOBILE INSURANCE. Complete automobile coverage would
require protection against bodily injury, property damage, collision,
fire, theft, and medical payment. Property damage and bodily injury
are commonly combined in the same policy and in a typical policy the
property damage costs considerably less than the bodily injury. The
cost of bodily injury insurance is based on the territory in which the
car owner lives and keeps his car. Thus, liability insurance costs will
be lower in Sleepy Eye, Minnesota, than in New York City because
the accident rate is so much smaller in a small town than in a large,
congested, metropolitan area.

The amount of coverage which each automobile owner should have
depends upon the law and upon his own particular needs. The advice
of an insurance expert should be sought here, as was suggested above.

PUBLIC LIABILITY INSURANCE. This provides protection against
a great many risks. Some of the common ones are: injury to a person doing a specific job for you, such as putting up storm windows or
working as a household employee; and injury to persons who are on
your property at your request, delivering milk, paper, groceries, etc.

Such accidents may cost a great deal of money and the property owner is legally liable. Public liability insurance provides him with protection from such costs.

Conclusion.—Insurance needs should be studied carefully so that they may be included in an individual's or family's budget. As was pointed out above, it would be foolish and expensive to insure against all risks. But it is important to insure against major or very costly ones.

Savings [11]

Saving Reduces Immediate Consumption.—Not all personal disposable income can be used in the purchase of immediate-consumption goods and services. If this were done, there would be no way to pay for any maintenance and increase in the man-made capital plant. Consequently, some use of purchasing power must be diverted from immediate-consumption expenditure into business investment if the economy of the community is to progress or even survive. In other words, the accumulation of capital plant for the commonwealth inevitably involves savings on the part of someone. Each individual (or family) is faced with the decision as to his share in the total volume and form of savings. In considering the matter it is pertinent to consider the effect of his action both on the commonwealth and on his own fortunes.

In this country part of our money income is taken by government, as taxes. Some of these tax funds are used in the construction of highways, public buildings, parks, and other physical things which contribute either to further production or to consumption. Thus there is a kind of "enforced savings" through this process.

Moreover, the management of corporations often decides to use part of the company's income for plant expansion rather than to distribute it to the stock-holding owners. This may be thought of as quasi-public "enforced savings." These two forms of savings reduce the socioeconomic necessity for savings from personal disposable income, but do not entirely remove it. They do account, in part, for the relatively small amount of personal savings referred to in Chapter 14.

Personal Savings Are Unevenly Distributed.—Not only are personal savings small in the aggregate, but they are very unevenly held

---

[11] Some aspects of the problem of savings are discussed in Chapter 14 and some data concerning the amount of personal savings are given there.

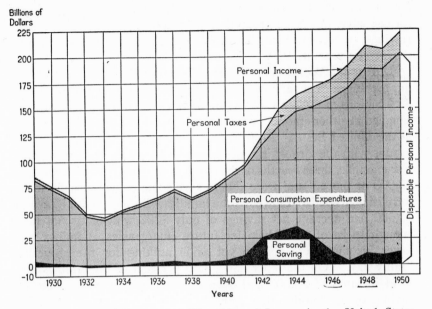

FIG. 35.—Personal Income and Disposition of Income in the United States, Annually, 1929-50

Source: W. N. Peach and W. Krause, *Basic Data of the American Economy* (Chicago: Richard D. Irwin, Inc., 1949), p. 12; *The Economic Report of the President*, January, 1951, p. 236.

by individual families. A considerable proportion of the total population is either unable or unwilling to take advantage of any of the facilities for saving during nonwar years. For example, in the prosperous year of 1929, it has been estimated that there were about $15,000,000,000 of individual savings, which was about 18 per cent of the total income produced.[12] Of this amount, the 59 per cent of families having incomes of under $2,000 saved only 1.6 per cent while the 2.3 per cent of families having incomes in excess of $10,000 contributed two thirds of the entire savings of American families. In other words, the nearly 60 per cent of families at the lower end of the income scale made total savings that averaged only $15 per family and even the lower 97.7 per cent of families saved an average of only $165 per family, while the upper 2.3 per cent saved an average of over $14,000 per family. In fact, the 21 per cent of families with incomes of under $1,000 actually consumed more than they produced by an aggregate amount of about $2,150,000,000 or an average of

---

[12] The data for 1929 are from Maurice Leven, *et al., America's Capacity to Consume* (Washington, D. C.: Brookings Institution, 1934), p. 93.

$365 per family; that is, instead of saving money or purchasing power for use later, this large group used past savings, increased their borrowings, or received contributions from charity even in the relatively prosperous year of 1929.

During the World War II period, because of patriotic and rationing pressures, "net savings of individuals" reached a peak in 1944 of 35.4 billions of dollars (see Figure 35), a peak never before or since equalled in either amount or per cent (19 per cent) of national income in the United States. A strong concentration of saving among the groups with the largest incomes was still the pattern in our country. For example, three fourths of the city families in 1944 had incomes of $2,000 or more [13] and were able to save some money, usually in the form of war bonds. However, the families with incomes of $2,000 to $2,500 had average net savings of only $122 which was not large enough to be of much help for future emergencies. Families with lower incomes were able to put aside nothing for the proverbial "rainy day." On the other hand, 12.5 per cent of the families with 1944 incomes of $5,000 and over saved 62 per cent of all the net savings of city families that year.[14] Obviously, it must be concluded that the rank and file of American families are failing to make, because they either cannot or will not, any adequate personal provision for old age, unemployment, or other future emergency. This circumstance has led to much public discussion and some legislation concerning compulsory saving for old age and insurance against unemployment. Some of the possibilities as well as the advantages and disadvantages of the various proposals are discussed in this chapter.

Purposes for Savings.—This brings us to a consideration of the personal reasons which induce individuals to save. Provision for the proverbial "rainy day" accounts, perhaps, for the first small savings. While the rank and file of our population tend to live from hand to mouth, as pointed out in Chapter 14, still a great many families have from one to several hundred dollars that can be called on in emergency. The cash or loan value of insurance policies and the insured deposits in savings banks and building and loan associations serve this purpose in many cases. So many families have not acquired even the small reserves needed for ordinary emergencies, however, that our social security legislation has provided compulsory insurance against

---

[13] Half of the families and single persons in cities in the United States in 1944 had net incomes, after the payment of taxes, of less than $2,700.

[14] "Expenditures and Savings of City Families in 1944," *Monthly Labor Review*, January 1946, p. 142.

unemployment for many classes of workers. The coverage is for short periods designed to tide over a period merely sufficient for the finding of a new job. There is considerable support, also, for compulsory insurance against the loss of time due to sickness, and for the same reason.

Another personal reason for savings is to provide for old age or perhaps for early retirement. Savings sufficient for this purpose are held by still fewer than those who can take care of short emergencies. Consequently, our compulsory social security program calls for individual contributions to provide small pensions at age 65. These pensions are so small that many individuals will still consider it wise to make additional savings for use after their retirement.

A third important reason for personal savings is that the money saved may be invested in such a way that it will earn a return that may become a substantial supplement to the current labor income of the individual. After the minimum requirements are met for emergencies and a moderate pension, this third reason becomes the main force motivating saving. It becomes, also, both the major force and the major mechanism for the start and growth of personal fortunes.

INVESTMENT

Types of Investment Possibilities.—Savings, if they are to work for one, must be invested. When we invest surplus funds we do one of two things: either we buy ownership rights in some form of property, or we lend money. Each of these things may be done in several ways and each has its special places in investment programs. Ownership of property includes the outright ownership of either urban or rural land, ownership of a personal business, share in a partnership, holding of stock in a corporation, membership in a cooperative society, and so on. Lending of money includes deposits in savings banks and building and loan associations, loaning on mortgages on land or other real property, or purchases of bonds of a corporation or public body.

Investment Illiteracy.—Despite our excellent educational facilities, the average person in the United States is poorly informed about matters of finance and investment. Worse still, instead of admitting they don't know and seeking out informed investment advice, most persons act on impulse or the advice of friends and acquaintances. The way in which glib salesmen can talk professional men and women as well as others into "investing" in unsound or doubtful schemes for making money is almost unbelievable. Many capable and intelligent individuals might be called financially illiterate. It is important for those who have money to invest to seek the counsel of reputable and informed investment advisors.

Relative Safety.—Individuals invest money in the hope of obtaining a reasonable return with a reasonable degree of safety. For most small investors, the degree of safety is more important than the rate of return. If a family's savings total $1,000, for example, the difference between a return of 3% and 8% is only $50 a year. While $50 is important to a low- or moderate-income family, it is not important enough to risk the loss of any considerable part of the original $1,000.

Government bonds and the guaranteed deposits in banks and savings associations are the safest forms of investment. Bonds of good private corporations also are reasonably safe. Mortgages on good urban or farm property are safe provided one knows the individual property and the persons operating it.

Bonds, savings deposits, and mortgages are forms of loans and are safe investments in the sense that the lender is reasonably certain to get back the money he invests. But as was pointed out in Chapter 6, money does not always have the same purchasing power. In periods of inflation, when the prices of things consumers buy are rising, the repayment of a loan does not carry with it as much purchasing power as the lender gave up originally. Conversely, of course, when prices are falling the money repaid will have enhanced purchasing power.

• The ownership of property, whether outright individual ownership or as stock in a corporation, is likely to fluctuate in money value more nearly as does the purchasing power of money. In this sense, therefore, ownership is a safer investment than lending; that is, the purchasing power as distinguished from the money value is more likely to remain reasonably constant. On the other hand, poor management may greatly lessen the value of any particular piece of property, whether held by an individual or by a corporation.

Investors Are Speculators.—All investment is fraught with risk. The persons who share the financial risks of economic enterprises are called speculators and the carrying of these risks is called speculation. Different investment possibilities and policies involve very different degrees of speculation. The launching of new industries, products, or corporations usually is a highly speculative and riskful undertaking. Old and conservatively managed companies and established governments present investment opportunities with minimum speculative risk. There are times when it is wise and reasonably safe to invest in common stock of good companies. There are other times when it is prudent to sell stock and buy bonds. So let us repeat, with emphasis, that those who have small amounts of money to invest usually will do well to consult competent and reliable investment counselors.

Quasi-Investments.—Purchase of durable consumer goods may be considered quasi-investment. As pointed out in Chapter 3, these goods give up their utilities slowly. Consequently, an automobile, for example, that is a year old and has been driven 10,000 miles, still possesses much of its original ability to yield utility. If the owner does not wish to harvest the remaining utility for his own use he can sell the car and use the money for any other purpose. This is especially true, perhaps, in the case of a house because of its long life and the lack of observable evidence of deterioration. While the purchase of durable consumer goods permits the recovery of some money value for the unused utilities, it is less likely that the value will have been increased by earning as is the case with investment in productive property.

Relation Between Saving and Investment.—Savings are available for investment and are a principal source of investment funds. Bank loans are another important source. Not all savings are invested promptly, however, and that is unfortunate. Unwise investments are unfortunate for the individual because his future income is smaller than it would have been had he followed a prudent investment policy. It is unfortunate for the commonwealth because some of the money paid out for production is not used either for further production or for purchasing the products of current production. Consequently, there is danger that the market will not be cleared of goods already produced and available. As a result, production programs will be curtailed, employees will be dismissed, the flow of income will be reduced, and the downward spiral to a depression will have started.[15] This may sound theoretical, as of course it is, unless for some reason many individuals fail to invest their savings at the same time. When that occurs the repercussions can be very serious. So perhaps it is fair to say that the individual owes it both to himself and to his community to make sure that his savings are placed so that the purchasing power they represent will be used by someone either for direct consumption or in further production.

---

[15] For discussions of some other forces that contribute to industrial fluctuations see the section on sales promotion in Chapter 14, and the section on credit in Chapter 6.

Wise Use of Consumer Credit

Instalment Credit an Important Type of Consumer Credit.— The term "consumer credit" has been used earlier in this book. Its gradual development in the United States, exhibiting a definite cyclical and expanding pattern of growth, was described in Chapter 6. Many types of consumer credit contributed to this expansion, but instalment sales contracts handled by specialized finance companies accounted for the most striking increases. Thus, charge accounts, lay-by plans whereby for a small down payment an article will be "earmarked" or set aside for the purchaser who will get possession of the good after further payments are made, small cash loans, and a miscellany of other types of relatively short-term credit are included in consumer credit, but instalment credit is the largest type. Table 49 shows what an important role instalment credit has played in the total consumer credit picture.

Thus we see that a major part of consumer credit is granted on the basis of instalment contracts which permit the purchase of more expensive commodities over a fairly long period of time. Although, as was pointed out in Chapter 6, instalment credit is used for the purchase of clothing, books, and other less durable consumer goods, it is usually more common and less risky to sell durable consumer goods in this manner.

It was pointed out earlier that "durable consumer goods" refers to goods used by people for their personal enjoyment, comfort, or satisfaction, but which are not used up, destroyed, or totally consumed for a considerable period of time. Houses are one obvious example, while automobiles, pianos, chairs, vacuum cleaners, and radios are others. Each of these things may be useful to its owner for a number of years and may be transferred from one user to another at any time. It is a conspicuous characteristic of such goods that a supply sufficient for consumption in a single day or hour cannot be separated physically from the total supply as can, for example, an orange from a boxful, or a sheet of writing paper from a ream. Consequently, if ownership of durable consumer goods is to be transferred, the transaction must involve a supply that can be consumed or fully used only over a considerable period of time.

Use of durable consumer goods can be provided to individuals by any of three methods of financing, namely: (1) the person may postpone such use until he has saved enough money to pay for the long-time supply, (2) the commodity may be rented to the user by the owner for a limited period of time, and (3) the individual may bor-

TABLE 49

TOTAL CONSUMER CREDIT, BY MAJOR PARTS

(In Millions of Dollars)

End of Year or Month	Total Consumer Credit	Instalment Credit					Noninstalment Credit			
		Total Instalment Credit	Sale Credit			Loans †	Total Noninstalment Credit	Single-payment Loans ‡	Charge Accounts	Service Credit
			Total	Automobile	Other					
1929	6,252	3,158	2,515	1,318	1,197	643	3,094	749	1,749	596
1933	3,439	1,588	1,122	459	663	466	1,851	303	1,081	467
1939	7,031	4,424	2,792	1,267	1,525	1,632	2,607	530	1,544	533
1940	8,163	5,417	3,450	1,729	1,721	1,967	2,746	536	1,650	560
1941	8,826	5,887	3,744	1,942	1,802	2,143	2,939	565	1,764	610
1942	5,692	3,048	1,617	482	1,135	1,431	2,644	483	1,513	648
1943	4,600	2,001	882	175	707	1,119	2,599	414	1,498	687
1944	4,976	2,061	891	200	691	1,170	2,915	428	1,758	729
1945	5,627	2,364	942	227	715	1,422	3,263	510	1,981	772
1946	8,677	4,000	1,648	544	1,104	2,352	4,677	749	3,054	874
1947	11,862	6,434	3,086	1,151	1,935	3,348	5,428	896	3,612	920
1948	14,366	8,600	4,528	1,961	2,567	4,072	5,766	949	3,854	963
1949	16,809	10,890	6,240	3,144	3,096	4,650	5,919	1,018	3,909	992
1950	20,093	13,468	7,923	4,134	3,789	5,555	6,615	1,326	4,227	1,062

† Includes repair and modernization loans insured by Federal Housing Administration.
‡ Noninstalment loans (single-payment loans of commercial banks and pawnbrokers). Revised beginning January, 1929 to exclude non-consumer loans. For description and back figures see *Federal Reserve Bulletin*, November, 1950, p. 1466.
Source: *Federal Reserve Bulletin*, February, 1951, p. 218.

row money and pay in full for the commodity, later repaying the loan from subsequent income. In this third method the buyer may borrow directly from the seller by using either an open charge account or an instalment contract, or he may borrow from some other source such as a bank or a credit union. It is mainly in connection with this third method of financing the use of durable consumer goods that the problems of consumer credit have arisen. As was pointed out above, it is durable consumer goods which have in the main been financed by means of instalment credit. In Chapter 6 we pointed out that the financing of automobiles on the basis of instalment contracts was very largely responsible for the expansion of consumer credit in the 20's and again in the later 30's and it was instalment credit which led the increase in consumer credit in the post-World War II period.

Consumers often need to curb their enthusiasm for this type of purchasing. That is, they must beware not to obligate their future too deeply. We commonly hear the statement that one who buys on instalment is mortgaging the future, but so is the man who rents a home and agrees to pay a stated amount per month for the next twelve months. The principal difference is that with instalment purchases one pays the full price during the first part of the period of use (but not so far in advance as when cash is paid in full), while in renting a house, payments are spread over the entire period of use. If the consumer has planned his future consumption as well as his present consumption, he should have no particular difficulty with his instalment payments. A working rule has been suggested for the family of moderate or low income, that total monthly instalment payments on consumer durables other than homes should not exceed 10 per cent of the expected monthly income.

Credit Is Used to Purchase Many Types of Goods.—Table 50 shows for the years 1948 and 1949, the percentages of retail sales for which consumers' credit was granted, in those stores where a sizable proportion of the total sales was on the basis of some form of credit. These data show that consumers make free use of credit in the purchase of many types of goods. With furniture, jewelry, household appliances, and automobiles (see footnote to Table 50) the percentage of credit buying is especially high, while in other stores, such as drugstores, variety stores, and filling stations (and thus not included in the table), the percentage is relatively low. Credit, when granted by these latter stores, is done largely as a service or convenience in order that customers may pay for their purchases once a month rather than every time anything is bought. Moreover, credit is usually extended

by them if they are neighborhood stores and their customers are well
known by the owner or manager. In the main, credit is more freely
used with durable goods than with those that are quickly consumed.

In Table 50 we see that automobiles, high-priced jewelry, large
and expensive items of furniture such as dining-room sets, and household appliances such as refrigerators and vacuum cleaners are sold to

TABLE 50

PERCENTAGE OF TOTAL SALES

Kind of Store	1948				1949			
	Cash	Charge Account	Instal-ment	Total Credit	Cash	Charge Account	Instal-ment	Total Credit
Department	54	36	10	46	52	37	11	48
Men's clothing	51	45	4	49	48	47	5	52
Women's apparel stores	45	51	4	59	44	52	4	56
Furniture	19	20	61	81	17	18	65	83
Household appliance ..	30	29	41	70	27	26	47	73
Jewelry	38	24	38	62	35	25	40	65
Hardware	42	54	5	59	41	54	4	58
Automobile dealers ...	60	20	26 *	46 *	57	17	20 *	37 *
Automobile tire & accessories	49	31	20	51	46	30	24	54

* The proportion of instalment sales reported by automobile dealers is believed
to be substantially understated because of accounting methods used in handling
instalment paper sold. The authors would point out that automobile finance companies and banks extend instalment credit on automobiles in addition to that extended
by the dealers.

Source: *Retail Credit Survey, 1949.*

a considerable degree on instalment contracts. The ordinary credit
arrangements in such cases require a moderate or even a small down
payment before the purchaser is given possession of the article and
the remainder in instalment payments which are generally arranged
to run from twelve months to twenty-four months. This is true in
noncritical times and when we do not have credit controls such as
Regulation W, which was enforced during World War II and during
a part of the time since. In the furniture field this method of selling
is very widely used as a means of consumer persuasion. However, it
appears to be true that the higher the proportion of instalment business done by a store, not alone in the furniture field, the cheaper the
goods it is likely to deal in. Thus the consumer should be very selective when dealing with a retail store which caters to instalment purchasers.

Of particular interest is the use of instalment selling in the automobile field because of its great influence on the total amount of consumer credit. Except for the war years, automobile credit has been about one half of all instalment credit and about a fifth of total consumer credit.

The Council of Economic Advisers has estimated that the total instalment sales in 1949 amounted to nearly $11 billion. Probably about 25 per cent of this was paid in cash, so that the instalment obligation accepted by consumers was about $6 billion, of which probably $4 billion was still outstanding at the close of the year. In other words, consumers decided in 1949 to spend about $4 billion in 1950 or later on for the further use of goods which they first obtained in 1949. Moreover, the reliance by consumers on the instalment method of financing their purchases has increased in relation to other types of consumer credit. In 1929 instalment credit amounted to about one half of total consumer credit whereas in 1949, twenty years later, instalment credit was about 65 per cent of the total. Thus, the increase in total consumer debt seems to have occurred largely because consumers have come to accept the slogan "pay as you ride" and it has certainly affected the consumption habits of a great many persons in the United States. They regard their instalment contract merely as a decision to spend ten dollars or twenty-five dollars or some other amount a month for the current use of a washing machine, a radio, an automobile, or the complete furnishing of a new house, and not as a debt incurred for something already finished or consumed, like the doctor's and the hospital's bills following an operation. This attitude is responsible, in part, for the marked increase in the purchase of electric refrigerators, new houses, and all other forms of durable and semidurable items, not just during the post-World War II period but during the last twenty-five to thirty-five years.

Instalment purchasing certainly, and this may apply to other forms of consumer credit as well, may be an expensive luxury for the consumer. Interest charges are frequently high and are likely to be padded with various "service" charges. The total charges are often larger than they seem to be. They may be stated as 6 per cent, for example, while actually 6 per cent is charged on the entire loan all the time in spite of the fact that it is being reduced each month. For example, if one hundred dollars plus interest at 6 per cent is to be repaid in twelve equal monthly instalments, many companies add $6 to the original $100 and divide by 12. Actually, this charges interest on the unpaid balance at the rate of nearly 12 per cent, for the principal sum is reduced each month and averages over the period only

To _____
(Name of Dealer)

Married _____ Number

Full Name _____ Single _____ dependents _____
(Please Print)   (Nationality)

Date of

Residence address _____ birth _____
(Number)   (Street)   (City)   (County)

How long ____|____ Phone No. _____ Previous address _____ How long _____
Mos.   Yrs.

Lived in that city how long _____ Present business address _____ Phone. No. _____

Employed now by _____ How long ____|____ Badge No. _____
(Name of firm)   Mos.   Yrs.

Week

Occupation _____ Income $_____ Month Date received_____

How

Previously employed by _____ Occupation _____ long _____
(Name of firm)   (Address)

Trade Union _____ Lodge affiliation _____
(Name and Number)   (Name and Number)   (City)

Total monthly expenses $_____ Name other sources of income _____

Pass-

Savings accounts with _____ Branch _____ On deposit $_____ book No.____
(Bank) (Address)   (Name)

Checking account with _____ Branch _____
(Bank)   (Street Address)   (Name)

Purchased last car from _____
(Name Dealer)   (Address)

To what Finance Co., if any, were payments made thereunder? _____

Have you ever suffered an automobile insurance loss? _____ What kind of loss? _____

Trade references with whom I (we) have had credit dealings:

1. Business reference _____
(Name)   (Street)   (City)   (State)   (Phone)

2. Business reference _____
(Name)   (Street)   (City)   (State)   (Phone)

3. Personal reference _____
(Name)   (Street)   (City)   (State)   (Phone)

Near Relative not living with you _____
(Name)   (Street)   (City-State)   (Relation)

I (We) own the following property	Title in name of	No. of acres or size of lots	Improved Yes or No	Total cash value	Amount of encumbrance	County	State

Address of property _____ Car will be used for: Business and Pleasure _____

Livery and Renting _____ Will be kept in private garage _____ Public garage _____

IF A FARMER, supply following information: I own $_____ worth of machinery, $_____
worth of live stock. Total amount owing on machinery and livestock $_____ My income
this year will be $_____ from Grain, $_____ from Hay, $_____ from Fruit, $_____
from Dairy, $_____ from other. My net income last year was $_____. I owe to banks
and others $_____. The undersigned warrants the truth and accuracy of the foregoing
information.

Purchaser signs _____

By _____

Dated this _____ day of _____ 19__   (Official Title, if Company)

FIG. 36.—Automobile Instalment Purchase Application

277

about $50. Anyone contemplating a purchase under an instalment contract should examine the various charges carefully as well as all other features of the contract. A typical instalment purchase application is given in Figure 36, and should be examined carefully.

A variation of instalment selling has been developed in the form of the "Thrift Corporations." Their sole business is granting loans to finance consumer purchases at local stores and they are usually owned by the merchants of the community. The consumer selects his merchandise, arranges a loan for the full amount of the purchase, pays the merchant "cash," and then repays the loan company the price of the goods plus interest.

There are, perhaps, several reasons which the seller has for granting consumer credit, one of which is to influence consumer purchasing. This influence may result in an increase in the total consumption of material goods. It is more likely, however, to result in the consumption of some types of goods at the expense of other types. Perhaps, as with competitive advertising, it is most likely to result merely in a shift of patronage between brands of commodities or between individual merchants. These and many other devices shuttle in and out of the picture as millions of daily purchases are made.

Consumer credit may be looked upon as a means of enlarging the consumer's useful income. It can be a most effective device for this purpose, if intelligently and carefully used. When the use of consumer credit was in its infancy those who hoped to use it to increase their sales were not fully appreciative of the importance of not overloading the consumer with debts. Today it is a common practice on the part of those selling to the consumer to require information as to the consumer's total debts outstanding and to advise the consumer as to the advisability of purchasing an expensive consumer good. Unfortunately, this is not done by all retailers and a good many consumers load themselves up with crushing consumer debt so that they not only lose their payments already made but the commodity itself. The consumer should budget his expenditures and carefully plan his consumer debt obligations as he would his cash expenditures. Credit unions and banks, as well as reputable finance companies, will give the consumer intelligent assistance on this problem.

PROJECT QUESTIONS

1. Obtain a budget book and prepare to keep an accurate record of your income and expenditures for a school year. It will be helpful to examine several so-called "model budgets" printed and distributed by insurance companies, banks, finance companies, and the like.

2. Obtain samples of instalment contracts for the purchase of an automobile, furniture, refrigerator, and television set, and discuss such aspects of the contracts as:

   a) interest rates; amount and how figured
   b) differences in the contracts
   c) repossession clause
   d) references and other data required of the borrower
   e) any other significant points

3. Obtain samples of various types of insurance policies. If possible, discuss their relative merits and weaknesses with a qualified representative of an insurance company. Do you now feel that you can plan for your future insurance needs? What are they and in what way do you expect to satisfy them?

4. Discuss what buying motives influenced your purchases of recent items such as a suit of clothes or dress, ties, underwear, shaving cream or cosmetics, etc. Do you approve of such motivation? What improvements, if any, can you suggest?

Chapter 18

CONSUMER-INITIATED AIDS
(THE CONSUMER MOVEMENT)

INTRODUCTION

From limited beginnings, the American economy has grown into a complex and powerful system. And, as was pointed out earlier, price operates as an important guide to individual action within the limits set by the rules of the game as they are set at any particular moment by customs and legal act. Other persons offer to each of us, individually, a price for our personal service or for the use of our capital. The upper limit of the price bargain is set by what the buyer believes the service or use of capital will be worth to him, either for personal consumption or as an aid to further production. The lower limit for an effective price offer—that is, one that will result in a deal—is set by our willingness to do the job or to dispense temporarily with the use of our capital. The interplay of judgment of buyer and seller finally results in a price somewhere between these two limits at which a trade is made or a deal consummated. If the good or service is reproducible like cans or automobiles rather than nonreproducible like the painting of a great artist, and if the price agreed upon is satisfactory enough to the seller, a supply will continue to be forthcoming. Similarly, if the satisfaction the buyer gets from his cans or automobiles is of the sort that bears repeating, and if it proves equal to anticipation, demand is likely to continue.

Broadly speaking, this mechanism of decision operates throughout the entire field of economic activity. It is present in the bargaining for labor at all levels, in the rent of a home, in the sale of crude oil, or eggs, or watches, or scrap iron, or steam yachts, or cabbage. Perhaps, however, the mechanism is used with less precision in connection with purchases for final consumption than elsewhere. If this be true, the cause probably lies in the inability of the consumer to exercise sound judgment in balancing the satisfactions to be expected from one purchase against those that would come from some other use of purchasing power. The reality of this lack of ability, together with some of its causes, has been discussed in earlier sections while some of the aids initiated by the consumer and others to assist the consumer in decision-making will be considered in this chapter.

On the assumption that consumers are somewhat at a disadvantage in the operation of the price mechanism, organized governments have undertaken certain things in their behalf. These include rules and regulations laid down by public legislatures in the interest of consumers, the pure food and drug laws, the standards of weights and measures, usury laws, prohibitions of misbranding and false description, and so on. In general, it will be pointed out that little has been accomplished in this field as yet beyond the setting of pretty low minimum standards for commodity qualities and limits for interest rates, the prevention of the crudest sort of misrepresentation, and the provision of minimum sanitation requirements, and so on. The ways by which government attempts to assist and protect the consumer will be discussed in Chapter 20.

The Consumers' Movement Is Group Action to Aid Consumers. —The opportunities for additional group action in this field would, therefore, seem to be large. This group action has taken a great many forms and has been labeled by many as the consumer movement. One may broadly define the consumer movement as consisting of all efforts—whether they be organized or unorganized and whether they be by individuals, groups, or institutions—which are designed to make the consumer a wiser buyer and user of the products and services which are required in his capacity as consumer; a more intelligent user of resources both individual and national; and an informed and alert citizen willing to play an effective role in the decisions that determine how the economic resources of the community, nation, and world are to be used.

If the consumer movement is defined in this way, it would comprise all activity in the interest of the consumer. Under this definition this entire chapter and the next, therefore, can be said to be devoted to a discussion of the consumer movement. It is a movement which includes a wide variety of greatly differing efforts, focused to a major or a minor degree, for either short or long periods, on the welfare of the consumer. Naturally, the sectors of the movement are constantly changing, constantly shifting their emphasis, and the size of the movement varies from time to time depending upon the well-being of our economy. During and following the very serious depression of the 1930's, for example, there was an upsurge of interest in improving the welfare of the consumer as well as in trying to awaken within the consumer a desire to help himself. During the latter part of the

1930's a great many organizations were brought into being for the express purpose of helping the consumer, and various national organizations already in existence took on such a program as a side issue. As a matter of fact, at one time during the latter part of the 1930's it was said that sixty such formally organized groups were participating in consumer interest programs. Of course, a great amount of the activity was unorganized and cannot be listed nor recognized in a presentation such as this one. We shall, however, be concerned with those organized activities which have been effective in aiding the consumer.

CONSUMERS' COOPERATIVES

One of the earliest and perhaps most effective of the consumer-initiated attempts to help themselves can be found in the consumer cooperative movement. Consumer cooperation, as will be pointed out below, is an attempt on the part of consumers to increase their real income and improve their scale of living by reducing merchandising costs and by making available the amount and quality of those things which the consumer wants. Some of the important things the co-operators hope to accomplish are: (1) to lower the cost of living by eliminating some market operations, and by taking over others and performing them more efficiently, (2) to give consumers more nearly what they want by dealing directly with producers and by avoiding a good deal of producers' sales promotion, and (3) to enable consumers to learn more readily and more accurately the truth about all commodities so that their choices will be more intelligent.

The Consumers' Cooperative Movement Is Old.—The consumer cooperative movement grew up out of the circumstances of the Industrial Revolution in Great Britain. It was a reaction against the early abuses, or at least the rigors of the capitalist industrial system. Finding themselves ground between the upper and lower millstones of high prices and low wages, the British factory workers sought some escape. There had been numerous sporadic ventures into "help your-self enterprises" of one kind or another in Great Britain for a considerable period of time before the first successful consumers' cooperative was established. For example, there are records of the building of a corn mill by subscription in 1767 and the Fenwick Weavers' Society was established in Scotland in 1769. Another interesting attempt was made from 1820 to 1830 in societies based on the social theories of Robert Owen. These societies were started both in England and in the United States. Owen was a successful businessman who revolted against the social conditions and economic teaching of his day. He refused to accept the Malthusian theory of population and the Ricardian Iron Law of Wages. Under Owen's paternalistic or even indulgent guidance, New Lanark, the town in which was located the cotton mills of which he was first owner and manager, became the model manufacturing town of Great Britain. He was responsible for reforms which were radical then but are either archaic or the accepted pattern today, such as shortening the working day to ten and three quarters hours, eliminating child labor, improving sanitation, and adult education. He believed in "a new moral world," meaning full collectivism instead of private ownership. Several communal associations were formed in which all property was collectively owned and in which everything was shared equally. After several unsuccessful attempts in Britain, Owen came to the United States and established the New Harmony Community in Indiana in 1824. Practically all such early communal attempts were unsuccessful, because of a lack of unity among the members, and this one was no exception. They did make a contribution to the consumer cooperative movement, however, in dramatically calling attention to the possibility of voluntary grouping for self-help.

THE ROCHDALE COOPERATIVE. There were also numerous other early attempts at consumer cooperation which failed for various reasons, mainly because of the practice of price-cutting and of giving members benefits before they had earned them. Although these attempts were short-lived, they undoubtedly set the stage for later successful ones. Finally, by 1844 the mass of working people in Great Britain were in debt in a very disagreeable way to companies which employed them—this was known as the truck system.[1] England, building her Victorian supremacy on coal, shipping, and manufactured cotton, paid a very bitter price in human life. Nowhere were conditions worse than in the early Lancashire mills. In the town of Rochdale there is a record which shows that 1500 persons each existed on 45 cents a week in 1841. After they had repeatedly been refused wage increases, twenty-seven male weavers and one woman formed what they called The Rochdale Society of Equitable Pioneers on October 12, 1844. They opened a store on Toad Lane, where it still stands.

---

[1] The industrial practice of paying very low wages and charging very high prices to workers who were forced to trade in company-owned stores. In this way, workers were constantly in debt to their employers. See Beatrice Webb, *The Discovery of the Consumer* (London: Ernest Benn, Ltd., 1928), p. 13.

Each of the twenty-eight members subscribed the meager amount of one tuppence each week to form the capital, and from this very small beginning the cooperative society grew and expanded. The Rochdale pioneers began to sell groceries to themselves through their cooperative for two reasons: to free themselves from the toils of the "truck" and also with the idea of accumulating a capital fund from which they might realize their ideal of self-employment in flannel weaving. But by 1900 the consumers' cooperative movement had reoriented its goals. The self-employment goal was forgotten and all efforts were bent toward maintaining and enhancing the superiority of cooperative business over private business.

ROCHDALE PRINCIPLES OF COOPERATION. Although the total of all cooperative ventures has probably had a much greater effect on the cooperative movement over the years than the Rochdale cooperative itself has had, yet the modern cooperative movement certainly was fathered by the twenty-eight Rochdale pioneers. The famous Rochdale principles of cooperation which have had and still have an important effect on the philosophy of consumer cooperation are strictly precise but are not always strictly followed by today's cooperatives. They are definite enough, however, to summarize schematically as follows:

Those that are largely social or sociological:
1. open membership
2. racial, political, and religious neutrality
3. democratic control
4. promotion of education

Those that are largely economic:
1. limited returns on ownership or capital investment
2. patronage dividends

Those that are largely business management:
1. sale at going market prices
2. cash trading
3. minimum emotional advertising or sales promotion

CONSUMERS' COOPERATIVES IN THE UNITED STATES. Various types and numbers of consumers' cooperative organizations were attempted in the United States preceding and following the establishment of the famous Rochdale Cooperative. Perhaps the earliest consumer buying club was started in Boston in 1845 by members of a labor union as a result of the urging of a tailor member, John Kulback. Although household supplies were bought jointly and distributed at weekly meetings, this buying club did not follow the Rochdale principles. Other such buying clubs were organized and grew, but they failed during the Civil War largely because of incompetent management and too liberal credit policy. The interest of labor in cooperative organizations was fairly widespread up to the Civil War because the union movement during this period looked upon cooperation as the best method of benefiting its members. However, other methods were adopted, such as strikes, the closed shop, etc., which seemed to be more effective techniques for achieving union objectives,

TABLE 51

ESTIMATED MEMBERSHIP AND BUSINESS OF CONSUMERS' COOPERATIVES BY TYPE OF ASSOCIATION (1948)

Type of Association	Total Number of Associations	Number of Members	Amount of Business
LOCAL ASSOCIATIONS			
Retail distributive	3,880	2,354,000	$1,229,500,000
Stores and buying clubs	2,400	1,256,000	828,000,000
Petroleum associations	1,350	960,000	358,000,000
Other	80	38,000	16,500,000
Service	786	395,290	29,223,000
Room and/or meals	180	22,000	6,000,000
Housing	125	13,000	3,000,000
Medical and/or other hospital care			
On contract	60	120,000	2,225,000
Own facilities	70	78,000	8,600,000
Burial			
Complete funeral	29	25,500	435,000
Casket only	2	590	8,900
Burial on contract	10	4,200	60,000
Cold storage	185	107,000	7,100,000
Other	125	25,000	1,800,000
Electric light and power	865	2,403,676	137,016,000
Telephone (mutual and cooperative)	33,000	675,000	10,000,000
Credit unions	9,329	3,748,628	633,783,555
Insurance associations	2,000	11,300,000	207,500,000
FEDERATIONS			
Wholesale			
Interregional	2	77	12,265,635
Regional	26	4,846	320,340,390
Districts	20	298	7,337,960
Service	19	1,685	3,276,500
Productive	16	302	83,739,000
Electric light and power	10	77	7,399,287

Source: *Monthly Labor Review*, October 1949, p. 401.

and only within very recent years have unions returned to their early favorable attitude toward the cooperative technique as a means of helping their members.

The weak cooperative movement probably would have died out in the United States during the latter part of the nineteenth century had it not been for the farmers, whose strong Grange Movement supported the cooperative idea and thereby kept it alive from 1867 on. Despite this support, by the turn of the century the consumer cooperative movement had dwindled to almost nothing. Since 1900 its size and strength have varied, growing during periods of depression and losing ground during periods of prosperity. Farmers' cooperatives have been considerably stronger in the United States than have consumers' cooperatives, both in terms of membership and volume of business, but they too have had a turbulent history. Even today consumers' cooperatives are less important than farmers' cooperatives although, in 1948, consumers' cooperatives had reached a new high in the United States. The data in Table 51 show the number of consumers' cooperatives, number of members, and volume of business, as estimated by the Bureau of Labor Statistics.

Consumers' Cooperatives Share of Business.—The cooperative movement has had a wide and substantial growth in Europe, especially in Great Britain and the Scandinavian countries. In the United States, however, cooperatives do only a very small proportion of the nation's total business. The data in Table 52 show the extent of participation of consumers' cooperatives in the national trade of various countries.

TABLE 52

PARTICIPATION OF CONSUMERS' COOPERATIVES IN NATIONAL TRADE

Country	Kind of Cooperative	Percentage
Austria	Retail Trade (food only)	10.0
Denmark	Wholesale and Retail Trade	25.0-30.0
Finland	Wholesale Trade	34.6
	Retail Trade	33.5
	Hotel and Restaurant Trade	22.4
France	Trade (not specified)	10.0
Great Britain	Wholesale Trade	9.0
	Retail Trade	14.0
Norway	Wholesale Trade	15.0
	Retail Trade	10.0-15.0
Sweden	Retail Trade	15.0-20.0
Switzerland	Retail Trade	12.0-15.0

Source: *Monthly Labor Review*, May 1949, p. 544.

It will be seen that even in Great Britain, where consumers' co-operatives are much stronger than in the United States, only 14 per cent of retail trade is conducted by consumers' cooperatives. In Sweden, 15 to 20 per cent of retail trade is controlled by consumers' cooperatives, whereas in Finland 33 per cent, and in Denmark from 25 to 30 per cent is cooperative controlled. In the United States, according to the most recent data, consumers' cooperatives do less than 1 per cent of the total retail business. However, there are certain regions and certain commodity fields where consumers' cooperatives are of considerable importance. This is especially true in the upper Great Lakes region, where consumer cooperatives are responsible for about 5 per cent of retail sales.

Philosophy of British and United States Cooperatives.—The philosophy of cooperation in the United States is similar to that in Great Britain, where the cooperative movement frankly asserts that it aims at a cooperative commonwealth. In Sweden, on the other hand, the aim of the cooperative movement appears to be to act as a yardstick or competitive prod to both private and governmental undertakings. In Sweden it is considered sufficient if the movement stimulates the adoption of efficient methods and the discarding of the obsolete, and prevents the development of monopolies operated in the interest of the owners. A report was made in 1938 by three of England's leading professors which throws considerable light on the movement in Great Britain. Their report suggests that the consumers' cooperative movement in Great Britain seems to have its limitations. In 1949, after more than one hundred years, the British cooperatives did less than 15 per cent of the total retail trade, this despite the fact that cooperative capital was well over $1,500 million and its annual sales were even greater and growing.

According to these students, the British cooperative movement did not appear entirely sound either in underlying philosophy or in management, and the criticism was made that it does not know where it is going. It is following a political philosophy that is not influential and has not been able to work out a new philosophy. Its educational work is conventional and without imagination; its press is dull and hard to read; it does not attract and keep the best brains, and it is unwilling to spend money for the best technical and professional services. Both in wholesaling and retailing, the cooperatives do not lead, they simply follow, which may result from the decentralized democracy which characterizes the movement in Great Britain. This criticism would suggest that the high hopes entertained of the part this movement would play in economic redemption of mankind are not going to be fulfilled in the immediate future.

Similarly, in the United States, although the cooperative movement has grown and is continuing to grow, its effectiveness in the total economic picture is not great. It is likely that we will follow the pattern of the British consumers' cooperatives inasmuch as our cooperative movement has been modeled pretty largely after the British. There seem to be definite and very strong restrictions to the growth of the consumers' cooperative movement inherent in the consumer members themselves. In the initial or pioneer part of the growth of the movement in the United States, societies could depend upon a loyal membership unified by the bond of foreign birth. For example, the very strong consumers' cooperatives in the Lake Superior region were organized and have been largely supported by foreign-born Finns. But it will become increasingly necessary for cooperatives to use other appeals to retain and enlarge a membership more and more made up of native-born people. This may mean, on the one hand, the end of the low-cost non-service consumers' cooperative with which we are familiar or it may mean, on the other hand, a rather noticeable growth in this type of retail outlet. Which direction the movement will go will, of course, largely depend upon what the economic picture is in the coming years. It is an opportunity for the consumers to help themselves and they will if the pressure for that help becomes great enough.

However, even though the consumers' cooperative movement may never be responsible for a large percentage of total retail sales in the United States probably there always will be certain areas in which it is a powerful retail unit. No doubt these areas will be similar to the rural community of Brule, Wisconsin, where the cooperative not only sells the villager and the farmer all that he needs, but satisfies his social and recreational needs as well. In addition, in such communities, as well as among small groups of people having an exceedingly high degree of homogeneity of interests in larger towns and cities, the buying association and consumers' cooperative provide a nucleus for social and political action.

Service Cooperatives May Be Consumers' Cooperatives.—
Closely associated to the retail cooperative are service cooperatives which exist primarily to render one or more services for their members. Among the numerous services rendered are financing, insurance, housing, medical care, telephone, electrical, burial, education, garage, laundering, publishing, milk distributing, and the provision

of library service. Although these service cooperatives may be associated with either producers' or consumers' societies or they may be separate organizations, it is well to examine them very briefly because they provide an opportunity for consumers to provide aid to themselves by group action. The following three service cooperatives are described to illustrate to the student how such associations come into existence and what assistance they provide consumers.

CREDIT UNIONS. A credit union can be defined as a cooperative small-loan bank. It is an association organized, either under state or federal law, by groups having a common interest as teachers, postal employees, farmers, and neighborhood groups. Credit unions have three primary objectives: to promote the habit of thrift, to loan funds to members at reasonable rates of interest, and to educate members to the value of savings, investments, and cooperative practices. Small loans always have preference over large loans, and all loans are made only for helping people get out of debt.

The first successful credit unions were started in Germany by two men, Frederick Raiffeisen and Herman Schulze-Delitzsch, about the middle of the nineteenth century. They were organized first as collective borrowing societies where persons with money were persuaded to place money at the disposal of needy farmers or artisans, the money to be repaid with low interest in monthly instalments. Raiffeisen worked with the farmers and Schulze-Delitzsch with the artisan group. These two types of self-help associations differed somewhat in organizational detail but in the main followed the same general plan. Most cooperative credit institutions have been patterned after one or the other of these systems.

The credit union movement in the United States was started in 1909 in Manchester, New Hampshire, by Alphonse Desjardins, a French Canadian from Quebec. It was modeled after the Raiffeisen organization. A prominent millionaire merchant of Boston, Edward A. Filene, was greatly impressed with the possibilities of credit unions and spent much time and money sponsoring them throughout the United States. The first state credit union law was passed in Massachusetts in 1909, but there was no federal law until 1934, by which time forty-three states had enacted credit union legislation.

The passage of the Federal Credit Union Act in 1934 stimulated the growth of credit unions in the United States. The credit union movement reached an all-time high in 1942 with 10,602 associations (54 per cent organized under state laws and 46 per cent under the Federal Act). The total membership exceeded three and a half mil-

TABLE 53

OPERATIONS AND ASSETS OF CREDIT UNIONS IN 1947 AND 1948

State and Type of Charter	Year	Number of Associations		Number of Members	Number of Loans Made During Year	Amount of Loans Made During Year	Paid-in Share Capital	Total Assets	Dividends on Shares
		Active	Reporting						
All	1948	9,329	9,327	3,748,628	2,684,329	$633,783,555	$603,393,780	$701,425,500	$7,940,882
	1947	9,168	8,942	3,339,859	2,170,685	455,833,601	509,713,962	591,126,677	9,964,201
State	1948	5,271	5,269	2,120,289	1,479,558	360,546,180	368,385,412	443,013,764	7,940,882
	1947	5,155	5,097	1,893,944	1,217,321	271,324,497	317,303,919	380,751,106	6,079,278
Federal	1948	4,058	4,058	1,628,339	1,204,771	273,237,375	235,008,368	258,411,736	3,884,923
	1947	4,013	3,845	1,445,915	953,364	184,509,104	192,410,043	210,375,571	....

Source: Serial No. R. 1969, from the *Monthly Labor Review*, September, 1949.

lions, and assets amounted to more than $322½ million. During and following World War II (see Table 53) growth was in terms of members, assets, and loans made. This growth continued through 1949 together with an increase in number of associations. The Minnesota League of Credit Unions reported credit union laws in forty-three states and the District of Columbia in 1949 with 10,205 credit unions (both state and federal associations), 4,250,000 membership, and total assets at $800 million.

There appears at present no noticeable opposition by commercial banks to the credit union movement, possibly because there is somewhat of a division of labor between the two types of institutions and also because credit unions themselves maintain accounts with banks and borrow from them.

COOPERATIVE INSURANCE SOCIETIES. Cooperative insurance is another of the rapidly growing activities of the cooperative movement —especially in the United States. It is one of the oldest branches of cooperative activity. The earliest of the cooperative insurance companies were the farmers' township fire mutuals organized more than 100 years ago. Rural insurance cooperatives provided fire, lightning, wind, hail, and miscellaneous types of farm insurance on a cost basis. Somewhat later, general insurance cooperatives were organized which provided fire, automobile, storm, loan, sickness, and hail (not on crops) insurance. It is difficult to estimate the actual number of associations because of the divergence of opinion among investigators as to what constitutes a true cooperative and because of the absence of information on farmers' and general insurance cooperatives.

COOPERATIVE HOUSING. In actual practice, only a relatively small proportion of the housing cooperatives in the United States adhere strictly to all the principles of cooperative housing. With a few minor exceptions this has been more or less true of cooperative housing in Europe as well. In a group of thirty-five associations studied by the Bureau of Labor Statistics in 1936, in only three was each member allowed to vote on administrative decisions regardless of the number of shares held.[2] In another study, published in 1949, one hundred associations are listed as housing cooperatives,[3] but most of them do not fulfill the requirements of a true cooperative. Some fall down in some respects and some in others. The characteristics of a genuine housing cooperative are:

---

[2] *Monthly Labor Review*, November, 1937.
[3] Elsie Danenberg, *Get Your Own Home the Cooperative Way* (New York: Greenberg, Publisher, Inc., 1949).

a) Each member has one vote, regardless of the number of shares held.

b) The buildings are bought or constructed by the association as such and not by the members individually.

c) Each member owns shares in the association to the value of the dwelling he occupies and does not receive title to any individual dwelling: legal ownership is held by the association as a whole.

d) Shares are nontransferable except with the permission of the association and usually not at more than par value.

e) Surplus savings accruing from the association's operations, which are not used for expansion or collective purposes, are returned to the tenant-members as savings returns, in proportion to the amount of their patronage or monthly payments.

f) Religious and political neutrality.

Consumer Information and Education

Selecting Merchandise Is a Complicated Process.—The qualities which are wanted in consumer goods are often very complex. Part of the complexity lies in the fact that some aspects of quality are intrinsic, tangible, and subject to physical measurement while other aspects are intangible and not easily measurable. The size of a shoe, for instance, may be measured objectively with length, width of instep and heel, shape of toe, height of heel, and as many other details as are desired included in the measurement. These are tangible and physically measurable aspects of quality having a direct bearing on the fit of the shoe. Comfort is perhaps an equally important aspect of shoe quality. It is not measurable in the same objective way as is size. Appearance is even less tangible and measurable. Individual tastes differ sharply with respect to matters of appearance and there is no unit of measurement with which to make comparisons.

Quality in merchandise is so difficult to measure that it is not certain that any organization, governmental or private, can ever make a good job of it. Take so simple a thing as a can of peaches, for example. The highest commercial grade of canned peaches contains a heavy sugar syrup, which adds little to the food value of the peach and may make it less well suited for use in salads. Moreover, color, flavor, firmness, and texture are all elements of quality in peaches, but there is no scientific way to combine these separate things into a single measurement of quality. If you believe it easy, just try to compare several brands of canned peaches, see if you can rank them in the same order on second taste, and then tell *why* you like one better than

another. Then try to say how much difference in price is justified by
the differences in quality; how much more, that is, you would be willing to pay for the one ranked first than for the ones ranked second,
third, or fourth. The money value of quality differences is hard for a
single individual to set, but when many people "vote with their dollars" in an open market they may hit the true value to society as
closely as would any other method.[4]

Even in the physically measurable aspects of quality it often is
difficult for the consumer to obtain adequate and precise information.
Considerable progress has been made in this field in recent years, but
there is room for further improvement. Many packages now display
on the label the amount of product contained, but this practice is not
a universal one. Some fabrics are labeled to show the materials out
of which they are made. Others are warranted against shrinkage.
Hosiery is labeled both as to the material from which it is made and
the number of threads to the inch. Even after all these things are
done, there are many aspects of quality which are left to the determination and judgment of the individual buyer at the time of purchase.
In many cases information could doubtless be given with greater
completeness and precision concerning some of the aspects of quality.
To the extent that this was done, purchases could be adjusted more
easily and quickly to the actual needs or desires of the purchaser.

In some cases where precise measurement of quality is not given,
the seller guarantees the quality in the sense that he will repair or
replace the commodity if it fails to perform in the manner claimed for
it. It is in this sense that refrigerators, television sets, and other
durable consumer goods sometimes are guaranteed either by their
manufacturers or their retailers. Many retail establishments will also
agree to replace many items of merchandise if they do not come up
to the consumer's anticipation. The amount of this sort of guarantee
differs widely among manufacturers and retailers. It is a method of
attracting patronage to some stores and it is also a policy which is
abused by some consumers.

Because of the inadequacy of information concerning quality and
the lack of uniformity concerning the guarantee of quantity and quality, consumers frequently are led to judge quality by price, believing
that the commodity with the highest price must be the best. In many
cases, however, price proves to give a poor indication of quality.
Merchants and manufacturers, through their advertising, often try to

---

[4] For a discussion of determining quality of canned foods see R. S. Vaile and
A. M. Child, *Grocery Qualities and Prices* (Minneapolis: University of Minnesota
Press, 1934).

make people believe their brand is worth more than those of their competitors even when there is no physical basis for the assumption. As a result, brands of similar quality may sell at quite different prices. The most conspicuous illustration of this phenomenon has been perhaps that of Bayer's Aspirin, which at times has sold at prices tenfold above those of chemically identical but less well-known brands.

Not only do brands of similar quality sell at different prices, but prices of identical brands vary greatly. For example, a brand of cooking oil was priced by one neighborhood store in Minneapolis at 67 cents a quart and by another, one block away, for 97 cents on the same day. A shopper in a large city recently priced an identical chair in three different stores in the city, at $48, $63, and $78. To be sure, in this case there were some differences in "services," such as credit arrangements, but in the main this difference in prices can be accounted for only by the differences in reputation and prestige of the stores. These things could have no effect on price, of course, if buying were done on a rational basis and if consumers could judge the quality of merchandise. Another recent case in which price failed to be a guide to quality is that of a purchaser who found an identical polo shirt priced differently in the basement, the men's department, and the boys' department of the same store. Moreover, the consumer has no information concerning "sale prices," and has little recourse when she buys a dress in one store "marked down" to $29.75 only to find that the dress actually retailed before the sale in that store and in other stores on the avenue at $26.50. Such price variations and discrepancies are major causes of "shopping"—the comparing of commodities—which, as we pointed out in Chapters 14 and 17, contributes greatly to the cost of retailing.

As long as such price variations exist consumers will be unable to do sufficient price-comparison shopping to assure the getting of the best values. Certainly a wiser use of consumer income might result from more uniform and dependable retail prices. Moreover, so long as these price variations exist, price is a poor guide to quality in some cases.

Price will probably remain a poor guide in some cases because of the intangible aspects of quality which make comparisons so difficult in any terms. For some purposes, glass is more valuable when fragile while for other purposes it should be durable and shatter-proof. In the former case, however, information concerning the fragility of the glass in a goblet will hardly serve as an objective measure of the value of the goblet. Other elements such as design, age, clarity of the glass, and so on probably are more important considerations.

This example merely emphasizes the difficulty of using even objective measurements of quality characteristics in conjunction with price to measure the relative value of specific purchases.

Consumers May Use Direct Action.—When consumers become convinced that prices are being held unduly high by manufacturers or merchants, they may use direct action.[5] Organized consumer boycotts are of fairly recent origin, but they can be very effective and their use may grow in importance. Labor unions have used them by boycotting goods offered for sale which do not bear the union label. A poorly organized attempt at boycott by consumers was made in 1920, when the price level reached a high point. Among other activities, New York City saw an overall-clad parade down Broadway early in the year. In England in 1922 a middle-class union was formed to fight high prices. Since then sporadic efforts at organized boycotts have been made and where determination has been strong they have accomplished their purpose. Among recent examples are the Amarillo, Texas proposed boycott of telephones for lower rates; the bread and rolls boycott in New York City in 1934; the famous meat strike in Detroit in 1935; and the Kosher meat strike in New York City in 1937. Well-organized boycotts are highly effective, but are not used often because it is difficult to organize consumers into effective groups and because the results attained may be at too great cost to those participating.

Group Action by Consumers.—In recent years, as was pointed out earlier in this chapter, many women's and other organizations which were formed originally for other purposes have joined their efforts in behalf of people as consumers. During and immediately following the depression of the 1930's there was an upsurge of interest of both organized as well as unorganized nature in improving the welfare of the consumer in addition to awakening within the consumer a desire to help himself. One national association carefully investigated the various national organizations which claimed to be bona fide consumer organizations and compiled a list of sixty such groups. To this list should be added all the government departments which were actively concerned with problems of consumer interest and which distributed consumer literature. The total number of people made aware of consumer problems in these various ways was well over five million. Many of the groups interested in legislation

---

[5] Some of the material in the paragraphs on boycotts and consumer movement is adapted from an article by Louis Bader and J. P. Wernette, "Consumer Movement and Business," *Journal of Marketing,* July 1938.

for the consumer have united forces in the Women's Joint Congressional Committee. A fair number of the organizations and groups contain men, and if they are all counted, the number affected may reach a third of the total population. This group of men and women may well become a strong force in obtaining support for legislation of interest to consumers in general and for disseminating useful information to them.

These groups are not yet as closely organized as they could be and, therefore, their effectiveness is not what it may possibly become. Even so, the movement cannot be treated lightly. Members of many of the organizations are leaders in other organizations and as such may be powerful factors in crystallizing consumers' thoughts along specific lines.

Consumer Organizations.—Consumer cooperative societies, consumer-organized testing bureaus, and the over-all type of organization that the Consumers' Foundation hopes to become, some of which have been mentioned earlier, are important parts of the consumer movement. There are two other over-all groups that are somewhat similar to the Consumers' Foundation in aims. These are the Consumer-Retailer Relations Council, a forum in which consumers and retailers can consider their mutual problems in accordance with the best interests of both, and the National Association of Consumers. The Consumer-Retailer Relations Council grew out of the work of the Advisory Committee of Ultimate Consumer Goods of the American Standards Association and the Consumer Relations Program of the National Retail Dry Goods Association. The present members are the American Home Economics Association, American Association of University Women, General Federation of Women's Clubs, National Retail Dry Goods Association, American Retail Federation, National Association of Better Business Bureaus, Inc., as well as certain individuals who have made significant contributions to the work of the Council.

The second group, the National Association of Consumers, headed by Helen Hall of the Henry Street Settlement, is a nonpartisan, nonprofit, nontechnical organization devoted to the advancement and protection of the economic welfare of consumers in the United States. It attempts to be a catalytic agent to fuse the activities of all organizations interested in the consumer, at least with respect to consumer relations. It is primarily interested in achieving a strong consumer movement as an essential to a sound economy. It undertakes to represent the consumer's interest through legislation and other means. For example, it has supported an international trade organization which would have certain safeguards to ensure that consumer countries and consumers would not be burdened by a short supply at high prices as a result of trade agreements.

The purposes of most of these over-all organizations are much the same. Perhaps someday they will pool their efforts and finally accomplish their aims, which may be summarized as follows:

1. To promote the use of informative labeling.
2. To promote the use of informative advertising.
3. To promote informative salesmanship.
4. To encourage practices which will tend to reduce abuses of such privileges as customer accounts, returns, deliveries, and similar services.
5. To foster local cooperation between stores or groups of stores and local consumer groups.
6. To promote the use of adequate standards for consumer goods.
7. To promote the use of uniform terminology in describing consumer goods and services.
8. To develop and promote the use of suggested codes of ethics for both retailers and consumers.

Organizations with aims such as these seem to offer the same approach to the solution of many of the problems of consumers. They merit the attention and perhaps the support of thoughtful persons. They certainly have a part in the general desire for consumer education.

Consumers Need More Formal Education.—But consumers today find themselves baffled and often frustrated by market situations. Certainly the average consumer in the decade of the 1950's lives in a much more complicated economy than did his counterpart in the 1750's. Under the simpler conditions of life in those early years, consumer problems were relatively simple and readily solved. This was true for a number of reasons, but a statement of the more important ones will be sufficient. The average person produced a large part of what he consumed. The variety and amount of products available for consumption were relatively small. Techniques of selling and distribution were simple and direct. Today this has all been changed, and we need to know more not only about nutrition, textiles, budgeting, and practical buymanship, but also about how our economic machine functions and why.

An important phase of the consumer movement is apparent in the growth of formal consumer education. The need for such training was recognized by the British cooperative movement in its early years of development and has been a major part of its program ever since. As a matter of fact, the consumer cooperative movement crystallized the awareness of the need for consumer education and spearheaded the action taken for satisfying that need. As was pointed out above, here in the United States a great many groups have effectively added their weight to this agitation. Progress has continued to the present time, although with some diminution during the war period. Interest in the subject is widespread. New courses in consumer problems are being introduced in elementary schools, colleges, and universities; and books are being written. Home economics courses which emphasize "buymanship" are being offered in an increasing number of secondary schools and colleges, and courses in the economics of consumption are being offered by many colleges and universities. The apex of this movement was, perhaps, the Institute for Consumer Education which was endowed by the Sloane Foundation at Stephens College, Columbia, Missouri in 1937. The purpose of this Institute was to devote time, effort, and thought to the increase and diffusion of economic education. The Institute, established as an independent agency which would be free of bias and pressure groups, was to have the following purposes:

1. To help the consumer to become a better manager of his resources of money, goods, time, and energy so that he secures the maximum satisfaction from these limited resources;

2. To aid the consumer to become a wiser buyer of goods and services so that he obtains the best possible values in making purchases in the market place;

3. To assist the consumer to become a wiser user of goods and services so that he gets the most utility from what he has;

4. To help the consumer to become an informed consumer-citizen so that he will act not only to improve his individual economic status but also to contribute through democratic means to the welfare of the consumers as a group.[6]

The Institute's objective was to assist schools, colleges, and adult groups to carry on more effective programs of consumer education. To achieve this goal the Institute set up two major programs of work which were designed to complement one another. One was a college

---

[6] The Institute for Consumer Education, *A Report of Work in Progress,* Mimeographed, March, 1941, pp. 1 and 2.

program which served as a laboratory for experiments which might be used in other schools and which taught students to become more efficient and socially more sensitive consumers. The other program was national in scope. It stressed research and popularization of research which dealt with such matters as the consumer movement in America and the role of the consumer as a citizen. The advent of World War II stopped the progress of the Institute, and at this writing the work has not been resumed on any broad scale. The important point so far as consumer education is concerned is that a large and wealthy foundation not only recognized the great need for providing a model consumer education program and for providing materials for use in other schools but also contributed money to operate such a program. If and when the war needs of our country and the world are diminished, it is to be hoped that this very important work will be resumed.

What is perhaps most important, however, is that business has come to realize that it is more profitable to work with and for the consumer than to disregard his needs and wishes. Furthermore, consumers are gradually realizing that if our economy is to grow or even to survive, the fundamental economic and business principles must be made realistic and widely understood by them.

Project Questions

1. Bring to class examples of grade labels and informative labels. Discuss these labels. Can they be improved? If so, what other information is needed?

2. Visit a self-service grocery store and find out, roughly, what proportion of the stock has grade labels and informative labels.

3. Investigate the extent of the Consumer Cooperative Movement in your community. List the names of the Consumer Cooperatives in your city or town (or county if there are no organizations in the city) and describe one Cooperative with reference to the following points:

    a) Organization
    b) Size (Membership)
    c) Capitalization
    d) Age
    e) Scope
    f) Advertising done
    g) Anything else you may think interesting

4. If you could buy equally fresh eggs from any one of the following places, from which would you buy?

From a regular private butter-and-egg man
From a private farmer directly
From a large chain
From a company operated by the state
From a consumers' cooperative

It is hoped that, by now, the student will realize the existence of the three criteria of desirability: convenience, quality of product, and price, and will be able to discuss their relative importance in a specific case.

Chapter 19

OTHER AIDS TO THE CONSUMER
(THE CONSUMER MOVEMENT)

Merchandise Identification

As our economy grew, business searched for different ways of competing for the interest and patronage of the consumer. Many types of merchandise identification have been used, not only to attract the buyer in his first purchase of the article but also to build a large group of "repeat buyers." These attempts were largely provided by business but, as will be pointed out later on, consumer groups initiated the agitation for more accurate and informative labeling and identification of goods as an aid to consumer buying.

The Brand or Trade-Mark.—One of the earliest devices used by business to identify products was the brand or trade-mark. By the use of either or both the owner hoped so to differentiate his product from all others that it would become known, recognized, and called for by the consumer. Many producers, wholesalers, and retailers have branded their goods and have attempted to convince consumers that their brands were superior to all others. Millions of dollars are spent annually by various types of business in the effort to build or to retain brand consciousness for their product or products among consumers. Much advertising is devoted to the establishment of brand prestige which, like good will, is an intangible element that is difficult to measure accurately.

Since the early 1920's many studies have been made in an attempt to measure the degree of influence which brands have upon the purchasing habits of the average consumer. Although there is considerable disagreement among the various studies as to the specific amount of influence which brands have on the consumer, there is general agreement that brands influence the consumer's decision to a considerable degree and that this influence is stronger among certain groups of consumers, especially the professional group, both men and women. There seems to be no question but that the existence of well-established brands does simplify buying by persons who do not have the time or who do not wish to take the time to compare quality, price, and other market characteristics of products. If a consumer finds a brand of hat, shoes, canned fruit, or anything else, with which he is satisfied, it takes less time, energy, and thought to buy that particular brand the next time. A study made at the University of Minnesota found that professional men and women such as doctors, lawyers, and teachers exhibited a strong brand preference for the particular commodities used in the study whereas the housewives from all income classes exhibited a low brand preference for the same commodities. Housewives, apparently, found the existence of brands to be of slight assistance in their job of doing the buying for the family whereas professional men and women found brands to be very helpful.

Labels for Consumers' Goods.—Consumers have been skeptical of the implied guarantee which business attempts to establish by the use of brands. They want this information put on a product's label and have expressed the desire for additional information and/or guarantee of the product. It is agreed that the real purpose of labeling is to enable the consumer to identify the qualities possessed by the desired product. There is no agreement, however, as to what kind of information would be most useful in quality and price comparison.

Two types of labeling have been advocated, straight grade labeling and informative labeling. Those who favor grade labeling argue that we should set up standards on the basis of which grades will be determined and then printed on the label. So far, the proponents of grade labeling have directed their attention mainly to canned foods. Their claim is that objective standards would eliminate differences of opinion and would insure uniformity of statements referring to the same qualities or characteristics.

Grade Labeling Is Voluntary in the United States.—The first movement toward grade labeling of canned goods in this country was made in August of 1916, in the United States Warehouse Act. The canners themselves promoted the Act because they needed some official certificate to present to banks in order to show the quality of canned goods on which they wished to borrow money.

The Act authorized the Secretary of Agriculture to establish and promulgate standards for agricultural products only, by which their quality and value might be judged or determined. Moreover, the standards thus set up were for use by growers and distributors and not by consumers. But the Warehouse Act was the beginning of a growing interest in the labeling of consumers' goods according to grades.

Then, in 1931, the Agricultural Marketing Service of the United States Department of Agriculture was given direct authority to establish A—B—C grades for the sale of canned goods to the public.[1] The A—B—C system was voluntary and a symbol was to be used on canned goods which would indicate that the canning had been supervised by government inspectors at the expense of the canner. In June of 1939 Congress authorized the Department of Agriculture to set up regulations governing the grading and certification of canned fruits and vegetables under the A—B—C system. The cost of having government inspection in the plant at all times during the canning season is borne by the canner at a small sum per can. All canners do not make use of this service; instead, many of them have elected to set up their own grading service under their own inspectors. However, any canner who wishes may use the A—B—C system. By the summer of 1940 two hundred canners had joined the movement to have constant inspection and grading of their produce by Department of Agriculture graders and by 1943, 55 per cent of all fruits and vegetables, whether canned, dehydrated, or frozen, were graded by government inspectors. There has been considerable disagreement on the advisability of this plan among the large companies and among allied associations. The grade labeling fight in the canned foods field came about in earnest, however, in 1943 when the OPA, as part of its program to level off prices, tried to put labels on all canned food at the retail level. Finally, through the Taft Amendment to the Commodity Credit Corporation Bill of 1943 the government regulation was ended, but the disagreement as to the proper type of labeling goes on. Women's and homemakers' groups favor the A—B—C grade labeling, as does the National Retail Dry Goods Association, the American Retail Federation, and the National Association of Food Chains in the National Consumer-Retailer Council. But grade labeling is still voluntary in the United States and only a small proportion of consumers' goods is marketed under standards which have been set up either by the government or by producers and which would permit meaningful grade labeling.

Cooperatives Grade-Label Canned Goods.—Cooperatives have been active in branding and labeling their own merchandise which is sold under the Co-op brand. Co-op brands are now grade-labeled at the cannery under the supervision of the National Cooperative Association. They are not U. S. graded but do adhere to the United

---

[1] "A" stands for excellent, for use on special occasions; "B" for good, for everyday use; "C" for fair, for thrifty buying.

States Standards. The red label is comparable to Grade A, blue label comparable to Grade B, and the green label is comparable to Grade C.

Grade Labeling and Informative Labeling.—Informative labeling is supported by certain consumer groups who argue that grade labeling does not provide the buyer with enough specific information to permit a comparison of various brands. Actually, the main difference between grade labeling and informative labeling [2] is that the informative labels carry much of the information by which the grades are determined. For canned peas, for example, facts on age, size, form, and color of the peas; the amount and content of the liquid; the flavoring used, etc., are examples of what is printed on labels. Those who advocate informative labeling assume that the consumer is able and will take the time to read all the information on the label and make an intelligent comparison of the various products on the basis of the information provided. They further assume that for many commodities most of the qualities of the product are measurable and can be reported accurately and with meaning to the average consumer.

Some Weaknesses of Informative Labeling.—Some of the specific qualities of some commodities can be determined with exactness. The width of a bolt of cloth, for example, or the weight of a leg of lamb is subject to unquestioned measurement. Consumers who purchase with reasonable care need never be surprised in these matters. The width of the cloth tells little, however, about its final usefulness. One needs, in addition, full information concerning the stuff from which it was made, its wearing qualities, the fastness of its dyes, the extent to which it will shrink on washing, and so on. And the weight of the leg of lamb tells little about its flavor or tenderness, or the proportions of bone and fat.

Even in the cases where accurate measurement should be fairly easy, and the information can be and is printed on the label, clever merchants frequently disguise their containers to their own advantage when selling to careless buyers. Thick bottoms are used in some glass bottles, and particular shapes or colors or designs on all sorts of packages have been carefully planned by commercial psychologists to give an optical illusion of size. Handsome containers have been used to give the impression of high quality. Figure 37 shows how the shapes and sizes of standard cans used in the food industry

---

[2] There are those who claim "informative" labeling to be the same as "descriptive labeling." Your authors question their identity. It would appear that a descriptive label need not be "informative," in the sense in which it is usually used. The term "informative label" has come to mean labels which carry information about quality, performance, quantity, and use and care of the product.

compare. From this diagram it is easy to see how much care consumers must exercise if they are to make accurate comparisons among the different sizes and prices of canned goods, even when very detailed information about the contents is printed on the labels.

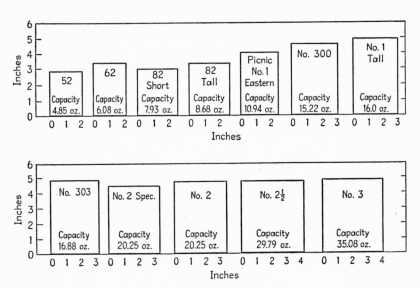

FIG. 37.—How Cans Compare

The chart shows the exact dimensions of some of the cans on the grocer's shelves. Capacity indicated on the cans is the distilled water which the can would hold if filled to its very top. Actual weight of the contents of cans of the same technical size varies with the kind of food and the degree of fullness. The label on the can gives the weight of each can's contents. Source: *Consumer's Guide*, October 5, 1936, pp. 10-11.

Moreover, in matters of taste, such as the flavor of a peach or a cigarette, the color of nail polish, the cut and design of a dress, there are no final or objective standards and the fashion is constantly changing. It is matters such as these that permit competing sellers to persuade customers to spend their money on one thing rather than another without full proof of the relative merits of the competing goods.

Federal, state, and local governments do some policing in the field of weights and measures. On the whole, consumer protection in this limited field is reasonably good, but consumers need to be on their guard against subtle misrepresentations. In the case of goods with many important qualities, the enforcement of either explicit or implicit guarantees is very difficult.

Consumers' purchasing would be greatly simplified with some saving of both time and money if more goods were produced under a plan of standardization and inspection. Producers in general have opposed standardization, and this is not surprising. So long as consumers can be influenced by emotional and even untrue claims, producers will continue to oppose attempts of standardization and uniformity. Moreover, consumers have never been entirely sure that they wanted goods standardized because, perhaps, they feared to lose some degree of individuality.

Conclusion.—Comparatively few goods are grade-labeled today. Various studies have been made in an attempt to determine the attitude of housewives toward grade labeling and toward informative labeling. The findings are not conclusive but they indicate that average consumers do not know much about grade labeling and do not distinguish clearly between grade labeling and informative labeling. Of course, consumers have had little opportunity to learn much about them through experience, since so few goods are so labeled. Also, perhaps the rank and file of consumers are not convinced that they will be able or willing to use the information which consumers' groups claim they want.[3]

INFORMATIVE ADVERTISING

Advertising Is an Effective Selling Tool.—Advertising contributes to the process of getting goods out of the hands of the producer and into the hands of the consumer. It is a step in the entire process of selling goods. Advertising performs a selling job which is, from one point of view, equally as important as packing, transportation, warehousing, or any other part of the distribution process. There may be an abundance of goods and very efficient transportation systems to carry these goods to every corner of our country but unless the goods are brought to the attention of the consumer and sold to the consumer those goods will not be used and there will be no point to producing them. Advertising is the best way business has found, so far, of telling the greatest number of persons about a product in the quickest possible time and at the lowest possible cost.

One writer has estimated that consumers have conscious wants for about half of the things they consume and that they depend upon suggestions and directions for the selections of the other half. Advertising is used by the producer and seller of goods to persuade the consumer to select certain goods for certain reasons. This may not

---

[3] For an excellent, detailed discussion of identification of consumers' goods see *Standards and Labels for Consumers' Goods,* by Jessie V. Coles (New York: The Ronald Press Co., 1949).

always be to the best interest of the consumer. It has been, however, a very effective selling tool.

Advertising Has "Come of Age."—Advertising is a fairly new selling device. In the fourth quarter of the nineteenth century advertising still was largely a cheap business for fakers and gamblers. Although patent medicine and lotteries gave early advertising a tremendous impetus, they also gave it a black eye. The business, however, was extremely profitable and the "tainted dollars" from such advertising provided much-needed revenue for newspapers and periodicals. In time, the better advertising crowded out the most objectionable. By 1893 advertising had taken on dignity and was recognized as a factor in the broad economic development of the United States. Advertising not only increased in quantity but also improved in quality. In the ten-year period from 1880 to 1890 total advertising in general magazines increased 200 to 300 per cent and by 1900 advertising had truly come of age. The main reasons for this marked growth were: (1) the widening gap between producers and consumers; (2) the rapidly increasing variety of new types of merchandise put on the market; (3) an increasingly greater need for product differentiation as the industrial system matured and manufacturers increased their capacity to produce more goods, and (4) the widening retail markets as the means of transportation steadily improved. This was especially true after the advent of the automobile.

Advertising Has Become More Informative.—From 1900 on, advertising has continued to improve in quality. There has been some federal regulation of advertising to eliminate untruthful statements and some attempt to limit the amount of exaggeration.[4] On the whole, however, the improved quality stemmed from the pressure of consumer demands for more informative advertising and the recognition by advertisers themselves that truthful and informative advertising was a more effective selling tool than any other type of appeal. Many manufacturers and merchants have combined in a long and somewhat successful campaign for truth in advertising, an effort which has been supported by many publishers, who refuse to accept false advertising. Some publishers have even gone further, establishing testing bureaus which issue labels of approval and recommendation for tested merchandise. The Good Housekeeping Bureau and the Jean Abbey Seal of Recommendation (Women's Home Companion) are cases in point. "Whenever you see this distinguishing

---

[4] See the discussion of government regulation of advertising in Chapter 20.

label on merchandise offered, in advertising or sales literature, you may be sure that both the product and the claims made for it have been carefully examined and fully approved." And yet the fact that the interests of the manufacturer and the publisher are so similar perhaps justifies the persistence of a bit of skepticism of these guarantees.

Word-of-Mouth Advertising—A Powerful Force.—Perhaps the oldest form of consumer protection is word-of-mouth advertising. People rarely converse long before the discussion turns to the merits of favorite brands of golf clubs, whisky, face creams, radios, washing machines, canned tomatoes, or something equally homely. Both the good and the bad points are paraded in these free-for-all debates and the results of use under home conditions are made known. Merchants as well as merchandise are evaluated. Certainly this informal sharing of experiences is a powerful force in consumer education and protection on the one hand, and in the directing of industry on the other hand.

The Consumer Must Discipline the Advertiser.—If it is true that consumers have conscious wants for only half of the things they consume it is not surprising that advertisements resort to an appeal to the emotions rather than an appeal to reason. The thinly veiled implication of most advertisements that there is only one product capable of insuring the consumer's satisfaction makes us somewhat skeptical of all advertising. Since all the products cannot possess this implied superiority, the consumer is likely to wonder whether any of them actually can be superior. It is perhaps expecting too much of the advertiser to discipline himself when there is no disciplinarian. It is up to the consumer to know what facts he wants the advertiser to present and to demand that such advertising be used.

INFORMATIVE SELLING

Although advertising is one of the tools of selling, one usually thinks of "selling" as personal salesmanship. It is probably impossible for the average consumer to know enough or learn enough about all the commodities which she buys to be an informed purchaser of merchandise. She, therefore, would like to depend upon qualified salespeople to give her the merchandise information she needs to make her purchases wisely.

The Consumer Wants More Informative Selling.—Too often, retail salespeople do not satisfy the consumer. In several studies it was found that among the ten most important qualifications which consumers expect of a successful salesperson, the leading five were: (1) a neat appearance, (2) a knowledge of the merchandise, (3) a willingness to volunteer helpful information, (4) courtesy, and (5) a willingness to suggest a substitute when the store doesn't have what the customer first asked to see. The fact that three of the five leading qualifications which customers want salespeople to possess have to do with a knowledge of the merchandise indicates the value which the average consumer places on informative selling.

The Growth of Informative Selling Depends on the Consumer. —A great deal has been accomplished in the improvement of informative selling since the turn of the century. Training programs in the larger retail stores emphasize the use of merchandise information. Some of the large department and chain retail stores in the United States have found it profitable to assemble merchandise information and make it available to salespeople. At frequent intervals, interesting data on the historical and present use of articles in stock and useful information on the construction, durability, color fastness, laundering and cleaning qualities, etc., of new products and new materials, as well as on products which have been stocked regularly, are circulated to the proper salespeople. Certainly, considerably more information on merchandise is available to the consumer than was available to her forefathers. Whether or not this information is passed on by the salesperson to the consumer depends pretty largely upon the training program of the respective stores. Certainly the consumer movement has had an important effect upon making the retailer aware of the need for this type of information. It remains true that the continuous and growing use of more information likewise depends upon the consumer's making known her desire for this type of informative selling.

Testing Services

Equally important, perhaps, and distinctly American are the several consumer groups that have been organized to test commodities, establish grades, and advise their members concerning the quality of various articles. These organizations generally limit their activities to research and recommendation, leaving the actual buying and selling to others. Among the aims of these organizations are a stronger food and drug law, better merchandise, established standards, grade labeling, lower prices, and truthful advertising.

The oldest of the group is Consumers' Research, Inc., for which Stuart Chase and others gave early publicity through their books, *The Tragedy of Waste, Your Money's Worth,* and *A Hundred Million Guinea Pigs.*[5] Consumers Union of the United States, Inc., is a similar though younger organization, having been established in 1936. Both organizations operate on a nonprofit basis, their income being derived entirely from fees and contributions of members by means of subscriptions to their published reports, each member having a vote in the control of the organization. Both organizations test products for quality and relate them to price. They report the results of the tests in monthly bulletins and summarize the results in annual manuals. Their own laboratories are used for testing, wherever possible, but private testing services as well as laboratories of colleges and universities are also used. The main difference between Consumers' Research and Consumers Union is the way they relate quality to price. Both report brands tested in three classifications. Consumers' Research classifies products A-recommended, B-intermediate, and C-not recommended. Consumers Union lists them as best buy, also accepted, and not accepted.

Limitations of Any Testing Service.—The two consumer organizations which have been mentioned and others which have not are relatively young. The depression of the 1930's gave them considerable impetus and they merit careful attention. Intelligent use of their services involves a careful study of the full discussion that accompanies the ratings in the reports, a very careful evaluation of the criteria used in rating a product, and a careful relating of these factors to one's own budget and the factors considered necessary in one's selection. Other limitations of any testing service have been pointed out by various students of the subject. Some are admitted by the services in their own publications. Some of the most important of the criticisms are listed as follows : [6]

Testing everything is not possible. Consumers' Research has called attention to the fact that by reason of the limitation of its funds it must confine the scope of its own investigation to such products as

---

[5] These are popularly called "debunking" books because they claim to expose and debunk certain conditions harmful to consumers. One of the first of such books was Upton Sinclair's *The Jungle,* which described the unsanitary conditions in the meat-packing industry.

[6] See the article by Ira I. Berman, "Comparison of the Ratings of Consumers' Research and Consumers Union" in the *Journal of Retailing,* October, 1940, pp. 76-81. Also, refer to article by Eugene R. Beem, "Consumer-Financed Testing and Rating Agencies" in the *Journal of Marketing,* January, 1952, pp. 272-285.

are of importance to the average consumer either because they are most commonly used or because their purchase involves a large initial expenditure. Consumers' Research goes on to point out that it can make no pretense to completeness or unfailing exactness of information because of the limitation of financial resources.

Rigid grading is not always possible. Industrial processes are not so well controlled or so constant that high precision in the judgment of their output is always warranted or even possible. Moreover, for certain products the establishment of scientific objective standards of quality are not possible. Two familiar examples are canned fruit and canned vegetables.

It is extremely difficult to judge a product on the appropriateness for the use to which it is to be put. Only the prospective user is in a position to make that type of judgment. This is closely associated with the problem caused by the differences in persons using a commodity. One person will drive an automobile in a manner very different from another, whose needs are different. This presents an almost insurmountable problem to any testing service.

One limitation, unknown to most consumers, is that the ratings are based on current retail prices at the time the tests are made. Changes in prices as a result of special sales events and differences in local conditions may and probably will throw off the ratings. These and many other limitations should be kept in mind by the consumer when using such testing services.

Government Serves the Consumer.—Government has supplemented the efforts of private groups of consumers in this area with various noteworthy attempts at organized protection. These will be discussed in greater detail in Chapter 20 but we may mention a few here. There are, for example, national standardization of weights and measures and various laws, such as the Federal Standard Container Law which establishes official sizes for many merchandise containers used in interstate trade. Although many states have laws regulating quantity, a number of states do not. Consumers are protected by the Food and Drug Administration, the Federal Meat Inspection Act, and many other laws which will be discussed later on.

BETTER BUSINESS BUREAUS

Trade practices which are unfair to the consumer are regulated to some degree, although much more might be done. There is a certain small amount of federal and state regulation which will be discussed in Chapter 20 as well as some private group regulation of misleading advertising. Also, most cities have ordinances against unscrupulous and fraudulent selling methods. Nevertheless, many business practices which harm the consumer, some not exactly illegal and others which are, would go on unchecked if it were not for the Better Business Bureaus.

Definition and Description.—The Better Business Bureaus are voluntary nonprofit associations established by businessmen for the protection of the consumer and legitimate business. The Bureaus aim at furthering and promoting honesty, truthfulness, and dependability in advertising and business, and fair competition in trade. The members believe that in so doing they increase public confidence in advertising, salesmanship, and business methods in general. The Bureaus were first organized about twenty-five years ago for the sole purpose of using all lawful means to eliminate fraudulent advertising. However, during the years of growth of the Bureaus a second, community, interest has been added—a desire to make the business world a better world. The Bureaus have developed programs to include not only fraud prosecutions but also the broader activities which they have assumed as part of their social responsibility. In at least one city in Minnesota a splendid aid to consumers is provided by the Bureau, which requires that every house-to-house canvasser, be he a research worker or a Fuller Brush man, must present his credentials to the Bureau in order to get a small card which authorizes him to "work the town" for a certain limited period of time. Every person is warned not to listen to any solicitor who has not such a card. Many fly-by-night schemes are thus prevented from being born and both time and money are saved for many consumers.

Fields of Consumer Protection.—Better Business Bureaus have given consumer protection and assistance in four fields, namely: (1) fraud prosecution, (2) fraud prevention, (3) promotion of fair advertising and selling practices, and (4) consumer education in money management, in buying, and in taking care of merchandise in everyday relations with business. Let us briefly see how Better Business Bureaus protect and assist consumers in these four areas.

PROTECTION AGAINST FRAUD. Fraud prosecution is the oldest of the programs of a Bureau and continues to be one of its very important functions. Consumers and businessmen are urged to register complaints and inquiries with the local Bureau, thus making it a clearing house. Every complaint is duly investigated by a staff member of the Bureau and where the facts warrant such action they are, with any additional evidence uncovered by the Bureau, referred to the appropriate government agency for prosecution. In general, the Bureaus attempt to stay out of legislation but in the field of fraud prevention they do assist in the enactment of some laws. Illustrations are the jewelry auction laws and some state advertising laws. Consumers may also obtain help by seeking information from the local Bureau *before* actually buying or investing money.

PROMOTION OF FAIR ADVERTISING AND SELLING PRACTICES. The promotion of fair advertising and selling practices has been of considerable help to consumers. The National Better Business Bureau [7] has published a booklet entitled *A Guide for Retail Advertising and Selling* and one for use by national advertisers entitled *A Guide for National Advertising*. The guides have done much to promote informative advertising and selling by prohibiting the use (by Bureau members) of terms and phrases which confuse and mislead consumers, as well as by promoting uniform terminology and standardized definitions or meanings of various terms. For example, cony (rabbit) garments are no longer advertised as various kinds of "seal" but as seal-dyed cony. Again, "Toya Panama" cannot now be used to describe braided paper hats from Japan. Bureaus require that members subscribe to and practice Bureau standards. In most cities, members are not permitted to use the name of the Bureau in their advertising and selling, nor do Bureaus endorse or recommend their members or their members' products or services. Members and nonmembers are supposedly treated alike and there are cases where the Bureaus have taken action against their own members through expulsion, publicity, or prosecution.

CONSUMER EDUCATION. The Bureaus' program of consumer education includes many of the activities under fraud prevention, fraud prosecution, and promotion of fair advertising and selling practices. In addition, it includes all forms of Better Business Bureau publicity. A great many agencies distribute free of charge such information as the Bureau publishes on unfair activities in advertising and selling, etc. Among these agencies are radio stations which give free time for calling attention to the activity of the Bureaus, and newspapers which carry Better Business Bureau advertisements as well as news stories covering the program of the Bureaus. In addition, the Bureaus have prepared and published bulletins and posters especially for consumers. They also publish car cards, payroll stuf-

---

[7] The National Better Business Bureau is located in New York City. About seventy local Bureaus are members of the National. All officers serve without payment although their responsibilities are great.

fers, etc., as a means of calling attention of the consumer to the type of assistance which the Bureau tries to give to the consumer.

Of particular importance to consumers are the booklets which were started several years ago and which present specific information on a great many subjects. The following few titles will indicate the variety of information which can be obtained free of charge by writing to one of the Bureaus: "Advertising," "Borrowing," "Budgeting," "Buying or Building a Home," "Buying Used Cars," "Cosmetics," "Health Cures," "Investment Companies," "Jewelry," "Legal Problems," "Life Insurance," "Oil Royalties," "Savings," and "Securities." The Bureau has attempted to keep up an endless flow of publicity to help consumers avoid deception and purchase more wisely.

Conclusion.—We have defined the consumer movement as including all activities, organized and unorganized, which make the consumer a more intelligent buyer and user of goods and services. In that sense, all the aids discussed in Chapters 18 and 19 are parts of this movement.

If the various parts of the consumer movement continue to grow and to gain importance, business methods will have to be modified somewhat to meet consumers' demands. The combined force of consumer cooperatives, consumer testing bureaus, consumer lobbies, consumer education, and consumer attempts to show laborers and employers the mutuality of their several interests, must lead eventually to a clearer understanding of the proposition that consumption is the purpose of all economic activity and that production is but a means to that end. Income must be produced; but income, after all, lacks substance except in consumption. Perhaps the consumer movement, in the combination of its phases, can so clearly express the desires of the people for specific goods and services that the wheels of industry will be built and turned more nearly in accord with consumer demand. Whether the movement expresses itself through the police power, government operation, consumer cooperation, testing bureaus, consumer education, or boycotts is, perhaps, of little importance. Maybe it will continue to use all the tools it can put its hand to. As a result of continued consumer pressure in many forms, however, it may well develop that total consumption income is increased; that fewer people are in want of bacon, orange juice, shoes, tennis rackets, gasoline, medical care, electric ranges, or whatever it is that the people want their consumption to consist of; and that the quality of the wants themselves will have risen to a new high level.

PROJECT QUESTIONS

1. Obtain copies of the reports of Consumers' Research and Consumers Union and compare the ratings of several commodities. To what extent do they agree and wherein do they disagree? Compare the reasons for the ratings given.

2. How many of your friends subscribe to or use any of the testing services reports? What are their opinions of the usefulness of the information provided?

3. Prepare definitions of "trade-mark" and "brand" which differentiate between them.

4. Visit several retail stores and "shop" for different commodities. Then write a brief essay on the type of salesperson who waited on you. Was there any "informative selling"? If there was, specify what information was provided.

5. Find out whether there is a Better Business Bureau in your town. How active is it? Does it serve the consumer in all four ways described in this chapter?

6. Furnish yourselves with the latest issue of *The Saturday Evening Post*. Cut out *one* advertisement to illustrate *each* of the *four* types of appeal. The classification of appeals is given in the following diagram. Indicate which combination of appeals is represented by each advertisement by placing in the upper right hand corner of the advertisement the number in the diagram which indicates that classification. For example, considering nothing else, the slogan "The skin you love to touch" in a Woodbury soap advertisement should be numbered "4."

Classification of Appeals

	Pioneer	Competitive
Rational	1	2
Emotional	3	4

7. Bring to class the food advertisement, the auto advertisement, and the cigarette advertisement which appeal to you the most strongly, i.e., make you want to buy. Tell what feature of each advertisement seems to be most influential.

Chapter 20

GOVERNMENT IN THE INTEREST
OF CONSUMERS

Competition as the Consumer's Protector

Caveat emptor, let the buyer beware, was long the accepted order of the day. The common law gave the consumer-buyer little protection against dishonest sellers. Early court decisions said in effect that since buyers and sellers bargain on equal terms, the buyers should take care of their own interests without special legislation on their behalf and with aid from the court only in case of flagrant misbehavior on the part of the seller.

During most of the nineteenth century, some of the accepted assumptions concerning political economy seem to have been about as follows:

1. Individuals attempt to maximize their own personal income from their efforts in production;

2. Income of individual producers can be increased only by more completely satisfying the wants of consumers;

3. Therefore, if individuals are given the greatest possible freedom and protection as producers, the interests of consumers will be served most adequately.

Early establishment of standard weights and measures, standard money, and terms descriptive of quality was undertaken largely in the attempt to keep competition among producers on a fair and honest plane. In other words, the early policing of sellers to prevent short weight, for example, was to prevent one seller's gaining an advantage over other sellers.

This general line of thought influenced and almost dominated our political control of industry until rather recently, and continues to exert some influence today. The development of the modern corporation, for example, with the accompanying economies of scale made possible by this form of organization, received political encouragement. This was in line with our belief that if we could increase productivity the lot of the consumer would automatically improve.

Late in the nineteenth century it became evident that some producing firms in this country might become so large as to injure other firms, even making it impossible for new ones to start. This, it was believed, might interfere with freedom of enterprise, lessen competition, remove the urge to improvement in production which competition is supposed to furnish, and possibly lead to actual restriction of output on the part of the large firms. Indirectly, each of these tendencies would injure consumers.

During the 1880's the fear of large firms became widespread, and in 1890 the Sherman Anti-Trust Act was passed. Its objective is to prevent the growth of individual firms, or the use of methods of competition, whenever such growth or use tended to create monopoly or injure competition unfairly. The assumption was implicit that protection of competitors protected consumers.

In 1914 the Clayton Act and the Federal Trade Commission Act were passed under the same assumption. They provided machinery by which competition unfair to competitors might be discovered and condemned. It was not until the passage of the Wheeler-Lea amendment in 1936 that the Federal Trade Commission was given authority over advertising or other business policies which appeared to be unfair to consumers.

This same philosophy of protecting competitors in the public interest is seen in both federal and state laws. Illustrations include some sections of the federal Robinson-Patman Act (1937), the various state Unfair Trade Practices Acts which limit the price reductions that may be offered to consumers, the federal and state laws legalizing resale price maintenance, state laws aimed at differential taxation of chain stores in protection of independent merchants, and so on. The hypothesis that competition protects the consumer, provided only that it is kept active and fair, has a long and distinguished history. Only recently have we come seriously to question its validity. Whether our doubts are well founded still is a moot question, the answer to which may lie in alternative ways of improving the lot of consumers. The efficacy of some of the alternatives is examined later in this chapter.

GOVERNMENTAL PARTICIPATION IN ECONOMIC MATTERS

Government as Referee.—There is an old adage that a government is best when it governs least. The political doctrine of laissez faire, let matters alone, is based on this assumption. It means that the most acceptable government is the one which has a minimum of restrictions and restraint, subsidies and special privileges, or actual direction of the use of resources. It presupposes that freedom of individual action is an end in itself from which comes some of the highest human satisfactions.

When this doctrine prevails—or to the extent that it does—the role of government is limited mainly to three areas:

a) The codification of rules of conduct
b) The function of a referee to determine if and when the rules have been broken
c) The function of a policeman to enforce the adopted rules.

The rules of conduct adopted under this doctrine or political philosophy would express the accepted moral code of the time. They also might express the accepted economic code. That is, if the freest and fullest competition is accepted as the most desirable economic situation, rules against any hindrance to competition would be in order. To the extent that laissez faire prevails, government action is limited to the adoption, refereeing, and enforcing of rules that conform to the accepted moral code and the social mores.

Government as Director.—A somewhat more tolerant attitude towards governmental direction of economic affairs might call for the regulation of some specific economic acts. Allocation of resources to specific uses, direct price or production control, minimum wage and maximum hour laws, compulsory old age and unemployment insurance, tariffs and subsidies favoring specific industries, each illustrate this degree of governmental participation. During the emergencies of serious depression or all-out war we have accepted this form of participation, perhaps with reluctance but without serious objection. The use of government in these ways appears to have grown, perhaps insidiously, independent of emergencies. The time surely has come for an examination of the inconsistencies, group favoritism, and interference with individual freedom associated with present and proposed government programs of this sort. It should not be inferred, however, that such programs should be condemned, but merely that they should be examined for consistency, balance, and net effect on individual welfare.

Paternalistic Aid.—Direct government aid sometimes is extended to certain segments of our economy. The wherewithal for such aid must come from other segments. Research by government agencies on problems of agricultural production and marketing, when no similar research is devoted to problems of manufacturers, is an illustration and subsidies to our merchant marine is another. The federal government collects taxes for highway purposes and then redistributes them in a different geographic pattern, causing New York, for example, to pay part of the highway costs in North Dakota. While this kind of government action may tend to equalize economic conditions among the several geographic and other segments of the country, it also may tend towards "the triumph of mediocrity," for any leveling within a given universe is likely to involve a leveling down of the peaks to fill the hollows. Here again it is not to be inferred that such leveling is either good or bad. Each case should be considered in the light of its direct accomplishments, its influence on the economy as a whole, and its indirect effects on human freedom and satisfaction.

The extreme case of paternalistic aid so far offered by government in this country is, perhaps, that given to agricultural producers through the medium of price support. This support is accomplished in various ways. In some cases the federal agency persuades farmers not to plant more than a designated acreage to commercial crops by paying them to plant soil-improving crops instead. Doubtless this has a long-run value to the commonwealth through the preservation or restoration of soil fertility, but it tends to hold current prices higher than they otherwise would be.

In other cases, the Commodity Credit Corporation either guarantees loans on stocks of farm products that are not offered for sale by farmers, or actually buys and stores part of the physical supply. Thus the supply available for immediate purchase is reduced and the price is raised. Since the demand for most farm products is inelastic, withholding part of the supply raises not only the price but also the aggregate money payment for the amount actually purchased for consumption.[1] As a result, consumers pay more for less product than they would without the government control. The socioeconomic question that properly should be raised in each case is whether the gain to farmers is sufficient to offset the loss to consumers. Each case has its own factual setting so that generalization is impossible, but certainly any scheme which keeps goods off the market must be viewed with some suspicion by anyone directly interested in the general level of consumption in the commonwealth. Perhaps any cases that work out as well as Joseph's administration of the Egyptian corn market over two thousand years ago should be welcomed, but not many administrations have been so successful.

---

[1] The effect of inelastic demand on total revenue from sales is described in Chapter 14

Development of Resources.—Development of the agents of production may be undertaken by government. The most conspicuous and well-known illustration in this country at present is the Tennessee Valley Authority (TVA), with its public development of power. Many other cases exist, both earlier and later in origin. Throughout the West, large-scale irrigation and land reclamation projects have been in operation, some of them for over fifty years. The furnishing of electric power to farms and rural communities through aid by the Rural Electrification Administration (REA) has developed rapidly during and since World War II and has resulted in increased farm production per person engaged in farming. Projects such as these add to the supply of resources available for use in private enterprise. Usually the government has undertaken such projects only when two characteristics clearly existed; first, the undertaking was large scale, costly, and its benefits available to many users; second, the costs could be recovered only over a considerable period of time.

There never has been much opposition to this type of government developmental action in principle. Many individual projects, however, have aroused intense controversy. Some have proved to be of great value to the commonwealth while others have failed to prove their worth. Perhaps it should go without saying that each case needs to be considered on its merits and that some undertakings will prove more beneficial than others. Direct government action may, however, be the only way by which some important reclamation projects can be carried out.

Operation by Government.—Sometimes government undertakes the direct operation of economic institutions or agencies. Public schools, the federal postal system, and public highways are long-accepted illustrations in this country. Municipal water and sewage systems, electric light systems, and liquor stores are other illustrations. In some other countries transportation systems, radio broadcasting, coal mines, national electric power grids, and collective farms are operated by government agencies. The extent to which the provision of housing and medical care should be undertaken through public enterprise now is a matter of hot debate.

Once government launches on the operation of economic agencies there is, perhaps, no logical stopping point. Consequently, it needs to be kept clearly in mind that each enterprise taken over by government lessens the opportunity for individuals freely to undertake that particular thing. This suggests that government operations might well be limited to those in which individuals cannot or will not act.

SOME SPECIFIC FIELDS OF GOVERNMENTAL PARTICIPATION

A General Outline.—Government agencies have been established over the years for the express purpose of protecting individuals as human beings, as competitors, and as consumers. Sometimes it is hard to distinguish among the three purposes, and perhaps such distinction is unnecessary. A mere listing of some of the fields in which government agencies now operate in this country will illustrate the very wide use of such agencies. Perhaps the individual reader can determine for himself in what manner each type of control affects him. The list of important fields includes:

1. Protection of human rights
    Freedom of speech and assembly
    Freedom to hold property
    Freedom from murder, theft, and other antisocial actions

2. Protection against fraud
    Misrepresentation of qualities of goods and services
    Sale of property that does not exist
    Misrepresentation of identity

3. Protection of health
    Quarantines and other medical requirements
    Sanitary regulations and building codes
    Food and Drug Act, milk ordinances, and other provisions to
        safeguard the quality of food supplies

4. Provision for education
    Tax-supported schools and compulsory school attendance [2]
    Adult education (home economics—county farm agents)

5. Provision for recreation
    Parks, playgrounds, recreational directors

6. Protection of the individual's finances
    Usury laws
    Government insurance of bank deposits
    Examination of stocks and bonds by Security and Exchange
        Commission (SEC)
    Credit and interest controls

7. Provision for security
    Old age insurance
    Employment insurance

---

[2] In spite of "public" education, it costs the individual $4,000-$6,000 to complete the work for a Ph.D. degree at state universities.

8. Aids to housing
    Public housing
    Guarantee of housing loans

9. Public services
    Police and courts, including Small Claims Courts
    Fire protection
    Streets and highways

10. Redistribution of income
    Through the tax system, with emphasis on corporation taxes
    and graduated income taxes

A Chronological Listing.—A brief chronological listing of some of the important legislation enacted and of some government-sponsored plans and activities during the first half of the twentieth century will show something of the recent development of aid to individuals.

1890. The passage of the Sherman Anti-Trust Act in 1890 was the first attempt to make illegal those business practices which destroyed or limited free competition. Unregulated competition was said by Adam Smith in 1776 to be the "obvious and simple system of natural liberty" and the best way to allocate resources to ensure the most efficient satisfaction of demands. He believed that it eliminated the least fit from industry and improved methods of turning resources to the satisfaction of demand. Soon exceptions began to increase and great doubt permeated our national thinking as to the capacity of competition to survive or, where it survived, to produce satisfactory results. At least as early as the 1880's, competition gave way to pools and agreements in the meat, whisky, steel, coal, cordage, explosives, and a number of other industries. Single corporations got control of a very large part of all the business in sugar, starch, oil, tobacco, and in many branches of the steel fabricating industry. Some of these corporations achieved control by methods both dramatic and ruthless. But, as Ida Tarbell shows in her book on *The Standard Oil Company*, these areas of control were regarded as manifestations of pathological tendencies. The possibility that this sort of development arose out of the very nature of competitive individualism was ignored until quite recently. It was felt that a law which would forbid monopolies, combinations, or conspiracy of trade, thereby compelling competitive behavior, would hold in line the exceptional cases of monopolistic activity. Of course, this Sherman Anti-Trust law was passed primarily to protect manufacturers, but it automatically protected consumers from the results of business methods which interfered with the operation of free competition.

1906. The first Federal Food and Drug Act was passed. It provided the first legal protection for the consumer against poisonous drugs and foods.

1907. The Federal Meat Inspection Law passed in 1907 was another attempt at protecting the consumer. This law provides that meat handled in interstate trade shall be inspected by trained veterinary inspectors and that the product which passes Government standards be marked, "U. S. Government Inspected." Many states now have their own inspection machinery for meat which is handled only within state boundaries and which therefore would not be inspected by federal agents. Thus, although the consumer was not protected as to price, he was protected as to quality.

1914. The Clayton Anti-Trust Act was passed. Armed only with words from the Sherman Act such as "restraint of trade" and "monopoly," the Supreme Court tried to compel competitive behavior. The attempt met with little success because of the loopholes quickly discerned by corporation lawyers. The Clayton Act was an amendment to the Sherman Act, expanding its provisions and specifically defining certain unfair practices such as exclusive contracts which prevented purchasers of goods from dealing in competing goods.

The Federal Trade Commission Act was also passed in this year. This act created the Federal Trade Commission, perhaps the most important legal agency in the control of trade practices. Here, as was noted of the Sherman Act, the consumer seemed to be protected somewhat indirectly. In contrast to the Sherman Act, however, consumer protection under the Federal Trade Commission Act was actually greater than its stated purpose would indicate. Whether the consumer had been deceived to the disadvantage of the competitor was set up, in Section 5, as a test as to whether or not a competitor had been harmed. Hence, although the Act was designed to furnish protection to manufacturers and tradesmen, its administration was directly advantageous to consumers.

1922. The Capper-Volstead Act was passed. It encouraged the organization of agricultural cooperatives by exempting such cooperatives from the provisions of the Sherman Act which forbade a group of individuals to act in concert with respect to price matters. Although the Clayton Act exempted nonstock and nonprofit agricultural organizations from such restrictions, it was not until the passage of the Capper-Volstead Act that agricultural cooperatives were specifically exempted. The Act does not, however, exempt agricultural cooperatives from other provisions of the anti-trust laws.

1923. The Bureau of Home Economics (the name was changed in 1943 to Bureau of Human Nutrition and Home Economics) was established by the Department of Agriculture. This Bureau started out to be and has remained one of the agencies of federal government most interested in consumer problems. Through its statistical research and information activities it has provided a large amount of practical data on a variety of subjects such as family expenditure patterns by income class, low-cost meal cookery, and development of substitute products.

1929. A special board of three members was set up by the Federal Trade Commission for the purpose of effecting more control of the issuance of untruthful advertising matter by individual firms. This Board reviewed all advertising matter carried in newspapers, magazines, and over the radio with the express purpose of reducing to a minimum, if not eliminating, false and misleading statements.[3]

1933. The Consumers' Council was established as a part of the Agricultural Adjustment Administration. In 1940, it was placed under the direction of the Agricultural Marketing Administration. For several years this agency had considerable success in bringing together all elements in the consumer movement to establish standards for more consumer goods and to support legislation favorable to consumer interests. Not infrequently, however, the Council and its director found themselves opposing the farmer-oriented, policy-making groups in the Department of Agriculture. Largely as a result of this conflict of interest, the Council has had little influence since 1942.

1933. The Banking Act passed this year made provision for a temporary and permanent plan to insure bank deposits up to $5,000. This amount was raised to $10,000 in 1950. To implement the insurance provisions, the Federal government established the Federal Deposit Insurance Corporation (FDIC) as a guaranteeing institution. All national banks must be members and a fair proportion of state banks have chosen to take part. In 1934, insurance of deposits was extended to savings and loan associations by permitting them to become members of the FDIC. Consumers are thus offered considerably increased protection.

1933. The Securities Act was passed to protect the individual in the field of security purchasing. There were various and inadequate laws in existence before 1933. For example, state "blue-sky" laws aimed at preventing the issuance of worthless stocks and bonds; sellers of such securities were prohibited from using the United States mail for the purpose. But the protection was inadequate because the state laws

---

[3] The Post Office Department has some control over direct mail advertising through its general power over the materials that may be sent through the mails.

were weak and the sale of securities was interstate business. Hence a strong federal law was needed.

1934. The Consumers' Advisory Board was set up by the National Industrial Recovery Act (NIRA). For the first time in the history of our country, the consumer was given formal recognition and status in the establishment of economic policies of the nation. This terminated, of course, when the NIRA was declared unconstitutional in 1935.

1934. The Federal Housing Administration was inaugurated in June 1934, to help stimulate recovery from the serious depression by assisting and protecting consumers in purchasing and financing homes.

1934. The Securities and Exchange Act was designed to control the sale of securities on the stock exchanges whereas the Securities Act of 1933 dealt only with over-the-counter sales.

1934. The Securities and Exchange Commission was organized on July 6 to administer the Securities Act of 1933 and the Securities and Exchange Act of 1934. Thus the supervision of registration of all security issues, the prohibition of fraudulent practices in the sale of securities, the supervision and regulation of transactions and trading in securities on stock exchanges as well as in other markets became the responsibility of the Commission.

1935. The National Industrial Recovery Act (NIRA) was declared unconstitutional, thus eliminating the Consumers' Advisory Board. However, many of its activities relating to consumers were shifted to other departments of the federal government, especially to the Department of Labor and Bureau of Human Nutrition and Home Economics. For example, a study of Consumer Purchases, a Works Progress Administration project, was conducted jointly by the Department of Labor and the Bureau of Human Nutrition and Home Economics.

1936. The President sent a Commission to Europe to study the cooperative enterprise (mainly consumer cooperatives) and to ascertain the movement's status and extent and its effects on the national economy and welfare of the countries selected. The Commission concluded that there was no reason to believe that cooperative enterprise would not expand to considerable proportions in the United States and that by 1970 or thereabouts the field of organization in the United States probably would be roughly (not equally) divided between private, government, and cooperative enterprise.

Fifteen years after the Commission reported it seems evident, from the discussion of the cooperative movement given in Chapter 18, that the forecast was much too optimistic. Cooperative enterprise in the marketing of agricultural commodities is of very considerable importance in the whole scheme of marketing farm products, but consumer cooperation still is of minor importance commercially and in some parts of the country it actually had lost ground as a social institution.

Also in 1936, the American Standards Association (a quasi-public body) organized an Advisory Committee for Ultimate Consumer Goods. This was another step toward the establishment of standards for consumer goods.

1937. The first compulsory fiber identification regulations were decreed by the Federal Trade Commission. These were known as rayon rules. For the first time, all fabrics containing rayon had to be labeled not only as to rayon content but also as to the particular kind of rayon fiber used. This rule applied to the manufacturers as well as the retailers of the fabric or garment.

The Consumers' Counsel of the Bituminous Coal Commission was established by Congress in this year. This was an important step in the growth of the Consumer Movement because it was the first consumer body to be set up by Congressional action. It was conceived of as an independent agency functioning entirely in the interests of the consumer. This Counsel was empowered by Congress "to protect the interests of the coal-consuming public as such interests may be affected by the administration of the provisions of the Bituminous Coal Act of 1937." [4] It was to "act in behalf of consumers of bituminous coal in practically every proceeding before the Bituminous Coal Division, as well as in initiating proceedings undertaken to alleviate apparent inequalities in the prices of coal, and in appropriate matters before the Interstate Commerce Commission." [5]

At first, the functions of the Counsel were placed in the Office of the Solicitor of the Department of the Interior. The extension of the Bituminous Coal Act of 1937 was approved April 11, 1941, and reestablished the independent character of the office providing for appointment of the Counsel by the President, by and with the advice and consent of the Senate.

This third attempt to set up machinery to implement the consumer point of view into the administrative process was a short-lived one. As Professor Campbell points out, "the Coal Consumers' Counsel came to regard himself as representing not only the ultimate consumer but the buyer at all stages of the industrial and distributive process, and

---

[4] *Annual Report, Office of the Bituminous Coal Consumers' Counsel,* Period July 1, 1940-October 31, 1941 (Washington: U. S. Government Printing Office, 1941), p. 1.
[5] *Ibid.*

the interests of these different groups proved at times to be in conflict." [6]

1938. The Consumers' Bureau of the Michigan State Department of Agriculture was the first state consumer agency to be created by executive order in the United States. This Bureau was the outgrowth of a four-year experimental program of the Wayne County Consumers' Council, a volunteer consumer group organized for the purpose of "recommending a concrete program to give the consumer representation in government." [7] The Bureau was to be directed by the Consumers' Counsel in cooperation with an Advisory Board appointed by the Commissioner of Agriculture, who also was to designate County Consumer Representatives whose function it would be to carry out the program of the Bureau in their respective counties. [8]

Let us examine the program of the Michigan Consumers' Bureau, which pioneered in planning for state aid to the consumer. The Bureau was divided into four divisions, namely, Research, Service, Federal and State Coordinating, and Information and Publications. The Research and Service Divisions were considered to be of primary importance, the other two being merely facilitating divisions. The Research Division planned to work in five areas which it considered fundamental to the consumer problem. Those five areas were:

1. Advertising—where it attempted to encourage the use of informative, factual advertising in order that the consumer might know whether or not the things he buys will meet his needs. [9]

2. Quality standards and Informative Grade Labeling—where it encouraged the use of grade standards and of informative grade labels so that the consumer might know the quality of the thing he buys.

3. Trade Practices—where it planned, through trade discussion groups, to show the effect of trade practice on the consumer, to encourage fair and just trade practices, and to promote informative selling.

4. Legislation—where it planned to show the effect on the consumer of legislation which affects his interests and to plead his case before those responsible for preparing legislation.

---

[6] Persia Campbell, *The Consumer Interest* (New York: Harper & Bros., 1949), p. 642.

[7] Consumers' Bureau—Michigan State Department of Agriculture, by Hester R. Fraser, Consumers' Counsel. Bulletin No. 1, 1938, p. 2.

[8] This Bureau never achieved the "action" stage. However, the authors believe the plan to be an important step in government relations with the consumer.

[9] Many authors refer to the consumer as "she," presumably because women are said to do a large part of retail purchasing. The present authors believe this is unrealistic, so at this point, lacking a bisexual pronoun, we shift to the masculine.

5. Consumer Exploitation—where it tried to protect the consumer against practices and schemes designed to exploit him.

The Service Division aimed at making available to the consumer the results of the work of the Research Division and any other data which would be helpful to him in his capacity as a consumer.

Although several other states set up consumer departments, bureaus, etc., few have attempted a program so broad as did Michigan.

1938. The new Food, Drug, and Cosmetic Act was passed by Congress after five years of vigorous lobbying by its supporters, but did not become effective until January 1, 1940. It prohibits interstate and foreign trade in adulterated and misbranded foods, drugs, and therapeutic devices. Under this Act, the Pure Food and Drug Administration is authorized to establish definitions and standards of identity, quality, and quantity of contents of containers for all except certain foods. A description of the Pure Food and Drug Administration and the way it enforces this Act will be given in a later section of this chapter.

1938. The Wheeler-Lea Amendment to the Federal Trade Commission Act was passed on March 2 by Congress. Years before its passage, the Commission had instituted (in 1929) a system to control more effectively the publication and dissemination of untruthful advertising matter by individual firms. This was done through the general powers of the Commission. The Wheeler-Lea Amendment gave the Commission specific powers for controlling false claims. The more important provisions of the Amendment are:

1. Broadening the Federal Trade Commission Act to deal with unfair practices adversely affecting the public without reference to competition;

2. Insertion of a section dealing specifically with "false advertising of foods, drugs, devices, and cosmetics";

3. Improving the method of procedure in the handling of cases;

4. Strengthening the power of the Commission to enforce final "cease and desist" orders by introducing a civil penalty of $5,000 for their violation.

Thus the Commission, in addition to controlling untruthful advertising, is given the power to control false advertising which aims at inducing the purchase of food, drugs, devices, and cosmetics. False advertising is defined as that which is misleading in a material respect. Not only are false statements punishable but so also is failure to reveal important facts about the product and its use. This was indeed an important step toward more effective consumer protection.

1939. The Federal Wool Products Labeling Act was passed to protect producers, manufacturers, distributors, and consumers from the un-revealed presence of substitutes and mixtures in spun, woven, knitted, felted, or otherwise manufactured wool products. It requires that product labels state the percentage of new and virgin wool, reprocessed wool, and reused wool. The Act is administered by the Federal Trade Commission. Because there are no chemical tests differentiating new and reused wool, evidence of the truthfulness of labeling will rest with manufacturers who are responsible for combining the fiber. For a violation of the Act the maximum fine is $5,000 and/or one year in jail. The Act does not apply to the manufacture or sale of carpets, rugs, and mats, or to upholsterers.

1940. On May 25, the President created the Office of Emergency Man-agement (OEM), appointed a Council of National Defense and, a few days later, appointed the National Defense Advisory Commission to work with the Council. He charged the Commission with seven major problems: (1) Industrial production, (2) Industrial materials, (3) Employment, (4) Agricultural production, (5) Transportation, (6) Price Stabilization, and (7) Consumer Protection. The designation of a separate division for consumer protection marked a high spot in the long struggle to get government recognition and support of the con-sumer.

Then came December 7, 1941. No longer were we an arsenal for other nations. We changed from the status of onlooker to participant and the national production machine shifted to a complete war econ-omy.

1942. In January, the President established the War Production Board (WPB) "for the purpose of assuring the most effective prosecution of war procurement and production," and the Office of Civilian Supply (in 1943 it became the Office of Civilian Requirements) which was "responsible for civilian needs and, therefore, for assisting the War Production Board regarding critical materials, facilities, and services as they relate to: (1) the health and productive capacity of the popu-lation of the country, or (2) essential work of business establishments other than war production."

At the same time the Office of Price Administration (OPA) was set up, which succeeded the Office of Price Administration and Civilian Supply of April 1941. Its three basic duties were:

1. To prevent inflationary increases in prices of commodities and rents in defense rental areas.

2. To ration commodities for civilian consumption whenever the WPB decided it was necessary to do so. The philosophy behind the nation's rationing program was summed up by President Roosevelt in his Cost of Living message to Congress on April 27, 1942: "It is obviously fair that where there is not enough of any essential commodity to meet all civilian demands, those who can afford to pay more for the commodity should not be privileged over those who cannot."

3. To protect consumer interests.

OPA's methods of control and regulation in performance of its three basic duties varied depending on the circumstances. Both selective and general techniques were used. For example, in the matter of price control, the first regulation specifically set dollars-and-cents maximum prices on secondhand machine tools. But when prices rose sufficiently to threaten a runaway inflation, a General Maximum Price Regulation was set up starting April 28, 1942. Under it prices were frozen at either the seller's maximum price during March, 1942, or, if no charge was made for the commodity or service, at the highest price charged during March by the most closely competitive seller of the same class. To take care of certain "squeezes" which developed, selective regulation was also used.[10]

Throughout the war and into the postwar period, the major governmental control devices in the interests of individuals, and specifically as consumers, were: price control to prevent exorbitant price increases; rationing to give reasonable equity to distribution of goods among individuals; and rent control.

Since the termination of price control and rationing the agitation for further aid to consumers has turned in somewhat new directions. Emphasis has been laid, for example, on public, low-cost housing, a field in which some important developments have taken place. More individuals have been brought under the provisions of the Social Security Act, especially in the matter of old age pensions. And there has been much discussion of various degrees of socialized medical care. Further protection of the consumer against unfair trade practices or misrepresentation apparently has, for the present, ceased to be an important issue. At the present time, the war and the defense effort have renewed emphasis on price control and rationing. Thus government aid to consumers continues in a state of flux.

---

[10] For a more complete discussion of government aids to consumers in time of war, see Kenneth Dameron, ed., *Consumer Problems in Wartime,* chap. xv, "Government Agencies and the Consumer in Wartime," by Helen G. Canoyer (New York: McGraw-Hill Book Co., Inc., 1944).

A Brief Description of Two Agencies

In order that we may see something about the way in which government agencies are organized and work, two important ones have been chosen for description. These are: The Food and Drug Administration and The Federal Trade Commission.

The Food and Drug Administration.—The first Food and Drug Act was passed in 1906. The Food and Drug Administration was created by Congress in 1927 to enforce this and certain other federal legislation designed to protect the consumer in his purchases of food and drugs. Between 1906 and 1938 there was a continuous struggle to improve the Act, and it was amended seven times. Finally, after five years of bitter argument, a new Food, Drug, and Cosmetic Act was passed in 1938 and amended in 1942. This Act is still in force.

The function of the Food and Drug Administration is the enforcement of five statutes or laws designed to ensure the honesty and purity of foods, drugs, devices, and cosmetics. These laws are the Food, Drug, and Cosmetic Act, the Tea Act, the Import Milk Act, the Filled Milk Act, and the Caustic Poison Act.

The personnel of the Food and Drug Administration includes chemists, bacteriologists, physicians, veterinarians, microscopists, pharmacologists, inspectors, administrative officers, and other specialists. The staff numbers about 300 persons in Washington and 600 in other centers. In order to develop and maintain active cooperation with all state and local officials enforcing state and local food and drug laws, a Division of State Cooperation is maintained. The United States is divided into sixteen districts, each with headquarters manned by chemists and inspectors and fully equipped with testing laboratories. Within these districts are three subdistricts with small laboratories and forty-one inspection stations. Each field or district is responsible for maintaining constant supervision. Factories are inspected for sanitary conditions, raw materials used, and controls exercised in compounding, processing, packaging, and labeling products destined for interstate shipment. When violations are suspected, shipments are reported for sampling at their destination. Each district also inspects interstate items shipped into its territory as well as imports at its ports. Thus it is possible to keep close check on adulteration and misbranding for the protection of the consumer.

Chief among the five statutes enforced by the Food and Drug Administration is the Food, Drug, and Cosmetic Act. The revisions of the original Food and Drug Act of 1906 have greatly extended the principles of consumer protection. For example, the labeling of foods, drugs, devices, and cosmetics now includes all written or printed matter accompanying the article as well as that in or upon the package or container. No labeling may be false or misleading in any way. Required information must not only be conspicuously placed upon the label but it must also be in terms the ordinary consumer is likely to read and understand under customary conditions of purchase and use. Also, any failure to reveal facts is misleading under the present law, and half-truths are insufficient. Moreover, even if the labeling of a food, drug, or cosmetic is adequate, containers must not be made, formed, or filled so that the consumer is misled. Thus containers with false bottoms or but partially filled would violate the Act.

Further, labels of drugs and devices must bear adequate directions and warnings specifying use, dosage, and administration. For example, habit-forming drugs and their chemical derivatives must bear on their label the statement "Warning—may be habit-forming." In addition, nonofficial drugs (i.e., drugs designated by a name other than that recognized in the compendia listed in the Act, such as any of the so-called cold cures or antihistamine tablets) must give more complete information concerning their ingredients than is required for official drugs.

Of primary importance are the new types of control established by the Food, Drug, and Cosmetic Act. For any foods there may now be fixed a reasonable definition and standard of identity, quality, and fill of the container. Food that does not conform to the definition and standard of quality or fill or container established in the Act must have the discrepancy clearly stated on the label. In cases of standards of identity, however, no deviations of any kind are permitted. For example, a product sold as tomato juice must contain nothing but the juice of pure tomatoes with or without salt. If the juices of other vegetables or other condiments are added it must be sold under another name such as V-8 Juice or tomato and celery cocktail. And on all goods for which standards of identity have not been set up by the Administration, the label must carry a full statement of the ingredients. Furthermore, all foods must state the presence of artificial flavoring, chemical preservative, or artificial coloring (except butter, cheese, or ice cream).

Violations may result in seizure of the offending goods and criminal prosecution of those responsible for the violations. Illegal acts may be restrained through application to the courts for an injunction.

An example or two will illustrate the type of protection the consumer is given by the vigilance of the Administration. It haled a macaroni corporation into court and there presented exhibits of rodent-contaminated raw materials and photographs of filthy equipment and operations observed during factory inspections. The firm was fined $15,000 even though by the time the case was tried the management had satisfied all standards of sanitation. In another instance, criminal actions were brought against two shippers of cream intended for butter manufacture. Here the exhibits were a can of cream which contained a dead mouse and a can of cream containing thousands of pieces of rodent hair with adhering flesh. Fines were assessed in each case and the inspection resulted in improved conditions.[11]

The endorsement activities of the Food and Drug Administration have generally been supported by the courts. Today the Administration is given considerable cooperation by business. Many firms now employ their own inspectors and experts to set up sanitation programs. However, an examination of the data in Table 54 will suggest how much protection the consumer has been and still is given by the Administration.

The Federal Trade Commission.—The Federal Trade Commission Act was passed in 1914. It provided "that unfair methods of competition are unlawful" and created the Federal Trade Commission to prevent such methods. Until 1938, "unfair" referred only to effect on competition, thus protecting the consumer by keeping competition free and uncontrolled. In 1938, the Wheeler-Lea Amendment to the Federal Trade Commission Act extended the test of whether or not competition is "unfair" to its effect on the consumer. Thus protection of the consumer under the Act became direct in certain areas such as false and misleading advertising, misbranding, espionage, bribery of competitor's employees, disparaging statements regarding competitors, etc.

The Federal Trade Commission is a quasi-judicial body and is the most important legal agency charged with administering the six statutes [12] under its jurisdiction, for the control of trade practices in

---

[11] *Annual Report of the Food and Drug Administration, 1948* (Washington, D. C.: U. S. Government Printing Office), pp. 541, 545.

[12] The six statutes are: Federal Trade Commission Act, Wheeler-Lea Act, Clayton Act, Webb-Pomerene Export Act, Wool Products Labeling Act, and certain sections of the Lanham Trade-Mark Act.

TABLE 54

SUMMARY OF VIOLATIVE SAMPLES FOUND IN INTERSTATE COMMERCE
WITH THE RESULTING NUMBER OF COURT ACTIONS
INSTITUTED DURING THE RESPECTIVE FISCAL YEAR

	Violative Samples					Resulting Court Actions				
	1945	1946	1947	1948	1949	1945	1946	1947	1948	1949
Foods	4,243	4,174	3,450	2,303	2,711	2,690	2,737	2,301	1,284	1,646
Vitamins and foods for dietary use	428	168	246	130	208	118	63	161	48	88
Drugs and devices	1,294	726	564	526	944	698	405	305	279	459
Cosmetics	56	28	12	37	24	20	14	8	21	14
Caustic poisons	1	3	2	2	0	1	2	2	2	0
Total	6,022	5,099	4,274	2,998	3,887	3,527	3,221	2,777	1,634	2,207

Source: *Annual Reports* of the Food and Drug Administration for the above years.

the United States. The Commission is composed of five members appointed by the President, with the approval of the Senate, for seven-year terms. Not more than three of the members may be of the same political party. A secretary elected by the members is also the executive director. The Commission has a working staff of six hundred employees including attorneys, economists, accountants, statisticians, and administrative personnel.

Until the Wheeler-Lea Amendment improved the method of procedure in handling cases, and strengthened the power of the Commission to enforce final "cease and desist" orders, the Commission sought to encourage compliance with the laws on a voluntary basis. After 1938, the Commission became a more effective enforcement agency and thus was able to give the consumer greater protection.

A case before the Federal Trade Commission may originate in any one of several ways : through complaint by a consumer or a competitor; from federal, state or municipal sources; or upon investigation by the Commission itself. When the Commission receives a complaint it decides through its legal division whether the complaint shall be docketed for investigation. When investigations are decided upon, the general procedure is to interview the accused party and ask for any evidence or information he may care to furnish in his defense. The investigator will often seek information from the general public or specific consumers, along with information from competitors of the plaintiff. When the investigator has developed all the facts he recommends the action which he thinks the Commission should take. The case is then reviewed by the Chief of Field Investigation, following which the Commission will either issue a formal complaint after which the case is tried, issue a cease-and-desist order, negotiate a consent decree whereby the accused person or firm agrees to stop the unlawful practices, or drop the case. Provision is made for appeal to higher courts which may affirm, modify, or set aside orders of the Commission. Orders to cease and desist, unless previously appealed, become final within 60 days. After they become final, violation results in civil penalties resulting from suits instituted by the Attorney General.

To expedite its work the Commission's staff is divided into seven major departments, namely, the General Counsel, the Director of Trial Examiners, and the Bureau of Administration, Bureau of Industry Cooperation, Bureau of Antimonopoly, Bureau of Antideceptive Practices, and Bureau of Industrial Economics. As an illustration of the magnitude of the task with which the Commission is charged, we present in Table 55 the work of one division of the Bureau of Antideceptive Practices, the Division of Radio and Periodical Advertising for six months in 1950.

TABLE 55

ADVERTISEMENTS EXAMINED AND SET ASIDE BY THE FEDERAL TRADE COMMISSION
MARCH THROUGH AUGUST, 1950

Month	Advertisements Examined			Advertisements Set Aside		
	Radio	Newspapers	Magazines	Radio	Newspapers	Magazines
March	77,420	22,205	15,204	1,331	807	656
April	59,758	12,563	12,406	1,201	537	512
May	67,746	17,671	12,485	1,551	782	654
June	52,966	22,106	9,719	1,247	1,380	467
July	55,114	16,418	7,542	1,324	1,121	598
August	45,146	19,500	8,489	1,206	989	544
Total	358,250	110,463	65,845	7,860	5,616	3,431
Per cent questionable				2.2	5.1	5.2

Source: Federal Trade Commission, "Monthly Summary of Work Reports," March through August, 1950.

The Division of Radio and Periodical Advertising conducts a continuous survey of advertising disseminated by means of radio and television broadcasts, magazines, newspapers, mail-order catalogs, and foreign language publications. In the six-month period, March through August of 1950, 534,558 advertisements were examined for probable misrepresentations which would injure the consumer. Of this total, roughly 3 per cent were set aside as being possibly false and misleading and requiring further careful examination. Thus thousands of inquiries and examinations are made and comparatively few violations uncovered.

A summary of all the cases in which the Commission (for all divisions) issued a complaint charging violation of one or more of the statutes it administers shows that during the four-year period, 1946 through 1949, 2,760 violations were charged by the Commission, of which only 724 were settled in one way or another. No formal complaints were issued, 283 cases resulted in cease-and-desist orders, 11 cases were settled by acceptance of Trade Practice Conference rules and 17 cases were closed without further procedure. Although the work is detailed and slow, consumers are more adequately protected in the specific areas of the Commission's jurisdiction than ever before.

Some Comments on the Welfare State

During the nineteenth century and the early years of the twentieth century, the American economy properly was spoken of as one of free enterprise, or an open and free-market economy. Under this system the individual was free to choose his occupation and a large proportion of our population worked for themselves as farmers, artisans, small shop and factory proprietors, and so on. While this was so, the individual's income usually depended directly upon the economic worth of his own services, as determined in the market place. Markets were consumer dominated and the work of the individual producer resulted in a large or small income to him in proportion as he pleased consumers. When one wanted more income he worked harder to please his customers, took on a second job, or increased his efforts in some other manner.

More recently we have become a nation of wage-earners. Today, at least four out of five gainfully employed persons work for others. In many cases both the amount of work one may do and the wage he may get are determined by the bargaining of a labor union to which he belongs. Whether or not he may work at all is frequently dependent upon the decision of the management of the firm for which he works. This dependence on the decision of the firm has led to consideration of annual-wage guarantees, but as yet only a few such schemes are actually in use.

Ever since we became a nation of wage-earners, periods of serious unemployment have occurred with unfortunate frequency. Involuntary unemployment has been accompanied by great instability of individual income, and it is evident that the free enterprise system has not provided individuals with stable incomes.

Income instability has led many individuals to urge a different form of economic control. Many different schemes have been proposed and a somewhat surprising number of them have been tried. These schemes are launched and usually carried out by government agencies. Collectively, they are spoken of as the Welfare State although there is no clearly defined outline or limit to the procedures included.

Some of the governmentally controlled items adopted during the past twenty years in this country in the hope of improving human welfare include:

1. Social security programs including old age annuities regardless of need

2. Insurance against involuntary unemployment
3. Publicly financed housing to be rented to low-income families
4. Public financial aid to private home building
5. Price support of certain agricultural products.

Another that is being urged in this country and has been adopted in England is general medical care at public expense.

The method of paying for each of these items includes the collection of money from firms and individuals who will not benefit directly from the program. Whatever activities the Welfare State undertakes, it almost inevitably lessens the closeness of the relationship between the individual's economic contribution to society and his income. This follows from the method in which the various projects are carried out. In general, the government imposes heavier taxes on the more productive individuals—that is, on the persons and firms that have the larger incomes—and uses the funds for the benefit of those whose incomes are smaller. Moreover, the state protects certain producers from price competition, by such devices as guaranteed prices for certain farm products and minimum markups for retailers.

Almost from the beginning in this country, aid has been given by government to some segments of the economy but not to others. The protective tariff has been used to help some industries meet foreign competition. Direct subsidies have been given to a few industries, notably to the merchant marine to help meet foreign competition in shipping. Railroads were built with the aid of some land grants. The synthetic rubber industry was given substantial financial help towards rapid development during World War II. But the programs of social welfare undertaken during the past twenty years appear different, both in degree and in kind, from anything previously used.

Most of the increase in government expenditures has come at the national level. For example, taxes paid by Minnesotans in 1930 and 1948 were as follows:

	In Millions of Dollars		
	1930	1948	Increase
For state purposes	45.2	145.9	3½ times
For federal purposes	30.1	700.0	23 times

Much of the federal expenditure is, of course, for past wars and future defense. Substantial amounts go to other things, however, as the following figures taken from the President's budget message for 1951 indicate.

In Millions of Dollars

National defense	13,798	
Veterans readjustment program	2,688	
Veterans life insurance dividend	563	
Other veterans expenditures	1,563	
Econ. Cooperation Adm.	3,250	
Government & relief, occupied areas	279	
Interest, retirement & trust funds, veterans pensions	7,783	
Subtotal		29,924
* Home mortgage purchases	990	
Postal deficit	160	
* Unemployment insurance	1,570	
* Farm price supports	952	
Reserve	175	
International	1,405	
Agriculture	1,241	
Transportation	1,524	
Natural resources	2,223	
* Social welfare	2,104	
General government	1,098	
* Housing	244	
* Education	434	
Other	272	14,392
Total		44,316

The starred items are clearly part of the new Welfare State program. They amount to nearly $6 billion for fiscal 1951 as recommended in the President's budget message. These funds are collected by government from individuals and firms. They are used for different purposes and for the benefit of persons other than would be the case under the conditions of complete freedom of choice. It is perfectly clear that this cannot be done and at the same time leave to individuals the opportunity to use the income from their efforts in their own sweet way.

There may be a gain in stability and security as a result of these programs, but there is an offsetting reduction in freedom. The net balance is measurable only in terms of human psychology and social mores. Such programs raise the question, how much individual freedom are we willing to give up in exchange for how much additional stability? Some argue that in addition to giving up freedom we give up part of the incentive to progress.

A literate citizenry should at least realize that security and stability cost something. Each time a proposal is made for some scheme that promises additional stability, its cost in individual freedom should be carefully assessed. It should be adopted only if its value balances its costs.

Project Questions

1. Write a description, somewhat similar to those given for the Food and Drug Administration and the Federal Trade Commission, of the work of any other government agency whose activities are in the interest of consumers. You are to give the source of your material in every case.

2. Does your state have a resale price maintenance law? If it does, get a copy of it and discuss the provisions in class.

3. Visit the Small Claims Court in your city to obtain information on the type of claim handled.

4. What are usury laws?

5. Look up the facts on the A & P Case. Discuss the implications of the government's action. How does it affect the consumer?

6. What recent action has the Federal Trade Commission taken to enforce the Pure Food, Drug, and Cosmetic Law? Examine newspapers, news magazines, and releases of the F. T. C. for this information.

BIBLIOGRAPHY

BOOKS

AMERICAN ECONOMIC ASSOCIATION. *Readings in the Theory of Income Distribution.* Philadelphia: The Blakiston Co., 1946.

ANDRES, E. M., and COCANOWER, C. D. *Economics and the Consumer.* Boston: Houghton Mifflin Co., 1942.

ANDREWS, B. *Economics of the Household* (rev. ed.). New York: The Macmillan Co., 1935.

ARONOVICI, CAROL. *Housing the Masses.* New York: John Wiley & Sons, Inc., 1939.

BABSON, R. W., and STONE, C. N. *Consumer Protection.* New York: Harper & Bros., 1938.

BARNETT, J. D. *More Co-operative Democracy.* New York: Richard R. Smith, 1941.

BARRETT, THEODORE, and SPAETH, L. B. (comps.). *What About Dollars?* New York: McClure Publishing Co., 1936.

BARTLETT, J. T., and REED, C. M. *Methods of Installment Selling and Collection.* New York: Harper & Bros., 1934.

BATHURST, EFFIE G. *Your Life In The Country.* New York: McGraw-Hill Book Co., Inc., 1948.

BEMIS, A. F. *The Economics of Shelter.* Vol. II. Cambridge: Massachusetts Institute of Technology Press, 1934.

BIGELOW, HOWARD F. *Family Finance.* Philadelphia: J. B. Lippincott Co., 1936.

BLAISDELL, THOMAS C. *The Federal Trade Commission.* New York: Columbia University Press, 1932.

BLANCK, A. P. *Foods and the Law.* New York: P. Smith, 1935.

BLODGETT, HARVEY A. *Making the Most of Your Income.* New York: The Macmillan Co., 1933.

BOOTHE, VIVA. *Salaries and Cost of Living in Universities.* Columbus: Ohio State University Press, 1932.

BORSODI, RALPH. *The Flight from the City.* New York: Harper & Bros, 1933.

BRAITHWAITE, D., and DOBBS, S. P. *The Distribution of Consumable Goods.* London: G. Routledge & Sons Ltd., 1932.

BRINDZE, RUTH. *How to Spend Money—Everybody's Buying Guide.* New York: Vanguard Press, 1935.

BROWN, AGNES. *Selection of Food.* Minneapolis: Burgess Publishing Co., 1944.

BURLEY, ORIN E. *The Consumers' Cooperative as a Distributive Agency.* New York: McGraw-Hill Book Co., Inc., 1939.

BURNS, C. D. *Leisure in the Modern World.* New York: Appleton-Century-Crofts, Inc., 1932.

BUSH, G. L. *Science Education in Consumer Buying.* New York: Teachers College, Columbia University, 1941.

BYE, R., and BLODGETT, R. *Getting and Earning.* New York: Appleton-Century-Crofts, Inc., 1937.

CAMPBELL, P. C. *Consumer Representation in the New Deal.* New York: Columbia University Press, 1939.

———. *The Consumer Interest.* New York, Harper & Bros., 1949.

CANOYER, HELEN G. "Cooperatives in Historical Perspective," in *Changing Perspectives in Marketing*. Hugh G. Wales (ed.). Champaign, Ill.: University of Illinois Press, 1951, pp. 243-65.

CARROLL, E. G. C. *Two for the Money*. New York: Doubleday Doran & Co., Inc., 1940.

CARR-SAUNDERS, A. M., *et al*. *Consumers' Cooperation in Great Britain* (rev. ed.). London: George Allen & Unwin, Ltd., 1938.

CARVER, T. N., *et al*. *Textile Problems for the Consumer*. New York: The Macmillan Co., 1935.

CHASE, STUART. *The Economy of Abundance*. New York: The Macmillan Co., 1934.

———. *Men and Machines*. New York: The Macmillan Co., 1929.

———. *The Tragedy of Waste*. New York: The Macmillan Co., 1929.

CHASE, S., and SCHLINK, F. *Your Money's Worth*. New York: The Macmillan Co., 1931.

CHILDS, M. *Sweden, The Middle Way*. New Haven: Yale University Press, 1936.

CHURCHMAN, C. W., *et al*. (eds.). *Measurement of Consumer Interest*. Philadelphia: University of Pennsylvania Press, 1947.

COLES, JESSIE V. *The Consumer-Buyer and the Market*. New York: John Wiley & Sons, Inc., 1938.

———. *Standards and Labels for Consumers' Goods*. New York: The Ronald Press Co., 1949.

COMISH, N. H. *The Standard of Living*. New York: The Macmillan Co., 1923.

CONSUMER CREDIT INSTITUTE OF AMERICA, INC. *Consumer Credit and Its Uses*. Charles O. Hardy (ed.). Co-authors: Fred H. Clarkson, E. M. Patterson, Charles W. Coulter, *et al*. New York: Prentice-Hall, Inc., 1938.

COWAN, ANNE LOUIS. *Consumer Mathematics*. Harrisburg, Pa.: Stackpole Sons, 1938.

COX, REAVIS. *The Economics of Instalment Buying*. New York: The Ronald Press Co., 1948.

DAMERON, KENNETH (ed.). *Consumer Problems in Wartime*. New York: McGraw-Hill Book Co., Inc., 1944.

DANA, MARGARET. *Behind the Label—A Guide to Intelligent Buying*. Boston: Little, Brown & Co., 1938.

DE FOREST, CHARLES MILLS. *Are You as Old Financially as You Are in Years? Make Sure*. New York: American Provident Corp., 1932.

DEWHURST, J. FREDERIC. *America's Needs and Resources*. New York: Twentieth Century Fund, Inc., 1947.

DIGBY, MARGARET. *Producers and Consumers*. London: P. S. King & Sons, Ltd., 1938.

DONALDSON, E. F. *Personal Finance*. New York: The Ronald Press Co., 1948.

DONHAM, S. A. *Spending the Family Income*. Boston: Little, Brown & Co., 1933.

DOUGLAS, P. H. *Social Security in the United States*. New York: McGraw-Hill Book Co., Inc., 1936.

EDWARDS, A. L. *Product Standards and Labeling for Consumers*. New York: The Ronald Press Co., 1940.

ELIOT, THOMAS D. *American Standards and Planes of Living*. Boston: Ginn & Co., 1931.

ELLIOT, S. R. *The English Cooperatives*. New Haven: Yale University Press, 1937.

ERKEL, A. M., and WAGNER, W. P. *Today's Consumer Family*. Minneapolis: Burgess Publishing Co., 1937.

ESKEW, G. L. *Guinea Pigs and Bugbears*. Chicago: Research Press, 1938.

EZEKIEL, M. *$2500 a Year; From Scarcity to Abundance*. New York: Harcourt, Brace & Co., Inc., 1936.

FLOYD, O. R., and KINNEY, L. *Using Dollars and Sense.* New York: Newson & Co., 1942.

FORD, J., and MORROW, KATHERINE. *The Abolition of Poverty.* New York: The Macmillan Co., 1937.

FOREMAN, C., and ROSS, M. *Consumer Seeks a Way.* New York: W. W. Norton & Co., Inc., 1935.

FOWLER, B. B. *The Co-operative Challenge.* Boston: Little, Brown & Co., 1947.

FRIEND, M. R. *Earning and Spending the Family Income* (rev. ed.). New York: Appleton-Century-Crofts, Inc., 1935.

GAER, JOSEPH. *Consumers All.* New York: Harcourt, Brace & Co., Inc., 1940.

GORDON, LELAND J. *Economics for Consumers* (2d ed.). New York: American Book Co., 1944.

GOSLIN, RYLLIS C., and GOSLIN, O. *Don't Kill the Goose.* New York: Harper & Bros., 1939.

GRAHAM, JESSIE, and JONES, L. L. *The Consumers' Economic Life.* New York: Gregg Publishing Co., 1946.

GREENWOOD, E. *Spenders All.* New York: Appleton-Century-Crofts, Inc., 1935.

HAMBLEN, S. B., and ZIMMERMAN, G. F. *Wise Spending.* New York: Harper & Bros., 1941.

HARAP, HENRY. *The Education of the Consumer.* New York: The Macmillan Co., 1924.

HARDING, T. S. *Popular Practice of Fraud.* New York: Longmans, Green & Co., 1935.

HAUSRATH, ALFRED H., JR., and HARMS, J. R. *Consumer Science.* New York: The Macmillan Co., 1939.

HAWLEY, EDITH. *Economics of Food Consumption.* New York: McGraw-Hill Book Co., Inc., 1932.

HAYES, H. G. *Spending, Saving, & Employment.* New York: Alfred A. Knopf, Inc., 1947.

HEIL, E. W. *Consumer Training.* New York: The Macmillan Co., 1943.

HENDERSON, FRED. *Capitalism and the Consumer.* London: George Allen & Unwin, Ltd., 1936.

HOYT, ELIZABETH ELLIS. *Consumption in Our Society.* New York: McGraw-Hill Book Co., Inc., 1938.

———. *The Consumption of Wealth.* New York: The Macmillan Co., 1928.

JACOBSEN, D. H. *Our Interests as Consumers.* New York: Harper & Bros., 1941.

JOHNSON, D. D. *Consume!* New York: Dynamic America Press, 1940.

JONES, J. HARRY. *The Economics of Saving.* London: Reed & Co., 1934.

JORDAN, DAVID F., and WILLETT, E. F. *Managing Personal Finances.* New York: Prentice-Hall, Inc., 1946.

KALLEN, HORACE M. *The Decline and Rise of the Consumer* (new ed.). Chicago: Packard & Co., 1945.

KALLET, A. *Counterfeit.* New York: Vanguard Press, Inc., 1935.

KALLET, A., and SCHLINK, F. *100,000,000 Guinea Pigs.* New York: Vanguard Press, Inc., 1933.

KENNEDY, ADA, and VAUGHN, CORA. *Consumer Economics.* Peoria, Ill.: Manual Arts Press, 1939.

KENNER, H. F. *The Fight for Truth in Advertising.* New York: Round Table Press, Inc., 1936.

KUZNETS, S. S. *Gross Capital Formation, 1919-1933.* New York: National Bureau of Economic Research Bull., 1934.

KYRK, HAZEL. *Economic Problems of the Family.* New York: Harper & Bros., 1933.

———. *The Theory of Consumption.* Boston: Houghton Mifflin Co., 1923.

LAIRD, DONALD A. *What Makes People Buy.* New York: McGraw-Hill Book Co., Inc., 1935.

LAMB, RUTH D. *The American Chamber of Horrors*. New York: Farrar & Rinehart, Inc., 1936.

LANDIS, BENSON Y. *A Cooperative Economy*. New York: Harper & Bros., 1943.

LAZO, HECTOR, and BLETZ, M. H. *Who Gets Your Food Dollar?* New York: Harper & Bros., 1938.

LEAVITT, JOHN A., and HANSON, CARL. *Personal Finance*. New York: McGraw-Hill Book Co., Inc., 1950.

LEVEN, M., *et al. America's Capacity to Consume*. Washington, D. C.: Brookings Institution, 1934.

LOUGH, W. H., and GAINSBRUGH, M. R. *High-Level Consumption*. New York: McGraw-Hill Book Co., Inc., 1935.

LUCK, J. M. *War on Malnutrition and Poverty*. New York: Harper & Bros., 1946.

LYND, R. S., and LYND, H. M. *Middletown in Transition*. New York: Harcourt, Brace & Co., Inc., 1937.

MACK, R. P. *Flow of Business Funds and Consumer Purchasing Power*. New York: Columbia University Press, 1941.

MACKAY, RUTH. *Money Without Men*. New York: Farrar & Rinehart, Inc., 1938.

MANN, G. C. (Comp.). *Bibliography on Consumer Education*. New York: Harper & Bros., 1939.

MEADE, JAMES EDWARD. *Consumers' Credit and Unemployment*. London: Oxford University Press, 1938.

MENDENHALL, JAMES E., and HARAP, HENRY (eds.). *Consumer Education*. New York: Appleton-Century-Crofts, Inc., 1943.

MONROE, DAY, and STRATTON, L. M. *Food Buying and Our Market*. New York: M. Barrows & Co., Inc., 1940.

MOULTON, H. G. *Formation of Capital*. Washington, D. C.: Brookings Institution, 1935.

————. *Income and Economic Progress*. Washington, D. C.: Brookings Institution, 1935.

NASH, B. *Developing Marketable Products and Their Packagings*. New York: McGraw-Hill Book Co., Inc., 1945.

NATIONAL ASSOCIATION OF BETTER BUSINESS BUREAUS. *Second Conference on Business-Consumer Relations*. New York: Nat'l. Better Business Bureau, Inc., 1940.

NATIONAL INDUSTRIAL CONFERENCE BOARD. *Cost of Living in the U. S., 1914-1936*, by ADA BENEY. New York: 1936.

————. *Cost of Government in the United States*, by L. H. KIMMEL and E. KADISH. New York: 1936.

————. *National Income and Its Elements*, by ROBERT F. MARTIN. New York: 1936.

————. *Wages in the United States, 1914-1930*. New York: 1931.

NEIFELD, MORRIS R. *Cooperative Consumer Credit*. New York: Harper & Bros., 1936.

NORRIS, RUBY T. *Theory of Consumer's Demand*. New Haven: Yale University Press, 1941.

NOURSE, E. G., *et al. America's Capacity to Produce*. Washington, D. C.: Brookings Institution, 1933.

NUGENT, ROLF. *Consumer Credit and Economic Stability*. New York: Russell Sage Foundation, 1939.

NYSTROM, P. H. *Economic Principles of Consumption*. New York: The Ronald Press Co., 1929.

OWENS, DAVID F. *Controlling Your Personal Finances*. New York: McGraw-Hill Book Co., 1937.

PACK, A. N. *Challenge of Leisure*. New York: The Macmillan Co., 1934.

PALMER, R. L. *40,000,000 Guinea Pig Children.* New York: Vanguard Press, Inc., 1937.

PATERSON, D., and DARLEY, J. *Men, Women, and Jobs.* Minneapolis: University of Minnesota Press 1936.

PEIXOTTO, J. B. *Getting and Spending at the Professional Standard of Living.* New York: The Macmillan Co., 1927.

PHILLIPS, MARY CATHERINE. *Skin Deep.* New York: Vanguard Press, 1934.

PITKIN, WALTER B. *The Consumer.* New York: McGraw-Hill Book Co., Inc., 1932.

POST, LANGDON W. *The Challenge of Housing.* New York: Farrar & Rinehart, Inc., 1938.

PURDY, F. *Mass Consumption.* New York: Talisman Press, 1936.

RADELL, NEVA H. *Accounting for the Individual and Family.* New York: Prentice-Hall, Inc., 1940.

RADICE, E. A. *Savings In Great Britain, 1922-35.* London: Oxford University Press, 1939.

REICH, EDWARD. *Selling to the Consumer.* New York: American Book Co., 1938.

REICH, E., and SEIGLER, C. *Consumer Goods.* New York: American Book Co., 1937.

REID, MARGARET G. *Consumers and The Market.* New York: Appleton-Century-Crofts, Inc., 1947.

———. *Economics of Household Production.* New York: John Wiley & Sons, Inc., 1934

———. *Food for People.* New York: John Wiley & Sons, Inc., 1943.

ROBINSON, L. W., and NUGENT, R. *Regulation of Small Loan Business.* New York: Russell Sage Foundation, 1935.

RONDILEAU, A. *Education for Installment Buying.* New York: Teachers College, Columbia University, 1944.

SHIELDS, H. G., and WILSON, W. HARMON. *Consumer Economic Problems* (3d ed.). Cincinnati: South-Western Publishing Co., 1945.

SHOUP, CARL S. *Principles of National Income Analysis.* Boston: Houghton Mifflin Co., 1947.

SMITH, AUGUSTUS H. *Your Personal Economics.* New York: McGraw-Hill Book Co., Inc., 1940.

SORENSON, HELEN L. *The Consumer Movement.* New York: Harper & Bros., 1941.

TEBBUT, A. *Behavior of Consumption in Business Depressions.* Cambridge: Harvard University Press, 1933.

TONNE, H. A. *Consumer Education in the Schools.* New York: Prentice-Hall, Inc., 1941.

TRILLING, M. B., and NICHOLAS, F. W. *You and Your Money.* Philadelphia: J. B. Lippincott Co., 1944.

TWENTIETH CENTURY FUND. *Does Distribution Cost Too Much?* New York: Twentieth Century Fund, 1939.

VAILE, ROLAND S., and CANOYER, HELEN G. *Income and Consumption.* New York: Henry Holt & Co., Inc., 1938.

WAITE, WARREN C., and CASSADY, RALPH, JR. *The Consumer and the Economic Order* (2d ed.). New York: McGraw-Hill Book Co., Inc., 1949.

WARBASSE, J. P. *Cooperation as a Way of Peace.* New York: Harper & Bros., 1939.

———. *Cooperative Way.* New York: Barnes & Noble, Inc., 1946.

WARD, BARBARA. *The West at Bay.* New York: W. W. Norton & Co., Inc., 1948.

WARE, C. F. *Consumer Goes to War.* New York: Wilfred Funk, Inc., 1942.

WERNE, BENJAMIN (ed.). *Business and the Robinson Patman Law.* New York: Oxford University Press, 1938.

WHARTON, JOHN F. *The Theory and Practice of Earning a Living.* New York: Simon & Schuster, Inc., 1945.

WILLIAMSON, E. G. *Students and Occupations.* New York: Henry Holt & Co., Inc., 1937.

WINGATE, ISABEL, et al. *Know Your Merchandise.* New York: Harper & Bros., 1944.

WOODWARD, D., and MARK R. *A Primer of Money.* New York: McGraw-Hill Book Co., Inc., 1936.

WOOTTON, BARBARA. *Plan or No Plan.* New York: Farrar & Rinehart, Inc., 1935.

WRIGHT, D. M. *Creation of Purchasing Power.* Cambridge: Harvard University Press, 1942.

WYAND, C. S. *Economics of Consumption.* New York: The Macmillan Co., 1937.

ZIMMERMAN, C. C. *Consumption and Standards of Living.* New York: D. Van Nostrand Co., Inc., 1936.

ZU TAVERN, A. B., and BULLOCK, A. E. *The Consumer Investigates.* Lincoln, Nebr.: University Publication Co., 1947.

ZWEIG, F. *The Economics of Consumers' Credit.* London: P. S. King & Son, Ltd., 1934.

PAMPHLETS

AGRICULTURAL ADJUSTMENT ADMINISTRATION. *Sources of Information on Consumer Education and Organization,* Pub. No. 1, 1936.

ALANNE, V. S. *Fundamentals of Consumer Cooperation.* Minneapolis: Northern States Cooperative League, 1936.

BAKER, HELEN. *Employee Savings Programs.* Princeton: Industrial Relations Section, Department of Economics and Social Institutions, Princeton University, 1937.

BOYCE, GEORGE A., and BEATTY, WILLARD W. *Mathematics of Everyday Life.* New York: Inor Publishing Co., 1936.

BRAINERD, J. G. (ed.). *The Ultimate Consumer: A Study in Economic Illiteracy.* Philadelphia: American Academy of Political and Social Science, 1934.

BUSH, ADA L. *Consumer Use of Selected Goods and Services by Income Classes.* U. S. Dept. of Commerce, Bureau of Foreign and Domestic Commerce, 1937.
———. *Consumer Viewpoint on Returned Goods.* Washington, D. C.: Government Printing Office, 1934.

Consumers' Bookshelf. Agricultural Adjustment Administration, Consumers Council Division, 1937.

COUNCIL OF ECONOMIC ADVISORS, *Economic Report of The President, 1951.* Washington, D. C.: Government Printing Office.

CRAIG, HAZEL T. *A Guide to Consumer Buying.* Boston: Little, Brown & Co., 1943.

CREWS, C. R. *Can We Establish a Consumer Society?* Minneapolis: Northern States Cooperative League, 1935.

DALE, E., and VEVHON, N. W. *Consumer Education* (Bibliography). Columbus: Ohio State University, 1941.

FILENE, E. A. "The Consumers' Dollar." New York: John Day Co., 1934.

GABLER, WERNER K. *Labeling the Consumer Movement.* Washington, D. C.: The American Retail Federation, 1939.

GALL, H. *Consumer Economics.* Columbia, Mo.: Institute for Consumer Education, Stephens College, 1940.

GALLAGHER, C. S., and GALLAGHER, F. C. *How to Cut Food Costs.* Detroit: F. C. Gallagher, 1941.

HALL, F. LaB. (ed.). *Consumer and Defense.* Columbia, Mo.: Institute for Consumer Education, Stephens College, 1940.

HARING, ALBERT. *The Installment Credit Contract.* New York: Consumer Credit Institute of America, Inc., 1939.

HELLER COMMITTEE FOR RESEARCH. *Quantity and Cost Budgets for Three Income Levels.* Berkeley: University of California, 1946.

KUZNETS, S. S. *Uses of National Income in Peace and War.* New York: National Bureau of Economic Research, 1942.

LAZO, HECTOR. *Subsidies as a Solution for the Squeeze.* Washington, D. C.: Hector Lazo, 1942.

LEAGUE OF NATIONS. *Wartime Rationing and Consumption.* Geneva, Switzerland: 1942.

MITCHELL, H., and COOK, G. *Facts, Fads, and Frauds in Nutrition.* Massachusetts State College Bulletin No. 342, 1937.

National Conference on Consumer Education, 1939. Columbia, Mo.: Institute for Consumer Education, 1939.

National Conference on Consumer Education, 1940. Columbia, Mo.: Institute for Consumer Education, 1940.

National Conference on Consumer Education, 1941. Columbia, Mo.: Institute for Consumer Education, 1941.

National Education Association. *Consumer Education Series.* Washington, D. C., 1947.
1. *The Modern American Consumer.*
2. *Learning To Use Advertising.*
3. *Time On Your Hands.*
4. *Investing in Yourself.*
5. *Consumer and The Law.*
6. *Using Standards and Labels.*
7. *Managing Your Money.*
8. *Buying Insurance.*
9. *Using Consumer Credit.*
10. *Investing In Your Health.*

NATIONAL RECREATION ASSOCIATION. *The Leisure Hours of 5000 People: A Report of a Study of Leisure Time Activities and Desires.* New York: The Association, 1934.

RISINGER, H. B. *Consumer Education.* New Brunswick, N. J.: Rutgers University Press, 1941.

SIEGLER, CARLTON J. *Consumer Problems.* New York: American Book Co., 1939.

STIEBELING, H. K. *Diets to Fit the Family Income.* U. S. Department of Agriculture, 1937.

STIEBELING, H. K., and WARD, M. M. *Diets at Four Levels of Nutritive Content and Cost.* U. S. Department of Agriculture, Circular No. 59, Nov., 1933. Washington, D. C.: Government Printing Office, 1933.

STIEBELING, H. K., *et al. Family Food Consumption and Dietary Levels.* U. S. Department of Agriculture, 1941.

U. S. Government publications (Government Printing Office, Washington, D. C.)
Department of Agriculture
"Are We Well Fed?" Misc. Publication 430.
"Changes in Rural Family Spending and Saving in Tennessee, 1943-44." Misc. Publication 666.
"Family Income and Expenditures," Part 2, "Family Expenditures." Farm Series. Misc. Publication 465.
"Family Income and Expenditures," Part 2, "Family Expenditures." Urban and Village Series. Misc. Publication 396.
"Family Saving and Spending as Related to Age of Wife and Age and Number of Children." Misc. Publication 489.
"How Families Use Their Incomes." Misc. Publication 653.
"Nutritive Value of the Per Capita Food Supply, 1909-1945." Misc. Publication 616.
"Rural Family Spending and Saving in Wartime." Misc. Publication 520.

Department of Commerce
"Retail Credit Survey," 1930 and 1935.
Department of Labor
"Clothing Expenditures; Family Income and Expenditures, 1947: Washington, D. C., Richmond, Va., Manchester, N. H." Bureau of Labor Statistics Reprint 1967.
"Consumer Spending: Denver, Detroit, and Houston." Bureau of Labor Statistics Reprint 1984.
"Family Income, Expenditures, and Savings in 1945; Birmingham, Ala., Indianapolis, Ind., Portland, Oreg." Bulletin 956.
"Family Spending and Saving in Wartime." Bulletin 822.
"Food Expenditures; Family Income and Expenditures, 1947: Washington, D. C., Richmond, Va., Manchester, N. H." Bureau of Labor Statistics Reprint 1960.
"Housing Expenditures; Family Income and Expenditures, 1947: Washington, D. C., Richmond, Va., Manchester, N. H." Bureau of Labor Statistics Reprint 1974.
U. S. National Resources Committee
"The Consumer Spends His Income." 1939.

VAILE, ROLAND S., with the assistance of Helen G. Canoyer. *Research Memorandum on Social Aspects of Consumption in the Depression.* Prepared under the direction of the Committee on Studies in Social Aspects of the Depression. New York: Social Science Research Council, 1937.

VAILE, ROLAND S., and CHILD, A. *Grocery Qualities and Prices.* Minneapolis: University of Minnesota Press, 1933.

WARBASSE, J. P. *Socialistic Trend as Affecting the Cooperative Movement.* New York: Co-op League of the U. S. A., 1940.

WARE, C. F. *Consumer in the Postwar Economy.* Washington, D. C.: American Association of University Women, 1945.

WILLIAMS, F., and ZIMMERMAN, C. *Studies of Family Living in the U. S. and Other Countries: An Analysis of Material and Method.* Washington, D. C.: U. S. Department of Commerce, 1935.

INDEX OF SUBJECTS

349

INDEX OF NAMES